The Edinburgh Festivals

The Edinburgh Festivals

Culture and Society in Post-war Britain

Angela Bartie

EDINBURGH
University Press

Dedicated to the memory of
Dr Neil C. Rafeek (1960–2006)

First published in hardback in 2013
This paperback edition 2014

Edinburgh University Press Ltd
The Tun – Holyrood Road
12 (2f) Jackson's Entry
Edinburgh EH8 8PJ

www.euppublishing.com

Typeset in Sabon by
Iolaire Typesetting, Newtonmore, and
printed and bound in the United States of America

A CIP record for this book is available from the British Library

ISBN 978 0 7486 7030 7 (hardback)
ISBN 978 0 7486 9405 1 (paperback)
ISBN 978 0 7486 7031 4 (webready PDF)
ISBN 978 0 7486 7032 1 (epub)

Contents

Acknowledgements

I have accumulated many debts during the time it has taken me to complete this book. First of all, I would like to thank Callum G. Brown, for 'lighting the spark', steering me successfully through the PhD during which much of the research for this book was conducted, and being a supportive and enthusiastic mentor, critic and friend. Robert Hewison, too, urged me to immerse myself in the writings of Matthew Arnold, T. S. Eliot and Raymond Williams, to consider more broadly the question of Scottish national identity, and to always keep my readers in mind, making this a better book by far. My oral history interviewees were wonderful, and I really appreciate their willingness to share their memories and experiences with me. There are others whose contributions I would like to take the time to thank them for: Jim Haynes for giving me the opportunity to fall in love with Paris, John Calder and Sheila Colvin (as well as Karolina Blåberg and Antonia Hoogewerf) for introducing me to oysters with champagne at a time when I was virtually penniless, Richard Demarco for sharing his enthusiasm for the arts and for being a historian's dream by creating such a valuable and impressive archive, and Alexander 'Sandy' Moffat for giving me new insights into the visual arts in sixties Scotland. Sadly, two of my interviewees are no longer with us: Cordelia Oliver, whose generosity, hospitality and wonderful home-grown fruit and vegetables were so welcome on those (rare) sunny Glasgow days, and Tom McGrath, with whom therapeutic shared grumbles about the art of writing sustained me during a particularly difficult stage. I miss Tom's mischievous sparkle and our much-relished conversations.

I would also like to acknowledge the support of the Arts and Humanities Research Board (now Council) for funding the doctoral research upon which much of this book is based. The team at Edinburgh University Press deserve special mention too, especially my editor John Watson, who has believed in this book from the beginning, and given me the time and space that I needed to take it from a sprawling draft to its present form. My copy editor, Jonathan Wadman, did a wonderful job of fine-tuning it, for which I am very grateful. A large number of archives were consulted for this study – many thanks are due to the staff of Edinburgh City Archives (particularly Richard Hunter), the Edinburgh Room in Edinburgh Central Library (especially Jane Mactavish), the Gallacher Memorial Library at Glasgow Caledonian University (especially Audrey Canning and Carole McCallum), the Mitchell Library (Glasgow), the

National Library of Scotland Manuscripts Division, the National Archives of Scotland and the Scottish Theatre Archives. Thank you to the Traverse Theatre, too, for permission to use the archives of the Traverse Theatre Club. For images I would like to kindly thank the family of Alan Daiches for permission to reproduce his evocative photographs, Sally Harrower at the National Library of Scotland for assisting in permissions and the digitising of the negatives, Eleanor Bell, Stewart Smith and Gillian Tasker for their sterling detective work in finding these images among many contact sheets, and Mark Buckland at Cargo Publishing for creating high-resolution copies for publication. I would also like to thank Richard Demarco and staff at the Demarco Archives (especially Terry Ann Newman and Holly Knox Yeoman) for giving me permission to reproduce photographs from Richard's wonderful collection and for kindly waiving copyright fees, and Scran Ltd for licensing the use of images from The Scotsman Publications Ltd.

A project like this demands a lot of time and energy, and I have been very lucky to receive support from a wide range of friends and family who are far too many to name. The following deserve special mention, however, for reading and commenting upon drafts of the book, discussing the ins and outs of the Festival, the arts and social and cultural change in post-war Britain, and/or generally putting up with the mild insanity that comes with writing a monograph: Susan A. Batchelor, Eleanor Bell, Lawrence Black, Mark Buckland, Tommy Callan, Becky Conekin, Roger Davidson, Andrew Davies, Malcolm Dickson, Dennis Dworkin, Alistair Fraser, Susan Galloway, Trevor Griffiths, Robert Hewison, Paula Hughes, Louise A. Jackson, Gordon Johnston, Joel A. Lewis, Euan McArthur, David McKinstry, Arthur McIvor, Claire Meikle, Lorraine Middlemas, Carolyne Mitchell, Sue Morrison, Mhairi Murning, Tom Normand, Frieda Park, Margaret Ritchie, Lucy Robinson, Jane Scullion, Gillian Tasker, Roma Thompson, Jim Tomlinson and last, but by no means least, Hilary Young (with whom I shared the rollercoaster of completing a PhD). I feel blessed to have had Neil C. Rafeek as a friend and guide, a colleague whose friendship, passion for the voices of the past, and humour are fondly remembered and sorely missed. This book is dedicated to his memory. I would also like to thank my colleagues in History, the School of Humanities and the Scottish Oral History Centre at the University of Strathclyde, and all those who have asked me questions and given me feedback on aspects of this research at academic conferences and seminars between 2003 and 2010.

My parents, Anne and George, and sisters, Karen and Lynne, have always supported, encouraged and believed in me. My wider family have been there for me too, urging me on and keeping me grounded. Thank you; it means more than you can know.

Above all, my love and appreciation go to my 'Family Bump', Andy and Orla. Their patience, understanding and tolerance have been tested to the limits, but they have repeatedly brought me back to the present when I've been rooting around in the past, and given me much needed diversion, laughter and affection.

Figures

Abbreviations

ACGB	Arts Council of Great Britain
BCC	British Council of Churches
BW	*British Weekly*
CEMA	Council for the Encouragement of Music and the Arts
CND	Campaign for Nuclear Disarmament
ECA	Edinburgh City Archives
ECL	Edinburgh Central Library
ED	*Evening Dispatch*
EEN	*Edinburgh Evening News*
EFC	Edinburgh Festival Council
EFP	Edinburgh Festival Papers
EFS	Edinburgh Festival Society
EIFC	Edinburgh International Festival Correspondence
EIFMD	Edinburgh International Festival of Music and Drama
ELFC	Edinburgh Labour Festival Committee
FFS	Festival Fringe Society
GA	General Assembly (of the Church of Scotland)
GH	*Glasgow Herald*
GML	Gallacher Memorial Library
IT	*International Times*
IWC	International Writers' Conference
LPC	Lord Provost's Committee
MoM	Minutes of meeting (of Festival Council)
MRA	Moral Re-Armament
NLS	National Library of Scotland
NRS	National Records of Scotland
SAC	Scottish Arts Council
SCDA	Scottish Community Drama Association
STA	Scottish Theatre Archives
TTA	Traverse Theatre Club Archives
TTC	Traverse Theatre Club
VAM	Victoria and Albert Museum

1

Introduction

On Sunday 24 August 1947, the first Edinburgh International Festival of Music and Drama opened with a service of praise in St Giles' Cathedral, the Mother Kirk of Scottish Presbyterianism. Present at this 'civic service of inauguration' were members of the local authority, Edinburgh Corporation, dressed in their ermine-trimmed robes, ministers of the Church of Scotland, members of the Episcopal and Free churches, civic leaders from around Scotland, representatives of law, medicine and the arts, and all 'distinguished visitors known to be in the City at that time'.[1] This ceremony officially opened the new festival with hymns, prayers and a blessing, as well as what a critic for *The Times* described as music of the English Renaissance (Hubert Parry's *I Was Glad*, normally used in royal coronations, and Ralph Vaughan Williams's *Te Deum*). This, he wrote, 'matched in sound the ocular splendour of official uniforms and academic robes'.[2] The inaugural opening concert was performed by L'Orchestre des Concerts Colonne, while the full programme served up a rich feast of European high culture: the Hallé, Jacques, Liverpool Philharmonic and BBC Scottish orchestras were all represented; there was chamber music, morning concerts, recitals of Scottish song, and the Glyndebourne Opera presenting *Macbeth* and *Le nozze di Figaro*. Sadler's Wells Ballet presented *The Sleeping Beauty*, and drama lovers could see the Old Vic doing *The Taming of the Shrew* and *Richard II* as well as La Compagnie Jouvet de Théâtre de L'Athénée performing *L'École des femmes* and *Giraudoux*.[3] A highlight of the inaugural event was the reunion of the Austrian composer Bruno Walter (who had been forced to emigrate, first to France and then to the United States, after the Nazi Anschluss of Austria in 1938) with the Vienna Philharmonic Orchestra. The singer Kathleen Ferrier recalled:

> It was unforgettable. The sun shone, the station was decked with flags, the streets were gay. Plays and ballet by the finest artists were being performed, literally morning, noon and night, and hospitality was showered upon guests and visitors by the so-called 'dour' Scots! What a misnomer![4]

Stereotypes of 'dour' Scots abounded in Lionel Birch's report for *Picture Post*. On arriving and seeing the 'brave but stingy' bunting on the roof of Waverley railway station, he wondered whether the whole Festival 'wasn't going to be a bit like that – brave but stingy'. How, he asked, were Edinburgh citizens going to react to 'this cultural and cosmopolitan invasion' in the 'land of the dour, reticent, wind-bitten Scottish'? Every night after the opera, he reported, 'the Princes Street trams were crammed with white ties and fur coats (mink, opossum and Scotch rarebit) and with long dresses tripping each other on the winding stair to the top deck', with the Scots much in evidence, enjoying themselves 'every bit as openly as the French or the Swedes' (despite having been told 'for centuries' that 'to enjoy oneself is probably a Bad thing'). Ultimately, Birch told his readers, Edinburgh citizens *made* the Festival:

> At least for the duration of the Festival, the tetchiness and ungenerosity [sic] which have disfigured post-war Britain were wiped away. In their place was a fresh spirit – the Festival spirit, or the Christian spirit, or the divine spirit, or the human spirit, or whatever you like to call it. People treating all other people with consideration, and indeed (I have to say it) with love, all through the day. Commonplace, d'you think? No, chum; revolutionary.[5]

When it began in 1947, the Edinburgh International Festival of Music and Drama encapsulated many of the new values given to culture in the immediate post-war world: a means of spiritual refreshment, a way of reasserting moral values, of rebuilding relationships between nations, of shoring up European civilisation and of providing 'welfare' in its broadest sense. Culture was also viewed as a useful new economic tool in the burgeoning tourist industry (the Scottish Tourist Board was founded in 1946) and as a means of attracting dollars into the beleaguered British economy. The Edinburgh International Festival was underpinned by 'high culture', and aimed to present the very best in music and drama performed by the very best artists the world had to offer. However, there was contest over 'culture' in Edinburgh, embodied most obviously in the activities of the Edinburgh Festival Fringe, which also began in 1947, and in wider cultural developments that influenced and affected the Fringe. From the mid-1950s, and particularly during the 1960s, tensions over the meaning and purpose of 'culture' and 'art' were to multiply and intensify across the western world, and these can be seen played out in microcosm in Edinburgh, the 'Festival City'. It has been argued that the very definition of the word 'culture' was the fundamental issue in the post-war critical debate.[6]

The Festival City provides an effective lens through which to explore critical debates over culture in the post-war world, changing practices in the arts, and broader social change between 1945 and 1970. We can trace the rise of the festivals as sites of controversy, notably in relation to the cultural debate on liberalisation in British society and to the challenges to dominant ideas about art that arose across the western world during the 1960s. As the site of a major international festival, Edinburgh had a clear importance in the arts during that period – an importance that has so far been neglected by cultural historians. We will focus mainly on the dramatic arts at the Edinburgh International Festival of Music and Drama and at the 'fringe' that grew up around it, as well as in other important theatres in Edinburgh, namely the Church of Scotland-owned Gateway Theatre, the independent Traverse Theatre Club and the civic-run Lyceum Theatre. Collectively, the Edinburgh festivals form a crucial – and curiously overlooked – site for the historian of cultural change in post-war Britain.

For too long, Edinburgh has been marginalised, ignored or glossed over in cultural histories of post-war Britain. Even when Edinburgh is cited in relation to the arts in society or the cultural upheavals of the 1960s, it is largely seen as marginal. It is often seen as peripheral in histories of modern Scotland too, viewed more as an annual 'invasion' of outsiders than as a vital part of national cultural history. When scholars have explored the arts in post-war Britain and the cultural revolution of the 1960s, they have tended to draw attention to London and the metropolitan arts.[7] But it is important to highlight the insights that the Festival City can give us into social and cultural change in post-war Britain: the growing influence of the arts in society, the way that youth had come to dominate the arts by the 1960s, and how 'high culture' was challenged and an emphasis on wider participation in culture popularised during the second half of the twentieth century. The Edinburgh festivals reveal, too, how cultural change was intimately linked to broader social change. Experimentation in the arts resulted in new artistic forms and challenges to censorship and traditional values. High-profile controversies on the Edinburgh stage, including that over the naked model wheeled across the gallery of the University of Edinburgh-owned McEwan Hall in 1963, created concern among ministers of the Church of Scotland, Conservative council-lors on Edinburgh Corporation, and others both within and outside Scot-land. An important thread running through this book concerns the relationship between the arts and organised religion. By exploring this changing relationship across a period in which the status of churches in society declined at the same time as culture was elevated in importance, new insights into the liberalisation of the arts from moral austerity and secular-isation can be revealed.

The Edinburgh festivals can also tell us much about the changing role of culture in post-war Britain, cultural policy and public funding of the arts, theatre history and theatrical censorship, and the growth of experimental and community arts. They are significant, too, in the emergence of Scottish culture and society from a long Presbyterian history. There is a pressing need to integrate the Edinburgh festivals into our understanding of how the new Scotland developed, casting off the shadow of John Knox and finding a new cultural confidence that paved the way for debates over devolution and Scottish independence.[8] By bringing artists and performers from all over the world to Edinburgh for three weeks every year, this brave post-war initiative was to have a far-reaching influence not only on the arts in Scotland but on the very character of modern Scotland.

ARTS FESTIVALS: HISTORY AND SIGNIFICANCE

Edinburgh is now a city of festivals, well known as the Festival City.[9] Despite the International Festival and the separate Festival Fringe – here referred to as the Edinburgh Festivals – being widely acknowledged as the model for the evolution of many of the world's estimated 10,000 arts festivals and constituting a major world festival themselves, their own history has barely been explored. What has been written about the Festivals has largely been from the personal perspectives of administrators, journalists and critics.[10] An exception is Eileen Miller's study of the 'official' Festival, published to mark its fiftieth anniversary. Using the official Festival archives, this explores the history of the Festival chronologically through its artistic directors, and offers an indispensable reference guide to programmes and finances during its first fifty years.[11] Similarly, histories of the Fringe have tended to be from the perspectives of those involved.[12] Alistair Moffat, Fringe administrator from 1978 to 1981, wrote a broader account of the development of the Fringe, which by the time his book was published in 1978 had become the largest arts festival in the world, eclipsing the 'official' Festival it sought to challenge.[13] Despite some references to the wider historical context of the Festivals at different stages in their development, to the Festivals in accounts of the Fringe and vice versa, and to wider cultural trends in post-war Britain, existing literature on the Festival City does not tie these all together. Large gaps are also evident. What, for example, do the Festivals tell us about the funding of the arts outside London during a formative period in state support for culture? How do the challenges from Fringe performers affect (or not) the programme of the official Festival? What about the broader shifts in ideas about the role of the arts in society? How are these reflected in and/or influenced by what was going on in Edinburgh, the site of the largest arts festival in the world?

When the Edinburgh Festival began there was little competition in the way of other arts festivals in Europe. While early Festival papers note that 'the general idea of such an International Arts Festival somewhere in Europe is in the air', it was believed that European pre-war venues like Salzburg, Bayreuth and Munich would be 'out of action' for some time due to the ravages of the Second World War.[14] The wider context of a post-war 'drive towards reconstruction, political stability and the forging of international linkages through trade (including through a fledgling tourism industry) set the tenor for economic and social advancement', meaning that a later 'upsurge' in the number of festivals being established formed 'important contributions to Europe's cultural infrastructure'.[15] The Edinburgh International Festival, as Jen Harvie has argued, sought to 'bolster a badly damaged sense of European identity by supporting the post-war revival of European arts and culture', an aim that will be explored in more detail in Chapters 2 and 3. She has also pointed to its 'significance as an institutional agent for articulating, rebuilding and possibly redefining post-war European culture' given the 'relative dearth of European institutions *per se* – not just arts institutions – at this historical moment'.[16] Even in the context of European arts festivals, the Edinburgh International Festival was distinctive. It was an arts festival that encompassed a variety of art forms (including opera, ballet, drama and music) and was not focused on the work of any particular artist, director or composer, or on the culture of any one nation or locale, unlike most pre-war festivals.[17] Harvie has observed how its 'multi-arts programming' allows cross-fertilisation between different art forms and for audiences 'to view various arts and artists comparatively, across categories that may otherwise be potentially exclusive'.[18] This was to prove important, not least in unintentionally creating the Edinburgh Festival Fringe in 1947. The term 'fringe' became hugely significant, first of all in relation to the Edinburgh International Festival and challenges to accepted definitions of culture and art, and then in the later 1960s to a particular brand of political and experimental theatre. It is generally acknowledged that the term as derived from the Edinburgh Festival was popularised by *Beyond the Fringe* and flourished through the counter-culture of the later 1960s and early 1970s. While an invitation from the director was required to be part of the Edinburgh International Festival, anyone could (and can still) take part in the Fringe. Although it is important to highlight that not everything on the Fringe was oppositional or experimental (and equally that drama in the official Festival programme could be challenging and innovative), the Edinburgh Festival Fringe still came to represent opposition and challenge to the programmed 'culchah' of the official Festival.[19]

In the modern world (especially over the last twenty years or so), the growth of festivals has been described as 'astonishing' and 'dramatic', with arts festivals rapidly becoming a 'worldwide tourism phenomenon'.[20] As early as 1983, reference was being made to the creation and revival of festivals 'on an unprecedented scale', while since the late 1980s, festivals have increasingly been utilised as 'a useful strategy for the contemporary city to adopt in the attempt to reposition and differentiate itself in an increasingly competitive world'.[21] Recent literature on arts festivals has tended to focus on globalisation, on more local considerations related to space, place and identity, and on the tangible impacts, whether economic, social or cultural.[22]

For a major post-war arts festival that is widely acknowledged as having powerfully shaped the 'festival as we think of it today' (along with Avignon) and one that 'provided a model for multi-arts festivals which has been conspicuously exported across the world', surprisingly little attention has been paid to the Edinburgh Festivals.[23] There are, of course, some exceptions. Jen Harvie recently explored the cultural effects of the International

Festival alongside some of its wider impacts in terms of the 'cultural practices and material resources that the EIF has not itself produced but has significantly provoked throughout its history'.[24] Wesley Monroe Shrum shows how the 'Fringe identity' feeds into the process of 'cultural mediation' between critics, spectators and performers, and influences where art forms are placed in the 'cultural hierarchy'.[25] The contemporary literature on arts festivals has much to offer the cultural historian interested in the arts in society, yet cultural historians have largely ignored twentieth-century arts festivals.[26]

Stanley Waterman has argued that a festival, whatever its format or cyclicality, 'can be regarded as a form of cultural consumption in which culture is created, maintained, transformed and transmitted to others [in ways which] usually involve production *and* consumption, *concentrated in time and place*'.[27] As an annual three-week extravaganza, the Festival and Fringe together provide rich pickings for those interested in exploring shifts in the arts as well as critical debates about culture. Pointing to the importance that has recently been attached to festivals, Bernadette Quinn observed:

> It is the very possibility of involvement and participation, and the potential to challenge, re-order, subvert and disrupt, that social scientists and others have held to be inherent in the concept of festivity [. . .] Cultural commentators conceive of festivals as risk-takers, as opportunities to challenge the *status quo* and push out boundaries.[28]

During the middle decades of the twentieth century, new ideas about the role of culture in society were aired, challenges were made to elite culture, there were attempts to break down hierarchies of culture, and assaults were mounted on the barriers between art forms such as the visual arts, drama, literature and music. In Edinburgh, tussles quickly began to take place as the official and fringe elements of the Festival staked their claims to 'culture', presenting the conceptions of culture that they saw as most important and relevant to their intended audiences. Starting out as 'Additional Entertainments' or 'Festival Adjuncts', the unofficial offerings during Festival time quickly developed their own Fringe identity. In contemporary society, fringes are an established feature of modern arts festivals, in which the former have, to some extent, democratised the latter. The Edinburgh Festival Fringe was central to this process. We will trace how it developed into an established feature of the annual Edinburgh Festival, and highlight how this influenced the official Festival. Feeding into this arena in the Festival City were ventures that symbolised new approaches to culture in post-war Britain and which reflected the shifts that were occurring in ideas about the role of the arts in society.

Recent studies by geographers have underlined the importance of arts festivals as 'authored landscapes': 'festivals are not natural occurrences [but] are social constructions that bear heavy signs of authorship'.[29] Festivals have been shown to be crucial arenas in which culture is contested, giving space to fight 'battles' over the role and meaning of culture and the place of the arts in society, and to focus broader concerns about the direction and pace of social change. Robert Hewison's conception of the arts as 'a battleground for the conflicting forces of social change' is a useful one; applying it to the Festival City can give us new insights into cultural and social change in post-war Britain.[30] In the late 1940s and early 1950s, for example, the kind of elite culture presented by the Edinburgh International Festival and supported by the Arts Council of Great Britain was being increasingly challenged by left-wing theatre groups, the Labour movement, Scottish folk singers and nationalists. We can see how these challenges helped to lay the foundations for the cultural upheavals of the 1960s (Chapter 3). We can observe, too, how a theatrical happening staged as part of an international drama conference in 1963 provoked concern about the social changes associated with the 1960s finding their way from London onto Scottish soil, focused anxiety about the forces of secularisation, and raised major questions about morality and religiosity in Scotland (Chapter 5).

CULTURE IN POST-WAR SOCIETY

Raymond Williams – arguably the founding theorist of cultural studies – observed that words like 'culture' are so difficult to define because they involve ideas and values.[31] 'The idea of culture is a general reaction to a general and major change in the conditions of our modern life', he argued:

> It might be said, indeed, that the questions now concentrated in the meanings of the word *culture* are questions directly raised by the great historical changes which the changes in *industry*, *democracy*, and *class*, in their own way, represent, and to which the changes in *art* are a closely related response. The development of the word *culture* is a record of a number of important and continuing reactions to these changes in our social, economic, and political life, and may be seen, in itself, as a special kind of map by means of which the nature of the changes can be explored.[32]

By the mid-1950s, the importance of culture as a key social issue had become more widely recognised. Writers such as Williams, Richard Hoggart and Stuart Hall together helped to develop the new field of cultural studies. The Centre for Contemporary Cultural Studies, the first academic department dedicated to the study of culture in society, was created at Birmingham University in 1964. This had grown out of 'cultural Marxism', a movement that fused cultural and political protest and sought to redefine the 'social struggle' in the light of recent social changes wrought by the new welfare state in conjunction with rising affluence.[33] Changes like these were contributing to the idea of transformation in the working-class experience in Britain. Hoggart in particular feared the erosion of 'working-class' culture in the face of a new 'mass culture', spread via the popular press, radio, cinema and television.[34] For some, the study of culture in society held the key to understanding such far-reaching social change. But to understand the growing importance of culture in the critical debate, we must first look at changes to ideas about the place of culture in society brought about by the Second World War and the creation of a welfare state in Britain.

Until 1939, there had been little direct state involvement in the arts in Britain.[35] The arts, especially music and drama, had largely depended upon a mixture of private patronage, commercial enterprise and subscription.[36] However, the experience of the inter-war depression, the spread of adult education and the popularity of amateur theatrical and musical organisations and activities had contributed to a growing belief in the value of the arts in and to society. This was consolidated by the experiences of the Second World War. The Council for the Encouragement of Music and Art (CEMA) was created during the war, in December 1939, by an organisation financed from America, the Pilgrim Trust, which was dedicated to supporting cultural activity.[37] Just three months after its creation, the British government awarded it a grant of £50,000, marking the shift to increased state responsibility for funding the arts. When CEMA was founded, the first clause of the memorandum sent to the Treasury to request financial assistance had committed the body to the 'preservation in wartime of the highest standards in the arts of music, drama and painting' while subsequent clauses called for their 'widespread provision' and 'the encouragement of music-making and play-acting by the people themselves'.[38]

Robert Hewison has argued that an unexpected outcome of the Second World War was that 'people had realised spontaneously that "culture" was one of the things for which they were fighting'.[39] There was a sense of idealism, with the war having been won by Britain and her allies, the welfare state in its infancy and the idea of social reform in the air. In August 1946, CEMA became the Arts Council of Great Britain, a body subsidised by the British government with the aim of providing 'State support for the arts, without State control'. However difficult the times, the Arts Council noted, 'we need the solace and stimulus of the arts'.[40] The Arts Council allocated funds received from the Treasury, answering to Parliament for its expenditure, but the choice of who should receive funds was ultimately decided by the organisation – this became known as the 'arm's length' principle.[41] When the Scottish Committee of the Arts Council was created in 1946 (see Chapter 2), it was at 'arm's length' from government and from the Arts Council, giving it 'double arm's length' position and thus greater autonomy over policy and funding decisions.[42] This commitment to the arts was consolidated with the Local Government (Scotland) Act of 1947, which gave municipal authorities the power to raise a fivepenny rate to support the arts.[43] Taken together, these developments were expressions of the Labour government's commitment to the idea of the welfare state and to widening access to culture as part of a broader social democratic consensus.

But in the immediate post-war period, the writings of the nineteenth-century poet and critic Matthew Arnold were still pervasive in ideas about culture in society. Arnold had inaugurated 'a particular way of seeing, a particular way of mapping the field of culture' and in doing so, 'established a cultural agenda which remained dominant from the 1860s to the 1950s'.[44] To Arnold, culture was the remedy to anarchy, bringing order to (potential) chaos:

> The whole scope of this essay is to recommend culture as the great help out of our present difficulties; culture being a pursuit of our total perfection by means of getting to know, on all the matters which most concern us, the best which has been thought and said in the world; and through this knowledge, turning a stream of fresh and free thought upon our stock notions and habits.[45]

A fundamental part of Arnold's thesis was that culture was the best substitute for a religion that was no longer effective; that culture would go beyond religion in that it sought a fuller development of personal and social qualities than the narrower strictures of organised religion.[46] Despite his contention that culture should make 'the best which has been thought and said in the world current everywhere' – and his assertion that 'the men of culture are the true apostles of equality' – in practice, Arnold's conception of culture helped to maintain the idea of a hierarchy of culture, due mainly to his emphasis on 'the best which has been thought and said in the world', and to the idea of culture as a 'civilising power'.[47] We can observe this in the way that the Arts Council developed, in public debates about the role of culture in the new post-war world and, as Chapters 2 and 3 will show, in the conception and programming of the Edinburgh International Festival. Furthermore, as Alan Sinfield has pointed out, the Labour Party manifesto of 1945 had 'hardly questioned the conventional idea of high culture'.[48]

A vocal critic to the idea of widespread diffusion of culture was the poet, writer and dramatist T. S. Eliot – who, according to his biographer, enjoyed 'almost shamanistic authority' in the post-war period.[49] Whereas Arnold saw culture as a substitute for religion in society, Eliot saw culture and religion as inextricably linked, categorically stating that 'no culture can appear or develop except in relation to a religion'.[50] Stephen Spender commented that Eliot's *Notes towards the Definition of Culture*, published in 1948, presented the reader with an either/or: 'Either we have a Christian culture or we have nothing.'[51] Eliot believed in the need for a 'graded society' (in terms of classes) and different levels of culture, arguing that while the whole of the population should take an active part in cultural activities, these should not be 'all the same activities or on the same level'.[52] Sinfield argued that the new emphasis on 'welfare-capitalism' in the immediate post-war years created panic among literary intellectuals as it 'implied that now all the people were to share in those good things that the upper classes had generally secured to themselves'.[53] Eliot was also against the idea of a classless society, an idea that had gained currency during the war years, and this put him firmly in opposition to contemporaries like the writer, reviewer, novelist and play-wright J. B. Priestley. Priestley was attracted to the idea of a 'nationalized culture' brought about by greater equality in a reconstructed Britain, and in 1941 had written in *Picture Post* that 'the soul demands the arts as the body demands exercise . . . In the [new] Britain we want to build, then, there will be plenty of art of every kind.'[54]

In the immediate post-war period, then, the meaning of the term 'culture' and its place in society had become a focus of discussion and dispute in the public arena. Tensions between approaches that favoured widening culture in society and those that sought to maintain elitism in the arts were clearly evident. As Mary Glasgow, the first secretary of CEMA, noted, there was 'a built-in conflict between the claims of art and those of social service, and in the lifetime of C.E.M.A. it was never fully resolved'.[55] These conflicts were bound up in the aim of CEMA to provide 'the best for the most'.[56] But Euan McArthur notes that a policy for the arts was not clearly set out, and that instead the remit was defined broadly so that it could accommodate both those who wanted to encourage the highest standards and those who wished to make the arts more accessible. Partly, this related to the 'genuine horror' of officially approved culture, which was associated with fascist and communist regimes, resulting in a view that any state-funded arts organisation should be reacting to what artists were doing rather than directing them.[57] In 1945, when announcing the formation of a permanent chartered body for the arts – what became the Arts Council of Great Britain – its first chairman, Lord Keynes, stated:

> The work of the artist in all its aspects is, of its nature, individual and free, undisciplined, unregimented, uncontrolled. The artist walks where the breath of the spirit blows him. He cannot be told his direction; he does not know it himself.[58]

Yet decisions were made about what was eligible for receiving funding, and these could hardly fail to reflect the preferences of those who sat on the committees making the decisions. Robert Hutchison has argued that the 'profoundest source' of the Arts Council's power 'lies in its official capacity to conceptualise and to identify the arts and the artistic'.[59] But this was not without challenge, and the post-war period was one of ongoing 'culture wars' as a range of voices defended, contested and renegotiated meanings of culture and definitions of art. As McArthur points out, the vexed question of what constituted the highest standards in the arts encouraged critical debate in society. Standards could not just be handed down as 'unquestionable givens' and 'there never was a passive public awaiting the stamp of elite or state culture even when society was at its most stratified and education least widespread'.[60]

In *Culture and Society, 1780–1950*, first published in 1958, Raymond Williams had shifted focus outwards from the narrower interpretation of culture, in which it referred to the 'principles of discrimination and values within the arts' (as a means of defining what works could be described as 'serious' in terms of having 'clear artistic merit') to a broader and more anthropological conception.[61] To Williams, a key achievement and major contribution was made by Eliot when he used culture to mean 'a whole way of life' and considered 'levels' of culture within that meaning.[62] In 1961, Williams set out to reinterpret and extend the framework of the cultural theories and debates analysed in *Culture and Society* in *The Long Revolution*.[63] Hailed by Dennis Dworkin as a 'landmark in the theorisation of culture', it sought to understand the complexity of the theory of culture, its place in society, and the way culture interacted with wider social, political and economic trends.[64] Williams redefined culture as 'the study of relationships between elements in a whole way of life. The analysis of culture is the attempt to discover the nature of the organization which is the complex of these relationships.'[65] That Williams was writing at a time of complex cultural and social change is evident throughout the text, and indeed formed the key impetus for his attempts to understand the process of cultural change and its relationship with the wider society. In short, Williams argued that Britons were living through a 'long revolution' that was difficult to define, was occurring unevenly across a long period, and was an exceptionally complicated process – but that its progress was most evident in the field of cultural change. The 'deeper cultural revolution', he argued, was 'being interpreted and indeed fought out, in very complex ways, in the world of art and ideas'.[66] The hierarchical model of culture that was prominent in the immediate post-war years was challenged and, to some extent, broken down during the 1960s, a process that had already begun in the 1950s. In 1964, Stuart Hall and Paddy Whannel argued that the 'cultural map is no longer so clearly defined. The older culture has been put under pressure, not only from the new media, but also from the art and experiment of the *avant-garde*.'[67] We can see this unfold in the Festival City.

It has been argued that by the late 1960s, the art of theatre had taken on a central cultural role in British society – at precisely the same time as going to the theatre had become more of a minority activity, adversely affected by the growing prevalence of television and the related shift from public to private forms of leisure.[68] Theatre, it can be argued, 'functions as a context in which a society can examine its sense of self, and the stresses upon it'.[69] To the theatre critic Michael Billington, the 'fluctuations' of post-war society can be traced through the work of dramatists, while for Martin Priestman, the theatre of the 1960s 'focused the many changes taking place in society more sharply than any other then-established art-form'.[70] Williams saw drama 'not only as a social art, but as a major and practical index of change and creator of consciousness'.[71] The middle decades of the twentieth century were a significant period of development for theatre in Britain, linked in to wider social change and upheaval. But although Edinburgh is often mentioned in connection with the term 'fringe theatre' or as the location of the Traverse Theatre Club, founded in 1963, the Festivals are barely mentioned or often omitted entirely in histories of theatre in Britain.[72]

Exploring the Festival City can also contribute much to our understanding of the development of theatre in post-war Scotland. The Edinburgh Festivals have in the past been referred to as 'impositions', events that were 'not Scottish' on account of them being in Edinburgh (a city sometimes charged with being more 'English' than 'Scottish'), being concerned with the international arts, and being run by people who were 'outsiders'.[73] Right into the 1960s the Festival was regularly charged with being a largely foreign import grafted on to an Edinburgh setting.[74] The substance of this accusation has endured and many historical studies of Scottish theatre in the twentieth century give relatively little attention to the Festival for this precise reason – that there is a significant gap between theatre in Scotland and Scottish theatre.[75] Adrienne Scullion suggests that this stems from the manner in which academic interest in Scottish theatre developed in the late 1970s and early 1980s, when emphasis was given to left-wing and working-class theatre in Scotland in the first half of the twentieth century.[76] This helped to determine the critical framework that historians of Scottish theatre worked within, meaning that writers, developments or theatres that were not specifically Scottish (in terms of origin, content or form) did not gain as much attention as those that were. Although Scottish theatre historians have not ignored the Festival, it has never been properly considered. To Owen Dudley Edwards, the place of the Edinburgh Festival in Scottish theatre 'might be usefully likened to the place of England in Scottish nationalism: flamboyant in impact, sometimes pivotal in effect, but not fundamental in essence'.[77] Randall Stevenson concedes that the Festival contributed 'to a widening Scottish interest in drama', and cites the particular contribution that two Edinburgh theatres, the Traverse and the Lyceum, made to the theatre scene in Scotland. David Hutchison, on the other hand, wrote that the Festival's contribution to Scottish theatre 'has been disappointing'.[78]

But, as this book demonstrates, the Festival was an important influence on Scottish theatre, theatre in Scotland, and on the Scottish arts scene more broadly – even when it appeared aloof. As McArthur has argued, 'the high arts, more than popular culture, are still entangled with ideas of national identity, which they seem to both reflect and, to a degree, produce'.[79] The exclusion of Scottish drama from the inaugural Edinburgh International

Festival – as not being of a high enough standard to take its place in an international festival – had major repercussions (as Chapter 3 will show). Tensions between the Festival's location in Scotland and the content of its international programme provoked artistic endeavour and cultural challenge, not least the creation of the Fringe itself. In reference to contemporary arts festivals, Stanley Waterman has observed that the 'fringes construct important informal discursive arenas in which social identities are constantly constructed, deconstructed and reconstructed'.[80] In Scotland, the Fringe was to provide a space in which ideas about Scottish national cultural identity could be explored and tested, while exploring the Festival City reveals major changes taking place in ideas about the arts in Scotland.

LOCATING THE FESTIVALS IN POST-WAR SOCIETY

What gives the Festivals their edge is their location in Edinburgh. This is a city that has often been associated with the 'great grey hand' of Presbyterianism and moral conservatism.[81] In a place known now as a cosmopolitan and international festival city, with some of the most liberal licensing laws in Europe, it is difficult to picture the very different Edinburgh of 1947. George Rosie has argued that there is a 'fairly plausible' theory that 'it is impossible to understand Scotland without understanding Scotland's religious history'.[82] Certainly, the cultural history of the Edinburgh Festivals must be understood in conjunction with the history of the Church of Scotland, and with the broader narrative of declining religiosity and increasing secularisation in the middle decades of the twentieth century.

Right into the 1960s (and arguably well beyond this), the Presbyterian value-system pervaded Scottish civic authority and society more broadly. As a Presbyterian church, the only time the Church of Scotland (also known as the Kirk) speaks 'as one' is during its General Assembly, held annually in May. The General Assembly held an authoritative voice and its position was usually taken as the Church of Scotland position, and by extension that of the Scottish people. The Scottish sociologist John Highet commented in 1960 that the General Assembly was the 'nearest Scotland comes to having a "Parliament"' and that it was supposed to act as 'the voice and conscience of the people of Scotland'.[83]

After the Union of 1707, Scotland retained distinctive legal, educational and religious practices and institutions (and therefore its own distinct civil society) and, from 1885, when the post of Scottish Secretary was created, a measure of administrative devolution in the form of the Scottish Office (which was a department of the United Kingdom government).[84] Roger Davidson and Gayle Davis have recently shown how influential religion remained in policy-making in Scotland. Fear of alienating the Scottish churches, in particular the Church of Scotland and the Roman Catholic Church, was 'an enduring concern of officials, not least because church

leaders retained disproportionate influence within government and municipal politics'.[85] There were also strong links between local government and
the Church of Scotland. Many members of municipal government were also
Kirk elders, church officers elected by their congregation to assist the
teaching elder, the ordained minister, in the government of the Church.[86]
David McCrone has found that survey data from the 1950s and 1960s
suggests that 'strong religious connotations were continuing to be played out
in Scottish politics', revealing the power of conservatism in Scotland in the
1950s.[87] On Edinburgh Corporation, the conservative Progressive Party was
the majority party throughout the period 1945–70.[88]

The Church of Scotland did not hold support for one party over any other,
so that members of any of Scotland's political parties were often members of
the Kirk, an influence that could have a strong bearing at local, Scottish and
British government levels. Between 1964 and 1970 the Secretary of State for
Scotland, whose role was to represent Scottish interests in Parliament, was
Willie Ross, a Labour MP and Church of Scotland elder, who represented the
conservative agenda of the Kirk in his response to the issues of relaxing liquor
licensing, legalising homosexuality, reformation of the divorce laws and
other 'permissive' issues.[89] The links between the Church of Scotland and
Edinburgh Corporation did not stop with Presbyterian influence through
personal affiliation with the Church. All newly elected Edinburgh Corporation councillors and town council bailies, as well as newly appointed Lord
Provosts, were inducted to their service through the practice of 'kirking', a
religious ceremony held in St Giles' Cathedral, with all civic authority
members dressed in ermine-trimmed robes and cocked hats.[90]

Until 1963, Callum Brown has argued, Britain was a 'highly religious
nation', one in which 'Christianity infused public culture and was adopted
by individuals, whether churchgoers or not, in forming their own identities'.[91] Hugh McLeod has pointed out that in the 1950s, most people in all
Western countries 'were at least nominal members of one of the Christian
churches [. . .]; the churches remained extremely powerful institutions; the
clergy of the larger Christian denominations generally enjoyed high status
and considerable influence'. Religion was pervasive in Scottish society in the
1950s and most adults in Scotland remained affiliated to the Church.[92]
Despite lower levels of church adherence in other parts of Britain, it was still
accurate to describe Britain as a Christian country. But during the 'long
1960s', this all changed and almost every Western country – Scotland
included – saw drops (sometimes dramatic) in churchgoing, markers of
religiosity, like christenings and marriages, and clergy numbers. The place
of the churches in British society also weakened: this was a period of
'decisive change'.[93] Brown argues that in the 1960s, 'a short and sharp
cultural revolution' caused religion to undergo a sudden and remarkable
decline as 'the complex web of legally and socially accepted rules which
governed individual identity' were swept aside and Britain broke with

traditional 'religious discourses of moral identity'.[94] But this 'break' was not a clean one, and varied across Britain. Debates about the pace, timing, extent and causes of secularisation continue, although there is general agreement on the significance of the 1960s as a 'hinge decade'.[95]

In 1960, Highet wrote that the Church was in competition with the 'new morality'.[96] By the mid-1960s there was often quite open conflict with the values of the new 'permissive society', a term which became used to describe the increasing freedom individuals had to express liberal attitudes to morality, the shift from public to private decision-making with regard to morality, and the legislation introduced to enshrine these shifts towards tolerance in law. Although there was a liberalisation of both attitudes and legislation, there remained a difference between attitudes and behaviour, with moral conservatism still exerting some power throughout the population.[97] Nevertheless, among many churches in Britain there was a clear shift towards a more permissive stance with regards to morality in the 1960s. This shift – and the tensions that arose from it – can be explored in the debates that occurred over the arts in Edinburgh, Church of Scotland involvement in theatre, and the content of specific performances. These give us a window onto how one of Britain's largest churches was responding to aspects of social change in post-war Britain, and to our understanding of the Scottish context.

In 1969, in one of the first major appraisals of the 1960s, the journalist Christopher Booker began his book with: 'As the Nineteen Sixties pass into history, most people in Britain sense to a more or less conscious degree that in the past fifteen years or so they have been through some kind of enormous and shattering experience.'[98] The sense of the 1960s as a time of major, fundamental, and all-embracing change has endured. Arthur Marwick has argued that in the 'long sixties' there was an 'international cultural revolution' that swept away old attitudes, social behaviours and patterns of morality, and brought about significant and fundamental changes to the wider society and culture.[99] The editors of a new journal launched in 2008 to focus on the 1960s argued that 'no recent decade has been so powerfully transformative in much of the world as have the Sixties'.[100] But it remains a contested era, one in which change was, as Mark Donnelly argues, 'uneven, with the impact varying across boundaries of class, gender, generation, region and ethnicity (notwithstanding the fact that the validity of these identifying categories were themselves called into question in the sixties)'. 'What was it', asked Donnelly, 'that transformed 1960s Britain – in many respects just another decade in the country's history – into "sixties Britain", a heavily edited and reworked concept that is saturated in symbolism, meanings and myth?'[101] Jeremy Varon, Michael S. Foley and John McMillan drew a distinction between 'the Sixties *as a period*, accessed through careful research, from "the Sixties" as a *popular mythology*, spun largely by mass entertainments, middlebrow commentary, commercial bromides, and pedagogic clichés'.[102] It is the popular mythology of 'the Sixties' that pervades Richard Finlay's overly simplified assessment:

> The swinging sixties passed Scotland by, and the best guess is that sexual intercourse did not begin north of the border until sometime in the seventies. There was no flower power, few hippies, no love and peace, nor anything usually associated with western decadent youth culture. There was no storming of the left bank of the Clyde, no Highland love-in festival, no Timothy MacLeary to advocate the expansion of Caledonian consciousness. Nor was there much of a permissive society, even though a great many went looking for it. The closest most people got to it was on the telly.[103]

But Scotland was not peripheral to the major cultural upheavals of the 1960s. An examination of the Festival City contributes much to our understanding of Scotland's distinctive experience of that transformative period – although the Festival is not the only evidence that the kind of social and cultural changes we associate with the 1960s were taking place on Scottish soil. An exciting variety of ideas, influences and initiatives were cross-fertilising with one another and important literary and cultural connections were being made. We can see this in other Scottish cities such as Glasgow, at the CND Late Club, for example, or the Citizens Theatre and its experimental studio, The Close Theatre Club (opened in 1965), and in folk song, literature, visual arts and theatre circles.[104] Eleanor Bell has shown how a number of Scottish poets adopted concrete poetry in the early 1960s, and in doing so connected the Scottish literary scene to the international avant-garde, challenged the continued hold of the Scottish Renaissance on writers and posed questions about what it meant to be Scottish in contemporary society.[105] One problem has been the continuing power of the 'media Sixties', while another is the relative paucity of research on the arts and culture in 1960s Scotland.[106] In many ways, the points made by Ross Birrell and Alec Finlay in 2001 still stand:

> There is a pressing demand for new cultural histories of the period – why not a study of the justified sinners of the 1960s, John Calder, Jim Haynes, Alex Trocchi, Edwin Morgan, Mark Boyle, Ian Hamilton Finlay and Tom McGrath [. . .] When will Scottish culture be able to sustain a body of criticism worthy of its cultural production?[107]

Thankfully, new research is beginning or already underway on these 'justified sinners' (all of whom feature in this book), marking renewed interest in this era.[108] All too often, the 1960s have been seen as a period of stasis – even a 'cultural desert', as Tom Nairn so famously charged – with the more significant shifts not occurring until at least the 1970s, largely because this was a period in which Scottish national identity flourished in the field of culture.[109] But the post-war period was a transformative period for Scotland and, as we shall see, laid a number of valuable foundations for later developments.[110]

NOTES

1. *The Times*, 25 August 1947; Edinburgh City Archives (hereafter ECA), Early Festival Papers, Festival Notes, 8 October 1946.
2. *The Times*, 25 August 1947.
3. The full programme for this (and every subsequent Festival up to and including 1996) can be found in Miller, *The Edinburgh International Festival*, Appendices.
4. Kathleen Ferrier cited in Miller, *The Edinburgh International Festival*, 31.
5. Birch, 'Edinburgh's Festival'.
6. Hewison, *Culture and Consensus*, 34. See also Dworkin, *Cultural Marxism in Postwar Britain*; Sinfield, *Literature, Politics and Culture in Postwar Britain*.
7. For perspectives on Scotland, see McArthur, *Scotland, CEMA, and the Arts Council*; Galloway & Jones, 'The Scottish Dimension of British Arts Government'. For the north-east of England, see Vall, *Cultural Region*; for Wales, Jones, 'An Art of Our Own'.
8. Surveying the historiography, it often seems that the Festival is the proverbial 'elephant in the room', mentioned only in passing (if at all). See e.g. MacDonald, *Whaur Extremes Meet*; Cameron, *Impaled upon a Thistle*.
9. The Edinburgh Military Tattoo (founded in 1950) also had its roots in the inaugural Festival, growing out of displays of piping and dancing on Edinburgh Castle esplanade, while the Edinburgh Film Festival developed from the Edinburgh Film Guild's International Festival of Documentary Film (see Hardy, *Slightly Mad and Full of Dangers*). Six festivals currently take place in Edinburgh each August, with more at other times of the year.
10. George Bruce, a BBC arts producer and writer, published his personal history of the Festivals in 1975, *Festival in the North*. Later, Iain Crawford, the Festival publicity manager (1973–82), published his own eyewitness account of the Festivals and the personalities associated with them, *Banquo on Thursdays*. A number of photographic books have also been produced – see, for example, Scotsman, *Festival City* and Wishart, *Celebration!*.
11. Miller, *The Edinburgh International Festival*.
12. McGlone, *(Behind the) Fringe*; Dale, *Sore Throats and Overdrafts*. A short commemorative book was also produced by *The Scotsman* to mark the fiftieth anniversary of the Fringe in 1996: Bain, *The Fringe*.
13. Moffat, *The Edinburgh Fringe*.
14. ECA, Early Festival Papers, EIFMD Report, summer 1945.
15. See Quinn, 'Art Festivals and the City', 929.

16. Harvie, 'Cultural Effects of the Edinburgh International Festival', 14. See also Harvie, *Staging the UK*.

17. Bayreuth celebrated the work of Wagner, for example, and Salzburg Mozart.

18. Harvie, 'Cultural Effects of the Edinburgh International Festival', 16.

19. 'Culchah', writes Raymond Williams, was a mime word that came out of the association between culture and class distinction in the reaction to Matthew Arnold's *Culture and Anarchy*. See Williams, *Keywords*, 92.

20. Bradby & Delgado, 'Editorial', 3; Quinn, 'Art Festivals and the City', 931; Prentice & Andersen, 'Festival as Creative Destination', 7–8.

21. F. E. Manning, cited in Quinn, 'Changing Festival Places', 238; Quinn, 'Art Festivals and the City', 927.

22. Much of this work has been from the perspectives of geographers and researchers in tourism and cultural policy. See e.g. Jamieson, 'Edinburgh'; Prentice & Andersen, 'Festival as Creative Destination'; Quinn, 'Arts Festivals and the City'; Waterman, 'Carnivals for Elites?'; Wehle, ' "Avignon, Everybody's Dream" '.

23. Bradby & Delgado, 'Editorial', 2.

24. Harvie, 'Cultural Effects of the Edinburgh International Festival'. See also Harvie, *Staging the UK*, Chapter 4.

25. Shrum, *Fringe and Fortune*.

26. Historians have explored some aspects of festivals in nineteenth-century Britain e.g. Drummond, *The Provincial Music Festival in England*. In the twentieth century, the Festival of Britain of 1951 has merited some attention: see Atkinson, *The Festival of Britain*; Conekin, 'The Autobiography of a Nation'.

27. Waterman, 'Carnivals for Elites?', 65.

28. Quinn, 'Arts Festivals and the City', 934.

29. Quinn, 'Symbols, Practices and Myth-making', 332; Quinn, 'Arts Festivals and the City', 937.

30. See Hewison, *Too Much*.

31. McGuigan, ' "A Slow Reach Again for Control" ', 105; Williams, *Keywords*, 17.

32. Williams, *Culture and Society*, 16.

33. Dworkin, *Cultural Marxism in Postwar Britain*, 3, 79. It is important to acknowledge the importance of the Hungarian Uprising of 1956, too, in creating the New Left. Intellectuals who had been expelled from the Communist Party of Great Britain, or who had left in protest at the brutal Russian suppression of the uprising, came together to form the New Left. This created an 'injection of fresh thinking from a newly independent, radical Left [which] had a stimulating effect on the orthodox Labour movement' (Hewison, *Culture and Consensus*, 106–7).

34. Hoggart, *The Uses of Literacy*; Hewison, *Culture and Consensus*. There was also a long-standing fear of Americanisation linked to anxieties about mass culture in post-war Britain.

35. Gray, *The Politics of the Arts in Britain*, 35.
36. Leventhal, ' "The Best for the Most" '.
37. The Entertainments National Service Association (ENSA) was also resurrected to provide entertainment for troops, as it had done during the First World War. CEMA had roots in adult education: see McArthur, *Scotland, CEMA and the Arts Council*.
38. Hewison, *Culture and Consensus*, 33–4. See also Leventhal, ' "The Best for the Most" '.
39. Hewison, *In Anger*, 6.
40. Conekin, '*The Autobiography of a Nation*', 119.
41. Shellard, *British Theatre since the War*, 6. See Sinclair, *Arts and Cultures*.
42. Galloway & Jones, 'The Scottish Dimension of British Arts Government', 29.
43. Similar provisions were made for England and Wales in the Local Government Act of 1948, except that the rate limit was sixpence.
44. Matthew Arnold (1822–88) was highly influential in the mid-Victorian period, especially in the spheres of religion, culture and education. Although *Culture and Anarchy* was first published in book form in 1869, the basis of his arguments had been presented throughout 1867 and 1868, in lectures and in articles in the literary journal *Cornhill*. Storey (ed.), *Cultural Theory and Popular Culture*, 3.
45. Art and culture were 'crudely associated' with public order in the early part of the nineteenth century too. See Bennett, 'Cultural Policy in the United Kingdom', 207–8. Arnold's writings on culture responded to fears that the enactment of the Reform Act (1867) would create anarchy when the working classes achieved more political power. Arnold, *Culture and Anarchy*, xxxiii, 44–5, 100, 204.
46. Ibid., 6.
47. Arnold, *Culture and Anarchy*, 70, 108–9; Bennett, 'Cultural Policy in the United Kingdom', 207.
48. Sinfield, *Literature, Politics and Culture in Postwar Britain*, 50. For a longer view of ideas underpinning cultural policy in Britain see Bennett, 'Cultural Policy in the United Kingdom'.
49. Peter Ackroyd, cited in Hewison, *Culture and Consensus*, 51.
50. Eliot, *Notes towards the Definition of Culture*, 27.
51. Spender, *Eliot*, 231.
52. Eliot, *Notes towards the Definition of Culture*, 36–48.
53. Sinfield, *Literature, Politics and Culture in Postwar Britain*, 44–5.
54. Hayes, 'More than "Music-While-You-Eat"?', 209–10.
55. Secretary of CEMA from 1939 to 1944, Glasgow was also secretary general of CEMA (1944–6) and secretary general of the Arts Council (1946–51). Glasgow, 'The Concept of the Arts Council', 262.
56. For more on this, see Leventhal, ' "The Best for the Most" '.
57. McArthur, *Scotland, CEMA and the Arts Council*, 233–4.
58. Cited in Glasgow, 'The Concept of the Arts Council', 261.
59. Hutchison, *The Politics of the Arts Council*, 13.

60. The latter point was argued by Jonathan Rose, cited in McArthur, *Scotland, CEMA and the Arts Council*, 318–19.
61. Laing, 'The Politics of Culture', 72.
62. Eliot wrote that 'culture is not merely the sum of several activities, but a *way of life*' (Eliot, *Notes towards the Definition of Culture*, 41). See Williams, *Culture and Society, 1780–1950*, 229 (see 224–38 for a focused discussion on Eliot).
63. Williams, *The Long Revolution*, ix.
64. Dworkin, *Cultural Marxism in Postwar Britain*, 96.
65. Ibid, 42–3, 46. Williams has been criticised for leaving the new field of cultural studies with a very loose anthropological definition of culture. McGuigan, ' "A Slow Reach Again for Control" ', 110.
66. Williams, *The Long Revolution*, xi, 273.
67. Hall and Whannel were influenced by Williams's arguments in *Culture and Society* and *The Long Revolution*, particularly those on the role of the media in cultural change and in the formation of new social relationships. Hall & Whannel, *The Popular Arts*, 22, 45.
68. Priestman, 'A Critical Stage', 131.
69. Stevenson & Wallace, *Scottish Theatre since the Seventies*, 14
70. Billington was deputy to Irving Wardle on *The Times* (1965–71) and has been theatre critic for *The Guardian* since October 1971. Billington, *State of the Nation*, 5; Priestman, 'A Critical Stage', 118.
71. Williams, *The Long Revolution*, xi, 273.
72. See e.g. Billington, *State of the Nation*; Elsom, *Theatre outside London*; Hinchliffe, *British Theatre*; Shellard, *British Theatre since the War*; Shellard, *The Golden Generation*. Arthur Marwick has given the work of the Traverse some attention, while *Scotsman* drama critic Joyce McMillan published a history of the Traverse itself. See Marwick, *The Sixties*, 348–52; McMillan, *The Traverse Theatre Story*.
73. For more on this see e.g. Edwards, 'Cradle on the Tree-top', 48.
74. Bruce, *Festival in the North*, 14.
75. Stevenson & Wallace, *Scottish Theatre since the Seventies*, 14.
76. A player was 7:84: Scotland, a theatre company that reignited interest in Scotland's theatrical past by presenting 'Clydebuilt' in 1982, a season of Scottish plays from the 1920s, 1930s and 1940s. Scullion, 'Glasgow Unity Theatre', 215–16, 250.
77. Edwards, 'Cradle on the Tree-top', 34.
78. The Traverse and Lyceum theatres will be explored from Chapter 5. Stevenson, 'Scottish Theatre'.
79. McArthur, 'The Cultural Front', 192.
80. Waterman, 'Carnivals for Elites?', 63.
81. Stevenson & Wallace, *Scottish Theatre since the Seventies*, 14.
82. Rosie, 'Religion', 78.
83. Highet, *The Scottish Churches*, 198.
84. See e.g. Cameron, *Impaled upon a Thistle*.
85. Davidson & Davis, *The Sexual State*, 147.

86. Elders also represented their church at presbytery meetings, and could potentially represent their districts and areas at the next two 'layers' in the church courts, synods and the 'supreme court', the General Assembly.
87. McCrone, *Understanding Scotland*, 112.
88. Even in 1971, when the Labour Party won the most seats for the first time (twenty-eight to the Progressives' twenty-seven), the Conservatives had nine seats, meaning that there was still a right-wing majority. Grateful thanks to Jane Mactavish, ECL, for providing this data.
89. The office of Secretary for Scotland was raised to a full secretary of state in 1926. See Cameron, *Impaled upon a Thistle*.
90. Whitley, *Thorns and Thistles*, 25.
91. Brown, *The Death of Christian Britain*, 175–80.
92. Brown, 'Religion and Secularisation', 52.
93. McLeod, *The Religious Crisis of the 1960s*, 1. The 'long 1960s' covers from around 1956 to 1974.
94. Brown, *The Death of Christian Britain*, 175–80.
95. McLeod, *The Religious Crisis of the 1960s*. For a review of the secularisation debate, see Morris, 'The Strange Death of Christian Britain'.
96. Highet, *The Scottish Churches*, 184.
97. Donnelly, *Sixties Britain*, 116. The very term 'permissive' remains contentious and debate continues about just how permissive 1960s Britain really was, particularly in light of the moral backlash that occurred in the late 1960s and early 1970s. See Collins, *The Permissive Society and Its Enemies*.
98. Booker, *The Neophiliacs*, 12.
99. Marwick *The Sixties*, 5–20.
100. Varon et al., 'Time Is an Ocean', 1.
101. Donnelly, *Sixties Britain*, xiii. See also Sandbrook, *Never Had It So Good*; Sandbrook, *White Heat*.
102. Varon et al., 'Time Is an Ocean', 4.
103. Finlay, *Modern Scotland*, 249.
104. For more on the Citizens, see Coveney, *The Citz*; Oliver, *Magic in the Gorbals*. For a personal perspective on the cultural scene in early 1960s Glasgow, see Bartie, 'EXPLORER'.
105. Bell, '"The Ugly Burds without Wings"'; Bell, 'Experimenting with the Verbivocovisual'.
106. There are notable exceptions. See e.g. Birrell & Finlay, *Justified Sinners*; Normand, '55° North 3° West'.
107. Birrell & Finlay, *Justified Sinners*.
108. Eleanor Bell and Linda Gunn are due to publish a new book, *The Scottish Sixties*; Bell and I revisited the Scottish cultural scene on the eve of the 1960s 'cultural explosion' in *The International Writers Conference Revisited*. A number of research students are also working on aspects of the Scottish culture in the 1960s, for example Stewart Smith (on Ian Hamilton Finlay and Alec Finlay) and Gillian Tasker (on Alexander Trocchi).

109. Nairn, 'Festival of the Dead'; see e.g. Stevenson & Wallace, *Scottish Theatre since the Seventies*.
110. Varon et al. wondered 'whether a more circumspect language of repetition with variation or change is not more appropriate to characterize the period's transformations – in part or as a whole – than a vocabulary of watershed, rupture, or epistemic shift' (Varon et al., 'Time Is an Ocean', 4).

2

The Cultural Resort of Europe: The Creation of the Festival, c. 1944–1947

At a reception prior to the opening of the inaugural Festival, the Lord Provost of Edinburgh and chairman of the Edinburgh Festival Society, Sir John Falconer, remarked:

> The human mind needs an occasional stretch into an overflowing fountain of grace and beneficence to confirm its weak faith, and to anchor it to something higher than itself. This city may become the cultural resort of Europe, where men and women will find a haven, not merely to hear and see, but to be quiet and respond to a life of spiritual and intellectual refreshment and inspiration.[1]

Coming after the long years of the Second World War, in a year beset by the harshest winter in living memory, austerity measures, continued rationing and an ongoing sterling crisis, the 'cultural feast' of the Edinburgh International Festival of Music and the Arts seemed at odds with the society in which it took place. Yet it also symbolised the optimism and possibilities of the postwar world, part of the new, stable and inclusive society that many sought to build in the aftermath of war, and one in which the spread of culture was anticipated as part of the broader welfare state.

THE INITIAL PROPOSAL

The idea of creating an international festival of the arts in Britain originated from Rudolf Bing (1902–97), general manager of Glyndebourne Festival Opera in the Sussex Downs.[2] Built for the purpose of staging a Mozart festival in 1934, Glyndebourne had become a world-famous institution famed for its summer opera festivals. As it had had to close during the Second World War, Bing was concerned that it would be impossible to revive it in 'the dark, petrol-less years immediately after the war' and so he hit upon the idea of having an arts festival that would pay tribute to Britain's struggle during the war, but also support Glyndebourne so that it could be revived later. According to Bing, Oxford was the first choice but he had been unable to 'bring town and gown together in a joint venture'.[3] Edinburgh was not even the second choice; apparently Bath, Chester, Cambridge and Canter-

bury were considered before attention turned to the Scottish capital. The oft-
repeated 'legend' is that in 1942, while walking along Princes Street in
Edinburgh, Bing was inspired by his surroundings to start an arts festival to
help solve Glyndebourne's financial problems.[4] In his autobiography, Bing
recalled that during a trip to Edinburgh in 1940 he had noted that the castle
on the hill 'had a Salzburg flavour'.[5] Edinburgh's picturesque setting combined with more practical advantages secured it as the location for this new
festival.

After the failure at Oxford, Bing met with representatives of the British
Council during a visit to London in December 1944. This meeting saw the
'seed take root' when Henry Harvey Wood, Scottish representative of the
British Council offices in Edinburgh, suggested Edinburgh as a venue for the
proposed festival (though he noted that Bing was at first sceptical 'because of
the Scottish climate').[6] But after visiting Edinburgh and lunching with some
of Wood's friends – who included Professor Sidney Newman (conductor of
the Reid Orchestra), Murray Watson (editor of *The Scotsman*) and the
Countess of Rosebery (a keen patron of the arts) – Bing received a response so
enthusiastic that plans were made to approach the city fathers. Edinburgh did
not boast a long-standing love of the arts or a proven record for encouraging
music and drama, but had more practical reasons going for it: the city had
suffered very little bomb damage, had a natural beauty and a 'colourful
history', was capable of accommodating 50,000 to 100,000 visitors, had
good rail connections and enough theatres, and was an area in which the
British Council operated.[7] The idea was officially proposed at a meeting
between Bing and the Lord Provost, the town clerk, the city treasurer and the
city chamberlain in February 1945. It was not made in specifically cultural
terms because, according to Bing, the Lord Provost, though 'an awfully nice
little man', had 'not the foggiest notion of what I was talking about' (we will
see that Falconer actually took a very active role in early preparations for the
Festival). Rather, it was put forward in terms of what such a venture would
do to benefit the city of Edinburgh's international standing and, perhaps,
economy.[8] While Falconer was enthusiastic from the outset, Bing and Wood
encountered problems from other members of the corporation between
February 1945 and September 1946, when the town council finally approved
the plans. As Eileen Miller notes, Falconer 'had the enthusiasm to inspire his
colleagues on the council and the determination to steer the scheme safely
through the mass of civic obstacles that would inevitably be raised in its
path'.[9]

There was some resistance to the idea of an international festival of the arts
being held in Edinburgh. Bing wondered 'whether the sombre Scottish capital
could acquire the necessary "festival spirit", as understood in the European
festival centres'.[10] Within Edinburgh Corporation, Bing and Wood had to
work hard to convince councillors that the plan had a 'reasonable chance of
success'.[11] One unnamed civil servant at the Scottish Office thought that

having an international arts festival in Edinburgh in August 1947 was 'quite reckless' and the surest way to defeat any hope that it could become an annual event:

> To bring people from lands of plenty to a Scotland where hardly a taxi can be had when it rains – as it will surely do – and where wine, spirits and confectionery are virtually unobtainable except in minute quantities and at preposterous prices, is the surest way of driving them to give Scotland a miss in future, and to advise their compatriots to do likewise.[12]

The public were notified in November 1945 that consideration was being given to a festival in Edinburgh to take place in summer or early autumn 1947 in a press release appealing for the help of all interested 'in the creation of an Arts Festival of the highest standard in the Scottish capital'.[13]

SHAPING THE FESTIVAL

Work began on shaping and organising this ambitious venture. The Edinburgh Festival Society Limited (EFS) was officially created a year later, in November 1946. According to the memorandum of association, its first object was to 'promote and encourage the arts, especially opera, plays, dramas, ballets and music'.[14] The articles of association also specified that the company would consist of 150 members, with all 'such members present and future of Edinburgh Town Council' automatically becoming members. Any transaction of business at meetings required at least six members present; no fewer than two of these had to be town council members. Furthermore, the chairman of the Festival Society, whose role was to oversee the administration and organisation of the Festival each year, was named as the Lord Provost of Edinburgh. Edinburgh Corporation (the term commonly used to refer to the Town Council) was to have a significant degree of control over the newly created EFS, at least on an administrative level. Within the society, several committees were formed: Finance and General Purposes, Programme, Catering, Reception and Addition of Members.[15]

But despite this evidence of careful planning, responsibilities for the organisation of the first Festival were not clearly defined and were reworked as the plans for the Festival progressed. Individuals appear to have played a larger part in organising funding and choosing the programme than the committees. Although there was a Programme Committee, headed by Henry Harvey Wood, it was Rudolf Bing, as artistic director, who was largely in charge of the programme for the first Festival, and who wrote all of the initial reports on the programmes and finance. Lord Provost Falconer also took on a significant role in organising the inaugural Festival, including corresponding and meeting with representatives of the Arts Council and drumming up financial support. Discussions surrounding the Festival and its organisation were not restricted to the committees of the EFS, but also took place through existing channels of local government, for example town council and Lord Provost committee meetings.

Between September 1946, when plans were finally approved by the corporation, and the opening of the Edinburgh International Festival on 23 August 1947, attention was given to the actual organisation of the Festival, in terms of its administration and content and also, crucially, securing enough funding for the venture. Bing was arguably the most important individual in both the development and final shape of the inaugural Festival. In an early report, it was agreed that Glyndebourne, 'as originator of the Edinburgh Festival' and itself Britain's leading pre-war festival centre, would offer its services for the organisation of the Festival and, in consultation with the various committees, also prepare its programme.[16] In this respect, Glyndebourne was to act as 'organising centre' without payment, other than the reimbursement of outlays and overheads – as a 'servant' to the EFS.[17] Nonetheless, securing external funding for the venture was crucial. Glyndebourne itself could not offer financial support (and, indeed, was depending on the Edinburgh Festival to support its programme). Bing wrote in his memoirs that Sir John Christie, Glyndebourne's owner, did not personally get on with the chairman of the Arts Council, Lord Keynes, and that this was why Glyndebourne did not receive support from the Arts Council.[18] Mary Glasgow, then Arts Council secretary general, recalled that Keynes and Christie had a 'continuing battle', that Christie had 'pleaded hard' for subsidy from CEMA for Glyndebourne Opera for when it reopened after the war 'and his resentment when it was refused was great and lasting'.[19] Bing knew that a venture on the scale he anticipated for Edinburgh would require government support; he thought that by having the Festival in Edinburgh, he could bypass the Arts Council through the British Council.[20]

The recently created Arts Council of Great Britain was 'at first somewhat aloof' to Edinburgh's festival plans. While Wood had been involved right from the first mention of an arts festival, being instrumental in Edinburgh becoming the chosen location, giving practical advice on promotional material and heading the Programme Committee, it was September 1946 before the Arts Council formally agreed to be associated with the venture and offered a grant of £20,000.[21] This came after some prompting. Falconer formally invited the Arts Council to support the proposed Edinburgh International Festival in November 1945. That same month, he also invited Osborne Henry Mavor (1888–1951), better known as the playwright James Bridie, to join the general committee organising the proposed Festival.[22] At that time, Bridie was also chairman of the Scottish Committee and a member of the General Council of the Arts Council. In February 1946, after some months of prompting, the Arts Council responded to state that it was 'not prepared to enter into formal association with the Festival Committee or to offer any financial help at this early stage'.[23] By April 1946, however, Bridie had written to Keynes, pointing out that the British Council people in Edinburgh and Tom Johnston (in his capacity as chairman of the new Scottish Tourist Board) were 'very anxious' about the forthcoming Festival and felt that the Arts Council should take a prominent role in it. Bridie felt that the venture was unlikely to succeed without Arts Council support, and even suggested to Keynes that the theatre director Tyrone Guthrie should replace Bing as artistic director because, despite having 'performed the remarkable feat of rousing enthusiasm in Edinburgh', he did not consider Bing a 'very reliable guide'.[24] Later, concerns were raised about the role of Bing and Glyndebourne in the organisation of the Festival; a number of Arts Council representatives (including Glasgow) expressed their unease with this arrangement and sought confirmation that Bing would not be acting as a representative of Glyndebourne while artistic director of the Festival.[25]

Another arts festival, focused primarily on drama, combining civic support and government funding for arts, and with the joint aims of tempting tourists and promoting the arts, was discussed the year that the Edinburgh International Festival was officially proposed, albeit on a smaller scale and in a different location. Bridie had participated in an informal conference held in Perth in October 1945 to discuss a Scottish theatre festival planned for July 1946. It was felt that such a festival was 'highly desirable as an adjunct to the Highlands as a tourist centre', in order to offer some permanent attractions for the 'mind' of the visitor, and perhaps more importantly, to 'make Scotland, as a whole, more theatre conscious to the benefit of Scots Theatres'.[26] Indeed, in August 1945 the first Perth Theatre Festival had been held with Bridie as patron, and in his letter of acceptance he had congratulated Perth theatre on the way it had revived drama all over Scotland. In fact, he commented, 'I look forward to the time when Perth will invite [Scottish theatres] to co-operate in making Perth a Scottish Salsburg [sic]. Everybody who loves the noble art of the drama must wish them well.'[27] It was planned that the festival would be organised by the Scottish Committee of the Arts Council, with the help of an organising committee comprising representatives from the Scottish repertories, the Arts Council, tourist organisations and Perth civic authorities.[28]

Bridie was a champion of Scottish theatre and while in CEMA, and then the Arts Council, was in a 'good strategic position' to make a structured contribution to Scottish drama beyond his own plays.[29] On his appointment as chairman of the Scottish Committee of CEMA, the Scottish Secretary of State, Tom Johnston, had given Bridie private instructions to be 'Scotland's man'.[30] Certainly, Bridie had been disappointed with CEMA's attitude to Scotland, charging that it viewed Scotland's status as 'equivalent to an English provincial city or area'.[31] As early as 1943, Bridie had argued that the London office did not appreciate the heavy workload of the Scottish Committee, and commented on the necessity of 'selling' CEMA to Scotland, 'where a certain amount of prejudice still exists'.[32] In fact, between 1940 (when CEMA first appeared in Scotland) and 1943 (when its Scottish Committee was formally established), negotiations over the practical autonomy of Scotland as part of the fledgling Britain-wide organisation were taking place. These largely arose due to the way in which CEMA was founded as part of the Board of Education, without consideration that Scotland and Northern Ireland had devolved education systems. In the end, Northern Ireland was excluded from CEMA's remit, while Scotland was included; Northern Ireland created its own arts organisation, and Scotland negotiated a devolved body within a wider British organisation.[33] Euan McArthur emphasises that there was a difference between political nationalism and cultural nationalism during this period:

> Cultural nationalist feelings were expressed consistently by Scottish Committee members, but although sometimes linked to political aspirations, the Committee's determination to secure its ambitions, if at all possible, within a British structure is striking. Separation was only contemplated under the direst pressure. Hostility within CEMA's Council to Scottish nationalism was marked by a general failure to distinguish between its political and cultural aspects.[34]

Keynes, chairman of CEMA from April 1942, was particularly guilty of this kind of hostility, and tensions between London and Scotland were not resolved by the formation of the Scottish Committee in 1943. Between 1945 and 1946 – at the same time as the early Festival discussions were taking place – 'tense negotiations' were underway for the Arts Council's Royal Charter. Keynes had not consulted the Scottish Committee during his plans to turn CEMA into the Arts Council, which led to Bridie threatening to resign if the Scottish Committee was denied official status in the Royal Charter. Mary Glasgow wrote that the Scottish Committee was a 'particular source of irritation' for Keynes, due to its 'insistent demand' for a Goschen formula share of funds. Said Keynes, 'I would rather hand them over their share of the money, leaving them to stew in their own feeble juice, than agree to a separatist precedent which would allow them to get the best of both worlds.'[35] In the end, devolution was agreed: a Scottish Committee 'with powers to "advise and assist" the Council in the promotion of its objects in Scotland' was created after involvement from the Scottish Education Department and the Secretary of State for Scotland.[36] Andrew Sinclair has noted that Keynes was 'tetchy' about the Arts Council in Scotland and preferred a policy of centralism (in London). In 1945, Keynes had expressed his hope to restore the capital as 'a great artistic metropolis'.[37] Bridie later charged that the new Arts Council was over-active in London, which 'has less need for "encouragement" in Music and the Arts'.[38] Keynes died in spring 1946, before the Arts Council was incorporated under Royal Charter, but he was hugely influential in shaping its development out of CEMA.[39]

It is significant that the embryonic festival was being organised and discussed at the same time as negotiations were taking place for the development of the Arts Council, and particularly during debates about devolved control for nations within the Union. The correspondence between those involved in the development of the Edinburgh International Festival and representatives of the Arts Council (roles that overlapped in the case of Bridie) reveal a range of concerns about the form and content of the proposed Festival. For one, an international arts festival in the Scottish capital conflicted with Keynes's vision of London as the 'great artistic metropolis' of post-war Britain. There was also a very palpable fear that involving the Scottish Committee of the Arts Council would lead to a more nationalistic festival, like the Scottish Theatre Festival envisioned by Bridie in October 1946. Some members of the Arts Council's Scottish Committee were considered 'too nationalistic and difficult to work with' by the London office.[40]

The records of the Arts Council on the Edinburgh Festival certainly reveal ongoing concerns about how Scottish the programme was to be. For example, a letter from Glasgow to Stewart Cruickshank, manager of the King's Theatre in Edinburgh and member of the EFS Programme Committee, asked of the Festival:

> Is it to be British, so far as this country's contribution is concerned, or mainly Scottish? Is it to be Scotland acting as host to distinguished foreign artists and giving them in turn the best that Scotland can offer; or is it to be Great Britain acting as host, with Edinburgh as the chosen seat of entertainment?[41]

Four months later, Glasgow wrote in a letter to Keynes that the Edinburgh Festival organisers

> do not seem to have decided properly whether it is to be a Festival of British art for foreigners or of International art for everyone. (Probably, it will be, in fact, a Festival of Scottish art, although the Lord Provost disclaims that suggestion.)[42]

Arts Council members were keen to ensure that the Festival did not become a vehicle for the promotion of the Scottish arts. As the Arts Council director of art, Philip James, noted: 'If there are to be exhibitions they *must not* be of Scottish art. Should we not have some say in the design of the publicity and indeed of the productions themselves lest these become too much *à l'écossaise*?'[43] The period between November 1945 and summer 1946 was one of protracted negotiation between the Festival organisers and Arts Council representatives in London.[44]

In June 1946, Bridie received a letter from Glasgow stating: 'Personally, I like the look of the Festival less and less.' The Arts Council director for Scotland, Mrs S. Shirley Fox, responded that she had ingenuously supposed that the Arts Council would wish to have at least a finger, if not a hand, in a big arts festival [. . .] As I see it, of all the buses that the Council has had an opportunity of missing, the Festival is just about the largest and fastest. The position now appears to be that any money that we might be able to give would be so small a proportion of the total sum required that it would give us no more than a side-show concession. And the opportunity that we might have taken of acting as general artistic consultants is now long past. Moreover, the Festival Directorate now has the unfortunate impression that we regard the whole thing as a potential gold brick.[45]

The Arts Council finally awarded the Edinburgh Festival formal association and financial support in August 1946, subject to certain conditions including 'that the programme of the Festival is approved by the Arts Council'.[46] This was despite its policy of not interfering 'with the arrangements of our associated companies and orchestras'.[47] Since Lord Provost Falconer was an 'energetic champion of the cause', Edinburgh Corporation was rallied into providing funding, making a grant of £20,000 towards the costs in the first year. Application was also made to the Secretary of State for Scotland for a scheme of public utility under Section 16(1) of the Local Government (Scotland) Act to meet expenditure not exceeding £1,000, while the remainder of the money required to fund the venture came from donations. The Earl and Countess of Rosebery had famously donated the money made when one of the earl's horses, Ocean Swell, won the Derby and Jockey Club Cup in 1944.[48] The issue of funding made the plans for the Festival a little fraught in those early years, especially since the costs involved were not modest by contemporary standards for public culture.[49] Indeed, the funding provided to the Festival by Edinburgh Corporation became a source of contention in later years, including the charge that ratepayers' money should be spent on amenities and repairs required in the city rather than a festival that was often accused of being for visitors, not for Edinburgh.

HOSTESS OF THE ARTS

The Royal Charter of the Arts Council of Great Britain stated that its purpose was:

> Developing a greater knowledge, understanding and practice of the fine arts exclusively, and in particular to increase the accessibility of the fine arts to the public throughout Our Realm, and to improve the standard of execution of the fine arts and to advise and co-operate with Our Government Departments, local authorities and other bodies on any matters concerned directly or indirectly with those objects.[50]

This emphasis on the fine arts was also reflected in broadcasting. The 'cultural elitism' of the BBC manifested itself in 1946 with the creation of the Third Programme, a BBC radio channel dedicated to the arts with an unashamedly 'high-brow' content. It was envisaged that listeners would be led (as their tastes became more refined) from the Light Programme to the Home Service and finally to the Third Programme, the pinnacle of this 'broadly based cultural pyramid'.[51] Likewise, the Arts Council was intended to lead people on to 'finer' arts; at this time, it gave most of its funding to the most expensive arts, namely opera and ballet.[52]

The Edinburgh International Festival was clearly a product of its time. The artistic standard was intended to be 'superlative', as an early report (written in summer 1945) noted.[53] In the foreword of the first programme, Lord Provost Falconer stated that the Festival was presenting the 'highest and purest ideals of art in its many and varied forms'.[54] However, there appeared to be some confusion among the public and press concerning the aims of this new arts festival. In May 1947, 'Vagula Blandula', of local Edinburgh newspaper the *Evening Dispatch*, tried to remind readers that they were not on a 'cultural mission' and that the enterprise was *not* for 'Scotland's cultural enlightenment', since 'Scotland just couldn't afford to organise such an expensive cultural treat for herself'. Rather, 'Blandula' argued, the 'real purpose of our Festival is to provide a good draw for visitors – in the shape of what they want to see and hear, not what Scots think they ought to'. S/he summarised the 'Hard-Fact Basis' of the Festival: 'With no cultural aces of her own to strengthen her hand, she has scooped the pool – become a No. 1 centre in a paying commercial line, the commerce of culture.'[55] There was a vital economic aspect to the venture, and this is where the term 'the commerce of culture' manages to encapsulate two very important developments in post-war Britain: the new role of culture in society, supported by state funding, and its use as a means of attracting tourists and therefore boosting the economy. Indeed, initial reports on the Festival and early press releases emphasised tourism. While the Festival was organised with the 'highest' ideals in mind, to promote art of the highest possible standard performed by the best artists in the world, and so enliven and enrich international cultural life, at a practical level it was intended as an attraction for tourists and an economic boost. One of the central driving forces was to 'draw to the British Isles the World's Tourist Traffic', and right from the earliest planning stages, the British Travel Association, Thomas Cook, and the newly created Scottish Tourist Board were all involved.[56] This was particularly important given the sterling crisis experienced throughout 1947 and the pressing need to attract dollars into the British economy.[57]

According to the EFS, Edinburgh was to be 'hostess to other nations, inviting them to bring their best in the arts and to bring, also, their travellers and holidaymakers'.[58] Taking advantage of the number of visitors expected to arrive in Edinburgh, the Chamber of Commerce arranged to devote all of the windows in Princes Street to an exhibition presenting Scotland's industries, arts and crafts for the duration of the Festival. Furthermore, an

Enterprise Scotland exhibition was organised and held throughout and beyond the Festival period in the Royal Scottish Museum in Edinburgh. The timing of the Festival was planned to make it a holiday festival and, since Britain was still faced with rationing and austerity measures, special arrangements were made for visitors.[59] The General Committee of the Festival Society arranged for a subcommittee to 'purvey Edinburgh's hostery to the visitor', including having 'Scottish items' like piping and dancing available for tourists, and organising a group of reliable guides whose mission was to make sure visitors got the 'true story' of Edinburgh.[60] 'Blandula' commented that Edinburgh's 'real vocation' was to 'win good-will, dollars, and crowns by providing tourists with the accommodation, entertainment and activities that tickle them best and make them want to come back'.[61]

However, the Festival was not just a chance for Edinburgh to attract tourists and boost its local economy. With the eyes of the world on Edinburgh, this was a chance for the city fathers to renew its long-held reputation – as the seat of Scottish Presbyterianism, home of the eighteenth-century Scottish Enlightenment and centre of the more recent Scottish literary renaissance. Edinburgh had once been widely known as the 'Athens of the North', and during the Scottish Enlightenment, the city had been regarded as the 'cultural capital of Scotland' and civic importance attached to the pursuit of the 'polite arts'.[62] Festivals had taken place in Edinburgh more than 100 years before the International Festival (a number of musical festivals had been held between 1815 and 1871).[63] Yet, in the run-up to the Festival, James Bridie remarked that during the eighteenth century, Edinburgh had grown so

> proud and haughty that nothing below the standard set by these astonishing men [Enlightenment thinkers such as David Hume] was good enough for her. She founded a school of criticism that blasted and withered the creative arts for hundreds of miles around [. . .] Edinburgh was left with the Kirk, the Law and the practice of medicine. The arts became attenuated and sporadic.[64]

Nonetheless, during a spot on the Third Programme in April 1947, Bridie declared that 'Edinburgh has already smoothed out her habitual frown and is taking on an Athenian aspect. When the fiddlers tune up this August they may be playing in a new era.'[65] The Festival afforded a fantastic opportunity to renew Edinburgh's reputation as a city of great faith and importance. It had been a leave city for American, Norwegian, Polish and Dominion troops during the war years. In 1947, Sir Robert Bruce Lockhart, writer and Foreign Office diplomat, wrote that during the war, 'drunkenness, rowdiness, and immorality were unbridled' and that in Edinburgh, 'I felt the presence of a dying civilisation'. To Lockhart, Scotland was losing its 'virtues' and 'without a national revival' Scotland would be 'doomed beyond salvation'.[66] The approach that both civic government in Edinburgh and the national Church of Scotland took to the arts was bound up in many ways with concerns about moral decline and national revival.

For Falconer and Edinburgh Corporation, the Edinburgh Festival was an integral part of that revival. Falconer announced that the Festival was to become an annual event 'sustained on the very highest level so that the capital city might become the cultural resort of Europe'.[67] This was a 'proudly planned' festival with civic identity at its very heart, and it was not just Edinburgh's revival that Falconer hoped to achieve. In connection with the aforementioned Enterprise Scotland Exhibition, Falconer – in a highly symbolic ritual – revived a centuries-old Highland tradition using the 'Fiery Cross'.[68] This was a cross made of birch wood bound with leather thongs, and was 'traditionally the call to Scottish clans to join battle or give assistance'. Falconer reignited the ancient ceremony, last observed in the eighteenth century, in Edinburgh at the beginning of August 1947, during which he lit a number of crosses, then allegedly extinguished the flames in goat's blood before attaching a small flag of the nation that each cross was destined for to its charred edges; these included England, the United States of America, Australia, New Zealand, the Netherlands, Denmark and France.[69] Here the Lord Provost was using a novel and highly symbolic means to ask Scots all over the world to support the 'new Scotland', of which the Festival was an important part. In a message to the Lord Mayor of London, on the day that the Fiery Cross reached the capital, Falconer proclaimed: 'To-day we are raising the Fiery Cross in friendship, but it signifies danger [. . .] We are rallying with it the spirit of Scotsmen all over the world to restore our position.'[70] Edinburgh was marketed as a 'spiritual haven', and the Fiery Cross was not the only symbol of Christianity that was utilised, since the Festival began, and ended, with a religious ceremony.[71] Indeed, during the inaugural opening ceremony at St Giles', the Very Revd Dr Charles Warr, Minister of St Giles' and Dean of the Thistle, described the occasion as 'historic' since it 'emphasised the unity between churchmen and the civic authorities regarding the Festival'.[72] It was evident during the first Festival that issues of moral and economic regeneration, as well as national identity, were to be bound up with religion and its associated symbols.

WEAPON OF ENLIGHTENMENT

One of the most interesting developments in the post-war period was the way that churches began to formally utilise the arts. The influence of the Kirk has often been blamed for Scotland's 'sporadic' theatre history, due to its suppression of theatre and its regular submitting of churchgoers to sermons 'of fire and brimstone, or figural conflict between the Beast and the Lord, Heaven and Hell, quite dramatic enough to overwhelm anything the stage itself could offer'.[73] However, even before the Second World War, churches had begun to get very interested in the use of drama. From about 1890, church drama groups had been popular and by the 1920s and 1930s they were part of congregational life in many suburban churches. Amateur drama in Scotland experienced a 'boom period' of activity, with church groups making up a large proportion of the amateur groups in existence.[74] Indeed, this was a period of unprecedented interest in the theatre, with repertory theatres established in a number of towns and cities, including St Andrews (1933), Perth (1935), Dundee and Rutherglen (both 1939), and subsequently Glasgow (1943) and Pitlochry (1951). Perth & Kinross County Council, in a 'quite unprecedented move', formed a committee of management to run the Perth Repertory Theatre Company. The idea of 'civic theatre' became popular as theatre was increasingly seen as having a function that 'served the common good' in social and economic terms, as well as being a 'useful tool in the growing industry of tourism'.[75] Adrienne Scullion points to the immense success of amateur theatre organisations like the British Drama League and the Scottish Community Drama Association (SCDA) during the inter-war period, both of which 'promoted a quintessentially bourgeois ethos of improvement through culture' and helped to popularise the 'fashionable and increasingly influential' idea that 'drama is good for you'.[76] The Church of Scotland had even set up a Kirk Drama Federation, which ran competitions and co-ordinated drama groups across Scotland (and, from 1950, an annual festival of drama). However, drama then was predominantly a recreational activity, looked on somewhat disdainfully by critics, with the arts largely used for amusement or entertainment and the material presented often seen as 'unadventurous' and 'parochial', kailyard inspired and conservative.[77] But after 1945 the use of the arts changed. The Kirk began to see drama as more than simply a means of entertainment. Drama became a 'weapon of enlightenment' and in 1946, the Church of Scotland officially welcomed the arts by opening its own theatre in Edinburgh, the Gateway Theatre.[78]

Despite some evidence of a revival of faith during the Second World War, historians have generally argued that the war helped to undermine the role of religion and traditional Christian morality in people's lives. A Mass-Observation report found that saying prayers and continuing to profess faith in Christianity were evident throughout the war years but that, for Protestantism, the war 'made matters worse than ever'. Angus Calder argues that this was in part evidenced by the physical destruction of churches, a decline in churchgoing, a shortage of manpower (including clergy), and the questions raised by reports of 'the war's horrors' – essentially, 'How could God let these things happen?' Nevertheless, the success of T. S. Eliot's work, particularly his sequence of poems *Four Quartets* (published together for the first time in 1946), demonstrates the persistence of religious ideals in popular culture. These four poems were religious in tone, but ultimately concerned with shared spiritual experience – something that had resonance with a population living through the war.[79] In order to bolster morale, the government had adopted a 'work hard, play hard' ethic which some argued contributed to the undermining of the Christian religion in Britain and accelerated the decline of religious puritanism in Scottish society.[80] Churches across Britain responded to this perceived weakening of Christian belief, and also to the growing responsibility that the state was taking for the British population through the implementation of the welfare state. The historian George I. T. Machin stated that churches were keen to point out that people required more than material needs, and that it was the duty of the churches to provide spiritual welfare.[81]

The Church of Scotland showed some anxiety about the influence of the Second World War. The growth of a 'merely secular outlook' had, according to the Committee on Church and Nation, led to a marked decline in church attendance, as well as the 'weakened hold of religion upon the human mind and consciousness'.[82] The Kirk had embarked on a number of methods designed to 'find suitable ways of getting the Message of the Gospel over in terms which this generation can understand'. In 1946, the Home Board instituted a declared policy of evangelism, notably using religious broadcasting as means of communicating the values and teachings of the Kirk, supported by the BBC under its Scottish controller, Melvin Dinwiddie. In 1945, the Committee on Social Service had told the General Assembly that the use of the 'dramatic interlude as a means of proclaiming religious truth has shown what a power the technique of radio has in the field of evangelical instruction'.[83] In the immediate post-war years the Church of Scotland was experimenting with new ways to relay the Christian message to Scotland's population and this included using the arts as one of the Church's answers 'to the problem of our changing world'.[84]

The Kirk's new openness to the arts was part of a widespread surge in ecclesiastical interest in theatre and the arts that had developed during the war years. In 1946 the *British Weekly*, subtitled *A Journal of Social and Christian Progress*, announced a revolution in the theatre and referred to a movement that had been growing, spearheaded by the British Drama League, which claimed that the art of theatre could be a factor in the cultural and educational progress of the population. The churches, the article concluded, 'are at last alive to this weapon of enlightenment'.[85] The arts, and drama in particular, comprised an interesting experiment in the expression of religion on the part of the Church, and its main function was as an educational and evangelistic tool in order to achieve reconciliation between generations.[86] This created interest within the Church in actively using drama in Christian outreach work. In 1944, the Home Board of the Church of Scotland was gifted Elm Row Community Centre in Edinburgh by an anonymous benefactor, a property then in use as a community centre and cinema. Plans were immediately made to run part of the property as a theatre. In 1945, the Home Board reported to the General Assembly that it had taken possession of Elm

Row as a challenge, a 'chance to make a great experiment to meet new circumstances with new equipment and new technique' since home mission work had changed so much that the usual methods used had become outdated.[87] The General Assembly gave its approval for the endeavour in 1946, and in October that year the new Gateway Theatre was officially opened under the direction of the Revd George Candlish (director) and Sadie Aitkin (manager). Here, the Church of Scotland, a body that had long been negative in its attitude to the theatre, and sometimes downright oppressive, had become a direct patron of the dramatic arts, and so 'entered upon an experiment unique in the history of the Church'.[88] As Winifred Bannister exclaimed, 'at last the theatre's old enemy, the Kirk, had come to accept it, even to give it hospitality!'[89]

In 1946, the Home Board reported that the theatre would be used for 'worth-while presentations of the highest standard', echoing the aim of the EFS in its initial press release of November 1945: to create 'an Arts Festival of the highest standard in the Scottish capital'.[90] In fact, it is difficult not to see the similarities between the aims of the EFS and those of the Church of Scotland in their approach to the arts. While the Home Board had initially stated that presentations would be 'dictated by a basic concern for content and Christianity', the Gateway did not restrict itself to specifically religious drama and its *raison d'être* was not to preach sermons in a dramatic form, but instead to present plays 'of educative, artistic and human value'.[91] By the time of the opening ceremony of the first International Festival, the Church was taking responsibility for 'centuries of aesthetic indifference' in Scotland and, according to the local press, taking on the duty of 'fostering and promoting aesthetic appreciation'.[92] Charles Warr recalled being visited by Rudolf Bing in 1946, who said that 'both he and Sir John [Falconer] felt strongly that it would be out of keeping with the traditions of Scotland if the Festival were not to open with a religious service' (albeit one that was in keeping with the Kirk but welcoming to other denominations).[93] The forthcoming Festival also dovetailed nicely with the Kirk's new stance on the arts.

During the opening ceremony, Warr remarked that the arts had been 'deplorably neglected in this country, to its grave and serious cultural and spiritual loss; and nowhere has this neglect been more apparent than in the Presbyterian Church'.[94] In a significant gesture, he noted, the inaugural ceremony was 'done in a church where, in the latter half of the century, first John Knox and then other ministers had laid the arts of drama and music under the ban of their zealous displeasure'. Warr voiced this change in Presbyterian policy: 'Christianity is and must be a friend of the arts. Harmony and beauty are the keynotes of creation; ugliness and discord are the negation of Christ.'[95] This was a time of idealism, a time for the Kirk to try to counter the 'cruelty, persecution, and sufferings of these dark years' and use a novel means of spreading Christian teaching.[96] To justify its new role, a philosophy was developed that linked the Church of Scotland and the artist in a symbolic alliance termed the 'New Cultural Renaissance'.[97] Through this, the Church wanted to ensure that the relationship between itself and the artist was clearly understood – that both were dedicated to the same ends, to the 'essential ideal of Beauty, Truth, Goodness, and of man as a creative being'.[98] The Gateway was intended to provide a 'common ground' for those 'seeking the Truth by way of religion and those seeking the Truth by way of Art', and was also a significant addition to theatre space in Edinburgh.[99]

For Edinburgh, the Festival was a chance to create a new post-war identity as the 'cultural resort of Europe' and reclaim its position as the 'Athens of the North', a place of major cultural and spiritual importance. As well as reasserting both a civic and a national identity through its internationalism and the high standards promised, the Festival was also a symbol of civic and religious bodies uniting through an appreciation of the spiritual power of the arts. The Church of Scotland Home Board was making plans for the property in Elm Row at the same time as the Edinburgh Festival was being negotiated and organised by Edinburgh Corporation; it is hard to believe that there was no interaction and discussion between the City Chambers and the Church of Scotland. The opinion that an arts festival would act as a 'beacon of light' in a world darkened by war and destruction appealed to the Christian ideals of the Kirk, especially since it too was looking for new and experimental ways of reaching a generation affected by war. Thus, the link between religion and the Festival had been established and, although it was to become severely strained in the years that followed (particularly during the 1960s), it was one that was to be continually renewed. In 1971 the Festival opened with a televised church service, during which the Minister of St Giles' commented that the first Festival was 'in many ways the first streak of dawn, of light after long years of all-pervading gloom, pain and hate, destruction and brutality'.[100] It is to the cultural challenge that arose from the exclusion of Scottish drama at the inaugural Festival that we must now turn, in order to understand both the development of Edinburgh as a site of cultural contest and its importance as a lens for exploring the 'culture wars' that shook the western world in the 1960s.

NOTES

1. Edinburgh Central Library (hereafter ECL), *Submission on Behalf of Edinburgh Festival Society for Nobel Peace Prize*.
2. Being of Jewish descent, Bing had been dismissed from his post as assistant administrator of the Charlottenburg opera house in Germany by order of the Nazi Party. See Forbes, 'Bing, Sir Rudolf Franz Joseph'.
3. Bing, *5,000 Nights at the Opera*, 79.
4. Miller, *The Edinburgh International Festival*, 1.
5. Bing, *5,000 Nights at the Opera*, 70.

6. Donaldson, *The British Council*, 149; National Library of Scotland (hereafter NLS), Acc. 11309, James Bridie: Edinburgh International Festival Correspondence (hereafter EIFC), 1946–9, Wood, *Notes on the Origins of the Edinburgh International Festival*.

7. Miller, *The Edinburgh International Festival*, 2; Bing, *5,000 Nights at the Opera*, 84.

8. Bing, *5,000 Nights at the Opera*, 85.

9. Miller, *The Edinburgh International Festival*, 2.

10. Ibid., 8. See also for amusing anecdotes about local councillors trying to jeopardise plans for the Festival.

11. ECA, Early Festival Papers, press release from Lord Provost of Edinburgh, 23 November 1945; NLS, Acc. 11309, Bridie: EIFC, Wood, *Notes on the Origins of the Edinburgh International Festival*.

12. National Records of Scotland (hereafter NRS), ED61/45, letter, 24 July 1946.

13. ECA, Early Festival Papers, press release from Lord Provost of Edinburgh, 23 November 1945.

14. ECA, Early Festival Papers, memorandum and articles of association of EFS, 22 November 1946.

15. These committees changed over time.

16. 'Glyndebourne' effectively meant Bing and his assistant, Ian Hunter. ECA, Early Festival Papers, EIFMD Report, undated.

17. See e.g. Victoria and Albert Museum (hereafter VAM), ACGB, EL5/62, Edinburgh Festival, November 1945–December 1946.

18. Bing, *5,000 Nights at the Opera*, 84.

19. Glasgow, 'The Concept of the Arts Council', 267. Christie had also been excluded from CEMA: see Leventhal, ' "The Best for the Most" ', 301.

20. Bing, *5,000 Nights at the Opera*, 84.

21. ECL, EFS, *Edinburgh Festival*, 12; ECA, Festival minutes, minutes of meeting (hereafter MoM) of Programme Subcommittee, 17 September 1946.

22. NLS, Acc. 11309, Bridie: EIFC, letter, 23 November 1945. See also Linklater, 'Mavor, Osborne Henry'.

23. VAM, ACGB, EL5/62, letter from Glasgow to Falconer, 23 February 1946.

24. This was not replied to, since Keynes died on 21 April 1946. Bridie resigned from the Arts Council in summer 1946, on hearing that Sir Ernest Pooley was to succeed Keynes. Guthrie was a Scottish theatre producer, playwright and actor, then running the Old Vic Theatre Company in London. NLS, Acc. 11309, Bridie (5): British Council and Arts Council (BC&AC), letter, 9 April 1946.

25. See VAM, ACGB, EL5/62.

26. NLS, Acc. 11309, Bridie (5), notes from the conference, 16 October 1945.

27. *The Scotsman*, 24 August 1945. Bridie's version of 'Scottish theatre' was subject to challenge – see Chapter 3.

28. NLS, Acc. 11309, Bridie (5), notes from the conference.

29. Coveney, *The Citz*, 49.
30. Cited in McArthur, 'The Cultural Front'
31. NLS, Acc. 11309, Bridie (5), undated memo on Arts Council.
32. Ibid., letter, 14 December 1943.
33. McArthur, 'The Cultural Front'; McArthur, *Scotland, CEMA and the Arts Council*.
34. McArthur, *Scotland, CEMA and the Arts Council*, 109.
35. For an outline of the Goschen formula (set at 12.08 per cent of total funds), see McArthur, *Scotland, CEMA and the Arts Council*; Glasgow, 'The Concept of the Arts Council', 268.
36. Galloway and Jones, 'The Scottish Dimension of British Arts Government', 29. See McArthur, *Scotland, CEMA and the Arts Council* for close analysis of these negotiations.
37. Sinclair, *Arts and Cultures*, 63; Keynes cited in Leventhal, ' "The Best for the Most" ', 307.
38. NLS, Acc. 11309, Bridie (5), undated memo on Arts Council.
39. McArthur argues that the 'devolution conflict' over Scotland's level of autonomy in the Arts Council would have dragged on had Keynes lived. See McArthur, *Scotland, CEMA and the Arts Council*, 313. On Keynes, see Upchurch, 'Keynes's Legacy'.
40. NLS, Acc. 11309, Bridie (5), undated memo on Arts Council.
41. VAM, ACGB, EL5/62, letter from Glasgow to Cruickshank, King's Theatre, 27 December 1945.
42. Ibid., letter from Glasgow to Keynes, 10 April 1946.
43. Ibid., note on 'Glyndebourne-Edinburgh Festival', 24 November 1945.
44. See VAM, ACGB: EL5/62, 5/63.
45. NLS, Acc. 11309, Bridie (5), letter, 20 June 1946; letter, 22 June 1946.
46. It was also dependent on approval of detailed financial estimates submitted in advance. The Arts Council stipulated that a sum 'not less' than £40,000 had to be provided from other sources before the venture was launched. See VAM, ACGB, EL5/63, Edinburgh Festival, 1945–1946, Finance Subcommittee, 19 September 1946.
47. VAM, ACGB, EL5/62, letter from Glasgow to Bing, 25 January 1946 in response to Bing asking 'what sort of active steps' the Arts Council would be prepared to take in establishing a programme for the Festival.
48. ECA, *Minutes of the Town Council of Edinburgh, 1945–6*, Meeting of Magistrates and Council.
49. £20,000 in 1947 equates to £1.43 million in 2010, using the retail price index (purchasing power of pounds sterling), See http://www.measuringworth.com/ppoweruk/ (last accessed 6 December 2012).
50. Charter cited in Hewison, *Culture and Consensus*, 43.
51. Sinfield, *Literature, Politics and Culture in Postwar Britain*, 51.
52. Conekin, 'The Autobiography of a Nation', 119. See also Minihan, *The Nationalization of Culture*.
53. ECA, Early Festival Papers, EIFMD Report, summer 1945.
54. Ibid., EIFMD Programme, 1947.

55. *Evening Dispatch* (hereafter *ED*), 7 May 1947.
56. ECA, Early Festival Papers, press release, 27 September 1946.
57. See for example Newton, 'The Sterling Crisis of 1947 and the British Response to the Marshall Plan'.
58. ECL, EFS, *Edinburgh Festival: A Review*, 9.
59. See Miller, *The Edinburgh International Festival* for more details.
60. *Scottish Daily Express* (hereafter *Express*), 5 September 1947.
61. *ED*, 7 May 1947.
62. This title had been 'bestowed' on Edinburgh by the painter 'Grecian' Williams because of the Grecian buildings around the Calton Hill area of the city. In 1949, in a symbolic gesture during a civic ceremony held before the Festival's opening ceremony, the president of the Municipal Council of Athens, Mr Demetrius Skouzes, presented the gift of an ancient urn containing earth taken from the Acropolis in acknowledgement of Edinburgh's claim to the title. For full details, see *The Times*, 8 August 1949.
63. See Miller, *The Edinburgh International Festival*, xi–xiii.
64. *The Scotsman*, 12 April 1947.
65. Bruce, *Festival in the North*, 16.
66. ECL, 'Edinburgh Notes', *Edinburgh Evening News* (hereafter *EEN*), 15 November 1947.
67. *The Times*, 25 August 1947.
68. *Express*, 25 August 1947. The Church of Scotland Youth Committee had revived the idea of the Fiery Cross in February 1947 as a symbol to be used as 'a call for the Church to action' (*The Scotsman*, 20 February 1947).
69. *The Times* reported that Falconer had 'extinguished the flames in goat's blood' (*The Times*, 12 August 1947) while *The Scotsman* reported that he had dipped the crosses in a bowl and raised them 'dripping red', which made many *recall* the ancient custom of extinguishing the fire in goat's blood (*The Scotsman*, 7 August 1947).
70. *The Times*, 12 August 1947.
71. ECA, EIFMD Programme, 1947.
72. *ED*, 25 August 1947.
73. Stevenson & Wallace, *Scottish Theatre since the Seventies*, 14.
74. See e.g. Brown, *Religion and Society in Scotland since 1707*.
75. Campbell, *Playing for Scotland*, 120.
76. Scullion, 'Glasgow Unity Theatre', 221.
77. Hutchison, *The Modern Scottish Theatre*, 33. 'Kailyard' is a term used to refer to overly sentimental and nostalgic (often rural) Scottish writing. Of course, there were exceptions, not least Glasgow Unity Theatre – see Chapter 3.
78. *British Weekly* (hereafter *BW*), 7 November 1946.
79. Mass-Observation report cited in Calder, *The People's War*, 477–81; Spender, *Eliot*, 157.
80. Lord's Day Observance Society, *Our Yearbook, 1945*, 1; Brown, *Religion and Society since 1707*, 162.
81. Machin, 'British Churches and Social Issues', 347–9.

82. *Reports to the General Assembly of the Church of Scotland* [hereafter *GA*] *1946*, 239–55.
83. *Reports to GA 1945*, 257.
84. *The Scotsman*, 25 August 1947.
85. *BW*, 7 November 1946.
86. *BW*, 24 October 1946.
87. *Reports to GA 1945*, 206.
88. 'Report of the Home Board on the Function of the Gateway Theatre', in *Reports to GA 1961*, 312.
89. Bannister, *James Bridie and His Theatre*, 191.
90. *Reports to GA 1946*, 173; ECA, Early Festival Papers, press release, 23 November 1945.
91. *Reports to GA 1961*, 311.
92. *The Scotsman*, 25 August 1947; *ED*, 25 August 1947.
93. Warr, *The Glimmering Landscape*, 182. The Presbytery of Edinburgh suggested that churches could 'most effectively identify themselves with the Festival' by holding special services on the closing Sunday (7 September). NRS, CH2/121/62, Church of Scotland Presbytery of Edinburgh Minute Book, 4 March 1947.
94. *The Scotsman*, 25 August 1947.
95. *ED*, 25 August 1947.
96. *Reports to GA 1945*, 271.
97. Reid, *Kirk and Drama*, 6; *BW*, 28 August 1947.
98. *BW*, 28 August 1947.
99. Reid, *Kirk and Drama*, 5.
100. Whitley, *Thorns and Thistles*, 57.

3

Cultural Challenge: The Creation of a 'Fringe' 1947–1955

Aspiring to be 'the Athens of the North' once more, Edinburgh had, in the International Festival, presented an event in 1947 that emphasised 'high culture' and successfully attracted many of the best artists Europe had to offer to the city, at a time when austerity measures were still in force and European nations were emerging from the upheaval of the Second World War. In the run-up to the inaugural Festival, Rudolf Bing found himself going beyond the usual duties of an artistic director by organising the de-requisitioning of a number of Edinburgh hotels and negotiating the de-rationing of curtain material. With Britain in the grip of vicious rationing, the Board of Trade had had to assist by securing supplies of crockery and household goods for visitors. A controversy also occurred when the Minister for Fuel and Power, Emanuel Shinwell, banned the floodlighting of Edinburgh Castle; a compromise, that of lighting the castle during specific hours in the evening, was reached in the face of widespread outrage.[1] Arts impresario Richard Demarco, then a seventeen-year-old schoolboy, recalled:

> I was still staggered by the idea of the castle being floodlit because remember the war had been and everything was blacked out [. . .] There was rationing of clothes, you had coupons to buy clothes, coupons to buy food, and suddenly there was this incredible commitment to international culture.[2]

Despite these shortages, it was declared that the Festival would be sustained on the 'very highest level'. The arts were seen to reinstate civilised values, promote peace, bring people of the world together on the 'common denominator of an appreciation of the Arts', and thus provide a 'moral and intellectual guiding force'.[3] In many ways these claims echo the social qualities that Matthew Arnold had attributed to culture.[4] In 1953 Ian Hunter, by then artistic director of the Festival, asked the composer Bruno Walter (reunited with the Vienna Philharmonic Orchestra for the inaugural event) why he had accepted the invitation to appear in 1947. Walter replied:

> When the invitation came to me I felt it was enormously important. It was just after the end of the war. Regardless of anything else, I found that from the humane and cultural standpoint it was of the utmost importance and

most to be desired that all the ties which had been torn should be re-united [. . .] What you have seen here in Edinburgh is one of the most magnificent experiences since the war. Here human relations have been renewed.[5]

In 1947, paying tribute to Lord Provost Falconer, Walter said that the Festival demonstrated 'to the whole cultural world the power of the spiritual values'.[6]

But there was another artistic landscape being created in Edinburgh at this time, one of cultural contest and challenge. The Festival organisers had apparently 'written out' Scottish cultural representation at the inaugural event, arguing that the standards were simply not high enough to sit alongside the best that Europe had to offer. While Scottish music did find a place in the official programme that first year, Scottish drama was entirely absent. This initiated cultural challenge, seen in the development of an artistic fringe and the short-lived Edinburgh People's Festival (1951–4).

POST-WAR BRITISH SOCIETY

The period 1947 to 1955 has been described as 'deeply old-fashioned', an era dominated by consensus in politics and society.[7] The first few years were overshadowed by austerity measures, a dependence on the USA due to the devaluation of sterling, and a loss of prestige linked to the decline of the British Empire.[8] Kenneth O. Morgan wrote that in the immediate post-war years Labour, 'in its pursuit of the New Jerusalem, [. . .] looked to the past, through the eyes of relatively conservative, conventional leaders', and this sense of harking back to the pre-war past was reflected in the behaviour of the wider population.[9] Callum Brown has referred to a widespread adherence to the Victorian moral codes of thrift, respectability and sexual restraint throughout the 1950s, while the popularity of the coronation of Elizabeth II in June 1953, when 56 per cent of the adult population watched the ceremony on television, arguably helped to 'symbolically renew' the old domestic order by restoring comfortable patterns of class hierarchy and deference.[10] This sense of a 'conservative era' was renewed when the Conservative Party was re-elected in 1951 and returned with a large majority in the 1955 general election.[11] The coronation heralded the arrival of the 'New Elizabethans' and the return of the ceremonial and the careful use of tradition and ritual (the 'touchstone' of cultural conservatism).[12] During the first ten years of the Festival, opening and closing ceremonies were developed that were rooted in the traditional rites of the civic authorities and the Church, the Festival opening each year with a church ceremony on a Sunday morning. In the lead-up to the inaugural event, the question of whether it would be acceptable to have Sunday concerts had been aired. Some members of the organising committee wanted only a sermon, since it was 'not considered that an opening could really be made worthy of the occasion on a Sunday'. In the end an opening concert did take place on the Sunday evening, performed in Usher Hall by L'Orchestre des Concerts Colonne from Paris.[13] 'Immensely popular' Sunday services also took place in Princes Street Gardens, services that made the Festival a 'target for Free Church criticisms' (as Brown has recently noted, the 'Sabbath endured as a contentious issue in twentieth-century Scotland').[14] Just as Scottish civil government was 'kirked' each year in church ceremonies, the Festival too was sanctified by religious ceremonies that were tied into the renewal of Christian and conservative culture in 1950s Scotland.

The conservatism of the period was partly due to continued austerity. Rationing of foodstuffs did not end until 1954, nearly a decade after the cessation of hostilities, and the effect of these shortages had a continuing influence on provision of the arts. The Festival had caught the public imagination in 1947 by the 'very boldness of its conception' and there had been an enthusiastic response to plans for a repeat in 1948.[15] But the conductor of the Royal Philharmonic Orchestra, Sir Thomas Beecham, famously announced in Glasgow in 1948 that 'the people of Scotland are damned fools to throw away £60,000 on a music festival', objecting that since 'we could not afford our necessities, it followed that we could not afford our luxuries'.[16] There were doubts from within government too. At the end of September 1947, Sir Stafford Cripps, in his new role as Minister of Economic Affairs (a newly created post) arranged a meeting with Lord Provost Falconer to try to persuade him to postpone the 1948 Festival.[17] Asserting that this was based on his own personal views and not those of the government, Cripps argued that plans would be impeded by restrictions on foreign travel and a 'scarcity of goods' expected for 1948 (as well as that the Olympic Games were due to be held in Great Britain).[18] Perhaps Cripps had objected to the 'almost wanton lavishness' of the scale on which the Festival was planned at a time when tight austerity measures were in place. Despite involvement from the Board of Trade too, keen to ensure that the Festival organisers should be confident of success 'even in the face of growing international difficulties', the EFS – with the support of Edinburgh Corporation and the Scottish Office – was determined to go ahead.[19]

Plans for the 1951 Festival of Britain were also well underway, and may have influenced Cripps's decision to meet with the Lord Provost. Cripps had declared his support for the idea as early as October 1945 and committed the Board of Trade to investigating it further.[20] The Festival of Britain was partly organised to celebrate the centenary of the Great Exhibition of 1851, and the introduction to the official programme announced: 'The Festival is our chance to show the world that Britain not only has a pride in its past, but a faith in its future.'[21] When the EFS heard about the plans, concerns were expressed that the Festival of Britain would divert attention and resources from the Edinburgh Festivals. A Scottish Office document in early 1948 refers to 'an almost complete pre-occupation with London functions'.[22]

Ultimately, the Edinburgh Festival received additional funding in order to put on an 'augmented' programme, while festivals of drama and the arts were also held in Aberdeen, Inverness, Perth and Dumfries.[23] The official programme flyer, *Scotland in Festival Year 1951*, began:

> Edinburgh's Fifth Festival of Music and Drama will be the outstanding cultural event of 1951 in Britain. For three weeks Scotland's capital city will offer the world's best music, drama, opera, and ballet in an atmosphere which cannot be duplicated elsewhere.[24]

In response to the Lord Provost's assertion that, with competition from the Festival of Britain, the Edinburgh Festival needed to have more of a Scottish flavour, the *Scottish Daily Express* quipped: 'Never mind the competition from London. We can whack the whole lot of them. They are only copying our example.'[25] As recent scholarship has shown, the Festival of Britain can tell us much about post-war British society and, given that it took place throughout the British Isles, about aspects of national identity – and yet its Scottish dimension has received scant attention.[26]

Cultural extravagance also conflicted with the rise of the Cold War. Indeed an effect of the Cold War, combined with Britain's economic difficulties and a drive towards conservatism in politics, culture and social values, was a 'culture of conformity'. From the mid-1940s, many Cold War programmes, articles and stories had been broadcast or published; some of these were serious, while some amounted to scare stories, but, Robert Hewison has argued, taken together, the effect was the creation of an atmosphere in which there was 'safety in conformity, and no encouragement at all to think freely'.[27] It was believed that the Cold War, combined with the pervasive cultural conservatism of the period, had a negative effect on the production of new artistic work during the 1940s and 1950s, and led to a tendency to rely on work that had already been performed elsewhere, work that was considered 'safe'. 'The unadventurous nature of the West End', wrote Dominic Shellard recently, 'mirrored the constrictions of early 1950s society.'[28] One commentator lamented the 'deadness' of the cultural scene, while another contemporary commented in April 1956 that the 1950s would later be seen as a right-wing orthodoxy.[29] In fact, it has been suggested that the intellectual left were displaced by the 'stifling conservatism' founded upon the revival of traditional values, which in turn stifled intellectual debate.[30]

But the tendency to see this period as a 'theatrical wasteland', 'awakened' by *Look Back in Anger* in 1956, has been challenged. Shellard, for example, points to the importance of a number of developments that run counter to this pervasive narrative, not least the foundation of the Arts Council, the increasing interest in foreign theatre, and the development of a new edgy theatre criticism led by Kenneth Tynan of *The Observer*. The latter's frustration at the 'theatre's stasis' in the early 1950s came through his criticism as he lambasted Britain's social, political and cultural insularity, which he saw as embracing fear of America, fear of the advent of commercial television, fear of criticism, fear of emotional engagement, fear of an open sexuality and a fear enforced by censors of film and theatre, who both discouraged political attacks on the establishment.[31]

It would be 'disingenuous' to see this period as a 'cultural wasteland'. For example, the foundation of a number of theatres outside London, encouraged by state subsidy from the Arts Council, 'provided a tremendous stimulus for regional theatre, and, in turn, created a new training ground for actors, directors, designers and technical staff, previously restricted to employment in the commercial sector.'[32] There was a clear rise in general interest in theatre during this period, as well as in the arts more broadly. The first British university department of drama opened in Bristol (1946); the Society for Theatre Research was created (1946); the Royal Scottish Academy of Music opened the Glasgow College of Dramatic Art (1950); new drama periodicals were founded, including *Theatre Notebook* (1946) and *Plays and Players* (1953); and theatres opened up in towns and cities across Britain, including Ipswich (1947) and Canterbury (1951). The Edinburgh International Festival also inspired new festivals; during 1948 alone 'small sister' festivals were added in Bath and Cheltenham, the 'youthful' Yorkshire Symphony Orchestra made a trial run of a festival in Huddersfield, and the Aldeburgh Festival was founded by composer Benjamin Britten, singer Peter Pears and writer Eric Crozier.[33] However, just as CEMA had been a force for 'cultural conservatism', so the Arts Council developed a reputation for funding only art that was established and generally conservative (and usually London based).[34]

In many ways, culture was still conveyed through fairly strictly controlled channels, most apparent in the system of theatre censorship. The Lord Chamberlain's office operated as censor under the Theatres Act of 1843, although there had been an official censor, established by the Crown, of some description since the sixteenth century. Every new theatrical text to be publicly performed in Britain had to be submitted to the Lord Chamberlain for inspection and approval and, without a licence from him, the play could not be performed. During the 1950s the Lord Chamberlain as censor still had, as one historian put it, 'broad, arbitrary and sinister powers' and, even after he had issued a licence for a play, could change his mind and veto a line, scene or even a whole play with no appeal.[35] The grounds for censoring a play were based on the results of a parliamentary joint select committee of 1909, although from 1945 the Lord Chamberlain's readers referred to both 'past precedent' and their own 'personal whim' when reaching decisions regarding the licensing of plays.[36] During the 1950s a play could be censored for a range of reasons: for example, if it was deemed 'indecent', contained an act of 'alleged sexual impropriety' or a moving naked body, showed representations of God or Christ onstage, or made reference to 'the forbidden subject' (as the Lord Chamberlain described homosexuality in 1957).[37] Theatre was also censored for political reasons: for example the play *Strangers in the Land*, about Malaya, was refused a licence in 1954, while cuts and changes were requested in other plays, too.[38]

At the heart of conventions in the early 1950s lay a religiously defined moral core that often harked back to Victorian mores – for example, patriarchy, respect for authority and the importance of religion. Callum Brown has described a 'world profoundly conservative in morals and outlook, and fastidious in its adherence to respectability and moral standards'.[39] The period 1945–60 has been described as one of 'reconstruction' in Britain, with attempts made to rebuild the institutions of the past, particularly in terms of the religious life of the population.[40] As well as the physical reconstruction of churches, the Church of Scotland embarked upon a policy of reconstruction using evangelism to retain and attract members and was, for the first half of the 1950s at least, largely successful. The driving force of the Kirk's evangelical campaign of the early 1950s was the 'Tell Scotland' movement, followed by the Glasgow-based crusade of the American evangelist the Revd Dr Billy Graham, who, between 21 March and 30 April 1955, attracted more than a million people in Scotland to meetings in the Kelvin Hall, Hampden Park and other venues.[41] Graham's religious services offered excitement in Scotland (and indeed across Britain), with high levels of funding and the backing of a thousand-strong choir contributing to 'its buzz of Hollywood and its razz-matazz'.[42] These gains were short lived, however, and challenges to Scottish Presbyterianism snowballed from the late 1950s.

But during its first years, the Edinburgh Festival was clearly framed by Christian spiritual values. Although the religious sermon preached during the Festival's opening ceremony was different each year, the message was similar: art was a 'bond of reunion in a disintegrated world' and the Edinburgh Festival formed a chance for visitors 'from all over the Old world and the New to forget for a while the things that divide them, and to breathe together a tranquil atmosphere of spiritual unity'.[43] This idea of harmony in a disharmonious world was the focus for the role of the arts that the Festival established and developed throughout its first ten years. The EFS attempted to promote the arts as a means of achieving 'the light of concord and goodwill' in 'dark, unsettled times'.[44] Indeed, during the inaugural opening ceremony it had been declared that 'harmony and beauty are the keynotes of creation; ugliness and discord are the negation of Christ', while a sermon preached at the 1948 service, by the Revd Dr A. Nevile Davidson of Glasgow Cathedral, reflected that art 'in its supreme manifestations' had 'something of a spiritual quality'. But Davidson warned that

> nothing was more dangerous, however, than to think of music and art or science and philosophy as a substitute for religion. What was immensely

needed now was a new alliance of friendship and mutual trust between religion and art and music and science. Such a renaissance would result in a wonderful enrichment of life and a wonderful deepening of our decaying civilisation.[45]

In August 1952, the Lord Provost, James Miller, described the arts of music and drama as the 'divine arts' and members of the EFS, by using the arts to bring together 'men and women of all races and creeds, of all ranks and classes', as 'serving God's will'.[46]

Figure 3.1 Picture taken inside St Giles' Cathedral during the opening ceremony of the Edinburgh International Festival, 1961. (© The Scotsman Publications Ltd. Licensor www.scran.ac.uk)

It is interesting that the arts were presented as a means of promoting harmony and order, especially since the Church of Scotland had previously been against them for being *dis*orderly, particularly the art of drama. In the official Festival Programme of 1949, a short history of the relationship between the Kirk and drama was included, perhaps as a means of conveying how supportive of the arts the Church of Scotland had become. The piece noted that the Covenanting Kirk had 'set its face hard against the Temples of

Belial' (theatres) because they were 'disorderly houses' in contrast to the Kirk, which stood for 'law and order'.[47] During the sermon at the 1952 opening ceremony, Charles Warr preached:

> This Festival is a testimony to the harmony which is at the heart of creation. It witnesses to the survival power of beauty amid ugliness, of harmony amid discord, or truth amid insincerity, fake and lies. [. . .] Let us then offer our Festival to the Glory of God and let its music challenge the strident noises of the world.[48]

The Festival in conjunction with the Gateway Theatre offered a perfect opportunity for the Church of Scotland to redefine its attitude towards the arts and to stake a claim in cultural provision – then seen as an integral part of the post-war reconstruction of civilised society.

Messages about harmony, stability and order pervaded these sermons, and surely resonated with an audience recovering from the war years. In the 1950 opening ceremony, Warr said:

> During the coming weeks this Festival will transform our city into an isle of international harmony and friendship, set in surrounding seas of international animosity and discord [. . .] With faith, hope and courage, let us begin our Festival. The light still shines, there is still music on earth.[49]

Themes from Matthew Arnold's *Culture and Anarchy* are clearly evident in these sermons: culture as a means of creating harmony and order; the idea that the arts would bring 'light'; and the sense that culture could 'rescue' civilisation. Furthermore, Davidson's assertion that it was 'dangerous' to 'think of music and art or science and philosophy as a substitute for religion' could be seen as a direct criticism of Arnold's argument for culture as a substitute for religion.[50] T. S. Eliot's argument that culture and religion were inextricably linked found more resonance and probably influenced the sermons. Eliot was then a well-known and respected cultural figure and a prolific writer on (and defender of) conservative and Christian values, and parts of what became *Notes towards the Definition of Culture* had appeared in essay form in the four years preceding its publication. Davidson's comments on the need for an 'alliance' between 'religion and art and music and science' reaffirm Eliot's assertion that 'the artistic sensibility is impoverished by its divorce from the religious sensibility, the religious by its separation from the artistic'.[51] Eliot put this idea into practice in his own writing, and after his conversion to Christianity (in 1929) the theme of his plays was 'the discovery by heroes, and one heroine, of their religious vocation'. This was the central theme of his *The Cocktail Party*, which was commissioned by the EFS and premiered at the International Festival in 1949. Eliot was clearly attracted to the Festival and it to him; two of his other major plays – *The*

Confidential Clerk and *The Elder Statesman* – were also commissioned by and premiered at the Edinburgh Festival in 1953 and 1958 respectively.[52]

DEFINING 'CULTURE'

In spring 1951, William Emrys Williams took over the job of secretary general of the Arts Council. Robert Hutchison notes that the concluding sentences of the 1951/2 Annual Report 'bear his stamp':

> In reconsidering the exhortation of its Charter to 'Raise and Spread' the Council may decide for the time being to emphasize the first more than the second word [. . .] High standards can be built only on a limited scale. The motto which Meleager wrote to be carved over a patrician nursery might be one for the Arts Council to follow in deciding what to support during the next few straitened years – 'Few, but roses' – including, of course, regional roses.[53]

However, the 'few roses' were largely metropolitan ones, as the Arts Council gradually closed down its regional offices in the 1950s and sought to concentrate its resources on building 'centres of excellence'.[54] The Arts Council's Scottish Committee, on the other hand, was able to continue funding 'direct provision' in the form of tours of drama, music and art exhibitions around Scotland due to its 'considerable independence from both ACGB and the government'.[55] The Arts Council had stopped directly funding the Edinburgh International Festival from 1952, instead asking that it be funded out of the Scottish Committee's budget. This was much to the consternation of the EFS, who pleaded for the existing arrangement to continue and pointed out that the Festival 'is not merely a Scottish one but international in all respects, and one the results of which affect tourism in the country as a whole'.[56] They felt that the grant should come from the central fund, rather than the comparatively smaller (and declining) proportion available to the Scottish Committee.[57]

Who decided what the highest standards of art were – and what 'deserved' to be funded by the Arts Council – remained contentious during this period, in the Festivals and more broadly. At the beginning of 1952, Edinburgh's claim as a great cultural centre manifested itself in an ambitious proposal when Sir John Boyd Orr made a submission on behalf of the EFS for the Nobel Peace Prize (which Orr had won in 1949).[58] This was made on the basis that the Festival was 'a constructive effort on behalf of European civilisation, for it was clear that should the traditional civilised values, already weakened by the war, be allowed to fail, hope of peace would surely fail with them'. The Festival, it was argued, had made a 'contribution to peace and understanding through the arts', a 'duty which could not lightly be put aside'.[59] The transcript of the submission lays out the role that the EFS envisioned for culture by drawing mostly on the words of successive Lord Provosts conveying the policy and aims of the Festival. Sir Andrew Murray, the second Lord Provost to act as chairman of the EFS, promoted the Festival to the position of 'interpreter' of the arts. Addressing a conference of British press editors in March 1949, he stated that the Festival had to be a means of resolving conflict to lift the 'levels of human thought and welfare.' He went on:

> Aught that we can do to bring together men and women from all parts of the world; aught that we can do to assist them to find a common interest and mutual understanding in the revelation of the music and art of the great masters; aught that we can do to establish an incorruptible love of truth, to create a lofty spirit of freedom and to blend a moral and intellectual guiding force in the future of the world – aught that we can do in this respect will meet the greatest need of mankind and confer the greatest gift upon a wavering civilisation.[60]

The organisers of the Festival finished by stating their belief that they were 'making some small contribution towards a basis for mutual understanding between the different peoples of the world, the establishment of which must necessarily be a pre-requisite of enduring peace'.[61]

But the policy of presenting the music and art of the 'grand masters' meant that there was little room for those who wished to create new culture, rather than interpret existing culture. The EFS maintained strict control of what was on offer in the official programme. All decisions made by the artistic director of the Festival were also considered by the Programme Committee, which was composed of representatives of cultural organisations, members of the Town Council and other interested parties who had helped to found the Festival. This sometimes frustrated Rudolf Bing. The Festival was undoubt-edly an 'elite' affair, and Bing's standard of programming was continued by his successor, Ian Hunter, who was artistic director from 1950 until 1955. Hunter had been assistant director to Bing and, furthermore, had also worked for Glyndebourne, although Bing's departure had 'loosened the ties' between the EFS and Glyndebourne. Hunter was described in his obituary as 'a grand elitist in the days when elitism in the arts was something to be sought after and admired'.[62] The need to open the Edinburgh International Festival up to a broader audience was not a major concern during its earliest years, despite some criticisms of elitism and exclusivity being aired. However, this was soon to change.

THE BIRTH OF THE FRINGE

Challenges to the Festival's interpretation and presentation of culture began before the inaugural event in 1947. In the run-up to the first Festival there had been a number of complaints regarding the programme and the Festival's professed aims. Hugh MacDiarmid, the Scottish poet at the centre of the Scottish literary renaissance of the 1920s and 1930s, was a particularly vehement critic. He had previously refused to allow his poetry to be read out in a city he despised as a 'stronghold of bourgeois decadence' and in a letter to the correspondence column of *The Scotsman* before the inaugural event, he bluntly remarked:

> It is to my mind absurd that a city which has always treated the arts so meanly can suddenly blossom forth as a great centre of world-culture. It is like giving the content of a University Honours course all at once to a class of mentally defective children.[63]

MacDiarmid, like many others, was particularly dismayed to see that the inaugural Festival, although situated in the Scottish capital, did not include much that was 'Scottish'. In May 1946, Rudolf Bing had suggested Scottish contributions would be 'regimental sword dances, Scottish folk dances and bagpipe music' – illustrating an outsider's romanticised perception of Scottish culture.[64] But James Bridie had also downplayed the Scottish contribution to Lord Keynes in London, stating in April 1946 that it would be 'incidental [. . .] the big attractions are to be from London and abroad'.[65] In the end, the inaugural programme had included the BBC Scottish Orchestra, concerts of traditional Gaelic and Lowland songs, and a performance by the Glasgow Orpheus Choir. Scottish drama was excluded in 1947, however. It had been intended that a new play by Bridie (set during the era of Mary Queen of Scots) would be part of the inaugural programme, but 'insurmountable difficulties' between Bridie and the Old Vic meant that it was dropped.[66] Overall, it was felt that there was a distinct lack of Scottish material, especially drama.

Yet this absence was filled, and Scottish drama was performed during, but not as part of, the 'official' Festival when eight theatre groups turned up 'uninvited and unheralded', organised performance spaces for themselves and put on their own shows. Of those first eight groups, six were from within Scotland (they are considered on the following pages) while the remaining two were from England: the Lanchester Marionette Theatre, who put on puppet plays in an Edinburgh cinema, and the Pilgrim Players from the Mercury Theatre in London, who presented T. S. Eliot's *The Family Reunion* and *Murder in the Cathedral* at the Gateway Theatre.[67] The coining of the term by which they became known has often been attributed to the playwright Robert Kemp who wrote, in an *Edinburgh Evening News* article in the run up to the 1948 Festival: 'Round the fringe of the official Festival drama, there seems to be more private enterprise than before.'[68] In fact, the term predates this article by almost one year. Another article in the same paper in September 1947 had described the Edinburgh District of the SCDA's performance as being 'only on the fringe of the official programme', while Alistair Moffat cites a critic who remarked 'that it was a shame the show [*Everyman*, performed in Dunfermline Cathedral, nearly 20 miles north west of Edinburgh] was so far out "on the fringe of the Festival" '.[69]

In that first year, however, events held outside the aegis of the Edinburgh International Festival were not referred to as 'the Fringe'. Rather, articles started to appear about the 'semi-official' and 'barnacle' events or 'Festival adjuncts' being held in venues around the city. *The Scotsman* said: 'Assessing them dispassionately in their self-appointed role, we may truthfully say that they add balance to the Festival.'[70] That balance was derived from the observation that the majority of plays being performed on the official stages were written some 'three centuries ago' while the semi-official plays were all modern plays and, furthermore, that of the eight theatre groups that turned up, six were Scottish. They were: the Christine Orr Players (an amateur theatre company from Edinburgh), who presented *Macbeth*; Edinburgh People's Theatre, doing Robert Ardrey's *Thunder Rock*; the Edinburgh District of the SCDA, who presented Bridie's *The Anatomist*; Edinburgh College of Art Theatre Group, performing August Strindberg's *Easter*; a production of *Everyman* sponsored by the Carnegie Trust; and the Glasgow Unity Theatre, who presented Maxim Gorky's *The Lower Depths* and Robert McLellan's *The Laird o' Torwatletie*.[71]

Moffat observes that it was 'unlikely that any one of these groups had the idea of performing on the Fringe and subsequently contacted the others'.[72] Yet the role that the Glasgow Unity Theatre group played in the establishment of that first fringe festival is a considerable one. They can, in fact, claim to have founded the Edinburgh Festival Fringe.[73] Glasgow Unity had, 'in the face of official and establishment opposition', proposed a season at an Edinburgh theatre during the three weeks of the official Festival.[74] This proposal was made in a letter written by Eveline Garratt, then assistant director of Glasgow Unity, and published in the *Glasgow Herald* in January 1947 (although Unity's artistic director, Robert Mitchell, had already booked the Little Theatre in Edinburgh in August 1946, following the success of its season there).[75] Noting her sadness at the 'high prices to be charged for both material and spiritual accommodation' at the forthcoming Festival, Garratt lamented the lack of Scottish culture in the Festival programme, pointing out that Unity had approached Bing and asked whether Scottish theatre had been asked to participate in the Festival and, if not, whether Unity's season of plays might be included. In response to the answer that 'No Scottish theatre is up to standard', Garratt challenged Bing and 'all guid Scots bodies on the Festival committee' to see 'Scottish theatre at its most vital in an original Scottish play', then, if they were still not satisfied that the standards were high enough, to consider bringing together the cream of Scottish dramatists, performers and producers and presenting the result 'as a composite example of Scottish theatre'. Garratt ended her letter with Unity's bold proposal:

> Meanwhile, in the event of the committee's not considering this worth while, we shall continue to endeavour to prove on our own that there is a Scottish drama by presenting three original Scottish plays in the Little Theatre, Edinburgh, during this exciting period. If we are considered then not worth visiting in the light of more glittering, more expensive, and more famous efforts we shall go down with our heads high secure in the knowledge that there is a growing Scottish theatre, and that we, unlike the Festival committee, are humbly helping to build it.[76]

Garratt's letter provoked a flurry of letters to the *Glasgow Herald* in which Unity's proposal, the place of Scottish culture in the Festival, and indeed the purpose of the Festival, were debated by public figures, including Bridie and MacDiarmid, and members of the public.[77] Mitchell also recalled being asked to come and meet Bing, at which Bing tried to persuade Unity to withdraw as 'the standard is not good enough'.[78]

A plausible reason for the appearance of the other Scottish groups in Edinburgh outside the official Festival was to challenge the snub to the Scottish theatre community and to support Unity's protest. The principle at stake was whether Scotland would 'accept the denigration of its own art in its own country and expose itself to the world as if culturally barren'.[79] Moffat considered that the first Fringe might 'be seen as a show of strength of amateur drama in Scotland' and related it to the post-war 'atmosphere of enterprise and missionary zeal in Scottish amateur drama'.[80] Furthermore, in that original letter to the *Glasgow Herald* Garratt asked: 'But what of the renaissance in Scottish theatre? Is it to find no place in this Festival?'[81]

Glasgow Unity was one branch of the Britain-wide Unity theatre movement, a left-leaning federation of amateur theatre groups committed to 'people's drama'.[82] Unity sought to present theatre that had a strong sense of social commitment and would attract working-class audiences to an activity that remained a predominantly middle-class pursuit.[83] To Colin Chambers, the experience Unity offered became 'like an extension of a political meeting into the cultural field, with an assumed union of values between actor, audience and play'. Yet, although Communist Party members were in a majority on Unity's management committee, Chambers has argued that there was no direct involvement from the national leadership of the party, except to discuss and agree on the value of the project, and that Unity was not financed directly by the party. Often seen as merely a 'communist front' theatre, from its formation Unity preferred to avoid the restrictive terms 'communist' and 'Marxist' and instead favoured the broader term 'worker's theatre'. Nevertheless, at national level, Unity was 'clearly a theatre of the Communist left'.[84] Glasgow Unity, argues Linda Mackenney, fundamentally 'saw itself as an artistic entity, albeit an artistic entity with social and political responsibilities'.[85]

The Glasgow branch of Unity was certainly left wing but its political identity was inextricably linked with its specifically Scottish identity. Unity's attempts to create a 'Scottish People's Theatre', wrote John Hill, were bound up with the 'two interrelated problems' of creating a socialist or people's theatre in terms of a recognisably Scottish theatre. By 1946, their policy became 'understood in more exclusively Scottish terms'.[86] Glasgow Unity had been founded in 1941 out of five companies (brought together as a result of wartime shortages) – the Glasgow Workers' Theatre Group, the Clarion Players, the Glasgow Players, the Transport Players and the Jewish Institute Players. This assembly, Scullion has argued, was crucial both to Unity's identity and its choice of productions:

> Because of its unusual genesis, Unity was always a group of political and social diversity – deeply conscious of its Scottish context and identity. As a company it never proposed or projected an overtly communist thesis – it was too much of a broad church for this to be the case – but the company did present the most politically and socially challenging theatre being made in Scotland in the 1940s.[87]

The challenge that Unity made to the official Festival in August 1947 was largely instigated by the lack of Scottish theatrical representation on the official programme, as well as in the group's concern with developing an explicitly Scottish political theatre. As Adrienne Scullion has noted, 'Glasgow Unity effectively demonstrated an interest in and commitment to socialist theatre *and* Scottish theatre, seeking out and nurturing new Scottish writers, and encouraging them to find the raw material for original plays in their immediate working-class and urban contexts'.[88] Hill suspected a problem in the way Unity used the term 'people', and argued that to Unity 'the "Scottish people" could easily do service for the "Scottish nation"; and the struggle for a "Scottish People's Theatre" become little more than that for a Scottish one'.[89] But it is important to highlight that Glasgow Unity's focus was not exclusively Scottish. As their 1947 Souvenir Brochure noted, their 'aims for the immediate future are simple:- to present side by side with the best works of international literature as many new and virile Scottish plays as we can find'.[90]

Linda Mackenney has argued that when Mitchell refused to back down, 'new and unethical pressures were applied' to Unity.[91] Although Glasgow Unity had received Arts Council association status in 1946, at a meeting held on 3 August 1947 between Unity, Dr James Welsh (the chairman of the Arts Council's Scottish Committee) and Bridie, it was informed that formal association with the Arts Council was to be suspended 'as from the commencement of the Festival period'. The group was told that it could reapply for formal association after the termination of the first Festival.[92]. The reasons given to Unity for this suspension of association were threefold: that Unity had failed to consult with the Arts Council regarding its future plans, that the theatre it planned to use in Edinburgh during the Festival period had not been popular with the public hence its visit was 'likely to be a financial failure', and that it would be 'competing with the best international Artists with standards considerably higher' than those of the Glasgow Unity Theatre group (the inference being that it was simply not good enough).

Glasgow Unity was not deterred from its main motive, which was to present Scottish drama performed by a Scottish company, and in response to the Arts Council's withdrawal of support, it launched an appeal through the Scottish press for £800 in order to 'ensure the appearance of a Scottish theatre in the Festival' – and it got it.[93] On the opening night of its critically successful run during the Festival, MacDiarmid 'made a swingeing attack' – one widely reported in the press – denouncing the Arts Council, the EFS and all those who had failed to support Scottish representation at the inaugural Festival.[94] Miron Grindea of *Tribune* highlighted the irony of a company 'considered by some people in authority as below international standards' being 'greeted by critics and public alike as the best group of players at the Festival'.[95]

It has been suggested that Bridie influenced the Arts Council's decision to withdraw support from Glasgow Unity. It was publicly known that there was division and 'not much love lost' between Bridie's sort of theatre and the 'aggressively realistic' sort produced by Unity.[96] According to John Hill, Glasgow Unity challenged the failure of Scots drama 'to come to terms with the urban, lowland experience of most of the nation'. In fact, Hill specifically cited the failures of Bridie and James Barrie 'with their eyes on the West End and their isolated class milieux'. In October 1946, Joseph MacLeod had written: 'In the new Scottish theatre there are two divisions: primarily middle-class repertoire and writers whose art is seen in Perth, the Glasgow Citizens Theatre and elsewhere: and the tougher working-class dramas and performances to be seen in Glasgow Unity Theatre'.[97] Bridie, who was instrumental in founding Glasgow Citizens Theatre and was at that point running it, had attracted criticism for hiring non-Scottish actors and actresses in the troupe; Unity was clear that all its performers should be Scottish and, indeed, demanded 'new Scots plays by new Scottish writers to be performed by native actors'.[98]

A fundamental conflict may have existed between Unity and Citizens (with Bridie as its spokesperson) about what constituted 'Scottish theatre'.[99] Both Bridie and Glasgow Unity were seeking to further the development of Scottish theatre, but had different ideas of the form and content it should take. Bridie had long been a champion of Scottish theatre, but had treaded an 'Anglo-Scottish path', seeking a compromise between Scottish theatre and theatre in Scotland. In many ways, this can be understood in terms of the broader theatrical landscape of inter-war Scotland – when Bridie was developing as a playwright and champion of a national theatre in Scotland. As late as 1939, there had only been one Scottish professional theatre (Perth Repertory, opened in 1935) and most theatres in Scotland were either English owned or largely used for repertory theatre groups who travelled around Britain. Donald Campbell said of the late 1930s that there was 'simply nowhere in Scotland for a professional actor to work'.[100] The launch of the Citizens company in 1943 was part of Bridie's dream to create a Scottish national theatre.[101] But Bridie – and the Citizens – came under some attack for not employing enough Scottish actors or presenting enough plays on Scottish life. Loud challenge came from Glasgow Unity Theatre. Winifred Bannister, who worked with Bridie and was involved in the formation of the Citizens Theatre, referred to Unity as the 'first really vital force towards a Scottish national theatre – the sustained attack':

> It grew apace and with great vigour. It was the first Scottish theatre to break clean away from English manners and it made a determined grasp of fundamentals. It was a clamorous, uninhibited voice calling on the audience as if Calvinism had never been! [. . .] It was a company that gave a welcome blood transfusion to the Scottish theatre, and it provided the newly arrived Citizens' Theatre with an east wind to battle against.[102]

Bannister noted that Bridie had been unprepared for the rate at which agitation for national drama was increasing.[103] At the same time, Glasgow Unity was attracting large audiences for its plays reflecting contemporary Scottish life. The competition between the two had even extended as far as physical theatre buildings. Glasgow Unity had set up home in the Athenaeum, a theatre in the city centre, until Bridie – with the backing of CEMA – took it over for the Citizens Theatre with the intention of developing it into a Scottish national theatre.[104] The tensions between Bridie and Glasgow Unity were therefore long-standing, with the 'battle lines' drawn long before Eveline Garratt published her challenge in the press.

Nevertheless, Scullion counsels caution against 'casting Bridie as a preying figure of bourgeois culture' and points out that, despite Unity's successes on the 'fringe' in 1947, its 'high-profile opposition to the Arts Council and many within Scottish theatre [. . .] burned bridges, alienated support at home, and, at the very least, embarrassed the Arts Council'. Linda Mackenney, on the other hand, argues that 'Unity's ultimate sin was that it had been too quick to take the initiative in areas which the Scottish authorities sought to preserve for themselves'.[105] Unity was forced to rely on commercial success and therefore spent more and more time in London. With the added complications of 'financial mismanagement' and the aforementioned tension with the Arts Council, Glasgow Unity disbanded in 1951.[106] Unlike Scullion, Mackenney sees Bridie as a more culpable figure. In response to his public criticism of Unity for failing to consolidate its success, she comments that this is 'hardly fair' given that 'he was part of an establishment which so discouraged Unity's efforts, by evicting them from theatres and withdrawing their financial support'.[107]

But by defying the Festival organisers and very publicly mounting a challenge to the exclusion of Scottish theatre from the new Edinburgh International Festival, Glasgow Unity helped to create a cultural force that today is bigger than the official Festival. Although other enterprising groups may have come anyway, the high-profile challenge from Unity and its very public opposition to the official Festival helped to define the embryonic fringe as oppositional in stance and inclusive in appeal and – furthermore – to kick-start the process by which their 'outsider' stance gradually became mainstream. As Garratt commented, when interviewed nearly forty years later,

> funnily enough, all the things we were trying to do and insist on – that Scotland could have a theatre of high enough standard to match up to international standards – well, the establishment eventually cottoned on to that and was trying to do that with the Citizens.[108]

In the days and weeks after the 1947 Festival, reviews appeared in the local and national press. Although overwhelmingly positive, there were some criticisms that appeared and reappeared in various publications: namely that a 'native root to an international festival' was required and that, although the Festival was an 'authentic feast', there had been 'too high a proportion of old familiar dishes on the menu.'[109] Although characterised by a 'spirit of excitement, adventure and enterprise', the content of the programme had been seen as too conservative. One writer for *The Times* suggested that the Festival might be invigorated by the inclusion of 'new or seldom performed works, which by an honourable tradition has come in our country to be almost an axiom of festival policy'.[110] But in that first year it was conceded that having a festival on that scale was risky enough in a 'world made tetchy by shortages' and it was understandable, therefore, that the organisers would be conservative in their choice of programming.[111] This conservatism, in conjunction with the precedent set by Unity and the others who came to perform outside the official Festival, gave space for the Fringe to develop, as well as acting as a catalyst for the further development of theatre in Scotland.[112]

The Times reported in 1949 of a 'younger generation' of Scottish writers and artists that sought to revive older Scottish traditions in the arts, but also cited 'the lack of a strong native tradition in the arts' as a real weakness in the Edinburgh Festival.[113] In defence, the Lord Provost, Sir Andrew Murray, tried to justify the Festival's position on the inclusion of Scottish material at a conference held in March 1950:

The Festival of 1947 gave incentive to the newly found interest and vitality in the arts in Scotland and her capital. But our Festival was conceived on a truly international basis, endeavouring to draw to our city the best from every individual nation and contributing ourselves only the best of our national material and such as could take a worthy place according to international standards.[114]

The issue of Scottish drama caused friction between the artistic director and the Programme Committee in the first few years of the Festival, just as it did in wider theatre circles in Scotland. In a letter to Bridie in November 1947, Rudolf Bing wrote that, although he had been 'quite severely attacked' in various papers, he would gladly face more severe attacks 'for the sake of quality and against nationalism'.[115] In some ways, Bridie and Bing were in agreement. In his letter to the *Glasgow Herald* in response to Unity's proposal, Bridie wrote: 'Unity is quite right to chance its arm in Edinburgh: but the Festival Committee would be rendering a poor service to Scottish drama if, at this stage, it sponsored a match against some of the finest artists in the world' (Bridie compared putting Scottish drama on during the inaugural Festival to pitting a group of junior footballers against seasoned internationalists).[116] But after the first Festival, Bridie was keen to make sure that Scottish drama was represented in the programme of the Edinburgh International Festival.

In 1948, David Lindsay's sixteenth-century morality play *Ane Satyre of the Thrie Estaitis*, directed by Tyrone Guthrie and adapted by Robert Kemp, was presented to critical acclaim. This was a 'full-blooded satire' (last performed in 1552) on the corruption of the Church, state and people of sixteenth-century Scotland, although most of the satire was directed against the Church. It was interesting, therefore, that the play was performed in the Assembly Hall, where the Church of Scotland held its annual General Assembly (it has been suggested that one reason for the Kirk's permission to present this play might have been that the General Assembly had long been regarded by some as the successor to the three estates).[117] In order to make it fit for production in halls owned by the Kirk, some of the 'bawdier' lines had been cut; Henry Harvey Wood wrote in a letter to Bridie that 'provided we can cut or disguise some of the bawdier passages [. . .] there should be no difficulty about persuading the General Assembly to let us use their hall'.[118]

Still, the performance was not without controversy; a complaint to the Lord Provost in September 1949 said the play was insulting to Catholics, especially given the widespread persecution of Catholics 'in every country behind the Iron Curtain'.[119] In his reply, Lord Provost Murray confessed his own anxiety about the 1949 production 'because there was a burlesque which was additional and almost verging on the offensive' – about which he immediately contacted Guthrie.[120] This might help to explain why, for its third year of production in 1951, Guthrie revised it with the object of 'still further elucidating the ethical values of the piece'.[121] But a more significant outcome of the play being presented in the Assembly Hall was the innovation of the 'apron stage', built over the moderator's throne, to transform the space into a theatre. This was to have a far-reaching influence on the performance of theatre in the twentieth century and to revolutionise theatre building in Britain and America.[122]

Within the Programme Committee, tensions continued over the question of Scottish drama in the Festival programme. In October 1948 Wood suggested that Guthrie be made honorary adviser on drama to the EFS (a suggestion that Bing had apparently interpreted as a slight on his own competence). Together Bridie and Wood also suggested a meeting 'as it is high time that we took the drama side, and particularly the Scottish drama side, of the Programme Committee more seriously than in the past'.[123] When it was mooted that the Citizens Theatre company might present two plays at the 1950 Festival under the direction of Guthrie, Bing and Ian Hunter asked that the company appear as the 'Edinburgh Festival Players' rather than Glasgow Citizens Theatre. Bing's argument was that, since Bridie would be reinforcing the company, it would in effect be an ad hoc company, but this was countered by Wood, who insisted that just as the Old Vic or any other 'reputable company' would appear under its proper title so too would the Glasgow Citizens Theatre. Wood also pointed out that Glyndebourne was itself an ad hoc company yet had never offered to be called the 'Edinburgh Festival Opera Company'.[124] Bing charged that 'this business of Scottish drama' was so close to Bridie's heart that he might persuade himself into accepting standards he would otherwise not tolerate.[125]

At the Festival, high standards equalled costly ticket prices. In February 1947, responding to Garratt's letter, Bridie had written:

> The fine arts are very expensive and the guarantors of the Festival will probably have to make a present of a five-figure sum to the public. Is it not too much to ask the people who wish to enjoy the Festival to make their own contribution and to begin saving for it now?[126]

The ticket prices excluded attendance by many in a population still coping with shortages in the aftermath of world war, even though the Festival had been promoted as a means of using the arts to bring people together.

The Fringe, which offered more affordable alternatives to official Festival productions, was joined by another unofficial festival in 1951 (the year that Glasgow Unity disbanded). The Edinburgh Labour Festival Committee (ELFC) was established 'to initiate action designed to bring the Edinburgh Festival closer to the people, to serve the cause of international understanding and goodwill', echoing the professed aims of the official Festival.[127] Made up of representatives of the Communist Party, Edinburgh Trades Union Council, the National Union of Mineworkers and the Labour Party, as well as cultural groups, community organisations and independent art groups, the purpose of the ELFC was to present a 'People's Festival'. This week-long event, first held in August 1951, was committed to attracting working-class families, therefore affordable ticket prices and an atmosphere of inclusion were required. In doing this, the 1951 People's Festival exposed the tension over the aims of the International Festival: it asked how the Festival could use art to educate and to act as a means of bonding and reuniting people when so many were excluded by high ticket prices. Norman Buchan, who was heavily involved in the first People's Festival, wrote:

> Aw Princes Street was in a rout
> An' plagued by every kind o' tout
> The rich hae tickets but we're without –
> They're ower dear at the Festal-o.[128]

Bing had reported in August 1946: 'The high prices, which are inevitable and indeed desirable for artistic presentations of the standard aimed at, may reduce the number of "local" visitors.'[129] Martin Milligan, Communist Party member and one of the key organisers of the 1951 People's Festival, noted that the International Festival 'has a "Keep Out" notice posted for the working people of the city in which it takes place. This takes the form first, of high prices, and second, of a ludicrously cultivated air of "snootiness".'[130]

Jeff Hill has argued that the Labour governments of 1945 to 1951 were concerned with the enrichment of the country's cultural life and with bringing culture within the reach of the people, but that most of what they actually achieved related to 'elite' cultural activities.[131] The key motive of the People's Festival organisers was to counter this notion of elite culture with something that (they felt) originated from the people themselves, and this is why folk song culture was central to its inception and development. In fact, the legendary People's Festival Ceilidhs have been recognised as the starting point of the subsequent folk song revival in Scotland, and their influence on the British folk song revival has been widely acknowledged.[132] Hamish Henderson, 'poet, cultural and political activist, singer-songwriter and folklorist' as well as central organiser of the Edinburgh People's Festival, noted that he was inspired by Antonio Gramsci, writing: 'Gramsci in action *was* the People's Festival.'[133] As Corey Gibson has pointed out, Henderson was influenced by Gramsci's recognition of the potential and power of folk culture:

> That which distinguishes folk-song in the framework of a nation and its culture is neither the artistic fact nor the historic origin; it is a separate and distinct way of perceiving life and the world, as opposed to that of 'official' society.[134]

Henderson also said that 'the powerful stimulus behind the whole People's Festival enterprise' was Ewan MacColl, founder of the 1950s folk revival in Britain and an inspirational and revolutionary figure in oppositional culture.[135]

Born Jimmie Miller to Scottish parents, and brought up in Salford, MacColl had a long association with left-wing politics and agitprop theatre and believed in the potential of theatre and song to raise political conscious-ness among the working class.[136] By the 1950s MacColl, increasingly dissatisfied with the potential of theatre to convey a strong sense of political consciousness, had gravitated to folk song (a medium in which he had been thoroughly immersed since early childhood through his parents and the Scottish émigré community in which he lived). During visits to Scotland while on tour with Theatre Workshop, a pioneering theatre group that experi-mented with new ways of dramatic expression with the aim of reflecting the 'dreams and struggles of the people', MacColl had met Scottish writers such as Hugh MacDiarmid, Sydney Goodsir Smith and Henderson.[137] In a letter to Henderson in February 1951, MacColl had suggested that Henderson meet up with Alan Lomax, an American Communist Party member and 'just about the most important name in American folk song circles', to work together collecting traditional folk songs.[138] Many of the singers they recorded over the summer of 1951 then performed at the Edinburgh People's Festival.[139]

Following on from the success of the 1951 event, a three-week celebration was organised for August 1952 with the theme of post-war frustrations. Its aim was that 'the people's voice may be heard and the people's needs may be met' and to broaden its appeal, the name of the committee was changed from the ELFC to the People's Festival. In 1952 it was supported by fifty organisations and looked set to occupy a significant place in the festival season, but the 1950s were in the grip of the Cold War. At the beginning of the 1950s McCarthyism was reaching its zenith in the USA, and in Britain there was a general concern about communist propaganda despite there being no comparable 'witch hunts'. After the successful 1952 event, two 'right wing' members of the committee raised concerns about Communist Party propaganda in MacColl's *The Travellers*, performed by Theatre Workshop at that year's Festival.[140] In December 1952, one of the Edin-burgh People's Festival's key supporters, the Scottish Trades Union Con-gress, proscribed the People's Festival as a 'Communist front' and was closely followed by the Labour Party, who cited their objections to the 'pro-Stalinist line' of *The Travellers*.[141] The Edinburgh City Labour Party and the Edinburgh Trades Council defiantly continued to support the Festival (Councillor Jack Kane was chair of both the People's Festival Committee and the Labour Party in Edinburgh).[142]

The People's Festival was also significant to wider debates about the role of culture in society. It had opened with a one-day conference, attended by more than 170 people and described in the Communist newspaper the *Daily Worker* as 'the first general conference of the Labour movement in this country to discuss the crisis of culture'.[143] This conference, titled 'Towards a People's Culture', unanimously passed a resolution 'recognising that working people have pressing cultural as well as material needs and that in this field there exist a number of urgent problems', and called for working-class and cultural organisations around the country to establish committees similar to the ELFC as a matter of urgency. In fact, Milligan noted that, although Communists were 'only a small proportion of those present', the conference had made 'the leading role the Communist Party can play in the defence and development of British culture' evident.[144] There was a concern that imported American culture posed a threat to Britain's culture and cultural heritage. The National Cultural Committee (NCC) of the Communist Party (founded in 1947) highlighted this at their conference, 'The American Threat to British Culture', held in London in April 1951. Sam Aaronovitch, secretary of the NCC, had repeatedly emphasised the encroaching threat of what he termed 'cultural imperialism', a common fear in Cold War Europe.[145] This concern was also keenly felt by Scottish folk singers and other individuals involved in the People's Festivals. Milligan had pointed out to readers of the *Communist Review* that the 1951 People's Festival Ceilidh had 'helped to give living substance to phrases about our national cultural heritage' and, moreover,

> by the end of the evening it had very obviously moved the whole audience with a quality of pleasure and pride that made more intolerable than could many speeches the violence and tawdriness of the imperialist-American films and dance music that clutter up our cinema and radio programmes, etc.[146]

In the two years after the first People's Festival, the NCC had become more active in relation to the role of culture in British society. It held a national conference on Britain's cultural heritage in May 1952, and later in the year drew up and disseminated a plan of work that outlined the importance of cultural work 'as part of the mass work of the party'. That same year, the Communist Party also began to publish *Daylight*, a cultural journal aimed at readers outside the party.[147] Nonetheless, this was not a new idea. Jeff Hill notes that during the war, socialists had begun to realise that the struggle to change society had to be 'waged' on cultural, as well as political and economic, ground: 'The weapon to be used was an independent and assertive brand of socialist culture which fostered creativity, a communitarian spirit and a new socialist way of life.'[148]

Thus, the challenge to 'culture' as conceptualised by the Arts Council, the International Festival and other 'elite' institutions had begun to take shape. As Adam MacNaughton has commented, 'in the 1950s we needed a folksong revival in which the people, and particularly young people, did not feel that "culture" was being forced upon them from above'.[149] These early challenges to the International Festival were both political and cultural. A key aim of the People's Festival organisers was to encourage political consciousness among working people via the medium of culture. Plans for the 1952 event indicated that the content of the programme would

> make an important direct contribution to the fight for Peace and Friendship between peoples, and to heightening our National consciousness and pride in our traditions; and the making more vivid the vision of Socialism and the appreciation and strength of the working class.[150]

The NCC was also explicit about this political use of culture, proposing that a significant aim of its 1953 conference would be

> to show and discuss the development of man and his culture made possible by the abolition of class society i.e. the consequences of the basic law of socialism; and the active role of culture and ideology in bringing about these changes.[151]

Another important feature of the People's Festivals, like the Fringe, was an emphasis on new and contemporary work. Indeed, the *Daily Worker* reported that the 'dread of losing money' had resulted in a 'notable lack' of premieres in the official programme: 'Nearly all the exciting ventures which have saved the official Festival from dullness have been the work of unofficial bodies which have seized the opportunity to show what can be done when money is not the first consideration.'[152]

The People's Festival had appeared at a time when the official Festival was starting to attract criticism in the press for its 'stuffy' programme. The Fringe was becoming more popular and at a meeting of the Edinburgh Festival Council (EFC) in November 1950, the EFS referred to the 'unofficial events' held in Edinburgh during the Festival each year, 'over which the Society exercised no control'. Since the events were becoming more numerous and the publicity material they distributed did not 'make it clear' to the public that they were not part of the official Festival programme, it was suggested that 'steps should be taken to prevent any further misunderstanding'.[153] In August 1950 an article in the right-leaning *Scottish Daily Express*, a newspaper with a very high circulation in Scotland at the time, asked: 'But why not a Festival that isn't so Stuffy?' Critic John Barber accused the organisers of forgetting 'the glory of youth' and 'the joy of experiment', commenting: 'Nobody without fame gets a chance here of winning it.' He came up with an alternative Festival programme which he suggested would be held in Brighton or Blackpool rather than 'aristocratic Edinburgh or dainty Bath'. It would have dance bands instead of orchestras, clowns, acrobats, jugglers and strongmen instead of cellists and classic farces or penny gaff hits instead of Eliot or Sartre.[154] One letter that appeared in response to Barber's article defended the Festival: 'Away with the pretence that a dance band is entertainment and a symphony orchestra is snobbery. Away with that glorification of the lowbrow. Away with the sniffs at culture.'[155]

1953: CULTURAL CLASH IN EDINBURGH

In 1953, the Festival and the Fringe clashed publicly. By then, the programme of the Festival 'proper' was being more widely criticised. In August 1952, after discussing the 'unofficial events' held in the city at the same time as the Festival, a decision was made by the EFS not to incorporate the Fringe, nor allow it any publicity in official Festival publications. Until that point, some moves had been made to try to get the Fringe incorporated into the Festival programme (or at least obtain official acknowledgement), but from 1953 it became clear that the Fringe was to remain separate from the Festival. It therefore became increasingly important to define what the Fringe was and what it offered in comparison to the official Festival. In this period we can see the first signs of a 'Fringe identity' developing.

Certainly the Fringe, though not always referred to by this title, was attracting more attention by 1953. During that year's Festival, *The Times* alerted its readers to what it called 'the other theatre' in Edinburgh: 'Edinburgh in festival time now attracts to itself a number of theatrical enterprises over and beyond those specifically promised in the official programme'. These additional theatre productions served a 'useful as well as a delightful purpose', that of providing more choice for the enthusiastic theatregoer, since the Festival offered 'almost more music than the enthu-siastic music-lover can conveniently find time for' while the nature of theatrical production meant that there was usually several days between different productions.[156] But 'the other theatre' did not just provide more drama to balance up the music on offer from the official Festival.

On 24 August 1953 a review appeared in the *Scottish Daily Express* of a Fringe revue at the Palladium Theatre, *See You Later*, which, the critic wrote, takes a 'sharp look at all that is stuffy in Scotland's culture jamboree [. . .] and kicks it gaily out of the window'. The revue was presented by some of London's 'brightest newcomers' with the Scottish actor Duncan Macrae as guest artist. The Festival itself promised 'plenty of solid fare' but, wrote the critic, there were 'too few frivolities'. Accompanying the review was a photograph of one of the dancers in *Les Folies Ecossaises*, the eleven o'clock show also on at the Palladium: a young woman dressed in a halter-neck top and bikini shorts, showing her midriff. In that same issue of the *Express*, an article had appeared charging that the 'old Festival magic is missing': 'Something happened this year to the rapturous enthusiasm we called the Festival spirit. Remember it? It has lost its former sparkle and efferves-cence.'[157]

The following day Ian Hunter reacted to these articles and in doing so demarcated the lines between Festival and Fringe. In response to the picture, he said:

> When I see these 'sexy sketches' of the Fringe in the newspapers this morning, it is a little bit discouraging. While I have anything to do with the Festival, we will keep to the articles of association to present the very highest art.[158]

This comment hints at the reputation for being risqué that the Fringe was to attract during the 1960s, although in the early 1950s it was seen as risky in relation to artistic standards. Hunter went on: 'We are a serious festival and we must be. The International Festival of Music and Drama is a serious artistic event. If certain sections think that is stuffy – well, there it is.'[159] The Festival was built upon the belief that the arts served a higher purpose and had a serious function, while the type of material available on the Fringe was seen by the EFS as being 'light' and more for entertainment than spiritual refreshment.[160] These boundaries between 'high' art and 'popular' culture reflected the broader terrain and underpinned arts funding, and it was the 1960s before an effective challenge broke through.

Nonetheless that initial accusation that the Festival was too serious instigated Hunter's later admission that it meant 'nothing to the ordinary citizen'. In 1951, the *Daily Worker* had proclaimed that the People's Festival was aiming at the 'ordinary man'. 'What is more,' it continued, 'it is hitting the target.'[161] In part, this was about offering culture that was affordable (a major objective of the People's Festivals). But it was also about offering theatre and music that resonated with the local population. Glasgow Unity had enjoyed great success in the immediate post-war years with plays that reflected the lives of ordinary working-class people around Scotland. To Linda Mackenney, these plays

> reject specific categories of Scottish drama which project specific images of Scotland. Unity rejects tartanry and, with it, the kind of Scottish historical dramas that mythologise the past, but it also rejects the kinds of plays that over-idealise rural and, in particular, Highland life, which are likewise divorced from contemporary reality.[162]

Duncan Macrae adopted a similar approach, blending the hugely popular variety show format with theatre to create a form that would challenge what he saw as the Anglicisation of Scottish theatre and to remedy the lack of a 'native drama'. The commercially successful *Scottishows*, which ran during 1952–5 (including a three-week run at the Edinburgh Festivals), were part of Macrae's desire to create a theatre that was Scottish 'in style, form and content'. The language was modern Scots and the style was variety, which had been given 'new vigour' in the 1950s with the popular *Five-past-Eight* shows at Glasgow's Alhambra Theatre and with the adoption of the style for television.[163]

By September 1953, it was reported that Hunter was suggesting that more needed to be done to interest 'the man in the street'. His ideas were: to revive the century-dead Grassmarket Fair and bring in folk dancers from Scotland and Norway as well as tribal dancers from Africa to dance on the street; to publicise the famous musicians and artists so the 'man in the street' would recognise them and know why they were famous (in the spirit of Eliot, Hunter was suggesting a communication of culture here); to decorate Princes Street; and finally, to erect a big top and invite a 'world-class' circus.[164] This last proposal draws on a trend that was popular and even encouraged by the government during the Second World War as a means of providing entertainment for the wider population. Sandra Dawson argues that during the 1930s, but particularly during World War II, the circus had been heavily marketed as a 'unifying and democratic institution', one that transcended class and nationality.[165] It was interesting that an issue had arisen in 1950 when the Lord Provost of Glasgow had snubbed the Festival's opening ceremony to visit the circus instead, telling guests at the luncheon that day that he would much prefer to face the circus lions than 'the literary and social lions in Edinburgh'.[166] In response to Hunter's suggestions, the opinion page of the *Express* commented that the Festival did not offer enough to people who 'like a little colour and fun with their culture' and that both the Corporation and the Edinburgh Festival Society should 'examine sympathetically suggestions now being made to brighten the Festival for the non-artistic citizen'.[167]

Nonetheless, despite recognising that the Festival did not offer much for 'ordinary' citizens, these festivities were not to be part of the official Festival, and certainly not to be funded by it. Rather, Hunter envisaged that a 'corporation of private enterprise' would shoulder the responsibility.[168] During the war it was believed that 'good' culture should be supported by government subsidy while popular culture should be left to the 'dictates and uncertainties of commercial viability'.[169] It appears that the plea went largely unheeded since the issue of having a carnival to 'arouse interest among the general public' was raised again during an EFS meeting in February 1956, except this time it was suggested that the society organise it, since it would 'derive considerable revenue therefrom'.[170] In October 1955, a writer for the *Scots Magazine* had argued that for some in Edinburgh 'the Festival might as well be on the moon' and questioned how the organisers might bridge the gap:

> If the organisers of the Festival would come down from the top of the ladder just by a couple of rungs, it might be that this could help many to approach grand opera, the symphony concert, and chamber music with less trepidation.[171]

The relationship between the Festival and the Fringe during the first ten years has been described as 'avuncular' rather than competitive and it seemed that, for the most part, relations were founded on Lord Provost Murray's welcome in the 1950 Programme: 'You have come to take part in a Festival, the living symbol of which is friendship.'[172] Early Festival programmes had actually included references to some of the 'Additional Events' taking place during festival time in Edinburgh.[173] But the EFS in 1952 made a decision to effectively ignore the Fringe. *The Scotsman* asked what might happen if the position were to remain as it was, noting that organisation of the Fringe would help to maintain the 'standards and atmosphere of the Festival'. The Fringe did get more organised as the 1950s progressed, though at the behest not of the EFS or the corporation, but rather of performers who were part of it. They realised that in order to gain publicity and thus some measure of financial success, even if it only meant breaking even, they had to introduce some level of organisation. In 1951 a group of Edinburgh University students opened a reception centre for Fringe groups and, after being refused permission to advertise in the Festival Programme, an Edinburgh printer put a common programme together in 1954, titled 'Additional Entertainments'. Around 1954, the first steps were taken towards the organisation of the Fringe – in terms of a programme that could provide visitors with listings of all that was on at the Fringe and the locations of the performances, as well as some sort of central box office for selling tickets – when a meeting of Fringe groups was called 'to set up an "official" unofficial festival'. The following year, 1955, Edinburgh University students set up a central box office. All of these developments symbolised the self-help element that the Fringe grew out of and also signified its growing visibility and influence in the city. Indeed Hunter, as reported in *The Scotsman*, had commented that in 1955 Duncan Macrae 'was making an extremely big contribution to the Edinburgh Festival, and whether it was official or unofficial was, in a sense, immaterial'. Alistair Moffat has noted that this statement showed that 'the Festival Society had by 1955 recognised the Fringe as an integral (but not integrated) part of the Edinburgh Festival'.[174]

The People's Festival also helped to give the Fringe a more visible identity, in terms of presenting culture that was creative and contemporary and represented some measure of protest against 'elite' culture. Linda Mackenney has written that the Fringe became 'the arena where hitherto unrecognized local Scottish drama could assert itself'.[175] But the significance of the Fringe extended well beyond the Scottish scene. Even in 1949, companies from Canada, Norway and France took part at the invitation of the SCDA. Furthermore, the burgeoning Fringe was increasingly providing a space for very publicly challenging the existing politics of the arts in post-war Britain – in terms of values, costs, purpose, content and resonance with audiences.

On 8 September 1953, Macrae 'advanced' (the *Express* was suggesting a warlike arrival) into Edinburgh's George Street to lead a skirmish on behalf of the Fringe against the official Festival, its organisers and its ideals during a visit to the Three Weeks Club near the Festival headquarters. There he announced: 'Let's have the best for the lowbrows, too.' In his speech, Macrae criticised the EFS for not having recognised all the opportunities presented to it, asked that it decorate Princes Street in the future and, more importantly, invite the Fringe in. Glyndebourne opera, he argued, was 'a bit of glamour and luxury beyond our means' while the Fringe was 'for the people who cannot afford the big shows'. Macrae argued that Hunter, in making suggestions to try and interest 'the man in the street', 'has at last realised the gap between the arts and popular art'. At a Fringe show the people could 'hear language not too remote from their own language at a fifth of the price they would pay to see a great opera' – this, argued Macrae, would lead to the beginnings of discernment, without which 'they will not be able to appreciate the Glyndebourne Opera'.[176] Macrae's 'skirmish' on behalf of the Fringe was clearly still couched in post-war terms – that of the progression from popular culture to high art through exposure to culture – but was also firmly in favour of a culture that mattered to the majority of the population.

These were two key aims of the People's Festivals: to present affordable alternatives to the official Festival offerings, and to perform culture that had more resonance with the local population. Furthermore, the People's Festivals helped to cement the political element that had been a part of the Fringe since that first year, when Unity had been a key feature. In this sense, the challenges the Fringe and the People's Festivals made to the 'official' Festival straddled both political and cultural spheres (the two were not mutually exclusive). Nevertheless, the main difference that Macrae noted between the drama offered by the Festival and that by the Fringe was in terms of originality:

> Why do we have to waste our time on the Highland Fair, the Thrie Estates, and the Gentle Shepherd? Why go back to these museum pieces? The Festival Society seems to think that antiquity has a special quality. But art must be creative and contemporary.[177]

As F. M. Leventhal argues, the Arts Council that 'emerged after the war bore the imprint of Keynes's conception of public patronage. Unabashedly elitist, he disdained those, mainly on the political left, who extolled the merits of popular culture or who sought to revive participatory folk traditions.'[178] Jen Harvie has written that in its first decade, the Arts Council 'entrenched a bias of superiority, priority, and indeed productivity for the metropolis and one of inferiority and inactivity for the regions'.[179] But the growing influence and impact of more contemporary art and its creators was to become more keenly felt in Edinburgh, as it was more broadly. The challenges to the Festival explored here were early skirmishes in what were to widen and deepen into important cultural clashes. Furthermore, by the 1970s the challenges from the left and from 'below' were to become central concerns of arts bodies as the social and cultural changes of the 1960s and an increased emphasis on community-based culture began to influence state provision. In these early years of the festivals, it was mainly the issues raised by left-wing theatre groups, the Labour movement, Scottish folk singers and nationalists that influenced the direction and essence of the Fringe, creating a space for cultural collision that was to grow in stature and significance.

NOTES

1. Miller, *The Edinburgh International Festival*, 5–9. In some ways, this was understandable – if shortsighted – given the coal crisis of winter 1946–7, for which Shinwell had been widely criticised.
2. Richard Demarco, 6 October 2004.
3. *The Times*, 25 August 1947.
4. Arnold, *Culture and Anarchy*, 44, 69.
5. Walter, cited in Miller, *The Edinburgh International Festival*, 31.
6. *The Scotsman*, 27 September 1947.
7. Brown, *The Death of Christian Britain*, 6. See Morgan, *Britain since 1945* for more on 'consensus'.
8. The period 1945–51 was described as an 'age of austerity'; see Sissons & French (eds), *Age of Austerity*.
9. Morgan, *The People's Peace*, 28, 104–11.
10. Brown, *The Death of Christian Britain*, 5.
11. Hewison, *Culture and Consensus*, 69–74.
12. Allsop, *The Angry Decade*, 39–40; Hewison, *In Anger*, 53.
13. ECA, Early Festival Papers, Report on Programme and Finance, August 1946; Festival Notes, 8 October 1946; *The Times*, 19 August 1947.
14. See Brown, 'Spectacle, Restraint and the Twentieth-century Sabbath Wars', 171.
15. *The Times*, 3 September 1948.
16. Beecham, 'The Edinburgh Festival 1949', 271.
17. This post only lasted until Cripps became Chancellor of the Exchequer in November 1947, and was not reintroduced until 1964.
18. NRS, ED61/45, Copy to Mr Donnelly of Details of Meeting Between Lord Provost and Sir Stafford Cripps, 30 September 1947.
19. NRS, ED61/45, Notes on Meetings, February 1948.
20. Atkinson, *The Festival of Britain*, 8.
21. 'The Festival of Britain 1951', in *Scotland in Festival Year 1951*, 3.
22. NRS, ED61/45, letter, 8 January 1948.
23. Glasgow was an official Festival of Britain centre, housing the Kelvin Hall Exhibition. Sixteen festivals of the arts were also held in England and Wales. See 'The Festival of Britain 1951', in *Scotland in Festival Year 1951*, 7.

24. *Scotland in Festival Year 1951*.
25. *Express*, 30 August 1950.
26. See Atkinson, *The Festival of Britain*; Conekin, *'Autobiography of a Nation'*.
27. Hewison, *In Anger*, 24.
28. Shellard, '1950–54', 38.
29. Allsop, *The Angry Decade*, 21; Hewison, *In Anger*, 60.
30. When the Communist Party leadership supported the Soviet invasion of Hungary in November 1956, swathes of members left in protest. The Central Committee of the party remained suspicious of intellectuals, who had often questioned their leadership. See e.g. Dworkin, *Cultural Marxism in Postwar Britain*.
31. Shellard, '1950–54', 39.
32. Ibid., 30.
33. *The Times*, 3 January 1949.
34. See e.g. Gray, *The Politics of the Arts in Britain*; Sinclair, *Arts and Cultures*.
35. Shellard, *British Theatre since the War*, 12; Findlater, *Banned!*, 10.
36. Shellard, *British Theatre since the War*, 9.
37. Kathryn Johnson notes that the ban on the depiction of God on stage was 'absolute' until the mid-1960s. Johnson, 'Apart from *Look Back in Anger*, What *Else* Was Worrying the Lord Chamberlain's Office in 1956?', 125.
38. See for example Nicholson, 'Foreign Drama and the Lord Chamberlain in the 1950s', 44.
39. Brown, *The Death of Christian Britain*, 6.
40. Davie, 'Religion in Post-War Britain', 167.
41. Highet, *The Scottish Churches*, 90; Allan, *Crusade in Scotland*.
42. Brown, *Religion and Society in Scotland since 1707*, 193.
43. *The Times*, 22 August 1949; ECL, *Submission on Behalf of Edinburgh Festival Society for Nobel Peace Prize*.
44. ECL, *Submission on Behalf of Edinburgh Festival Society for Nobel Peace Prize*.
45. *ED*, 25 August 1947; *The Times*, 23 August 1948.
46. ECA, Early Festival Papers, Lord Provost's speech on the Castle esplanade, 17 August 1952.
47. ECA, EIFMD Programme 1949.
48. ECL, *Submission on Behalf of Edinburgh Festival Society for Nobel Peace Prize*.
49. *Express*, 21 August 1950.
50. Indeed, Raymond Williams noted that Arnold's argument for culture as a substitute for religion helped to continue the hostility expressed to the very term 'culture' and also provoked hostility 'from defenders of the existing system' (Williams, *Culture and Society*, 134).
51. Eliot, *Notes towards the Definition of Culture*, 26.
52. In fact, Stephen Spender commented that the theme of religious vocation 'must have seemed excessive' to the audience watching *The Cocktail Party* (Spender, *Eliot*, 189, 211). Arnold Hinchliffe noted that despite trying to

appear secular, his plays all fulfilled 'his maxim of religious usefulness'; they 'were supposed to surprise people into the meanings and implications of Christianity but audiences could feel that they had not been to the theatre so much as tricked into attending church' (Hinchliffe, *British Theatre*, 37–9).

53. Hutchison, *The Politics of the Arts Council*, 60.
54. See e.g. Hutchison, *The Politics of the Arts Council*; Minihan, *The Nationalization of Culture*.
55. Galloway & Jones, 'The Scottish Dimension of British Arts Government', 30.
56. NRS, ED61/45, letter from financial officer of EFS to secretary general of ACGB, 4 January 1952.
57. The Scottish Committee's grant allocation fell from the Goschen level of 12.08 per cent in 1952/3 to 6.6 per cent in 1962/3 (Galloway & Jones, 'The Scottish Dimension of British Arts Government', 30).
58. The Norwegian Nobel Prize Committee decided that none of the 1952 nominations met the criteria for the prize, although Albert Schweitzer was awarded it retrospectively in 1953.
59. ECL, *Submission on Behalf of Edinburgh Festival Society for Nobel Peace Prize*.
60. Ibid.
61. Ibid. The bid was resubmitted in 1953.
62. *The Herald*, 12 September 2003.
63. Miller, *The Edinburgh International Festival*, 18–19.
64. ECA, Early Festival Papers, EIFMD Report by Mr Rudolf Bing, May 1946. There is real scope for a focused study of the post-war tourist industry in Scotland as well as the connections between the Edinburgh Festivals and constructions of 'Scotland' for tourists (especially along the Royal Mile).
65. VAM, ACGB, EL5/62, letter from Bridie to Keynes, 17 April 1946.
66. Another 'extracurricular' Scottish event was the display of piping and dancing on Edinburgh Castle esplanade. This was organised by the Army's Scottish Command and was so popular that it developed into the Military Tattoo in 1950. See Miller, *The Edinburgh International Festival*, chapter 1.
67. Moffat, *The Edinburgh Fringe*, 15–16. The reasons these two groups chose to appear in Edinburgh at the same time as the Festival are unclear, although the potential of having the attention of the world's press, critics and audiences must have been a strong incentive.
68. *EEN*, 14 August 1948.
69. *EEN*, 9 September 1947; Moffat, *The Edinburgh Fringe*, 17.
70. *The Scotsman*, 14 August 1947.
71. Moffat, *The Edinburgh Fringe*, 16.
72. Ibid., 15.
73. Hutchinson, *The Modern Scottish Theatre*, 105.
74. Scullion, 'Glasgow Unity Theatre', 244.
75. Mackenney, *The Activities of Popular Dramatists and Drama Groups in Scotland*, 224.
76. *Glasgow Herald* (hereafter *GH*), 30 January 1947.

77. See *GH*, February 1947.
78. Robert Mitchell interviewed in 1967, cited in Mackenney, *The Activities of Popular Dramatists and Drama Groups in Scotland*, 225.
79. Scottish Theatre Archives (hereafter STA), As3, Hill, 'Glasgow Unity Theatre' (dissertation), 26.
80. Moffat, *The Edinburgh Fringe*, 15.
81. *GH*, 30 January 1947.
82. Founded in 1936 out of the earlier Worker's Theatre Movement, the popularity of Unity peaked in May 1947, when its national society could boast a membership of over 10,000, as well as more than three million affiliates and fifty branches in towns and cities throughout Britain (Chambers, *The Story of Unity Theatre*, 280).
83. Scullion, 'Glasgow Unity Theatre'.
84. Chambers, *The Story of Unity Theatre*, 19–20, 49, 124–30.
85. Mackenney, *The Activities of Popular Dramatists and Drama Groups in Scotland*, 160.
86. See STA, A.s.3, Hill, 'Glasgow Unity Theatre' (dissertation).
87. Adrienne Scullion has pointed out that, while Glasgow Unity productions reflected the Unity movement's commitment to drama that was locally committed, left wing and strongly narrative, they were also keenly experimental in both the content and form of their plays. See Scullion, 'Glasgow Unity Theatre', 230–4.
88. Ibid., 218–19.
89. Hill, 'Glasgow Unity Theatre' (journal article), 31.
90. Findlay, *Scottish People's Theatre*, xii.
91. Mackenney, *The Activities of Popular Dramatists and Drama Groups in Scotland*, 225.
92. NLS, Acc. 11309, Bridie (5), letter, 11 August 1947.
93. *The Scotsman*, 12 August 1947.
94. Scullion, 'Glasgow Unity Theatre', 244.
95. Mackenney, *The Activities of Popular Dramatists and Drama Groups in Scotland*, 227.
96. *The Scotsman*, 14 August 1947.
97. Hill, 'Glasgow Unity Theatre' (journal article), 28–30.
98. Ibid., 29.
99. See, for example, Hill, 'Glasgow Unity Theatre' (journal article); Scullion, 'Glasgow Unity Theatre'.
100. Campbell, *Playing for Scotland*, 131.
101. For more on the Citizens Theatre, see Coveney, *The Citz*; Oliver, *Magic in the Gorbals*.
102. Bannister, *James Bridie and His Theatre*, 192–3.
103. Ibid., 220.
104. Glasgow Citizens Theatre transferred to the Royal Princess's Theatre in the Gorbals area of the city in 1945. See Bannister, *James Bridie and His Theatre*, 206–18. On Bridie and Unity, see also Findlay, *Scottish People's Theatre*, Introduction.

105. Mackenney, *The Activities of Popular Dramatists and Drama Groups in Scotland*, 228.
106. See Scullion, 'Glasgow Unity Theatre', 244–9, for a fuller examination of Unity's demise. For a critical appraisal of Bridie and Unity, see Mackenney, *The Activities of Popular Dramatists and Drama Groups in Scotland*, 225–37.
107. Mackenney, *The Activities of Popular Dramatists and Drama Groups in Scotland*, 231.
108. Garratt interviewed in 1984, cited in Mackenney, *The Activities of Popular Dramatists and Drama Groups in Scotland*, 229.
109. *The Times*, 5 September 1947; Birch, 'Edinburgh's Festival'.
110. ECL, *Edinburgh Festival: A Review*, 29; *The Times*, 5 September 1947.
111. Birch, 'Edinburgh's Festival'.
112. See e.g. Harvie, 'Cultural Effects of the Edinburgh International Festival'; Garattoni, 'Scottish Drama at the Edinburgh Fringe until the Seventies'.
113. *The Times*, 22 August 1949.
114. ECL, *Submission on Behalf of Edinburgh Festival Society for Nobel Peace Prize*.
115. NLS, Acc. 11309, Bridie (6), letter from Bing to Bridie, 14 November 1947. Many of those who responded and wrote to the *Glasgow Herald* after it published Garratt's letter were firmly in favour of including at least some Scottish representation on the Festival programme.
116. *GH*, 1 February 1947.
117. Bruce, *Festival in the North*, 25–6.
118. NLS, Acc. 11309, Bridie (5), letter from Wood to Bridie, undated (c. January 1948).
119. ECA, Minutes of Council, letter from Duchess of Atholl (chair of the British League for European Freedom) to Lord Provost, Sir Andrew Murray, 6 September 1949.
120. Ibid., Lord Provost to Duchess of Atholl, 8 September 1949.
121. It was also performed as part of the International Festival in 1949, 1959, 1973, 1984, 1985 and 1991. See Scullion, 'Political Theatre or Heritage Culture?'. This issue of cutting 'bawdy' material will be revisited in Chapter 6. *The Times*, 22 August 1951.
122. Miller, *The Edinburgh International Festival*, 14. Guthrie developed his idea further in new builds at Minneapolis and Stratford, Ontario, which subsequently influenced the Sheffield Crucible and Leeds Playhouse – see Scullion, 'Political Theatre or Heritage Culture?', 221. Its influence can also be seen in the Traverse Theatre Club (see Chapter 5).
123. NLS, Acc. 11309, Bridie (5), letter from Wood to Bridie, 5 October 1948.
124. Ibid., letter from Wood to Bridie, 1 September 1949.
125. Ibid., letter, 14 November 1947. It would be worth examining Bridie's status and influence in Scottish theatre at this time, especially given his concurrent roles on the Scottish Committee of the Arts Council, as director of the Citizens and as a member of the EFS.
126. *GH*, 1 February 1947.

127. Gallacher Memorial Library (hereafter GML), Final Draft Constitution of the ELFC.
128. Buchan was a teacher and a founder member of the Glasgow Folksong Club. He was Labour MP for West Renfrewshire from 1964 until 1983 and for Paisley South from 1983 until he died in 1990. He was involved in the Communist Party at time of the People's Festivals and was described as a 'cultural stalwart' of the party (MacNaughton, 'The Folksong Revival in Scotland', 183).
129. ECA, Early Festival Papers, Report on Programme and Finance, August 1946.
130. Milligan convened a meeting in Edinburgh in 1950 to advance the idea that the left should welcome the Festival and should also take advantage of so many internationally renowned artists being in Edinburgh by presenting a people's festival to both complement and outdo the official event. See Henderson, 'The Edinburgh People's Festival'; GML, Milligan, 'Edinburgh People's Festival'.
131. Hill, ' "When Work Is Over" ', 257.
132. See Cowan, *The People's Past*; Gibson, ' "Tomorrow, Songs" '. The folk song revival will be returned to in Chapter 4. MacColl, *Journeyman*, 273.
133. Hamish Henderson, obituary, *The Scotsman*, 11 March 2002; Henderson, 'The Edinburgh People's Festival', 38. See also Gibson, ' "Tomorrow, Songs" '; Steele, 'Hey Jimmy!'.
134. Gramsci cited by Henderson, cited in Gibson, ' "Tomorrow, Songs" ', 52.
135. Henderson, 'The Edinburgh People's Festival', 40. MacColl was a songwriter, a singer and a playwright. See Harker, *Class Act*.
136. See MacColl, *Journeyman*.
137. It was at this time, during his increasing involvement with Scottish writers and folk singers, that Miller changed his name to Ewan MacColl (Chambers, *Continuum Companion to Twentieth Century Theatre*, 773).
138. For the full text of the letter see Finlay, *The Armstrong Nose*, 46.
139. A number of these singers went on to become household names in Scotland (like Jeannie Robertson and Jimmy MacBeath). The songs collected were the first items to be archived in the newly created School of Scottish Studies, founded at University of Edinburgh in 1951. Henderson also began work collecting folk songs from around Scotland.
140. Henderson, 'The Edinburgh People's Festival'. *The Spectator*'s critic had commented: 'A good company and a good director zealously devoted to the presentation of propaganda thinly disguised as experimental drama.' Moffat, *The Edinburgh Fringe*, 20; Theatre Workshop had performed at the 1951 and 1953 People's Festivals, and had also performed on the Fringe in 1949, having been invited by Norman and Janey Buchan.
141. Finlay, *The Armstrong Nose*, 63–4.
142. GML, letter from Milligan to Mr Georgeson, 3 January 1953.
143. *Daily Worker*, 31 August 1951.
144. See Hewison, *In Anger* for more on the impact of US culture on Britain; GML, Milligan, 'Edinburgh People's Festival', 87–8.

145. John Callaghan argued that by the mid-1950s the earlier 'anti-American' momentum was 'beginning to flag' and new pressures – like the effect of a rising affluence among the working classes on political beliefs and behaviour – were receiving more attention from within the Communist Party (Callaghan, *Cold War, Crisis and Conflict*, 85–104). See also Johnston, 'Revisiting the Cultural Cold War'.

146. GML, Milligan, 'Edinburgh People's Festival', 88.

147. GML, Plan of Work of National Cultural Committee up to Summer of 1953 (Communist Party).

148. Hill, ' "When Work Is Over" ', 239.

149. MacNaughton, 'The Folksong Revival in Scotland', 182.

150. GML, Work of the Edinburgh Labour Festival Committee: Plans for the Edinburgh People's Festival 1952.

151. GML, Plan of Work of National Cultural Committee up to Summer of 1953 (Communist Party).

152. *Daily Worker*, 31 August 1951.

153. ECA, EFC, MoM, 8 November 1950.

154. *Express*, 25 August 1950.

155. *Express*, 26 August 1950.

156. *The Times*, 20 August 1953.

157. *Express*, 24 August 1953.

158. Moffat, *The Edinburgh Fringe*, 26.

159. *Express*, 25 August 1953.

160. Henry Harvey Wood had said during the inaugural Festival: 'I see no reason why the lighter side of art should not have its share in our festival' (*Express*, 27 August 1947).

161. *Daily Worker*, 31 August 1951.

162. Mackenney, *The Activities of Popular Dramatists and Drama Groups in Scotland*, 198.

163. Smith, '1950–95', 256–7.

164. *Express*, 8 September 1953.

165. Dawson, 'Selling the Circus'.

166. This caused a minor spat after the Lord Provost of Glasgow denied having been invited to the opening ceremony at all, only for the Lord Provost of Edinburgh to issue the complete correspondence between their respective offices, which showed quite clearly that he had been invited on 19 June, accepted on 21 June and then declined on 31 July 'owing to official dates in the city' which were 'entirely unexpected' (*Express*, 22 August 1950).

167. *Express*, 9 September 1953.

168. These ideas were first aired by Hunter as part of a plea at an Edinburgh luncheon of the Sales Managers Association.

169. Hayes & Hill, *'Millions like Us?'*, 29.

170. ECA, MoM, 23 February 1956.

171. *Scots Magazine*, October 1955.

172. Moffat, *The Edinburgh Fringe*, 21; EIFMD Programme 1950.

173. See EIFMD Programmes 1950–3, for example.

174. Moffat, *The Edinburgh Fringe*, 18–22.
175. Mackenney, *The Activities of Popular Dramatists and Drama Groups in Scotland*, 171.
176. *Express*, 9 September 1953.
177. Ibid.
178. Leventhal, ' "The Best for the Most" ', 317.
179. Harvie, *Staging the UK*, 20.

4

Convergence of Cultures: New Developments in the Arts, 1956–1962

In 1960, *Beyond the Fringe* was part of the official programme of the Edinburgh International Festival. It was a late-night satirical revue performed by four young graduates of Oxford and Cambridge universities, Jonathan Miller, Peter Cook, Dudley Moore and Alan Bennett. Sir Robert Ponsonby, artistic director of the Festival from 1956 to 1960, had written to each individually, and brought them together for the show. To some the decision to present a show called *Beyond the Fringe* on the Festival programme was official recognition of the popularity and success of the late-night revues that had appeared on the Fringe since the early 1950s, a compliment, if you like; to others, it represented the EFS's attempts to reclaim some ground from the increasingly popular and well-publicised Fringe festival, whose influence was being more keenly felt by the organisers of the official Festival.

Other changes were afoot. In 1962, an international writers' conference brought around seventy writers from all over the world to Edinburgh to debate, over five days in front of a paying audience, five key themes: contrasts of approach, Scottish writing today, commitment, censorship and the future of the novel.[1] One of the organisers, the publisher John Calder, told the press: 'We are imposing no prohibitions on the free expression of opinion, however controversial or unusual.'[2] The frank discussion of love, sex and homosexuality (as well as drug-taking) at both the conference and its daily press briefings caused shock. These were issues not commonly mentioned in public anywhere at the time, let alone in Edinburgh on the official Festival stage. This was still a society in which censorship was routinely practised, particularly in relation to sex. One correspondent for *The Times* commented: 'Even fairly worldly journalists at the press conferences held by writers have signified that they have been disturbed by the repetition of these themes.'[3]

There was a clear sense of rapid social and cultural change between 1956 and 1962. The early cultural theorists Stuart Hall and Paddy Whannel noted in 1960 that Britain was a 'society in transition, a society throwing out a number of confusing signals'.[4] Old certainties were being challenged: the moral authority of organised religion was under scrutiny (even from within the churches); the effects of increased affluence and consumerism were changing ideas about social relations (seen, for example, in the growing belief in a 'classless society'); the spread of television as a medium was raising questions about the distinctions between public and private leisure, and was linked to the growing concerns about the 'Americanisation' of British culture; the process of post-war decolonisation gathered pace as former colonies became independent (making Britain 'an imperial power on the wane'); the 'culture of deference' in British society was beginning to erode as the increasingly popular 'satire boom' of the early 1960s pilloried and lampooned the 'Establishment'. Overall, there was a pervasive sense of anxiety expressed by commentators and intellectuals, often summed up in the question 'What's wrong with Britain?'[5] Anthony Sampson's famous *Anatomy of Britain*, published in 1962, noted: '[A] loss of dynamic and purpose, and a general bewilderment, are felt by many people, both at the top and the bottom in Britain today.'[6] In part, this was a reaction to the feeling of being between two worlds, between tradition and modernity. On day three of the International Writers' Conference, Norman Mailer commented that 'the absolutely subtle, almost overwhelming, almost oceanic collision of values in the West has resulted in a complete chaos and confusion'.[7] Bernard Levin was later to write of the 'strains caused by the certain past letting go and the uncertain future taking hold'.[8] In 1962, *The Scotsman* reported:

> When the Festival opened after the war the atmosphere was almost nineteenth century. Whatever the purposes of the organisers, those attending represented the box-at-the-opera approach, the luxuriance of resting into a period of artistic wallowing, as far removed from the present intellectual, active, positive, respectful and unhesitating and easy familiarity with the arts as can be [. . .] It would almost be true to say that the central position then held by Glyndebourne epitomised one of the differences between then and now, which is that then the greatest emphasis was on the artist, the executant, the performer, and that now it is on the art (the greatest involuntary emphasis, that is to say, which is nothing to do with either the intentions or the actions of the management).[9]

The arts were in flux.

THE FRINGE AND *BEYOND THE FRINGE*

Beyond the Fringe was the hit of the official Edinburgh International Festival in 1960. Late-night revues had long been associated with the Fringe, beginning in 1951 when *After the Show*, a professional revue that had transferred from London's West End, appeared. By the late 1950s, revues had become a well-established feature of the Fringe. In 1956, the EFS had even approved of satirical revues in its ten-year review:

> All are welcome in the City for the evidence which they bring of youthful initiative, energy and high spirits. Some of their liveliest contributions have

been late-night revues of an intimate and satirical kind, with the Festival as one of the targets. It can be the case that a convocation of the arts may become over-solemn and a little genial mockery is the right solvent for that. It must always be remembered that it is one chief function of a Festival to be festive. The 'Fringe' has nicely added to the gaiety of the assembled nations.[10]

Sir Robert Ponsonby had tested out their popularity in 1957, the first year that 'Late Night Entertainments' appeared in the official programme, when he booked the musical comedienne Anna Russell to present a show called *Satire and Song*. In 1959, Russell returned to 'make fun of the Festival' while Michael Flanders and Donald Swann were booked to perform their hugely popular 'own brand of inoffensive, gentle but very witty and often satirical humour'.[11] However, it was the Oxford Theatre Group who stole the show in 1959, having appeared on the Fringe in an Edinburgh Corporation Parks and Burials-owned hall and received glittering reviews from both local and national newspapers for *Better Never* (in which the young student Alan Bennett was a performer). The critic for *The Observer*, Alan Pryce-Jones, complained that Edinburgh had become 'a testing ground for subsequent London productions, or a shop window for Scottish repertory companies' and noted that the Festival would do well to take note of the 'creative energy' in abundance on the Fringe, particularly that of the Oxford Theatre Group. This, he felt, was 'just the kind of fringe organisation which ought to be encouraged more actively by any city preparing a festival'.[12] Bennett believed that this comment in conjunction with the success of the revue prompted the Festival to actively seek talent from both the Oxford Theatre Group and Cambridge Footlights to put on a similar revue in 1960.

The EFS was reacting to growing criticism being directed against it for becoming stale. In 1957 one prominent playwright and commentator on theatre, Alexander Reid, had charged that the Festival had got 'bogged down' and was in danger of collapsing once its novelty wore off, unless the organisers found a continuing purpose for it. He suggested that it would gain from adopting a large unifying theme; instead of being a 'cultural hold-all, a royal rag-bag full of rich materials which however pleasing individually have little relation each to each', he proposed a theme of Contemporary Art: 'By shifting the main emphasis of the Festival from the interpreters to the creators, the Festival could possibly be made the recognised launching ground for the major art works of at least the Anglo-Saxon world.'[13] In fact, the Festival had marketed itself as an 'interpreter of the arts' since its early days, largely relying on established and well-known material for its programme, while the Fringe had developed as a space for experimentation with new material and with an emphasis on 'the creators'.[14]

Ponsonby had commented that the Festival was getting 'a bit pompous' at the same time that late-night entertainment on the Fringe was 'flourishing'.

So, when a plan to present a different revue for each of the three weeks of the Festival was threatened because one of the proposed performers was unable to make it, Ponsonby, who had 'been pretty irked by the constant theft of our thunder by clever graduates from Oxford and Cambridge' on the Fringe, said to his assistant, John Bassett: 'Let's put on our own revue, let's beat them at their own game.'[15] The title *Beyond the Fringe* was suggested by Festival organisers as soon as the performers had agreed to appear, in January 1960.[16] As Jonathan Miller recalled,

> it was quite clear from the title which was foisted on us that the Fringe had become a competitive irritant to the organisers of the official Festival and that *Beyond the Fringe* was an attempt to outbid the presumptuous outsiders who opportunistically pitched their tents on the edges of the REAL Festival.[17]

It seems there was good reason for the director of the Festival to be worried that the Fringe might steal the Festival's thunder, since by 1959 it had begun 'to look like an alternative festival existing to exploit the contrast with official offerings'.[18] Furthermore, the Fringe had begun to develop its identity as the 'Fringe Festival', becoming more organised, printing its own programmes, setting up a central box office and advertising itself more widely. In fact, by the end of the 1958 Festival, after a series of open meetings by those interested in organising the Fringe (of whom the Oxford Theatre Group played a central role), office bearers had been elected to the newly formed Festival Fringe Society (FFS), and a list of aims drawn up. All groups who planned to appear in Edinburgh during festival time (and who had not been invited to be part of the official Festival) in 1959 were required to contact the secretary of the FFS, Ian Cousland, and pay a nominal fee. In 1960, the FFS even opened its own Fringe Club. Lord Primrose, a local aristocrat asked along to officially open it, made a plea to the EFS to recognise the part played by unofficial companies, and to mention the Fringe in the official brochure.[19]

The impact and significance of *Beyond the Fringe* extended far beyond Edinburgh. A resounding success, it quickly transferred to the West End after its Edinburgh run (falling on London 'like a sweet refreshing rain') and in 1962 opened on Broadway.[20] Its influence was far-reaching. Humphrey Carpenter has written that it fractured the 'culture of deference' in British society by igniting a 'satire boom' that 'changed the rules about what could and could not be said in public, and the younger generation's attitude to authority'.[21] To Michael Billington,

> if any one event marked a genuine cultural turning point, it was not the first night of *Look Back in Anger* in May 1956; it was the slightly shambolic opening performance of a late-night revue at the Lyceum Theatre, Edinburgh on 22 August 1960 [. . .] it exposed the widening gulf between the gen-

erations, helped to change our attitude towards authority forever and made satire in Britain a practical possibility.[22]

It also led to the creation of a satirical nightclub, 'The Establishment Club', opened by Peter Cook in Soho, London; a satirical newspaper, *Private Eye*; and a short-lived but highly influential BBC television satire, *That Was the Week That Was*. Beginning in November 1961, *TW3* (as it was more commonly known) ended in December 1963 after an announcement by Hugh Carleton Greene, director general of the BBC, to the effect that it might have an impact on the outcome of the 1964 general election and was therefore being withdrawn.[23] Politicians had been one of the main targets of its satirical humour, with Peter Cook's parody of Harold Macmillan 'the first time that a living Prime Minister had been lampooned on the twentieth century stage'.[24] Mark Donnelly has commented that satire 'contributed to the sense that it was time for a change of direction', Britain having spent over ten years under Conservative government.[25] Overall, *Beyond the Fringe* helped to undermine what was loosely termed 'the Establishment', a 'term coined to explain the interlocking political, social and cultural institutions that seemed to conspire to prevent change'.[26] As such, it was one of many challenges to tradition that broke through during this period of transition in British society.

SOCIETY IN TRANSITION

The jazz singer, critic and writer George Melly commented that 'satire spanned the period between Rock and the Beatles'.[27] While satire played an important role in setting the stage for many of the social and cultural changes associated with the 1960s, a number of other developments need consideration. In 1961, in *The Long Revolution*, Raymond Williams had noted the crucial impact he believed young people were having on a 'cultural revolution' in progress, and on challenging existing social values and attitudes:

> Consciousness really does change, and new experience finds new interpreta-
> tions: this is the permanent creative process. If the existing meanings and
> values could serve the new energies, there would be no problem. The
> widespread dissent, and the growing revolt, of the new young generation
> are in fact the growth of the society, and no reaction is relevant unless
> conceived of in these terms. The most useful service already performed by the
> new generation is its challenge to the society to compare its ideals and its
> practice.[28]

Williams pointed to the complex relationship between the major cultural and social changes that were gathering pace in late 1950s Britain, and his work represented both the developing field of cultural studies and the growing acknowledgement of culture as a crucial lens for wider social analysis.[29]

In October 1960, Penguin Books was put on trial for publishing obscene literature, namely D. H. Lawrence's 1928 novel, *Lady Chatterley's Lover*. This 'test case by arrangement' is often viewed as a turning point, a symbol of a major cultural shift occurring.[30] To Bernard Levin,

> it turned out to be a test of very much more, a test in fact of whether there had been a change, not only in the law of the land but in a vast body of largely unspoken conventions and unwritten rules about public taste and what it will, and will not, tolerate.[31]

It is important to highlight, however, that the Obscene Publications Act of 1959 (and 1964) did not apply in Scotland, where it was felt that the existing laws and procedures were adequate for dealing with obscene publications. As Roger Davidson and Gayle Davis argue, public opinion, often led by the churches, 'expected the enforcement of moral issues to conform to local values and not some set of statutory norms laid down in Westminster or indeed Edinburgh'.[32]

A number of factors combined to undermine the centre of moral authority that characterised the 1950s, and challenges to traditional moral values grew.[33] There had been no effective revival of religion in the 1950s, and the churches' evangelistic campaigns were described as 'very impressive but generally transient in their impact'. Church of Scotland membership peaked in 1956, in the aftermath of the Billy Graham events; thereafter, church adherence declined on a 'staggering scale'.[34] Churches throughout Britain were losing members and attendance at services was in serious decline.[35] There was also a growing concern about the perceived lowering of moral standards among the population. Yet, despite these trends, it was still widely believed that Scottish society was distinct from its counterparts in the rest of Britain. Throughout the 1950s, the Scottish Office and the Broadcasting Council for Scotland worked to 'protect the moral identity of Scottish society'.[36]

One of the first real challenges to traditional morality came in 1957 when the report of the Wolfenden Committee, commissioned by the British government to consider the extent to which homosexual behaviour and female prostitution should come under the condemnation of criminal law, was issued. It recommended that homosexual acts between two consenting adults should be legalised, provided they were over the age of twenty-one and in a private place. Most of the major church leaders in Britain showed their support for its recommendations, but the Salvation Army, the Baptist Church and the Church of Scotland passed resolutions against the change.[37] But the Kirk was split on the issue. A subcommittee of the Church and Nation Committee, appointed to investigate the question of decriminalising homosexuality in June 1955, reported in favour of decriminalisation in line with Wolfenden in December 1957, but was overruled by the main Church and Nation Committee (by seventeen votes to five).[38]

The recommendations of the Wolfenden Committee, eventually enacted into law in 1967 (though not until 1980 in Scotland), symbolised the first steps towards a morality decided in the private rather than the public sphere. Levin commented that during the 1960s people had turned away from the Church and 'found better things to do'.[39] This was certainly a worry for the Church of Scotland from the late 1950s, as the various committees that reported each year to the General Assembly acknowledged that other influences were beginning to undermine the authority of the Kirk. This was despite the views of Scottish churches – and in particular the Church of Scotland – being regularly cited in policy briefings and parliamentary debate as reflecting 'the general views of the people of Scotland'.[40] Nonetheless, it was clear that many General Assembly discussions were underpinned by concern for the morality of the Scottish population, and in 1959, the Committee on Temperance expanded its remit in response to recent social change and became the Committee on Temperance and Morals.[41]

In 1960, the Church of Scotland noted that people were living in a period of 'immense social change' and that it should be alert to these new patterns of change, especially in relation to youth.[42] One area of concern was the 'new medium' of television; by 1962 there were 1,119,000 television sets in Scotland, compared to 41,000 in 1952.[43] The Royal Commission on Broadcasting (the Pilkington Committee) concluded in 1960: 'The way television has portrayed human behaviour and treated moral issues has already done something and will in time do much to worsen the moral climate of the country.'[44] The Church of Scotland, in its evidence to the Pilkington Committee, stated that it had the duty of 'maintaining ordinances of religion', noted that it deplored anything that tended to 'lower moral standards in the community', and asserted that 'plays or films which, whether directly or indirectly, appear to question the sanctity of marriage or family life should be avoided. Blasphemy in every form should be banned.'[45]

It is important to emphasise, however, that there were some liberal elements within the Church of Scotland and many willing to make rational concessions to remain engaged with the population. Kirk committees often presented liberal standpoints only to be overruled by the more conservative General Assembly, whose findings were published as the 'official' stance of the Church of Scotland and, as Davidson and Davis have so persuasively shown, taken to reflect the views of the Scottish population at large.[46] However, in 1959, even the General Assembly had caused some controversy when it avowed the principle of all men possessing equal human rights in its request that the British government give 'effective power' to Africans in Nyasaland (now Malawi) in a report that included some 'forthright criticism' of government handling of the situation.[47] The Kirk's special committee on central Africa stated it was time 'for a daring and creative transfer of power to the African people', thus signalling a striking move away from colonialism (a crucial subject for the government between 1958 and 1961).[48] The Church also sought to reassess its stance of the 'right observance of Sunday' against the background of the 'contemporary world, with its new shape and outlook and social habits'.[49] One Fringe performer complained in 1962: 'Why can't I give a performance on a Sunday? [. . .] Is it because I make people laugh? Is it wrong to laugh on the Sabbath?' while another recalled 'having to cut minutes off the Saturday late revue to be finished before the Sabbath'. Larry Marshall, comic and star of the popular lunchtime comedy *The One o'Clock Gang* on Scottish Television, complained that it seemed to be okay for orchestras and quartets to perform on Sundays, but not for comedians.[50]

Churches wanted to stay in touch with young people. In Scotland, the Kirk was concerned about the effect of the 'rapidly changing pattern of life in this space age' on the nation's youth. Secular influences were perceived to have produced a sense of insecurity and uncertainty. A Sunday Observance report of 1962 highlighted the need for young people to have places to meet, and suggested that the Church show hospitality by opening church halls in order to provide places where teenagers might gather in 'healthy surroundings'.[51] At the 1960 General Assembly, when the suggestion was first made, the Church and Nation Committee asked that the Church of Scotland administer '"preventative medicine" to the ills of contemporary youth':

> It might well seem at first sight that such purely 'secular' and even rowdy use of ecclesiastical buildings was an unworthy concession to the spirit of the age. But through such means, accompanied by infinite patience and understanding, young people might eventually be brought into touch with God.[52]

Grace Davie argues that in the post-war period, churches were trying to shake off their image of belonging to the past, and between 1960 and 1975 were focusing primarily on their 'relevance', particularly on attempting to minimise the distinction between the sacred and the secular.[53] The Church of Scotland had shown its desire to maintain contact with young people, and its policy of offering church halls for their use was crucial to the success of the Fringe. Without access to the many church halls in Edinburgh, the mainly young performers that made up the Fringe festival each year would have struggled to find enough places to perform their shows. Part of the reason for the Church's hospitality to these young performers was their need to connect with youth in a time of great change in society. Another reason was that the Kirk wanted to have a point of contact with the intelligentsia, a group not usually connected with organised religion.[54] The Gateway Theatre assumed importance during this period as part of the Church's need to maintain contact with a population drifting away from its teachings.[55]

Chapter 2 showed that taking control of its own theatre had been a surprising and fairly radical step for the Kirk in 1946, having for so long condemned and even suppressed drama in Scotland. Its evangelistic aims and desire to promote a view of the arts that was spiritual and uplifting worked well in tandem with the new Edinburgh International Festival, which shared the high value placed on culture by the Gateway.[56] However, just as pressing moral questions divided opinion within the Kirk, so too did its relationship with the 'secular' arts. Indeed, at the 1958 General Assembly, a Highland minister had attacked the Church of Scotland's 'direct participation' in the arts, calling for an impartial committee to examine the whole operation of the Gateway Theatre. However, in an assembly of around 1,500 commissioners, Revd Robertson managed to muster fewer than fifty supporters 'against the modernist host who rose to endorse the Gateway aim of presenting theatre and film of "cultural and religious quality" to prove that such can effectively promulgate the Christian case.' According to *The Times*, 'the old guard of dour Calvinism took a sound drubbing here to-day when the General Assembly of the Church of Scotland refused to be stampeded into a condemnation of the secular arts'.[57]

The basis of Revd Robertson's complaint was moral: drama at the Gateway portrayed 'drunkenness, sordidness and immorality'.[58] Since 1953, the Gateway had been home to an independent theatre company – The Edinburgh Gateway Theatre Company Limited – under the chairmanship of Scottish playwright Robert Kemp. This company was independent from the Church of Scotland in that it had responsibility for the production and choice of plays presented in the venue.[59] Nonetheless, it operated under the proviso that if there were any doubts about the suitability of a play, the director of the Gateway Theatre, the Revd George Candlish, would be consulted.[60] Although he had never been to the Gateway, Revd Robertson argued that all Kirk theatre productions 'should be in all ways above reproach' and that he could not imagine that any New Testament apostles or older prophets would engage in such a venture as the Gateway Theatre. The General Assembly defended the enterprise, 'overwhelmingly' giving its vote of confidence but, during the following year's proceedings, Robertson again challenged the propriety of the Kirk presenting plays in the Gateway, this time with 'greatly increased' supporting votes.[61] Having visited the Gateway twice in the intervening year, Robertson accused the then current play, Kemp's *The Heart Is Highland*, of having 'suggestive references, frequent swearing and the name of God taken in vain'.[62] However, within just a few minutes of his challenge, Revd Robertson collapsed and died.

After prayers and the adjournment of the Assembly, it was announced that the Home Board had established a special committee to come up with a new policy for the Gateway. Presented in 1961, it illustrates how the Church of Scotland had developed its conception of the arts since 1946 against the context of rapid social change and declining church attendance, as well as what was considered appropriate material for dramatic performance. The committee's report began with some reflection on the attitude of the Kirk to drama and theatre, noting that from the Reformation to the early twentieth century it had been 'for the most part negative and sometimes hostile'. But, it asked, 'need this attitude, which originated in particular historical circumstances, be perpetuated in a quite different situation, and permanently inhibit the Church from having liaison with, and exerting some influence upon, a medium of communication?' In an age of expanding communication and increasing secularisation, the Kirk feared that the arts might become one of the 'lost provinces of religion', those areas of life in which Christian influence had dwindled. It was therefore seen as important for it to maintain some influence, even though there were still some Christians who continued to view the stage as an 'evil thing'.[63]

The Church of Scotland was keen to offer reassurance that drama was a worthwhile art, its main purpose in its 'higher forms' being 'to hold a mirror up to humanity, to show up the world in which men live and the kind of creatures that human beings are'. Thus regarded, the report asserted, 'drama is surely not a matter of no concern to the Church'. The report stressed in some detail what the Home Board regarded as worthwhile drama, suitable for presentation on the Gateway's stage: plays did not need to exhibit concern for specifically Christian values but 'should at least be marked by compassionate understanding'; 'banalities relating to sex, slang and drink' should not appear on the Gateway stage 'or indeed any other stage'; finally, while coarse language or behaviour could not be denied since to do so would not reflect reality, it was considered important that 'objectionable matter' was seen to be objectionable by both playwright and audience.[64] In 1959 the General Assembly had recommended that Kirk Sessions examine the scripts of all plays before their production on Church premises, to avoid 'onstage realism with regard to the use of alcohol'.[65]

However, the report was keen to convey the committee's belief that drama, 'like the other arts, has a right to be judged by what it can be at its best rather than what it may be at its worst', possibly mindful of the controversy over a Gateway drama production in October 1960. The play *Lysistrata*, written by Aristophanes in ancient Greece and performed by Theatre Workshop in Edinburgh in 1953 as part of the People's Festival, was due to have been performed at the Gateway in November 1960. But, on examination of the script, it was cancelled due to its risqué content (see below). There was some preoccupation with moral standards evident, linked in some ways to the *Lady Chatterley's Lover* trial; enough members of the Committee on Temperance and Morals had read Lawrence's book to express the opinion that 'it is pernicious, pornographic, and in some passages positively blasphemous'.[66]

It was clear that similar concerns about moral standards were on the minds of other bodies in relation to drama during the 1960 Festival season. One young theatre company, Group One Productions, arrived to perform *Desire Caught by the Tail*, a play written by Pablo Picasso, in Cathedral Hall, run by St Mary's Roman Catholic Cathedral, but on arrival they were told that the priests had read the script and did not think that it was 'the kind of thing they should put on' on account of it being too 'spicy'.[67] Even the local police were reading scripts at the 1960 Fringe Festival; the other play that Group One Productions had been due to perform, *Fringe of Light*, was seized by the police after two plain-clothes officers arrived during rehearsals and asked the manager for the script to be taken away to be 'read and approved'. This, they assured the manager, was a 'routine matter' and told him that other Festival play scripts had been read.[68] As Davidson and Davis show, censorship took place on a local level throughout Scotland in the 1950s and 1960s, where the Burgh Police (Scotland) Act of 1892 and associated local laws held most sway.[69] Unlike literature, theatre in Scotland was subject to the rule of the Lord Chamberlain's Office – but by the late 1950s, it was clear that its readers were beginning to 'lose their grip' on control of the stage as they sought to deal with the new wave of theatrical works and growing emphasis on contemporary subject matter, which was confirmed when the absolute ban on homosexuality on stage was lifted in 1958. Discussions did take place about new legislation that would liberalise theatrical censorship in Britain in the late 1950s, but this was ultimately abandoned for a number of reasons.[70] During these discussions, officials involved 'were mindful of the conservatism of Scottish attitudes towards sexual issues and of the growing concerns of Scottish church assemblies at the immorality of modern plays'.[71]

Lysistrata is about a long-standing war that wearies the wives of the soldiers fighting it so much that they go on strike – for the soldiers, the choice is either sex or war. Apparently described as a 'rollicking excursion into impropriety', the play was withdrawn for being 'unsuitable' after Candlish wrote to the company in August asking that it be withdrawn. At the time of the controversy, the Gateway Theatre Company had remained silent on its reasons for withdrawing the play. However, notes from a special meeting of the council of the Gateway Theatre Company in October 1960 state, in reference to a course of correspondence concerning *Lysistrata*, that it was 'clear that the Church had strong objections to the performance and would terminate the tenancy of the Theatre if it were intended to proceed.'[72] The Gateway had little choice but to respect the wishes of the Kirk on this occasion. It appears that this controversy prompted the Kirk to reassure its members that the Gateway was worthwhile, and that the church and drama could work well together. Indeed, the last line of the 1961 report to the General Assembly on the Gateway was: 'After a long separation the Church and the Arts have begun to live together again and the renewed association can bring nothing but good.'[73]

The Moral Re-Armament group (MRA), which will be explored further in Chapter 5, also utilised drama during this period and was keen to demonstrate what a positive moral force the theatre could be. MRA was a right-wing, American-based Christian lobbying body that conducted world-wide missions throughout the 1950s against communism and for a 'superior ideology', which MRA claimed it represented: 'It is an ideology of renaissance which can put democracy once more on the initiative in the war of ideas.'[74] MRA swept into Edinburgh on an 'ideological whirlwind', having already visited the capitals and chief cities of twenty-six countries in Asia, Africa and Europe since June 1955. The main part of what was called 'MRA Week' was the presentation of ideological plays that posed 'Freedom or Dictatorship': 'To live in a police state under a dictatorship, without the freedom to express an opinion or choice of religion; or to live in a reorganised world under the guidance of God'.[75] These plays, including *The Vanishing Island* and *We Are Tomorrow*, were performed in front of crowds at the Empire Theatre in Edinburgh, with overspill shows put on at the Little Theatre and Epworth Hall. The group owned its own theatre in London, the Westminster Theatre. Theatre, it proclaimed, was 'the pulpit of this century'.[76]

In fact, drama was to prove an extraordinary force in the 'war of ideas' during this period: between old and new, conventional morality and the 'new' morality, tradition and experiment. British theatre was seen to be 'emerging from a prolonged post-war slumber and [. . .] there was a real scent of dynamic change in the air'.[77] Much of the impetus for this had come from foreign theatre influences. During 1955 and 1956, Samuel Beckett's *Waiting for Godot* and Eugène Ionesco's *The Lesson* were premiered in London at the Arts Theatre Club, while Bertolt Brecht's Berliner Ensemble made its first visit to London. Dominic Shellard has argued that these three playwrights 'broke radically with the conventions of drawing-room drama and encouraged writers to experiment with new styles of presentations, and between them they sketched out the path to take British drama into the sixties'.[78] This influence from the Continent coincided with the 'New Wave' of British theatre, as the 'Angry Young Man' burst onto the scene in 1956 when John Osborne's play *Look Back in Anger* was first performed at London's Royal Court. The main character was a young man called Jimmy Porter, who was frustrated and angry at both his own disillusionment and that of his generation. Although many critics had disliked it, Harold Hobson of the *Sunday Times* and Kenneth Tynan of *The Observer* both sang its praises. Hobson titled his review 'Tomorrow' and wrote 'It is bewildering. It is exasperating. It is insidiously exciting', while Tynan, 'The Voice of the Young', commented that it was 'the best young play of its decade'.[79] Similar writers, such as Colin Wilson, John Braine and Alan Sillitoe, were termed the 'Angry Young Men', although their 'common identity' was more a result of media labelling than any genuine collaboration between the writers.[80] Taken together, the trend (and the label) represented 'a fusion of the notions of "criticism of society" and "the young"'.[81]

There were new voices and styles evident in other arts too. This was also the era that rock 'n' roll made its breakthrough and transformed popular music – beginning with Bill Haley and His Comets' single *Rock Around the Clock*, which reached No. 1 in November 1955. British rock 'n' roll began with the release of Tommy Steele's *Rock with the Caveman* in 1956 and by 1958 the British charts consisted almost entirely of rock 'n' roll songs of some description.[82] A significant influence on British music, alongside rock 'n' roll, was skiffle, a do-it-yourself offshoot of traditional jazz that combined blues, jazz, folk and country and which began to appear in jazz clubs around the country from about 1952. Broom handles and wash-boards were used as instruments in conjunction with the relatively cheap and portable guitar.[83] Since the 1930s, though particularly after the Second World War when many Britons heard jazz on the American Forces radio network, jazz had been popular among middle-class, left-wing intellec-tuals.[84] During intervals in jazz clubs in the 1950s, some members of jazz bands had started to play American folk songs on string instruments, quickly spreading a craze among working-class youths for this affordable means of creating original music. In Scotland the popularity of skiffle peaked around 1957, when the All-Scotland Skiffle Championships at-tracted more than a hundred entries.[85] The effect of rock 'n' roll, jazz and skiffle in the 1950s cannot be overestimated, particularly as a symbol of the break being made with previously accepted attitudes and of the new role of youth as a metaphor for social change.[86]

But it is the folk song movement that is most significant here. Roots of the major folk song revival in 1960s Britain can be found in the Edinburgh People's Festival Ceilidhs of 1951–4. Norman Buchan argued that right from the beginning there was a strong connection between folk song and protest in Scotland. Adam MacNaughton has suggested that this was due to the motivation of the People's Festival founders: to create a counter-weight to the official Festival. Indeed, the whole essence of 'folk' in the 1950s was that it 'had something of the rebel underground about it', a connection that was strengthened when Scottish writers learned about American political singers such as Woody Guthrie, Cisco Houston, Lee Hays and Pete Seeger. Hays and Seeger formed the Weavers, a group persecuted by the McCarthy regime in America. In fact, Buchan argued that it was the recordings of the Weavers' explosive first reunion, at New York's Carnegie Hall in 1955, that had an 'enormously fertilising effect on the revival here – helping to create a natural alliance between protest and folk song'.[87] In his recent studies of Hamish Henderson, Corey Gibson has demonstrated the important political elements of the folk song movement and its embodiment of 'anti-culture'.[88] Folk song played an 'oppositional role' and was therefore, for Henderson, a precedent of Raymond Williams's 'long revolution' (Henderson had become increas-ingly drawn to the New Left in the 1950s).[89]

Founded in 1958, the Campaign for Nuclear Disarmament (CND) fused protest with jazz, folk song and festivity. Tom McGrath, Scottish jazz musician, poet and playwright, has recalled:

> Labour politics had been that you went to elections and voted and there were candidates and all of that, it was much more inbuilt, the parliamentary process and everything, whereas these things that were beginning then, Committee of 100 and CND, were movements that took to the streets and had clubs and had this whole social ramification, so it was very significant in creating culture, cultural forms.[90]

At early CND marches, trad jazz had played a prominent part, but gradually skiffle and folk become more common at protests.[91] Of course, it was not just at CND marches that folk songs were being played and sung in late 1950s Scotland.[92] When he arrived in Edinburgh in 1956, Jim Haynes, who went on to set up the Paperback Bookshop (see below), recalled that folk song culture was 'the *main* thing that was kinda bubbling up underneath'.[93] Folk song clubs were springing up around Scotland, including the Crown and the Howff in Edinburgh.[94] In 1962, the first performances by the Corries Folk Trio at a coffee shop on the Royal Mile were part of the Fringe. Formed by Edinburgh jazz and folk musician Bill Fyfe Hendrie, the Trio attracted crowds 'so big that the queues stretched right down the High Street to South Bridge', leading them to become not just the success of the Fringe but also nationwide favourites, signed to star in the popular BBC television series *Hootenanny*, which was broadcast from a pub in Edinburgh.[95] By 1962, folk music had reached an audience of millions through such avenues as the BBC's *Tonight* programme, on which the Glaswegian folk artists Jimmie McGregor and Robin Hall appeared weekly between 1959 and 1964.[96]

Demonstrating the shifts that had already occurred in the decade since the first People's Festival in 1951, folk song appeared in the official Festival's Late Night Entertainments programme in 1961, when Michael Barne, Rory and Alex McEwan, McGregor and Hall performed in *Songs of Battle, Bed and Bottle*.[97] Folk also inadvertently became part of the 1962 Festival when the 'Scottish Day' of the Writers' Conference ended with a burst of folk song and an acknowledgement of the CND campaigns to get Polaris out of the Holy Loch. Jazz, too, was part of the official Festival programme in 1962. The regular 'Jazz Beat' column in the *Scottish Daily Express* reported that the programme would include a gala Festival finish with the Fairweather-Brown Allstars, led by Al Fairweather and Sandy Brown, international jazz stars who had both studied at Edinburgh College of Art during the late 1940s and early 1950s. One performer at an official late night show, *Plain Song and All That Jazz*, was even appearing at the same time in classical recitals at the Freemasons' Hall, the announcement of which was compared to dropping 'a Festival-type bomb'.[98] This was not an entirely welcome development. Indeed, one member of the EFC, Dr George Firth (who had not actually attended any of the performances), wrote a very strongly worded complaint to the Festival Council: 'I am shocked to think of what took place under the umbrella of the Festival proper. So far as I know, jazz has not yet invaded the Festivals of Salzburg and Bayreuth to name but two which have stood the test of time.' People had been shocked by the 'sheer vulgarity' of the jazz, and by its satirical aspect, he charged:

> The band started with a roll of drums clearly indicating a prelude to the National Anthem. The audience rose to its feet but soon realised it had been taken in as the band went on to play jazz. This to some people might have been regarded as a comic effort but many I know took it as an insult to The Queen.

To Firth, jazz did not deserve to be part of a festival that aimed to present the 'highest and purest ideals of art in its many and varied forms' (jazz was not funded by the Arts Council until 1967). But ideas about art were beginning to change.[99]

The theme of protest also pervaded new literature. The beat movement became famous in 1957 after Allen Ginsberg's *Howl and Other Poems*, seized by San Francisco police earlier that year, was acquitted of being obscene and judged to 'have some redeeming social importance'.[100] The ensuing publicity ensured the protagonists' notoriety to the 'straight' world and attractiveness to those concerned about the increasingly materialistic world in which they felt they lived. Their fundamental philosophy was to get out, to get on the road – as Jack Kerouac so famously proposed in his seminal novel *On the Road* – and his writings were like refreshing drops of rain to individuals tired with the conformist and materialistic atmosphere of 1950s America (and Britain). From 1957, the philosophy of the beats influenced the burgeoning youth culture and, indeed, the counter-culture of the later 1960s. Their message struck fear into many mainstream critics, which was compounded by many of the beat writers' open admission of drug use (as part of their 'journey').

By the late 1950s Edinburgh had become a popular stop on the beat trail, a place for like-minded people from all over Britain to meet and to exchange ideas. Many of those involved in the 1960s counter-culture remember meeting in Edinburgh to hold poetry readings and meet new people, as part of an *On the Road*-inspired movement of creative energy around Britain. Mike Horovitz, arguably Britain's leading beat poet and founder of the influential poetry magazine *New Departures* in 1959, ran New Departures poetry nights at the Cellars Club in Edinburgh.[101] Johnny Byrne, 'one of Liverpool's leading beats', recalled there being around fifty beats among people he knew, of whom a very small 'hard-core' moved around Britain with one of their regular stops being Edinburgh. Byrne funded poetry readings in the city by working two weeks each year in the Army reserves, alerting others once a venue had been found including his friend, the leading poet Spike Hawkins, who noted that at the time 'London was no more the centre than anywhere else. There was constant movement. We were meeting people, communicating, establishing centres.' To Hawkins, 'Edinburgh was a brief respite where one would meet one's friends, swap ideas, very very exciting, highly powered, highly charged, new work, new faces, new women.'[102]

THE PAPERBACK BOOKSHOP

An important centre for meeting like-minded people and exchanging ideas was created in autumn 1959, when Jim Haynes opened the Paperback Bookshop at 22A Charles Street, right in the middle of Edinburgh's university district. Haynes was a young American who had lived in Louisiana and Venezuela before he arrived in Edinburgh in October 1956, as part of his national service, to work in the nearby British–American air force base at Kirknewton. Having asked 'to go to the smallest possible base, in western Europe, preferably in a major city, near a university', Haynes had arrived in Edinburgh almost accidentally but had fallen in love with the city, especially after attending his first festival season in 1957: 'I found the *influx* of visitors into the city exciting and, yeah, just the whole city suddenly coming *alive* and the energy level rising.'[103] He was granted permanent night duty so that he could attend the University of Edinburgh (where he began a degree in history and economics), living a student's life by day and spending his evenings as an airman listening to the Soviet air defence forces. He gained permission for an early release from the military early in 1959.[104] One day shortly afterwards Haynes entered a junk shop he discovered near the university, went in and asked the proprietor 'right there' if he could buy her shop, a proposal she readily accepted. He quickly established a reputation as a 'counter-culture entrepreneur extraordinaire'.[105]

Haynes converted the junk shop into Britain's first paperback-only bookshop.[106] The aptly named Paperback Bookshop opened its doors before the big 'paperback revolution' of the 1960s, which expanded those paperbacks available to the British beyond just those by Penguin and Pan and opened up the book trade to a wider audience. He was one of the first bookshop owners to treat paperbacks seriously and indeed, Haynes asserts that his was the first bookshop to organise paperbacks by their subject, rather than publisher as had hitherto been customary in British bookshops. The British publisher John Calder, described as 'guardian of the European post-war avant-garde', noted that the atmosphere of the bookshop – the lack of a till, Haynes' easygoing manner, the free coffee and tea he offered and the soft music he kept playing in the background – shocked the local book trade, whom he described as extremely conservative.[107] Further shock came from the books that he stocked. He told me: 'I did sell all these books that you could only

Figure 4.1 Jim Haynes, standing on right, and unidentified others outside the Paperback Bookshop, c. 1962. (© Richard Demarco, the Demarco Archives)

really buy in Paris at the time, all the Olympia Press titles, y'know like Henry Miller and, of course, Alex Trocchi, and [...] then I was importing *American* paperbacks', though he admits that some things were 'sold under the counter' and not displayed.[108] The Scottish artist Alexander 'Sandy' Moffat, then a young student at Edinburgh Art College, recalled:

> If you wanted to get books by these writers that you were discovering and [had] never heard of before, you were going to make your way to the Paperback Bookshop. That was probably the only place you could get these things [...] and the fact that Jim Haynes himself was always there, this guru as it were selling these things, giving you a cup of coffee or he was always in conversation with someone else [...] you felt, well, this is the kind of education that you needed.[109]

Figure 4.2 Agnes Cooper holding a copy of *Lady Chatterley's Lover* with coal tongs, inside the Paperback Bookshop, 1961. (© Alan Daiches, National Library of Scotland)

There was still a fear of the power of literature to corrupt. The Paperback became a focus for these fears when, in the aftermath of the Penguin trial, a retired missionary, Agnes Cooper, bought a copy of *Lady Chatterley's Lover* from Haynes, carried it outside with a pair of tongs, and set it on fire using a jar of kerosene (or something similar), as she denounced the 'iniquitous document'.[110] To Roger Davidson and Gayle Davis, her response was arguably 'symptomatic of a broadly conservative and Calvinistic attitude to sexually explicit literature in Edinburgh in the early 1960s, an attitude shared by many booksellers'.[111] This attitude was also shared by librarians. Like many British public libraries throughout the 1960s, Edinburgh's had a separate 'annexe' 'whose sole purpose was to stop citizens from getting access to "strong" fiction which their rates had gone to purchase', an issue that became increasingly contentious as the decade progressed.[112] The City Prosecutor, James Donaldson Heatly, actively enforced obscene publications clauses in local Corporation Acts (including bringing proceedings against the *Kama Sutra* in 1964, making Edinburgh the only city to do so).[113] Nonetheless, there was a growing demand for access to the literature that the Paperback stocked, with people coming from all over Britain to buy titles not available to them in their own areas. By 1964 it had become 'an institution [. . .] its existence and curious character has been the subject of articles and broadcasts in almost every country in the English-speaking world.'[114]

The Paperback Bookshop's influence in Edinburgh itself was far-reaching and it regularly features in the memories of many who lived in the city at that time. Part of its attraction was that it provided tea and coffee in a relaxed environment, remained open until eight in the evening, and also opened on Sunday afternoons. This was unusual in Edinburgh (and Scotland) at that time, though there was no Scots law to prevent it.[115] Furthermore, it seems that the Paperback, along with the growing impact of youths looking for places to congregate, encouraged the opening of more coffee shops in Edinburgh. These included Bungy's Coffee House, described as 'bourgeois in its appeal'; Studio 3, the hangout of aspiring intellectuals, poets and artists; and La Boheme, said to have a continental touch, playing jazz and skiffle until two o'clock on a Sunday morning.[116] Referring to London, Colin MacInnes had written about the creation of 'a new world of young people [. . .] set in the networks of skiffle parlours, jazz joints, rock and roll basements'.[117] As *The Scotsman* reported, one youth had written on the subject for a school essay competition, calling his winning entry 'Youth's Home from Home'. He described Bungy's as the 'haunt of non-conformist youth', the 'nearest thing – although not at all near – to a den of Beatniks' and decried the lack of similar places in Edinburgh, blaming the 'unsavoury aura' of their reputation as a likely reason. He also criticised the lack of access to the arts all the year round, a situation eloquently summarised by the *Scotsman* in 1960:

> One can sympathise with the transient hedonist who finds Edinburgh quite far removed from his dream of a Festival Centre – 'ye looked for much, and, lo, it came to little' – but the city's youth long ago came to face the fact that for 49 weeks of the year they must use their own initiative and improvise on the Festival's lost chord to meet their pleasure needs.[118]

There was a demand for more meeting places and entertainment for young people in the late 1950s and early 1960s. This was due to a range of factors, including 'the bulge' (the post-war baby boom, which saw an increase in the number of young people in society by the late 1950s), the Education Act of 1944 (which saw more young people able to access further and higher education), and in Edinburgh, the expansion of Edinburgh University and the introduction of the Junior Year Abroad scheme. The latter was run by American Ivy League universities from the 1950s, and saw their students come to an English-speaking university for a year as part of their studies.[119] John Flattau, now a New York-based photographer, was one of these exchange students who spent the academic year 1959/60 in Edinburgh. He recalled:

> Well, as I remember Edinburgh it was, first of all it was *much*, much smaller than it is now and I remember it as being, that the presence of students was really overwhelming in terms of the town. It was like half student, it seemed and . . . it was small, there were very few Americans here at the time . . . a lot of English . . . it was very friendly, it was *really* small town. It was small town and *extremely* provincial.[120]

To Sandy Moffat, the Edinburgh Festival offered the promise of an annual cultural feast:

> For us who were starved, as it were, living in this Presbyterian country, like starved of art and then suddenly for three weeks of the year there was this chance to see these people [famous writers, artists and performers], you know it was very, very exciting.[121]

It was this energy and excitement that Haynes sought to extend all the year round in Edinburgh. He argued that the Paperback Bookshop 'was one of the *first* things that was bubbling away in the city *all year round*, I mean, not just during the Festival but all year round, it was something going on.'[122]

This was one of the main reasons for the major impact that the Paperback had. One Edinburgh University student at the time remarked: 'The impact on the Edinburgh of the day of this liberal, easy-going meeting-place, where you could drink coffee and never be "hassled" to buy a book, is almost impossible to overstate.'[123] Flattau commented:

> It was always a place to kind of hang out, I mean you could always meet somebody there, you know, and [Haynes] was so friendly you could actually go in there and just kind of sit around and have coffee and talk and . . . it was just like that. It was *extremely* relaxed.[124]

To Haynes, the 'bookshop was not just a bookshop, it was also a salon, it was a coffee house, it was a gallery, it was a meeting place, it very quickly became a real centre'.[125] The effect of this centre was to bring together a number of important creative figures – including Richard Demarco and John Calder – who were to play a central role in many important developments in the arts and culture in 1960s Edinburgh: for example, the founding of the Traverse Theatre Club, the opening of the Demarco Gallery, and the seminal writers' and drama conferences of 1962 and 1963 (the latter of which was to instigate a crisis of morality in relation to the Festival and to the way that the Kirk dealt with issues of morality in general).[126]

Demarco emphasised the importance of the Paperback in bringing like-minded people together and forging contacts:

> All these people [like Calder and Haynes] mixed with the up-and-coming journalists, writers and students like Magnus Magnusson, young people, local people, David Steel and his wife Judy, because they were meeting these Americans and they were going to Jim Haynes's bookshop, which was virtually on the campus of Edinburgh University, it was part of Edinburgh University really, every student knew about it, it was where you got a free cup of coffee and you could read *Lady Chatterley's Lover* or all of the books by John Calder that were banned and no other bookshop in Edinburgh would touch with a bargepole.[127]

Calder also cited the importance of the Paperback as a 'social centre' in his memoirs.[128] The Paperback had an international outlook from the beginning, with its name printed on the outside in twenty-five languages. Haynes's business card described it as 'Europe's new international book-shop, coffee-cellar and gallery'.[129]

So, the Paperback quickly became a magnet for people in Edinburgh (and Scotland more broadly). It was casual and drop-in, much like the style of the famed City Lights Bookstore in San Francisco, established by Lawrence Ferlinghetti in 1955, and famed as the focus for the American beat movement.[130] The Paperback also attracted individuals from further afield, particularly since it was one of the very few places in Britain that stocked early beat material. Many of the people who visited, and often met there, became key figures in the counter-culture movement of the later 1960s. These included Jeff Nuttall (artist, writer of one of the defining 1960s texts, *Bomb Culture*, and co-founder of the fringe theatre group the People Show), Tom McGrath (jazz musician, poet and founder editor of the alternative newspaper *International Times* (*IT*)) and Barry Miles (who co-founded and ran the Indica Bookshop, described as 'the command centre for the London underground scene', as well as, with Haynes and others, *IT*).[131] John Lloyd, then 'sometime editor' of *Student*, a University of Edinburgh student paper, was also a 'habitué' of the Paperback and later became editor of the underground magazine *Ink* (launched in 1971). Haynes, recalled Lloyd, 'was a really powerful figure for people like me who were looking for something new, and we weren't sure what'.[132] When Haynes left Edinburgh in 1966, he became instrumental in a number of ventures in London that helped to define the 'Swinging Sixties', including the creation of the Arts Lab, a centre for the underground scene in London.[133]

The Paperback did not just sell books, it aimed to be an all-round cultural centre. Between 1959 and 1964, it hosted poetry readings, folk song nights, theatre productions and art exhibitions.[134] Michael Freudenberg, then publicity manager of Edinburgh University Drama Society, and Juan (now Breyten) Breytenbach, then a young artist and writer, created a gallery space in summer 1962. Freudenberg recalled:

> The origins of the emergence of the Gallery start with a chance meeting between Breyten (Juan as he was called then) and myself. We happened to click and we agreed to dig out the basement for a Gallery, there and then. Jim agreed. Hey presto, we had our first Expo within weeks, and Juan came back for the Festival with a new series of paintings specially for the occasion.[135]

One local arts critic wrote: 'Underground art movements are nothing new, but there is surely some novelty in an underground art gallery,' and the experimental aspect did not stop there, since its main aim was to give a free platform to young artists 'who have something to show'.[136] McGrath recalled an early visit to the Paperback:

> Oh, there was all these amazing new books by Henry Miller and Beckett and all of them, and it was just great sitting drinking coffee and reading these books and lots of nice people around. I also remember Jim coming in waving these tickets about saying 'Does anybody want to go to the theatre? Here's some free tickets'. There was an absolutely great feeling of what the art scene could be.[137]

The Paperback had also served as a meeting place for those disparate groups and individuals that made up the Fringe. Haynes quickly became involved in the organisation of the Fringe Festival, with the Paperback becoming a box office for Fringe productions from 1959 before, in 1960, becoming itself a venue for a Fringe production of David Hume's *Dialogues Concerning Natural Religion* (to major critical acclaim).[138] The Paperback was an early manifestation of that 1960s trend of bringing together different cultural forms under one roof and giving space for cross-fertilisation, cultural exchange and experimentation.

THE INTERNATIONAL WRITERS' CONFERENCE 1962

Out of the connections made at the Paperback Bookshop came the International Writers' Conference. This brought together world-renowned writers in Edinburgh University's McEwan Hall in an event held as part of the 1962 official Festival programme. It was organised mainly by John Calder, with the blessing and backing of the EFS, with assistance from Jim Haynes and Sonia Orwell, commissioning editor of a publishing house and the widow of

George Orwell.[139] Together they produced a stunning line-up: from Amer-ica, Norman Mailer, Henry Miller, Mary McCarthy and William Burroughs; from Scotland, Hugh MacDiarmid, David Daiches, Edwin Morgan and Alexander Trocchi; from England, Lawrence Durrell; from Austria, Erich Fried; and from India Khushwant Singh, to name but a few of the seventy or so who attended. Furthermore, the conference attracted a huge audience and filled the 2,300-capacity McEwan Hall most days; Haynes remembered watching 'an incredible queue form' to buy tickets in the hours before the opening and knowing then it would be a great success.[140] Reporting on the first day of the conference, Magnus Magnusson, then a *Scotsman* journalist, described it as 'a lively, impromptu, incoherent jazz session of literary attitudes, part critical, part theatrical, part entertainment'.[141] This was not the first time that Haynes and Calder had organised a literary event in Edinburgh, having brought a group of French writers published by Calder (Marguerite Duras, Alain Robbe-Grillet and Nathalie Sarraute) to speak at a 'crammed' meeting of university students in Edinburgh in 1961 (as part of a successful tour around Britain). This, alongside the widespread interest in the poetry readings held regularly in the Paperback, inspired Calder to introduce a literary element to the Edinburgh Festival.[142]

The week before the event, Calder told the press that discussions would explore the difficulties of the contemporary Scottish scene, the central conflict of the modern writer (defined as 'to what extent, in a world of violent political and ideological differences, he should use his work as a platform for his beliefs'), and censorship.[143] Calder also asked that the conference be thought of as a 'literary festival' and stated: 'We are imposing no prohibitions on the free expression of opinion, however controversial or unusual.'[144] Indeed, on the first day both writers and audience were invited to make comments, no matter how abusive, should they wish to do so – 'In a sense the more abusive the better,' commented that day's chairman, Malcolm Muggeridge – while Daiches, the second day's chairman, outlined that there would be 'every opportunity for interruptions, fights, flytings, abuse, differ-ences of opinion and so on'.[145]

The clash between MacDiarmid and Trocchi on the second day of the conference was the most famous and oft-repeated one. There are a number of different accounts of this incident, which was widely reported and is often cited when MacDiarmid or Trocchi are mentioned. Magnusson reported:

> The Scottish literary world put on a little domestic comedy for the benefit of visitors to the International Writer's Conference in the McEwan Hall yesterday. It was the familiar kitchen scene where the protagonists throw crockery at each other, where father-figure speaks of tradition, adolescent son flounces out to play Teddy-Boys out in the street instead of joining the family liturgy, and the neighbours look on in some embarrassment.[146]

In many ways, this spat represented generational conflict perfectly, with Trocchi telling MacDiarmid: 'You have a few rather old-fashioned quaintnesses that are not of my generation.'[147] Magnusson described it as a civil war, with nationalism (MacDiarmid) being pitted against internationalism (Trocchi). There have been so many different versions of what happened between MacDiarmid and Trocchi that the exchange has taken on a mythical quality, and yet in many ways it symbolised changes occurring in generational attitudes towards morality, identity, politics and the arts.[148]

Hugh MacDiarmid was the penname and public persona of Christopher Murray Grieve, the Scottish writer and poet who had more or less single-handedly started the Scottish literary renaissance of the 1920s, reconstructing and writing in Lallans, a dialect that drew on traditional Scots language. MacDiarmid's writings were closely tied up with questions of Scottish national identity and his most famous poem, *A Drunk Man Looks at the Thistle*, continues in many ways to symbolise Scottish nationalist sentiment. On 11 August 1962, the day that MacDiarmid celebrated his seventieth birthday, his *Collected Poems* was published and 'led to a general consensus of opinion that MacDiarmid was one of the greatest living poets'.[149] In reference to his birthday, when both national and international newspapers had 'carried long laudatory articles on my work', parties had been organised and a *Festschrift* published, MacDiarmid had remarked that it was 'an astonishing outburst of national and international recognition'.[150] Nonetheless, Alan Bold notes that MacDiarmid remained a 'controversial public figure, forever immersing himself in argument, forever fighting literary and political battles ... [he] took great delight in confusing his admirers'.[151]

Alex Trocchi was, essentially, a Scot in exile. Born and brought up in Glasgow, and a graduate of Glasgow University, he had established himself in Paris in January 1952 where he became editor of what became a hugely influential avant-garde literary journal, *Merlin*. It was sold in Amsterdam, London, New York and Paris, and published material by major writers such as Jean-Paul Sartre, Jean Genet, Eugène Ionesco, Henry Miller and Samuel Beckett, many of whom Trocchi knew personally.[152] This work brought him into contact with Maurice Girodias, manager of Olympia Press (founded in 1953 and committed to publishing 'erotic works with some literary quality'), which, in the six or seven years it operated, 'led an ultimately successful assault on the moral establishment of Europe and America, and helped to end the concept of censorship and the banning of literature on the grounds of obscenity'.[153] Olympia published Trocchi's first serious novel, *Young Adam*, a psychological thriller set on the canal that links Glasgow and Edinburgh, at around the same time as it published Vladimir Nabokov's *Lolita* and Burroughs's *The Naked Lunch*.[154]

It is worth exploring Trocchi further, since many of his experiences connect with key ideas of this period and are also reflected in the changing direction of the arts in the mid-to-late 1960s. During the mid-1950s, Trocchi had been experimenting with sex and drugs, and had subsequently (or consequently perhaps) become more out of touch with reality, leading him to look for answers in Lettrisme International in 1955. This was a small intellectual group that became the hugely influential Situationist International, 'the heart of existentialism', and a key player in the Paris rising of 1968. Described by founder Guy Debord as 'an active founding situationist', Trocchi became convinced that a revolution in attitudes was needed, writing to his brother and sister-in-law in 1955: 'I am outside your world and am no longer governed by your laws.'[155] On arrival in the United States in April 1956, this attitude immediately connected Trocchi with the New York and San Francisco beat scenes, and it was the mixture of French existentialism (which asserted that 'Man is a free agent, unbound by God, and he must accept responsibility for his actions in a seemingly meaningless universe') and the non-conformist and liberal philosophy of the beats that together influenced the key theme of Trocchi's novels, 'human isolation in a society marked by moral ambivalence and alienation'.[156] Trocchi created his most famous work, *Cain's Book*, published by New York's Grove Press in April 1960, while living on a scow on the Hudson River in New York. Trocchi was not just influenced in his writing and philosophy by the West Coast beat scene, he was a part of it and arguably influenced many of its key figures, who were often found at his apartment in Venice West, the epicentre of the beat movement, where he lived for a short time in 1957. The Scottish poet Edwin Morgan has commented that Trocchi had been desperate to 'deparochialise', and it was this that had swept him into the 'new internationalism of the later 1950s and the 1960s, especially on its French-American axis'.[157] It is amusing that while buying drugs in New York in the 1950s, Trocchi would carry a 'portable pulpit' to evade the police:

> If there was any sign of the police, he would unclip the wooden pulpit which he carried by a shoulder-strap, and, flourishing a Bible, would commence a fiery sermon, with traces of a good Scots burr in his oratory. Trocchi must have enjoyed the irony of impersonating the narrow-minded 'Holy Willie' Calvinist of small-town Scotland which his entire literary career had fulminated against.[158]

Trocchi found himself back in Scotland in 1961, having escaped the United States using illegal papers to cross into Canada to evade capture for supplying drugs to a minor, a crime that could result in the death penalty. He spent some time writing, travelling and trying to make some money (while dealing with various legal wrangles) before travelling to Edinburgh for the International Writer's Conference.

The 'Scottish Day' in 1962 began with some comments by Scottish writers on the history and current state of writing in contemporary Scotland before MacDiarmid was invited to make a contribution.[159] During this initial speech, and in front of writers from around the world, MacDiarmid announced that Scottish literature sought to rescue its national heritage from the influence of the English, announcing: 'As for English literature, it leaves me cold, as do the English themselves. It is a sort of fish world which is completely alien to me.' Morgan responded by asking that Scottish writers wake up to what was going on in America, as well as in Europe, and 'worry far less than they do about their tradition', describing contemporary Scottish writing as provincial and philistine and arguing that international events like atomic power, space exploration, 'the whole world cybernetics' were not being reflected in the intellectual life of Scotland. This, he felt, was what made Scotland 'truly provincial'. As chairman, David Daiches then asked: 'This question, "Is Scottish literature provincial or parochial?" I wonder what Alexander Trocchi has to say about that. He has probably seen more of the world, having lived in France and America, than the rest of us.' Wasting no time, Trocchi stated that he did not believe he had been mistaken in leaving Scotland since

> the whole atmosphere seems to me to be turgid, petty, provincial, the stale-porridge, Bible-clasping nonsense. It makes me ashamed to sit here in front of my collaborators in this conference, those writers who have come from other parts of the world, and to consider the level of this debate.

He then called MacDiarmid 'an old fossil' before declaring that in the previous twenty years of Scottish writing, of all that had been interesting, 'I have written it all'.[160]

This caused a great deal of shock. At the time of the conference Mac-Diarmid, the 'Grand Old Man' of Scottish literature, was 'at the very peak of his powers and sat on top of the Scottish literary tree' where, due to his large number of followers, it was inadvisable to provoke him.[161] Trocchi, on the other hand, although well known to many writers on the international scene, was nonetheless still relatively unknown in his native country.[162] Although *Young Adam* had received some praise in the Scottish press, Scotland's literary circles hardly knew him, and *Cain's Book*, which had been published with some success in the USA in 1960, was not published in Britain until February 1963. The spat was described in the *Scottish Daily Express* in terms of MacDiarmid as a 'defender' and Trocchi as an 'attacker'. In a newspaper that proclaimed itself a guardian of Scotland's heritage, the article described Trocchi as a man who wrote a novel on drug addiction, 'lean, dark and with an American accent', constantly smoking despite clear 'No Smoking' notices in the conference hall, and pointed out to its readers that he had illegally crossed from the United States into Canada.[163]

Figure 4.3 The Scottish panel at the International Writers' Conference, 1962. Alexander Trocchi, centre; Edwin Morgan, foreground. (© Alan Daiches, National Library of Scotland)

Trocchi's connections with America and American literature were the basis of MacDiarmid's retorts; he asked why writers should 'keep up with the Joneses' when America had 'gone absolutely rotten in the bulk of its production' before accusing Trocchi of seeming to 'imagine that the burning questions in the world today are lesbianism, homosexuality and matters of that kind'.[164] In an *Express* article later that week, MacDiarmid wrote that the central issues for writers at the conference had been 'sexual perversion, and the vicious habits of beatniks and lay-abouts'.[165] Trocchi argued that these were issues that related to questions of identity, which young American and French writers were dealing with best, and offered to continue the discussion in private sometime, to which MacDiarmid replied: 'I don't think we will get any further, even in a private conversation, because the things that you are prepared to accept [. . .] as a Calvinistic, Communistic Scot, I have no time for at all.' Quipping 'I am only interested in lesbianism and sodomy', Trocchi then asserted:

> I think the question of human identity is the only central question and it is a question of man alone and I don't give a damn if he's a Scotsman, or an American, or anything else. It is high time we transcended nationalistic borders.[166]

Key to Trocchi's criticism of MacDiarmid was the belief he had developed that 'absolute linguistics imprison men within conflicting dogmatisms', that totalitarianism and dogmatic beliefs were wrong. MacDiarmid's commitment to Scottish nationalism and communism, his belief in politics as a means of change, infuriated Trocchi, and indeed other writers when, during a discussion on the commitment of the writer the following day, he declared 'I think that probably I am the only fully committed writer present at this conference' before backing his statement by pointing out his Communist credentials.[167] It was clear by the end of the conference that Trocchi was firmly rooted 'in the same camp as the best European and American novelists', gaining support from, among others, Norman Mailer, Lawrence Durrell, Henry Miller and William Burroughs, the latter two also becoming close friends.[168]

The International Writers' Conference, and in particular the clash between MacDiarmid and Trocchi, was, as Eleanor Bell highlights, a 'particularly spectacular' expression of the growing impatience with parochialism, introversion and the 'seeming grip that MacDiarmid's Renaissance still had on Scottish culture at this time'. Referring to the deepening revolt and reaction in Scottish literary circles, Bell shows how a younger generation of Scottish writers (influenced by international literary developments, including concrete poetry) were seeking to widen the parameters of Scottish literature and culture, and to loosen the grip of the Scottish literary renaissance and its followers.[169] Edwin Morgan, for example, had written in the official programme for the 1962 conference: 'The main thing is to get our country to break out of its prickly isolation and have the self confidence to measure its creative life against the best and vividest examples from outside.'[170] The conference therefore provided a space in which these tensions could be aired, and connections between writers in Scotland and elsewhere forged.

It also sparked debate in the visual arts. Alexander Moffat attended as a young art student doing 'an almost Calvinist practical course' at Edinburgh Art College, playing in an avant-garde jazz band, and painting in an abstract expressionist style: 'Trocchi, Ginsberg, Kerouac, they were the free spirits that we wanted to emulate, as it were, and to free painting and all that. I mean improvising, like Pollock and everything, dripping the paint on and all that kind of stuff.' But his experience of attending the International Writers' Conference completely changed his direction and highlighted for him the possibilities of becoming a Scottish artist, of finding a means of expressing what it was to be Scottish in contemporary society through painting – just as MacDiarmid had through writing in Lallans:

> What came out of the Writers' Conference was life changing because all this stuff that we'd gone in with, you know, we'd gone in with Trocchi and beats and all that and we'd come out with MacDiarmid and communism and all this kind of stuff – it's amazing, isn't it? So we went in with one set of ideas and a year later, we'd come out and embraced a completely different way of positioning ourselves as artists [. . .] the Writers' Conference, it alerted us to this big, big world of stuff that we don't know anything about but we have to know about it, yes. [. . .] Suddenly we became aware that there was some kind of art world in Scotland; it wasn't negligible, it was actually really quite . . . it might be fragmented and underground but it was important. And that all began in August '62.[171]

Together Moffat and painter John Bellany mounted an exhibition of their paintings on Castle Terrace railings during the Festival in 1963, with a supporting 'manifesto' written by Alan Bold:

> 'What Knox really did was to rob Scotland of all the benefits of the Renaissance' wrote Edwin Muir in his study of the Scottish Calvinist, and the dead hand of Knox still grips the throats of many [. . .] while literature has become more and more international, painting in Scotland has remained isolated. There is no indigenous Scottish painting of any significance and the visual arts have manifested an appalling Romanticism and smallness.[172]

This was a response to what they saw as the conservatism of Scottish painting and exhibiting, directly provoked by the content of the Writers' Conference.

Many of the younger and less well-known writers in attendance also went on to become major figures in twentieth-century literature. In 1962, it is hard to believe that hardly anyone had heard of William Burroughs, who became one of the stars of the conference and whose career was effectively launched by it. Raymond Walters Jr wrote in a *New York Times* column:

> At Edinburgh, when Norman Mailer joined Mary McCarthy in proclaiming William Burroughs the writer of this century who'd most deeply affected the literary cognoscenti, the hall was drenched in puzzled silence. No one present, it seemed, had ever heard of Burroughs.[173]

As his biographer, Ted Morgan, noted, 'he had come into it unknown, and emerged a luminary'.[174] When Burroughs explained his 'fold-in' method of writing,[175] he was interrupted to ask if he was 'being serious'. On the back of the publicity arising from Burroughs's appearance at the Conference, his publisher, Barney Rosset of Grove Press, ordered extra copies of *The Naked Lunch*, which was eventually published in the United States in November 1962 (although it had first been published in 1959 by Olympia Press). Meagan Wilson has recently argued that the Writers' Conference 'launched him into celebrity' and 'was the impetus that Grove Press needed to distribute *Naked Lunch*'.[176]

Trocchi was to become famous in the British, as well as the international, counter-culture. In June 1962, his essay 'The Invisible Insurrection of a Million Minds' had just been published for the first time in Edinburgh's *New Saltire Review*. He argued that 'rigid categorisations had become an in-quisitorial rack to which the flesh of contemporary writing is to be twisted', and that political solutions did not work. 'The Invisible Insurrection' was to develop into an international phenomenon among major figures in the counter-culture in the form of Trocchi's *Sigma Portfolios*, which he started in July 1964. These were newsletter-style publications sent to a network of people, including Allen Ginsberg, Lawrence Ferlinghetti, Timothy Leary, William Burroughs, Tom McGrath, Edwin Morgan, Joan Littlewood, Jim Haynes and R. D. Laing, and were described as bringing together 'a possible international association of men who are concerned individually and in concert to articulate an effective strategy and tactics for [. . .] cultural revolution.'[177] Although they were never to achieve the aims that Trocchi had hoped for them, and in fact fizzled out by 1967, they demonstrate both the international counter-cultural network that was being established in the mid-1960s, which itself led to more fruitful developments, and the 'para-digmatic Sixties phenomenon, with its emphasis on revolt, liberation, alter-native lifestyles, anti-universities and worldwide cultural networking'.[178]

The International Writer's Conference of 1962 was a milestone, both to developments in the cultural life of Edinburgh and to highlighting a broader challenge to tradition in Scotland. It was also significant to cultural shifts in Britain more widely. Robert Hewison has argued that

> certain gatherings – increasingly tribal in character – reveal the burgeoning of this counter-culture, from the prophetic utterances of William Burroughs and Alexander Trocchi at the Edinburgh writers' conference in 1962, through the joyous poetry reading at the Albert Hall in 1965, to the sour 'Dialectics of Liberation' conference at the Round House in 1967.[179]

Writers, dramatists and philosophers were considering new ideas and new ways of living, rejecting the traditional values and mores that had previously governed most of western society. 'The breaking of taboos', wrote Hugh

McLeod, 'was a key theme of the early 1960s.'[180] Of course, this caused concern in the field of morality as the Kirk, like other representatives of organised religion, tried to tackle these changing attitudes. A *British Weekly* article observed in 1960 that the real 'crisis' of Christianity was that neither the Church nor individual Christians had managed to orient themselves 'to the world of mass materialism' while modern literature and drama had already begun to deal with the theme of the 'lack of meaning in contemporary life'.[181] John Calder has recently commented that 'the purpose of the avant-garde is exploration, probing the unknown, finding new ways to say important things which can no longer be adequately expressed the old way'.[182] The impact of the wider educational opportunities brought about by the Education Act of 1944 were becoming more sharply felt, particularly in relation to the arts, as one *Scotsman* writer noted in his description of the audience at the Writers' Conference: 'A cross-section of a society informed and nourished by the growing direct influence of the universities and their widening social impact.'[183]

But what was most striking about this period, in relation to a study of the changing role of culture in society, was the convergence of cultures, of different views and ideas, and modes of expression linking and coming together to produce the beginnings of a noticeable cultural shift. Indeed, this is a key feature of 'the sixties' that Arthur Marwick has repeatedly stressed: that the period was 'characterized by the vast number of innovative activities taking place *simultaneously*, by unprecedented *interaction* and *acceleration*.'[184] As a recent study of the Scottish counter-culture between 1960 and 2000 notes, one of the most interesting aspects to emerge was the 'interplay of the traditional or folk elements with those of the international avant-garde', an interaction that is particularly evident in Edinburgh at this time.[185] The balance, as *The Scotsman* highlighted, was shifting from interpreter to creator, and this was to become even more evident in the arts and in wider cultural policy. It was also becoming clearer that the arts were inextricably linked with the wider social changes of 1960s Britain (not least in the field of morality), developments that will be explored in the following chapters.

NOTES

1. Also see Bartie & Bell, *The International Writers' Conference Revisited*.
2. *The Scotsman*, 16 August 1962.
3. *The Times*, 24 August 1962.
4. Hall & Whannel, *The Popular Arts*, 272.
5. See e.g. Donnelly, *Sixties Britain*; Marwick, *The Sixties*.
6. Sampson, cited in Donnelly, *Sixties Britain*, 49.
7. International Writers' Conference (hereafter IWC), original transcript, Day 3, 21.
8. Levin, *The Pendulum Years*, 101.

9. *The Scotsman*, 25 August 1962.

10. ECL, *Edinburgh Festival*, 16.

11. There were no Festival Late Night Entertainments in 1958.

12. Carpenter, *That Was Satire That Was*, 68.

13. Reid, 'Has the Festival "Stuck"?'

14. ECL, *Submission on Behalf of Edinburgh Festival Society for Nobel Peace Prize*.

15. Interview with Ponsonby, cited in Carpenter, *That Was Satire That Was*, 69.

16. ECA, Edinburgh Festival Papers (hereafter EFP) 1960–2, Minutes of Meeting of Drama Subcommittee, 12 January 1960.

17. Cited in Bain, *The Fringe*, 7.

18. Moffat, *The Edinburgh Fringe*, 33.

19. *Express*, 22 August 1962. For more on the early administration of the FFS, see Jarman, 'Nascent Fringe'.

20. Bennett et al, *Beyond the Fringe*, 7. The EFS had failed to consider or negotiate any future productions, thereby missing out.

21. Carpenter, *That Was Satire That Was*, 2.

22. Billington was in the audience on the opening night as a young student critic and recalled 'sensing that the ground had genuinely shifted'. Billington, *State of the Nation*, 127.

23. MPs on both sides of the House called for its suppression. See Levin, *The Pendulum Years*, 319.

24. Billington, *State of the Nation*, 127.

25. Donnelly, *Sixties Britain*, 51.

26. Hewison, *Footlights!*, 132.

27. Cited in Carpenter, *That Was Satire That Was*, 310.

28. Williams, *The Long Revolution*, 353.

29. See Chapter 1. Also see Hewison, *Culture and Consensus*, 88–122; Dworkin, *Cultural Marxism in Postwar Britain*; Sinfield, *Literature, Politics and Culture in Postwar Britain*.

30. See e.g. Rolph, *The Trial of Lady Chatterley*; Sutherland, *Offensive Literature*.

31. Levin, *The Pendulum Years*, 290.

32. Davidson & Davis, *The Sexual State*, 221–2. This did not stop a group of Scottish Labour backbench MPs calling for the application of the Obscene Publications Act in Scotland and for the Lord Advocate to prosecute booksellers who sold *Lady Chatterley's Lover*.

33. Pym, *Pressure Groups and the Permissive Society*, 22.

34. Machin, 'British Churches and Moral Change in the 1960s', 224; Brown, 'Religion and Secularisation', 53.

35. Although this varied, depending on the church. The Roman Catholic Church, for example, experienced a short-lived increase in adherents in the 1960s. See McLeod, *The Religious Crisis of the 1960s*, chapter 3.

36. Davidson & Davis, *The Sexual State*, 147.

37. Machin, 'British Churches and Social Issues', 232.

38. Davidson & Davis, *The Sexual State*, 54–7 (see chapters 3 and 4 for a full account of the Scottish experience of Wolfenden and homosexual law reform in general).
39. Levin, *The Pendulum Years*, 102.
40. Davidson & Davis, *The Sexual State*, 57.
41. This occurred at the same time as the General Assembly considered the moral question of legalising homosexuality and prostitution.
42. *Reports to GA 1960*, 382.
43. Harvie, *No Gods and Precious Few Heroes*, 140. A Church of Scotland minister was in charge of BBC radio in Scotland during the 1950s.
44. *Report of the Committee on Broadcasting 1960*, paragraph 90.
45. *Reports to GA 1961*, 429. The Kirk was very concerned about the rise of gambling and alcohol consumption. See Machin, 'British Churches and Social Issues'.
46. Davidson & Davis, *The Sexual State*.
47. *The Times*, 19 May 1959.
48. *The Times*, 22 May 1959; Sandbrook, *Never Had It So Good*, 271. For more on this subject, see Breitenbach, 'Empire and Civil Society in 20th Century Scotland'.
49. *Reports to GA 1960*, 379. For a full account of changing attitudes to Sunday observance in Scotland, see Brown, 'Spectacle, Restraint and the Twentieth-century Sabbath Wars'.
50. Scottish Television was a new commercial station that began broadcasting in 1957. *ED*, 4 September 1962; Tim Brooke-Taylor, comedy writer and performer. See Bain, *The Fringe*, 16.
51. *Reports to GA 1962*, 387.
52. *The Times*, 14 May 1960.
53. Davie, 'Religion in Post-war Britain', 168. Note the change from the period of reconstruction (1945–60) described in Chapter 3.
54. Hugh McLeod argues that the intelligentsia was one of the first groups to break away from the influence of Christendom. McLeod, *The Religious Crisis of the 1960s*, chapter 1. Of course, extra revenue was another important reason for hiring out church halls.
55. It also became important as a venue for the performance of Scottish work.
56. Indeed, the Gateway was part of the official Festival programme in 1954, 1956–8 and 1960–1.
57. As they had been presented at the Gateway over the previous twelve years. *The Times*, 22 May 1958.
58. Ibid.
59. The company was formed after the Revd George Candlish, director of the Gateway Theatre, made an offer to Kemp and actors Tom Fleming and Lennox Milne. As an independent company it also qualified for Arts Council support.
60. Gateway, *Reports to GA 1961*, 313.
61. *The Times*, 21 May 1959.
62. STA, Af4: Press Cuttings, *Daily Record*, 21 May 1959.

63. Gateway, *Reports to GA 1961*, 315.
64. Ibid., 315–19.
65. *Reports to GA 1959*, 422.
66. *Reports to GA 1961*, 447.
67. *Express*, 11 August 1960.
68. There is scope for a study of censorship in action at the Edinburgh festivals, although there are difficulties in accessing sources for such a study. The licensing records of Edinburgh Corporation were reportedly 'incinerated' during local government reorganisation in 1975, while the Lord Chamberlain's files are organised according to when and where a play was first performed, making it a time-consuming and difficult task to trace many Fringe plays.
69. Davidson & Davis, *The Sexual State*, chapters 9 and 10.
70. See e.g. Shellard et al., *The Lord Chamberlain Regrets . . .*
71. Davidson & Davis, *The Sexual State*, 223.
72. STA, Cz2, Edinburgh Gateway Company Limited, Council Minutes, 1959–1970, Special Meeting of the Council of Edinburgh Gateway Ltd, 23 October 1960.
73. *Reports to GA 1961*, 321.
74. *Scotsman*, 15 May 1956.
75. *EEN*, 17 May 1956.
76. Howard, *Britain and the Beast*, 82.
77. Marowitz et al., *New Theatre Voices*, 11.
78. Shellard, cited in Sandbrook, *Never Had It So Good*, 177.
79. Shellard, *British Theatre since the War*, 43–4.
80. They were not exactly young, but were younger than had been usual in British theatre. Donnelly, *Sixties Britain*, 25.
81. Marwick, *The Sixties*, 55.
82. See Mitchell, 'A Very "British" Introduction to Rock 'n' Roll'.
83. Buchan, 'Folk and Protest', 181.
84. See McKay, *Circular Breathing*.
85. MacNaughton, 'The Folksong Revival in Scotland', 188.
86. See e.g. Osgerby, *Youth in Britain since 1945*.
87. Henderson, 'It Was in You that It A' Began', 8; Buchan, 'Folk and Protest', 170. This influence moved over the Atlantic in the opposite direction too – Seeger performed Scottish folk protest songs during American gigs and the American Folkways record company released a disc of these songs, *Ding Dong Dollar*, which was reissued several times. See Munro, *The Democratic Muse*.
88. Gibson, 'Tomorrow, Songs', 52.
89. Ibid.
90. Tom McGrath, 13 June 2005. Formally launched in October 1960, the Committee of 100 was made up of 'prominent figures from the world of entertainment and the arts' committed to the idea of mass civil disobedience. See Minnion & Bolsover, *The CND Story*.
91. See Campbell, 'Music against the Bomb', 115.

92. See Cowan, *The People's Past*.
93. Jim Haynes, 17 August 2003.
94. Outside Edinburgh, new folk song clubs opened in Aberdeen (1958/9), Glasgow (1959), Perth (1961) and Dundee (1962). See Munro, *The Democratic Muse*; Jim Haynes, 17 August 2003.
95. *Scots Magazine*, May 2004, 526.
96. Munro, *The Democratic Muse*, 38.
97. Miller, *The Edinburgh International Festival*, 202. The Corries were part of Late Night Entertainments in 1971.
98. *Express*, 3 August 1962.
99. ECA, EFC, MoM, 14 January 1963. Note that *Beyond the Fringe* also began by mocking the National Anthem, which Firth mentioned in his complaint.
100. George-Warren (ed.), *The Rolling Stone Book of the Beats*, 5–6.
101. McGough, *Said and Done*, 157.
102. Green, *Days in the Life*, 22–3.
103. Jim Haynes, 12 December 2003.
104. Haynes, 'A Love Story or How the Traverse Came to Be'.
105. Excerpt from *Weekend Scotsman*, 20 January 1973 in Haynes, 'C'est Ma Vie Folks!' Haynes, 12 December 2003.
106. Haynes believes that it was the first paperback-only bookshop in Europe. Haynes, *Thanks for Coming!*, 38.
107. *The Herald*, 2 October 2004; Calder, *Pursuit*, 183–4.
108. Jim Haynes, 17 August 2003. Tom McGrath recalled that Comet's Bookshop in Glasgow also stocked Olympia Press titles.
109. Alexander Moffat, 15 March 2012.
110. A full account can be found in Haynes, *Thanks for Coming!*, 41.
111. Davidson & Davis, *The Sexual State*, 237.
112. Sutherland, *Offensive Literature*, 8; Davidson & Davis, *The Sexual State*, 237.
113. For a rich account of literary censorship in Scotland (focused upon a case study of Edinburgh), see Davidson & Davis, *The Sexual State*, chapters 9–11.
114. ECL, *Evening News and Dispatch*, 7 March 1964. Comet's Bookshop in Glasgow also stocked similar titles.
115. See Brown, 'Spectacle, Restraint and the Twentieth-century Sabbath Wars'.
116. *The Scotsman Presents the Edinburgh Story*, 76.
117. Cited in Marwick, *The Sixties*, 57.
118. *The Scotsman Presents the Edinburgh Story*, 33, 76.
119. Richard Demarco saw this as important in creating a sense of internationalism in Edinburgh. Richard Demarco, 6 October 2004.
120. John Flattau (and Jim Haynes), 17 August 2003.
121. Alexander Moffat, 15 March 2012.
122. Jim Haynes, 17 August 2003.
123. McMillan, *The Traverse Theatre Story*, 12.
124. John Flattau (and Jim Haynes), 17 August 2003.
125. Haynes, *Thanks for Coming!*, 41.

126. This will be explored in Chapter 5.

127. Richard Demarco, 6 October 2004.

128. Calder, *Pursuit*, 184.

129. Article in *Stars and Stripes*, 9 October 1960, in Haynes, *Thanks for Coming!*

130. Haynes has said that at the time he set up the Paperback he 'knew *nothing* about City Lights'. Jim Haynes, 17 August 2003.

131. See e.g. Miles, *In the Sixties*; Green, *Days in the Life*. For more on the People Show, see Chapter 7.

132. Lloyd later edited *Time Out* and *New Statesman*. See Fountain, *Under Ground*, 14.

133. More can be read about Haynes's life in the London underground in almost any book that deals with London in the 1960s.

134. It closed and was demolished in 1964 as part of Edinburgh University's controversial expansion. Two sculptures marking its significance to Edinburgh were unveiled in what is left of Charles Street in August 2012.

135. Email from Freudenberg to author, 2 April 2012.

136. *EEN*, 11 February 1961.

137. Tom McGrath, 13 June 2005.

138. See Moffat, *The Edinburgh Fringe*.

139. Alex Neish, an Edinburgh writer and editor of *Sidewalk* magazine, was also named on early Conference correspondence. See Bartie & Bell (eds), *The International Writers' Conference Revisited*.

140. Haynes, *Thanks for Coming!*, 47.

141. *The Scotsman*, 21 August 1962.

142. Undated newspaper article by Magnus Magnusson in Haynes, *Thanks for Coming!* Along with the following year's Drama Conference, the Writer's Conference sowed the seeds for the Edinburgh International Book Festival, which in its present form began in 1983. See Bartie & Bell (eds), *The International Writers' Conference Revisited*.

143. 'Reports on the International Writers' Conference'.

144. *The Scotsman*, 16 August 1962.

145. IWC, original transcript, Day 1, 2; Day 2, 1.

146. *The Scotsman*, 22 August 1962.

147. IWC, original transcript, Day 2, 11.

148. The exchange was apparently fuelled by whisky. MacDiarmid commented in 1966: 'The "trouble" was that some wag had put on the speakers' table what we all took to be a carafe of water but which actually held pure malt whisky with which in the course of the proceedings we refreshed ourselves copiously' (MacDiarmid, *The Company I've Kept*, 190). Jim Haynes takes responsibility for this.

149. Bold, *MacDiarmid*, 416.

150. MacDiarmid, *The Company I've Kept*, 33.

151. Bold, *MacDiarmid*, 12.

152. Scott, *Alexander Trocchi*, 42.

153. Calder, *Pursuit*, 97; Scott, *Alexander Trocchi*, 43.

154. Calder, *Pursuit*, 98; Calder, 'Alexander Trocchi', 33.
155. Scott, *Alexander Trocchi*, 64.
156. Ibid.
157. Morgan, 'Alexander Trocchi', 56.
158. Scott, *Alexander Trocchi*, 87.
159. A fuller account of this conference (including lengthy extracts from the transcripts) can be found in Bartie & Bell (eds), *The International Writers' Conference Revisited*.
160. IWC, original transcript, Day 2, 4–10.
161. Bold, *MacDiarmid*, 416; Scott, *Alexander Trocchi*, 107.
162. After Trocchi's death in 1984 at the age of fifty-nine, Morgan remarked that in Scotland 'Trocchi never passed the scandal barrier, the drugs-and-sex-rootless-drifter reaction, and despite his obvious intelligence, and the controlled style of his prose, it seems likely that his unjust neglect as a writer was not unconnected with various sorts of moral disapproval'. Morgan, 'Alexander Trocchi', 56.
163. See Gallagher, 'The Press and Protestant Popular Culture'; *Express*, 22 August 1962.
164. IWC, original transcript, Day 2, 11.
165. *Express*, 25 August 1962.
166. IWC, original transcript, Day 2, 12.
167. Scott, *Alexander Trocchi*, 61; IWC, original transcript, Day 3, 4–5.
168. Scott, *Alexander Trocchi*, 108.
169. See Bell, 'Resisting "Prickly Isolation" in the Scottish '60s'; Bell, ' "The Ugly Burds without Wings" '.
170. Morgan, *The Novel Today*, cited in Bell, 'Resisting "Prickly Isolation" in the Scottish '60s'.
171. Alexander Moffat, 15 March 2012. To read the transcript of this interview, see Bartie & Bell (eds), *The International Writers' Conference Revisited*.
172. Bold, 'Introduction to the Paintings of Alexander Moffat and John Bellany At Castle Terrace Railings'.
173. Morgan, *Literary Outlaw*, 341–2.
174. Ibid.
175. The 'fold-in' method involved taking different pages of text and 'folding' them into each other, for example, taking text that Burroughs had written alongside pages from other authors and newspaper or magazine articles and rearranging them to create new texts. The 'cut-up' method associated with Burroughs is broadly similar.
176. Wilson, 'Your Reputation Precedes You'.
177. Hewison, *Too Much*, 107.
178. Letter written by Edwin Morgan, January 2002, cited in Birrell & Finlay, *Justified Sinners*.
179. Hewison actually wrote '1963', and indeed many still confuse the Writers' Conference of 1962 with the Drama Conference of 1963. Hewison, *Too Much*, xv.

180. McLeod, *The Religious Crisis of the 1960s*, 69.
181. *BW*, 4 August 1960.
182. *The Herald*, 10 June 2002.
183. *The Scotsman*, 25 August 1962.
184. Marwick, *The Sixties*, 7.
185. Introduction by Alec Finlay in Birrell & Finlay, *Justified Sinners*.

5

Culture and (Im)morality: The Year of the Happening, 1963

In the welcoming statement of the 1963 Edinburgh International Festival Official Programme, Duncan Weatherstone, the Lord Provost of Edinburgh and chairman of the EFS, declared that 'the mantle of the Festival is something which we carry proudly'.[1] By this time it was becoming more widely acknowledged that the arts had a valuable role to play in society, and indeed that year the Conservative government began an expansion to the Arts Council. This followed the publication in 1959 of views on the arts by the Conservative Party (*The Challenge of Leisure*) and Labour (*Leisure for Living*) as well as the findings of the Arts Council report *Housing the Arts in Britain*.[2] In 1963, John Calder and others organised an international drama conference to build on the success of the 1962 International Writers' Conference, during which leading voices in the dramatic arts were invited to 'discuss the meaning of drama today and the role that it must play, not only in their own lives, but in that of the public on whom it depends'. Participants included Edward Albee, John Arden, Martin Esslin, Jack Gelber, Harold Hobson, Joan Littlewood, Charles Marowitz, Sir Laurence Olivier, Harold Pinter and Arnold Wesker. This conference, wrote Calder, would be the 'most impressive gathering of theatrical personalities who have ever assembled in one place'. He warned: 'There will be hot arguments, there may be shocks, but once again the public will be treated to a concentrated course in one of the most vital arguments of today.'[3] There was certainly a shock during the conference, one that was to have a significant impact on the debate about morality, on responses within the Church of Scotland to social change, and on the development of new techniques in the dramatic arts. The year 1963 has been viewed as a critical one in the cultural revolution of the 1960s, one of crisis in the churches and one in which the burgeoning sexual revolution 'accelerated sharply'.[4]

'ANNUS MIRABILIS'

By the time of the Drama Conference in August 1963 there had been a great deal of public reflection and debate about the state of morality in British society. The year was to be seen as a crucial juncture in the development of what became known as the 'permissive society', as Philip Larkin famously highlighted in his poem 'Annus Mirabilis' (published in 1974). But many of the challenges made to traditional mores in that year were met with resistance from a range of individuals and groups.[5] What is clear, however, is that a number of significant challenges to traditional ideas about morality were mounted during 1963. Moreover, liberalised attitudes were beginning to emerge from unexpected quarters.

The very public obsession with morality was fanned in part by the daily reportage of the Profumo affair. This started with rumours in the press in March 1963, was exposed in a blaze of publicity in July, and continued to reverberate through to September. Britain's Secretary of State for War, John Profumo, had lied to the government about his relationship with Christine Keeler, a young woman previously connected to a Russian diplomat. Mark Donnelly has summarised it as 'a tale of sex, decadence and deceit at the heart of Britain's establishment'.[6] The scandal helped to undermine the Conservative government (Harold Macmillan resigned as Prime Minister in October 1963, citing ill health) and, according to John Seed, it had the wider effect of breaking down established assumptions of what was 'political', thus opening civil society and everyday life to a 'widely-diffused contestation of authority and tradition'.[7] Bernard Levin pointed to Profumo as the turning point in public attitudes in 1960s Britain: 'On that side stood a society which still felt obliged to maintain Puritan attitudes in public; on this side stands a society which no longer feels it necessary.'[8] Only three months after Profumo resigned, *Time* magazine declared that 'Britain is being bombarded with a barrage of frankness about sex'.[9] The 'new morality' had arrived.

The Church of Scotland highlighted a new stage in its reaction to these accelerating changes by amalgamating the Committee on Temperance and Morals with the Committee on Social Service, to create the Social and Moral Welfare Board. A key aim was to provide young people with 'sure standards' in order to 'keep a Christian scale of values in a world which so persuasively inculcates something very different'. Although the moral concerns that had preoccupied the Church of Scotland up to 1963 played a part in its development, its main stimulus was Professor G. M. Carstairs's Reith Lectures, particularly the 'charity versus chastity' debate. Carstairs had caused moral outrage when, during the third of his BBC Reith Lectures in November 1962, he had asked: 'But *is* chastity the supreme moral virtue?'[10] As the Canon Librarian of Southwark Cathedral, Douglas Rhymes, noted in 1964, writers, dramatists, psychologists and 'existentialist thinkers' had been, one after the other, questioning the whole foundation upon which morality was based but, from 1963, had been joined by voices from within churches.[11] A major influence was the Bishop of Woolwich, John Robinson, whose best-selling book, *Honest to God*, published in March 1963, 'placed God within humans, not outside of them' and 'emphasised God in our loving and ethical actions rather than in the next world and its promises'. Robinson supported the idea of a 'new morality' that was 'based on love, applied creatively to the needs of the actual situation, rather than on a legalistic ethical code'.[12] These were revelations that 'caused a storm' – and Scotland was not immune.[13] A Church of Scotland report acknowledged the important issue highlighted by Carstairs: 'that of the status of the Church in relation to such moral questions – by what right does the Church make moral demands of its members, much less of the nation as a whole?'[14] So we see that by 1963, even the moral authority of the Kirk in Scottish society was being challenged from within. An interesting perspective on this can be gained from exploring the challenges to traditional conventions in the arts (especially theatre) with new ideas about the nature of art, spaces for its performance and exhibition, and the relationship between different art forms, as well as between artist and audience.[15]

THE TRAVERSE THEATRE CLUB

On 2 January 1963, the Traverse Theatre Club opened its doors. Its name came from the layout of the tiny studio theatre where the seating for an audience of sixty was traversed by a two-sided stage.[16] During the second performance of Jean-Paul Sartre's *Huis Clos*, the leading actress, Colette O'Neill, was accidentally stabbed when a knife used in the play became tangled in her clothing and pierced her abdomen. She was helped at the scene by two doctors (after the audience had realised it was not part of the play) and quickly rushed to hospital, making the Traverse front-page news: 'the publicity was tremendous, advance bookings soared, and the theatre, in the words of its first director Terry Lane, "never looked back"'.[17] Sheila Colvin, then involved in the administration of the Traverse, recalled John Calder running upstairs and telling her to phone the press, saying 'We will *never* have better publicity than this'.[18] The publicity from the accidental stabbing of a lead actress was not the only reason that the Traverse never looked back. The club attracted international recognition in its first year of opening for its artistic policy, its aim to be far more than merely a theatre, its originality and the manner in which it developed. The Traverse was also famous for being located in a former models' lodging house (and ex-brothel) called Kelly's Paradise, situated in James Court just off Edinburgh's High Street. As Richard Demarco later claimed, 'it's not the place where you're going to start a revolution in the theatre, but in fact that's what happened'.[19]

   The Traverse has a contested history, one that continues to divide opinion. According to Demarco, Jim Haynes was the 'driving force' of the Traverse; art critic Cordelia Oliver credited Demarco and Haynes together; and Haynes takes credit for the idea, if not the energy, to bring it to fruition: 'There's always been a thousand discussions on who started the Traverse . . . It was my idea but everybody put in energy.'[20] One account suggests that the idea had been 'kicking around in the Haynes–Demarco circle for years', discussed many times among friends keen 'to keep the Fringe atmosphere in

Figure 5.1 Jim Haynes in front of the sign for the Traverse Theatre Club, at the entrance to James Court, 1963. (© Alan Daiches, National Library of Scotland)

Edinburgh alive all the year round'.[21] In *The Traverse Theatre Story*, Joyce McMillan named a cast of five key characters crucial to the birth of the theatre club in the following order of significance: Haynes ('the leading and most controversial character'), Demarco (then an art teacher, but already mounting exhibitions in the basement of the Paperback Bookshop), Tom Mitchell ('designer' and property developer, and owner of James Court, the building that housed the Traverse), John Malcolm (actor, who appeared in the summer of 1962 in the successful Paperback Bookshop production of Fionn MacColla's *Ane Tryall of Heretiks*) and finally Terry Lane (theatre director). To McMillan, the arrival of Malcolm was 'the crucial moment' that took the idea for a year-round arts club to the reality of the Traverse Theatre Club. In August 1962, part of the premises that later became the

Traverse had been used by members of Cambridge Footlights in their Fringe shows under the name The Sphinx Club and had been a great success.[22] Partly inspired by this, Malcolm had sought out Mitchell and persuaded him to buy the premises, before he, Lane and others began work on converting the dilapidated space into a theatre, restaurant and gallery.[23]

In most accounts, Malcolm and Lane are relegated into a supporting role, or seen as the stiff professionals on the Committee of Management in contrast to the radical and experimental 'amateurs'.[24] Lane, in particular, was criticised for repetitive casting and unadventurous programming, and his role and significance in the creation of the Traverse has been curiously underplayed or even, on a number of occasions, entirely overlooked. Malcolm undoubtedly set the gears in motion, finding the space, bringing on board Lane and others, and ultimately bringing the idea to fruition.[25] Lane – as designer of the unique space, integral organiser in the early planning stages, and artistic director for its first year – deserves far more recognition for his vital part in the history and successes of the Traverse than he has received so far. He had worked with Stephen Joseph in his Theatre in the Round in Scarborough, and already had extensive experience as both actor and director and a practical interest in experimental theatre when he was asked by Malcolm to join him in Edinburgh. Much of the widespread attention that the Traverse garnered in its first year was attributable to the favourable reviews given to Lane's choice of plays and direction in conjunction with the unique and intimate way in which he had designed the theatre.[26] Lane left in January 1964, for reasons as contested as those related to the Traverse's creation.[27]

While the exact circumstances behind the creation of the Traverse are likely to remain disputed, some of its roots are nonetheless visible in the Paperback Bookshop and the energy around the Fringe. When asked when and how the Traverse began, Haynes always dates it from the birth of the Paperback in 1959, but in particular its production of David Hume's *Dialogues Concerning Natural Religion* during the 1960 Festival season.[28] The Paperback undoubtedly contributed to the atmosphere and success of the early Traverse – as did Lane's experience of directing theatre in the round. The Paperback had provided a 'vital cultural centre', like Better Books in London, Peace Eye Books in New York, or City Lights in San Francisco, becoming 'both a focal point and inspiration of the cultural revolution'. But it was the Traverse that, in the words of Jonathon Green, became the 'landmark for cultural advance'.[29] Oliver regards it as 'the first fringe theatre', stating that it 'caught the attention of London critics, no question. They were raving about this new fringe theatre.'[30] Robert Hewison also argues that the Traverse was where fringe theatre first found a permanent home (see Chapter 7). It was certainly a first in Scotland and, it could be argued, in Britain. The Institute of Contemporary Arts (ICA) in London was perhaps the closest comparison at that time, but it was more of a 'straight' organisation with an atmosphere that was, according to Hewison, 'more inward-looking, cosy and staid'.[31]

During the 1960s, McMillan argues, the Traverse 'was at the epicentre of an intellectual ferment that rocked the capital's prissy façade and put it on the international map'.[32] It was not just a theatre, but 'an attempt to create a complete cultural environment'.[33] Demarco has complained that, while its significance as a theatre is widely recognised, the exhibitions and 'talk-outs' it presented have too often been forgotten. Demarco himself had an art gallery there, out of which sprang the Richard Demarco Gallery.[34] An important concept developed by the Traverse was that of an 'artistic open house' where 'drama does not exist in a capsule, but becomes part of the fabric of what has been called the quality of life'.[35] Tom McGrath recalled being excited about this idea:

> A very, very good atmosphere, yeah, and the art being there at the same time right next to you, that was very exciting too, seeing the Mark Boyle pieces so close and getting used to the idea of art being in there in the space where you were doing something that was literary or theatrical.[36]

In the early 1960s, the Traverse symbolised the idea of an all-encompassing world of the arts, in which the demarcation between art and life was broken down. In many ways, what was happening at the Traverse then was echoed by the counter-culture years later: just as the Traverse aimed to be a total cultural experience, so the counter-culture expressed itself as 'a living experience, a total way of life'.[37]

Within Edinburgh, the Traverse tried to break down social boundaries as well as artistic ones. Playwright Stanley Eveling, whose play *The Balachites* premiered at the Traverse in its first year of opening, commented that the original idea of the Traverse was to provide a place where people came to live and not just to see:

> The play was the centre, but just the centre, of a more generalised thing that was happening to them. They were being liberated, that's what. Then they would straighten their ties and fix their hair and go back to their nice Edinburgh flats. But it had an effect.[38]

The Paperback and the Traverse had started 'mixing people up'. Haynes recalled that the membership of the club was 'eclectic', while Sheila Colvin remarked that 'it got a wide variety of people in the audience even though it was such a tiny audience'.[39] The Traverse also helped to break down perceptions about what drama was, introducing new ideas in form and content and widening the parameters of 'Scottish drama'. McMillan commented that a powerful undercurrent in the story of the Traverse was the 'recurring tension between the theatre's Scottishness, its Britishness and its internationalism'.[40] It also contributed to the growing debate about the place of the Lord Chamberlain's office in 1960s Britain, mainly through its artistic policy of emphasising the experimental and the new. Its draft constitution, drawn up in autumn 1962, stated that the object of the new club was 'to present serious theatre productions of a type not usually presented for economic reasons and the renderings and encouragement of music, Scottish and other poetry and folk music, pottery, sculpture, painting, books and art'.[41] Colvin has commented that 'it was *always* about new work and if it wasn't absolutely, totally 100 per cent new writing, it was about stuff that you didn't get to see in Edinburgh at that time'.[42] In its first year alone, one world and eight British premieres were staged. In a speech at the club's first annual general meeting, Haynes, as chairman of the Committee of Management, commented: 'I think it is fair to claim that a large percentage of these would have never been produced in Edinburgh or in Scotland by anyone else.'[43]

The Traverse was more able than many other theatres to take risks with new plays because it was a club, and therefore received capital from annual membership fees. During the first AGM, Haynes noted that the Traverse had been formed without any financial backing by a group of people who felt 'that a theatre like the Traverse was a necessary ingredient to a civilised life' and believed that there were enough others in Edinburgh who felt the same to 'band together' in a club. The founders' belief was confirmed when the membership rose from a small number of enthusiasts to over 2,000 in the first year alone.[44] Another important reason that the Traverse was established as a club was in order to avoid the Lord Chamberlain's strict licensing laws. While any new play to be performed in a British theatre had to obtain a licence from the Lord Chamberlain's Office, club theatres were exempt and could even, if they wished, stage plays that the Lord Chamberlain had banned.[45] Thus, the Traverse did not have to pay the reading fee charged by the Lord Chamberlain's office for each script, saving the theatre money to invest in performances and, more importantly, giving it 'complete freedom in the selection of the repertoire'.[46] With this freedom, the Traverse was in a position to challenge the prevailing values of the city of Edinburgh, as well as those further afield. Indeed, in that first year, the Traverse presented Alfred Jarry's *Ubu Roi*, a play that begins with the word 'Shit'. One Edinburgh citizen told theatre historian John Elsom that it was the first time he had heard the word publicly spoken in Edinburgh, and that 'he trembled [. . .] at the impact such vulgarities would have on Culture' (note the capital 'C').[47]

THE INTERNATIONAL DRAMA CONFERENCE

The International Drama Conference was linked with the issue of censorship long before it began. The delegate list for the conference included representatives of Bertolt Brecht's Berliner Ensemble, an influential theatre group from the East German side of Berlin, as well as Brecht's widow. However, the British Home Secretary had refused to allow the representatives of what Kenneth Tynan referred to as 'the best company of actors in Europe' into the country, remarking: 'The present international situation is such that it was thought politic to refuse visas to persons of a country with a Government which we do not recognise.'[48] This was met with outrage, particularly since the Edinburgh International Festival, of which the Drama Conference was part, was founded on the principle of furthering international understanding and making itself open and welcoming to people of all countries, classes and races. The outrage was intensified by the knowledge that the Foreign Office issued around 200 visas each year to East Germans who wished to travel to Britain either for compassionate reasons or, more commonly, for trade purposes. Robert Ponsonby asked 'Is it really thought that the visits would have been dangerously subversive?', perhaps indicating the extent to which theatre was still seen as a subversive medium.[49] Tynan announced at the first press conference for the forthcoming Drama Conference: 'This is an example of censorship which has hampered, irritated, shocked and outraged us.'[50]

Questions of freedom and moral censorship were raised when John Calder was ultimately forced to retract an invitation to the American 'shock' comedian Lenny Bruce two months before the conference began. Bruce made his name in 1950s America with a fresh take on comedy that aimed to dent taboos, expose hypocrisy and, as Tynan explained, 'force us to redefine what we mean by "being shocked"' while all the time being extremely funny.[51] Bruce was hailed by the *New Statesman* as 'the evangelist of the new morality' while theatre director Charles Marowitz declared that he was 'fired in the same crucible' as the beats.[52] However, not everyone reacted to his comedy so favourably. Having already become regarded as a threat to conventional mores in the United States, Bruce was seen to pose a similar danger to Britain during his 'explosive' run at Peter Cook's Establishment Club in the spring of 1962. Sections of the press reacted with horror at his outspoken act and even an awed Jonathan Miller commented that 'Bruce was a bloodbath where *Beyond the Fringe* had been a pinprick'. By the time his run had ended Bruce 'was rushed out of the country with the conservative press baying at his heels' while two subsequent applications to bring him back to Britain – one by Cook and one on behalf of the International Drama Conference by Lord Harewood, then artistic director of the International Festival – were turned down by the Home Secretary.[53]

However, even if the Home Secretary had approved the invitation to Bruce to attend the conference, it is unlikely he could have appeared. In his memoirs, Calder recalled being summoned to a meeting with the recently elected Lord Provost, Duncan Weatherstone, who had apparently threatened to cancel the conference if Calder merely spoke to the press about the ban on Bruce.[54] One letter, sent to Edinburgh Corporation at the end of July 1963, expressed gratitude for the strong line that the Lord Provost and town councillors were taking against Bruce, while another declared that it was a 'disgrace to our City to invite a man of such character that the Home Secretary has ruled him unfit to enter the country'.[55]

These issues, among others, were raised during the course of the conference. On the fourth day of the conference, in discussions on the theme of 'Subsidy and Censorship', a resolution deploring censorship in the theatre and seeking the introduction of a theatrical equivalent to the X-certificate of the cinema was approved. Theatre producer George Devine, who said he had been engaged in conflict with the Lord Chamberlain's office over almost all of the eighty or so plays he had produced, moved that

> this conference [urges] the theatre-going public to bring immediate pressure upon the Government by all possible means to establish a theatre equivalent of the cinema X-certificate and thereby limit the out-of-date concept of dictating and controlling public taste which the present system of stage censorship imposes.

Although *The Times* reported that the resolution had been approved by all of the authors, actors and directors present at the time, it noted that there had been dissent from 'a small minority of the public present'.[56] The *Scottish Daily Express* was more critical:

> The Lord Chamberlain's Office – the nation's official conscience – was blasted, exposed, sworn at and ridiculed in a succession of 'tales of frustration' by speakers at the Conference. A speech by one delegate was reportedly 'filled with language that the Lord Chamberlain normally blue-pencils. And the audience seemed to appreciate his verbal freedom.'[57]

This resolution, supported by those leading voices in the theatre world in attendance, was another step in the growing public opposition to the existence of theatre censorship. But issues of censorship and public morality were aired in a more dramatic way on the final day of the conference.

'ACT OF SAN FRANCISCO AT EDINBURGH'[58]

In the first press conference for the Drama Conference, John Calder announced:

> The conference will build up each day. You can say the organisers promise much exciting argument and surprise . . . And the surprise? It will be most evident on the last day when avant-garde demonstrations concerning the future of the theatre will be made.[59]

The avant-garde demonstration was a 'happening', broadly defined as 'an improvised or spontaneous theatrical or pseudo-theatrical entertainment' that sets out to 'jolt the viewer from passivity in dealing with "the arts" '.[60] Calder wrote:

> In the theatre it is no longer enough to dispassionately follow the course of staged action. One must be involved by taking part, by being directly concerned in the action, by personally living the play that is being performed [. . .] the barrier between they and we, stage and audience, one's own life and the observed life of others must be removed.[61]

The Edinburgh happening was titled *In Memory of Big Ed*.[62] Charles Marowitz, an American theatre director and one of those who helped organise it, recalled the event:

> Gradually one became aware of the low, throbbing sound of an organ and an electronic tape feeding back carefully edited excerpts from the week's discussions. Then a nude on a trolley was pulled across the balcony above the speaker's platform. Carroll Baker, who had been seated on the platform, took this as her cue to descend and begin clambering over the seats as if hypnotized by Allan Kaprow (the American director) who, Valentino-like, was spooking her from the other end of the hall. By this time a group of strangers had appeared at the windows overhead hollering: 'Me; can you see me!' – and a mother ushered a baby across the stage pointing out the celebrities in the crowd. The final beat was when the curtains behind the speaker's platform suddenly tumbled down to reveal rows of shelves containing over a hundred sculpted heads illuminated by footlights. The actions had intended to disperse attention and create a number of different areas of interest, and by this time, they had fully succeeded. No one knew precisely what was happening nor where [. . .] For the first time since it had begun, that staid old conference with its dour Scottish squares and frumpy *litterateurs*, was bristling with feeling.[63]

The main organisers of the happening in Edinburgh were Kenneth Dewey, a young American director, Mark Boyle, a Glasgow-born artist, and his wife, Edinburgh-born artist Joan Hills (the mother carrying the baby, their son Sebastian, in the happening), who were at that time experimenting with assemblages and performance art.[64] Working collaboratively, but exhibiting and performing under the name Mark Boyle, Boyle and Hills had displayed *Erections, Constructions and Assemblages* in the Traverse Art Gallery earlier that summer. There they had met Dewey and been invited to collaborate on the Drama Conference 'event'.[65] The playwright Charles Lewson was also involved in the early planning stages.[66]

The happening represented a new direction in the world of drama, an 'irreverent attitude to the arts'. This made the conference chairman, Kenneth Tynan, burst out that happenings were 'totalitarian' and 'apocalyptic', in response to which Alexander Trocchi spat the word 'Dada' into Tynan's face. Journalist Magnus Magnusson commented that in Tynan's view, 'art should impose order on chaos, not merely reflect it'.[67] By 1963 it had become clear that in the world of theatre, something 'radical and destructive was in the wind' The editors of a collection of articles taken from the contemporary theatre magazine *Encore* noted:

> One caught glimpses of it in American plays like Jack Gelber's *The Connection* and Kenneth H. Brown's *The Brig*; in the anarchic experiments of the Happenings-men of New York and San Francisco; in the attitude behind improvisational satire, and in the daemonic, brooding person of Lenny Bruce; in an increasing preoccupation with the work and theories of Antonin Artaud and in the Theatre of Cruelty season launched at the LAMDA studio-theatre in London.[68]

Although they felt it was too early to define the new direction that drama appeared to be taking, they noted that, at the Edinburgh Drama Conference, it had been 'ominously alluded to' as 'the death of the word'.[69]

The happening took place on the last day, the theme of which was 'The Theatre of the Future'. Happenings were developed during the 1950s in the United States, particularly on the New York and San Francisco art scenes. They had grown out of concepts developed in the visual arts, concepts that threw off 'the fetters of convention' – for example, Boccioni and Italian Futurism, Bauhaus, Dadaism and Surrealism – and became incorporated into experimental theatre, notably by the American avant-garde composer John Cage.[70] To him, the purpose of art was to 'unfocus the spectator's mind, not something closed and apart, but to make the spectator more open, more aware of self and environment'.[71] Allen Kaprow, who took part in *In Memory of Big Ed* and also created *Exit Play*, a 'ritualistic walk along a barriered path jammed with auto tyres' through which the audience had to leave the Drama Conference, was an ex-student of Cage.[72] In his *18 Happenings in 6 Parts* at the Reuben Gallery, New York, in 1959, Kaprow had 'coined the term if not the concept' of the happening.[73]

In the Edinburgh happening, everything was overshadowed by the brief appearance of Anna Kesselaar, a nineteen-year-old nude art model, on the organ gallery that ran behind where the conference delegates were seated. She was pushed across the gallery at the same time as other parts of the happening were being performed, on a BBC lighting trolley by a BBC technician (not in a wheelbarrow, as so many accounts of the incident claim).[74] One article in *Encounter* magazine commented: 'Six days of intensive argument, hundreds of speeches, six Third Programme broadcasts, dozens of thoughtful press reports on the conference – all utterly obliterated by a forty-second appearance of a nude in a public place.'[75] Marowitz later wrote: 'In the papers the following day, the nude had become miraculously isolated from the Happening and most people simply got the impression that a "prank" had been played.'[76] To Calder, Kesselaar was

> naked, but within the law, as she was not moving, but being moved. She was a buxom blonde, but the railing covered the lower part of her body, so that only her head and breasts were visible and only for perhaps thirty seconds.[77]

Cordelia Oliver was in the audience that day and exclaimed, when asked if she had seen the happening:

> Look! The balcony is up *there*, the audience is being harangued by people on the stage and up on the platform. I'd be *surprised* if more than 2 per cent of people noticed the artist model being wheeled over. She was wheeled over the thing. Okay, she's an art school model, she's nude, but she wasn't standing *flaunting* the nudity.[78]

According to the law as it stood, Kesselaar was within its boundaries as the Lord Chamberlain did allow nudes on stage, provided they were motionless and expressionless in the face of the audience.[79]

Figure 5.2 Anna Kesselaar being pushed across the gallery of McEwan Hall during the happening at the International Drama Conference, 1963. (© The Scotsman Publications Ltd. Licensor www.scran.ac.uk)

For *The Scotsman*, Magnusson wrote sympathetically:

> Much will, no doubt, be made of the brief appearance of a nude model being wheeled across a gallery above the platform of a literary debate – and in hallowed McEwan Hall last night – but out of context, reactions are synthetic. Because the nude, and the casual elaborate series of 'Happenings' that were inflicted on the packed audience, were part of a fascinating illustration of futuristic experimental theatre.[80]

Magnusson reflects well how, in relation to theatre and the arts, the Edinburgh happening was significant. It represented the new direction that theatre was taking, the 'determination by those in the arts to blur the line between art and reality' that was to become ever more prominent as the decade progressed.[81] Indeed, that morning, before the happening took place, Joan Littlewood had described her 'dream theatre of the future – a Fun Palace at Bankside, where people could simply enjoy themselves in the art of living'.[82] This was a key observation of Raymond Williams in *The Long Revolution*: that while the traditional definition of art as a creative act had been 'profoundly important', the consequences of contrasting art with ordinary, everyday experience had been 'very damaging'.[83]

After the happening had been performed, Dewey explained to the audience:

> This kind of theatre is like jazz, at one level: it is held together not by law, not by control, but by the rapport between collaborators. We are trying to give back to you, the audience, the responsibility of theatre – performing your own thoughts, building your own aesthetics. Maybe you will get most out of it by disliking it.[84]

According to Calder, Dewey received much applause: 'He was after all doing what Artaud advocated, shaking the audience's sense of reality and making them realise that the world is an uncertain place where anything can happen.'[85] Boundaries between audience and performer were being broken down, as were traditional boundaries between art forms (and their classifications).

From the late 1950s, poetry had been developing as a powerful form of art, one that thrived in a network of cafés, pubs and clubs in towns and cities across Britain. An important feature of the 'New British Poetry' was its adoption of and experimentation with different art forms, particularly jazz, the visual arts and theatre.[86] Indeed, in *Erections, Constructions and Assemblages*, Mark Boyle's own 'interest in words' (he had started out as a poet and, indeed, had three poems published in the *Paris Review* in 1963) had 'spilled over into' the assemblages, thus combining the symbolism in the constructions with poetry.[87] Also in 1963, Edinburgh's own Ian Hamilton

Finlay published *Rapel*, the 'first definition of concrete poetry to be published in Britain'.[88] By the 1960s, Finlay had become associated with a group of American avant-garde writers influenced by the Black Mountain poet Robert Creeley, and in 1961 had established Wild Hawthorn Press and the poetry magazine *Poor.Old.Tired.Horse* (POTH), published in a different format each time it came out, and connecting international developments with contemporary Scotland in new and interesting ways.[89]

By the beginning of the 1960s, the main characteristics of what was later to become known as the 'underground' were beginning to form. Yet there was no sense of 'shared consciousness' or organised challenge to prevailing attitudes or authorities. Calder has commented: 'They were very exciting times . . . but we had no way of knowing then how things would turn out and what the 1960s would become. We were just discovering these fantastically big ideas and sharing them with young people.'[90] 'Fringe theatre was bubbling under the surface but had not yet become part of the "underground offensive",' Boyle has said. 'We weren't underground, we didn't think of ourselves as underground: we were an official part of the goddamn festival.' Most accounts cite the poetry reading at the Albert Hall in London in June 1965 as the seminal moment, when the real extent of this 'shared consciousness' first became apparent. Haynes has recalled:

> Everybody said the same thing: 'God, I didn't know we were so many.' It was a realisation that 'God, I thought it was just me and a few friends, but *this* many . . .' That was the revelation of the evening. There were lots of people out there like us.[91]

But, as Robert Hewison has pointed out, the International Writers' and Drama Conferences of 1962 and 1963 were important starting points for these kinds of gatherings.[92]

The happening in Edinburgh in 1963 aroused interest in the form and influenced others being created and organised in London (although European happenings also influenced this development). Boyle remarked that for him, happenings started at the Edinburgh Festival, although it has been argued that Adrian Henri, later known as one of the Liverpool Poets, put on the first happening to occur in Britain at the Merseyside Arts Festival in 1962.[93] This was a mixed-media event called *City*, 'a mixture of poetry, rock 'n' roll and assemblage'. Henri himself described it as the first happening to take place in England, although the chapter on happenings in his *Environments and Happenings* kicks off with a description of the Edinburgh happening.[94] Hewison has certainly argued that happenings had spread to Liverpool in 1962 and their impact was exaggerated at Edinburgh in 1963.[95] Others, like Hymie Dunn and Katharine Stout, cite *In Memory of Big Ed* as the first happening in Britain.[96] It certainly seems that it was the Edinburgh happening that caught the attention of artists in other parts of

Britain, particularly in London. Jeff Nuttall, then a London-based art teacher and artist and later a key practitioner of happenings and performance art, noted that 'everyone was wondering what the happening in Edinburgh had been about'.[97] The London-based Better Books, the ICA and a new venture, the Indica Gallery, began to both create and host happenings in the mid-1960s.[98]

But the significance of the Edinburgh happening was not just about the new avant-garde approaches to the arts that it symbolised, but the moral outrage that it provoked. Calder recently mused:

> I think it was a moment of Dadaism, something to satirise the intellectual pretension which had emerged in previous discussions. There were those who professed to be shocked, although I suspect that was hypocrisy and a bit of a class thing. Society was very mealy-mouthed then.[99]

'GODLESSNESS AND DIRT': MORAL OUTRAGE AND CULTURAL CONFLICT

John Calder was right to comment on the hypocrisy of the shock at the happening, and in his memoirs he blasted the popular press, particularly the *Scottish Daily Express*, which he described as 'a pillar of ignorance, prejudice, pretended Puritanism and reaction' and whose coverage helped place him at the 'centre of a scandal that was totally artificial'. While broadsheets such as *The Times*, *The Scotsman* and the *Glasgow Herald* devoted space to discussing the validity of happenings and covered the unfolding controversy over the 'alleged nudity' at the Festival, the popular press revelled in the scandal. The *Express* was particularly vocal in its denunciation of the model, the organisers, the Drama Conference and eventually the Fringe (even though the conference had been part of the official Festival). On the Monday following the incident it ran a huge banner headline, 'The Anti-Naked City – Nude Scene "Vulgar", Says Lord Provost', which was followed by a two-page article expressing some of the initial reactions to the episode. From left to right across the top of the article, under the headline, were photographs and accompanying snippets of opinion from the Lord Provost ('Action of a few sick in mind and art'), Calder ('I am not sorry for what happened'), Lord Harewood ('This stupid and pointless incident') and Carroll Baker ('It was very dramatic and very exciting'). The *Express* was not slow to give an editorial opinion on the subject – under the heading 'Pathetic', the whole conference was denounced a 'wallow of coarseness and vulgarity'.[100] Charles Marowitz quipped that Duncan Weatherstone, the Lord Provost, had 'bravely resolved to persevere in the midst of the barbarians'![101]

Most of the audience had hardly noticed the naked woman as the incident was brief and, being on the balcony, she was out of sight of many of them. However, to ensure that the story was not lost, the press (including the

Express) had taken her backstage afterwards, photographed her in more provocative poses than the audience had seen, and, as Calder says, 'had also given lurid accounts of the happening to the Lord Provost, who had, knowing nothing at all about the conference other than its presence in the Festival brochure, condemned it on their sensationalised report'. Indeed, when told of the incident on the evening of 7 September, the day the happening took place, he reportedly burst out: 'If what I am told is true, then my reaction will be violent.'[102] He made the most scathing attacks, calling it a 'piece of pointless vulgarity', and commented that it was 'a tragedy that three weeks of glorious Festival should have been smeared'. He also apologised to the principal of Edinburgh University – since the conference had been held in the university's McEwan Hall – for 'such an exhibition' having taken place in academic buildings. As Kenneth Dewey remarked when he left Edinburgh a few days after the happening, 'the angriest people now seem to be the ones who weren't there to see her'.[103]

The *Express* gave space to a campaign against the 'Godlessness and Dirt' of the happening, the conference and some parts of the Festival, though mainly the Fringe. This phrase, 'Godlessness and Dirt', first appeared on 13 September in an article by a Church of Scotland minister, Revd John Morrison, which urged Harewood, among others, to leave Edinburgh, and generally denounced 'the new morality'. From 12 October, almost all the articles relating to the nudity incident followed the banner headline 'Godlessness and Dirt', accompanied by an image of a religious figure (usually the statue of John Knox).[104] It is significant that 'Godlessness and Dirt' was also the slogan used by the leader of Moral Re-Armament (MRA), Peter Howard, to describe the moral decline of Britain.

The scandal over the happening developed quickly, fanned by religious and press interests, though it was the international MRA that arguably took the lead role.[105] In doing so, it brought itself into public conflict with the Church of Scotland over who held responsibility for, and authority over, morality in Scotland. The controversy prompted the Church to reassess its attitude to social and cultural changes, especially in relation to morality and the arts. The reaction to the naked model also gives an interesting insight into wider social issues.

Major concerns over morality, youth and faith had all converged when Anna Kesselaar was wheeled across the gallery of McEwan Hall. Within a week of the event, both Kesselaar and Calder, as the main organiser of the event, were charged in connection with the 'controversial incident' – Kesselaar for acting in 'a shameless and indecent manner' and Calder for 'having been art and part in this offence'.[106] The trial that followed, which took place at Edinburgh Burgh Court in December 1963, appears to have been the result of MRA agitation. Sections of the press had expressed outrage yet reprinted the apparently shocking revelations for their readers and the *Express* was no different.[107]

Like most of the press, the Scottish edition of the Protestant newspaper the *British Weekly and Christian World* had based its first report on the event on lurid descriptions, commenting on its front page: 'To stage a strip show for any purpose in the circumstances in which it was done was to violate to an offensive degree the public standards of the country, city, University and community in which Mr Dewey was a guest.'[108] Indeed, on 9 September, Revd Small of the Church of Scotland Social and Moral Welfare Board told the *Express*: 'I deplore this use of sex for cheap sensationalism', while the Church of Scotland's Edinburgh Presbytery called for a meeting to consider action against the 'vulgarity' and 'blasphemousness' of the conference.[109] Yet there was no cohesive reaction from the Church of Scotland since, as a presbyterian church, it could only speak through its annual General Assembly, which was not due to take place until May 1964. Nevertheless, representatives of the Kirk did make their voices heard in its only other 'official' voice, *Life and Work* magazine, as well as in Presbytery of Edinburgh meetings and the unofficial pronouncements of the *British Weekly*.[110]

The reaction was not a knee-jerk one. On 12 September, the front page of the *British Weekly* carried an editorial on the happening written by the managing editor, Revd Denis Duncan.[111] He expressed sympathy with the idea of a happening:

> [If the idea was to] startle and shock an audience into some degree of involvement and activity – and this seems to the uninitiated to have been the aim of American Mr Kenneth Dewey's staging, without public warning, his experiment at the Edinburgh Festival Drama Conference – Christians will not be unsympathetic.

The 'IDEA', he wrote, suggested possibilities especially if it could help audiences to think and not just watch; however, the 'CONTENT' was objectionable, a 'comment on the obsession of society that sex must get into the act'.[112] In the October edition of *Life and Work*, meanwhile, the editor, Revd John Wright Stevenson, asked 'Are We So Narrow-Minded?' in response to a comment made by Harewood describing Presbyterians as such. This, Stevenson told his readers, was 'because some of us had been critical of plays and discussions which seemed to have nothing to say of worth, which were no more than vivid reportage of human despair and moral defeat'. Quoting Matthew Arnold and pointing out his view that art must be a 'criticism of life', an interpretation of life, Stevenson then reasserted the Kirk's own particular view of the role of art, a view that had underpinned the Edinburgh International Festival in its formative years, and also influenced the policy of the Gateway Theatre:

> In a tragedy of Shakespeare we see men and women in the grip of evil; we see naked lust, pride, vengeance – and ambition which has become pathological.

But we are left in no doubt what are the qualities in human life which are enduring – of worth [. . .] Art is not a preacher of morals, but it does set out to find where worth is, in what qualities of human life. If a drama or a novel, or any other creative work, merely holds up the mirror to life, merely lets us see how certain people behave, and why, it is not art. It is not true art until it has revealed what men live by, however far they fall.

His final words reaffirmed the links between art and religion:

If we seem narrow-minded in our 'Presbyterian' artistic judgements it may not always be because we are dull and narrow-minded and convention-bound; sometimes it may be because, like Calvin, we do know what art is for – and that the Gospel and art have common ground.[113]

Representatives of the Church of Scotland appeared keen to ensure that it was not seen to be attacking the arts per se. Indeed, before the International Drama Conference had even taken place the *British Weekly* had considered the recent history of theatre, noting that it was a secular pursuit but that there was no going back on that, since 'we live in a secular world' in which the Church 'must be "secular" to have any effect in modern society'. Readers were told:

Automatic condemnation of our secular theatre by Christians is both cow-ardly and dishonest [. . .] Drama is like football. The spectator will support one team but should appreciate the opponent's play. The player will attack one goal but should learn from his opponents and realise that the game, which necessarily includes both teams, is what is most important.[114]

Even the strongly worded motion put forward at a meeting of the Presbytery of Edinburgh on 10 September, called in response to the happening, acknowledged that such artistic gatherings had value:

The Presbytery, strongly deploring the vulgarity and anti-Christian propa-ganda in the Drama Conference of the recent Festival yet believing there is great value in such conferences provided that they are organised by those who have the true interests of the people at heart and intend to uphold the best of our traditions in the theatre, instructs the Church and City Com-mittee to take the matter up with the Town Council and report to the next meeting of Presbytery.[115]

This motion was passed overwhelmingly, and on 14 January 1964, the Church and City Committee reported back that it believed the Presbytery of Edinburgh should overture (petition) the General Assembly to set up a special committee in order to examine the 'foundations upon which ethical judgements upon contemporary issues are based and to indicate the method and procedure to be followed in the determination of these judgements on that basis'. This was intended to help resolve the 'urgent pastoral situation' facing the Church in light of the 'present currency and influence of views alien to the patterns of sex morality hitherto accepted within the Church'. The incident at the Drama Conference had prompted the Edinburgh Presbytery to tackle the liberalised values of the 'new morality' perceived to be affecting Edinburgh through the 'keyhole' of the Festival. It proposed to set up this special committee and also send out a 'pastoral letter addressed to congregations and especially to the young, dealing with the present situation and its challenge'. The Church of Scotland was called upon to face up to the challenge of the 'new morality', although Kirk bureaucracy and theological disagreement (particularly 'the relation between theology or religion and morality') under-mined the initial urgency of the motion: it was not until October 1965, over two years after the Drama Conference, that the committee's report was finally presented to the Presbytery.[116]

This inability of the Church of Scotland to immediately make its voice loudly heard on moral issues invited criticism. In fact, churches in general were criticised for not doing enough to respond to the challenge of the 'new morality' during the 1960s.[117] During the controversy over the happening, it was MRA who most loudly criticised the authority of the Church and brought itself into public conflict with it. The front page of the *British Weekly* reported on MRA, giving one of its members, Michael Barrett, 'the cheek of the week' for saying at an MRA luncheon:

> There was a day in Scotland when her ministers were prophets and when the Kirk was the guardian of the people's soul and conscience. Now there is a strange silence. Why doesn't the Moderator of the General Assembly of the Church of Scotland proclaim where he and the Church stand?[118]

This attracted a barrage of letters to the publication in support of Barrett's challenge to the Kirk to declare where it stood 'with specific reference to the subversive nature of the Festival Drama Conference'. Barrett himself wrote in to point out that his comments were not a criticism of Prof. James Stewart, the Moderator for 1963, but said that 'anti-Christians and the nation need to know' where he stood in faith and morals. One correspondent, Catherine Hotchkiss of Edinburgh, noted:

> The Lord Provost acted at once, called together those responsible: organisers of the Conference, playwrights, critics, and directors and spoke out in no uncertain terms. Many Edinburgh citizens felt that this was a time when the Church could have spoken clearly and repudiated the foul language, the attacks on Royalty, the claims for freedom against all kinds of censorship, the avowed claim of the organisers and members of the Conference to

promote the kind of theatre which portrays sex, licence, pornography etc., and scenes like that of the nude model [. . .] We do not want that kind of rot and filth in the Festival or the theatre. We need a clarion call that will rouse people to stand up for what is true and pure and honest and lovely.[119]

That last sentence closely mirrored the four moral absolutes on which MRA based its teachings: Absolute Unselfishness, Absolute Purity, Absolute Honesty and Absolute Love.[120] In response to the letters sent in supporting the work of MRA, Duncan, as *British Weekly* editor, felt moved to write a full-page article on MRA, 'glad of the opportunity this surge of representative MRA correspondence creates for the time has come to write in absolute honesty about this whole MRA business'.[121] Duncan addressed the points that the writers made in turn, defended the Moderator, the Church of Scotland and the *British Weekly* from the accusations made in the correspondence, and challenged MRA itself. Duncan pointed out that Revd Morrison's letter misquoted the editorial to make it appear to say that 'Christians will not be unsympathetic to the nude episode', an act he said was not absolute honesty but 'diabolical dishonesty'. He ended by stating that he was sick of people like himself being 'the constant targets for MRA pressure' and asserted that the journal would not allow MRA 'to speak as if it alone in this world is an instrument of moral righteousness'.[122] MRA had certainly hijacked the controversy within the pages of the *Express* with its 'Godlessness and Dirt' campaign and one of its prominent local leaders, the Marquis of Graham, had even said during an address to an MRA meeting in London:

> The press, especially the *Scottish Daily Express*, have taken a lead in showing the disgust of the Scottish people [. . .] I would like to see the Church take a stronger line on these issues. It has spoken, but often very quietly and very late.[123]

It is highly likely that MRA was behind the *Scottish Daily Express* campaign over the happening, but not just because the campaign banner 'Godlessness and Dirt' was also Peter Howard's slogan for the moral decay of Britain. Howard frequently wrote editorials for the England and Wales edition of the *Daily Express*, while MRA adverts frequently appeared in its pages, including a full-page one in the 31 July 1963 edition to coincide with the trial of Stephen Ward over the Profumo affair.[124] In an article for the *New Statesman*, Bernard Levin focused on MRA's role in the controversy, noting that campaigners had 'kept up a ceaseless drumfire of letters' objecting to the Drama Conference based on what had happened during the 1962 International Writers' Conference. He quoted one writer as saying: 'After reading the press reports of the 1962 Writers' Conference [. . .] and being opposed to any attempt to lower the moral standards of the country, I decided to attend to see and hear at first hand.'[125] Levin's suspicion is also borne out by the contents of a folder located in Edinburgh City Archives, which is stuffed with letters from 'angry and concerned' people – sixty-seven in all, plus a petition against the filth of the Festival with more than 300 signatures from around Scotland, sent in October 1963 and drawn up during an MRA meeting in Edinburgh.[126] A large number of these letters have 'M.R.A?' marked on them, most likely by the Lord Provost's secretary, Francis Murdoch, who Levin said 'wielded considerable influence' over successive Lord Provosts, having held his position for around ten years by 1963. Calder has commented that Harewood used to say that MRA stood for 'Murdoch Rides Again'.[127] According to Levin, Murdoch was seen outside McEwan Hall on the day that the Drama Conference opened holding 'a curious document' consisting of

> a series of quotations by and about Mr Calder and Mr Tynan, all torn from context [. . .] designed to show that Mr Calder was a man chiefly employed in publishing obscene books, and that Mr Tynan was art and part of his offence, and an atheist to boot.[128]

It is the language used in the letters that suggests MRA involvement, with many emphasising the deliberate undermining of morals. According to the MP Tom Driberg, who wrote an influential book exposing some of their methods, MRA tended to avoid public discussions and instead favoured organising private pressure campaigns (mainly postal) in defence of its own interests. In 1965, the journalist Brian Inglis referred to its 'posse of trained correspondents'.[129]

One of MRA's tactics was to associate all liberal attitudes with communism, still perceived as a threat (especially with the recent Cuban Missile Crisis of 1962 still fresh in people's minds). By connecting the 'new morality' with a communist plot to take over democratic societies by first undermining them, MRA tried to play on public fears to gain more support.[130] On 2 September – the day that the Drama Conference opened – Howard published a book, *Britain and the Beast*, which emphasised the idea of a communist attack on morals in Britain (it was publicised in the *Daily Express*). Many of the letters in the Edinburgh City Archives folder use similar language to Howard, hinting at a plot to undermine 'British morality', though none explicitly mentions communism as such. For example, one individual wrote:

> It is obvious that the direction of the Festival has got into the hands of some who are determined to destroy the moral standards of the nation and it was a particularly bold and dastardly move to extend their activities to Edinburgh which has always stood for something very different. This is more than an attack on moral standards. It is closely connected with the future existence of the nation and the part we are to play in the moral leadership of the world.[131]

Another letter, from two Londoners, expressed their feelings that it was a 'tragic blow' that the 'honoured name of Edinburgh' should now be 'associated around the world with the filth and perversion' of the Festival, that the happening constituted an 'assault on morals and on faith that is world-wide in its scope and purpose', and that 'the attackers feel that if they can neutralise and mute the voice of Edinburgh they have won a world victory'.[132]

The controversy was a superb means for MRA to publicise Howard's book and reignite interest in MRA in Britain. Callum Brown has argued that its fortunes had 'started to falter after 1960 [. . .] by the early 1960s there was a groundswell of hostility to its conspiratorial methods and alien moral agenda'.[133] In November 1963, the editor of *Life and Work* asked readers: 'Are We Being Undermined?' Although he did not explicitly mention MRA, he wrote:

> It is plain from my correspondence and from my conversations that a considerable number of people think it is part of a Communist policy to encourage moral corruption in high places in our country – and not in high places only. Is there any evidence of a concerted attempt to undermine our moral standards and weaken the moral fibre of the nation [. . .]? This would be difficult to prove.[134]

Some years earlier, in May 1956, MRA had convened a meeting at the North British Hotel in Edinburgh, as part of its World Ideological Mission 'tour'. There, Peter Howard had claimed that western democracies 'lack a superior ideology . . . MRA is that ideology' and Scotland was 'meant to be the spearhead of the answer for the world'.[135] MRA clearly had support within Scotland, and within some Kirk circles too. Its influence is surely worth exploring – and strangely absent from accounts of religion in post-war Scotland. At a time when concern was being expressed about the 'moral muddle' Britain appeared to be in, and about the direction that ideas about morality and religion seemed to be taking, it appeared that Edinburgh proved attractive as a 'last bastion' against encroaching immorality.[136]

One London couple 'brought up with the highest regard and esteem for the great City of Edinburgh' stated that many still regarded Edinburgh as a 'legendary centre of high culture and faith'. The happening was seen to have undermined that reputation and many letters make reference to the 'degradation' of Edinburgh, for example: 'As a graduate of Edinburgh University, and proud of the history and traditions of our capital, I was infuriated to read of the degradation of our city occasioned by the scene in McEwan Hall.' Others express nostalgia for the 'old' Edinburgh: 'How very sad for dear old Edinburgh, the city of my birth.' Most interesting, however, was the feeling apparent from the letters that until the happening, Scotland had escaped the slide towards immorality occurring in England. One writer argued that 'things are going from bad to worse in England and now Scotland has risen to the occasion', while a Scot living in London wrote that he regretted 'that the filth we have in London should have been transferred to Edinburgh' and thanked Lord Provost Weatherstone for his 'fight to uphold the honour and moral standards of Edinburgh and Scotland'.[137] This was not an entirely uncommon view. Roger Davidson and Gayle Davis have shown how policy makers 'were sensitive to the moral conservatism of Scottish society in general and to the need to formulate legislation that respected public opinion north of the Border rather than indulge metropolitan values'.[138]

MRA supporters were not the only ones to feel that the nudity incident revealed that Scotland was no longer sheltered from the changes to morality felt to be gathering pace elsewhere in Britain. In October 1963, *Life and Work* reported an English Episcopalian minister's remark, 'Of course, England is no longer a Christian country', commenting that some people in Scotland 'must wonder if things are any better north of the border'. The nudity incident brought moral issues into sharp focus for the Church of Scotland and, alongside other factors, raised the question of whether the 'new morality' had significantly penetrated Scotland. During the 1963 General Assembly, the comment that Professor G. M. Carstairs had made during one of his Reith Lectures – that those who sincerely believed in the teachings of the Christian church were in 'a rather small minority' – had been refuted by a Committee on Church and Nation confident enough to make it clear that this was 'simply untrue' for Scotland. The Church of Scotland, the committee argued, 'is by far the largest organised body of men and women in the country', while the majority of Scottish people were reported to have a regular connection with some Christian church.[139] However, Callum Brown has argued that 1963 was the critical year for religion in Britain, a year when 'something profound' 'ruptured the character of the nation and its people, sending organised Christianity on a downward spiral to the margins of social significance', with the period 1963–5 described as a 'watershed in the religiosity of the Scots'.[140] As early as 1960, the Church of Scotland Presbytery of Edinburgh was calling for a special commission to be appointed 'in view of the declining number at Sunday Evening Church attendance'.[141] In the month after the happening, attempts were made to 'shield' the Scottish population as, in response to TV programmes of 'bad taste networked from London', the Broadcasting Council for Scotland (BCS) urged that these should be 'blacked out in Scotland' and alternative programmes to 'interest Scottish viewers' screened instead.[142] Two local councillors also motioned Edinburgh Corporation to 'consider what steps can be taken by the Corporation in conjunction with other like-minded bodies to ensure an improvement in the standard of television programmes'.[143] Throughout the 1950s, both the BCS and the Scottish Office had sought 'to protect the moral identity of Scottish society'.[144]

One of those who complained about the happening wrote that 'Edinburgh's Festival is a mirror of Scotland for the world', and that the Festival and its vision should either be protected or 'killed off' rather than be allowed to 'kill the spiritual and moral life of the country'. Some believed that it was 'outsiders', mainly English and American individuals involved in the arts, who were threatening the status and the reputation of Edinburgh and the Festival. One visitor told the Lord Provost that he was 'appalled at how your noble city is being used to spread obscenity and degradation by perverts from other countries'. In fact, the Festival itself came in for criticism, with some letters raising concern about Edinburgh Corporation funding a Festival 'now being used to give moral decadence to the nation'.[145] Furthermore, Revd John Morrison blasted the attacks on the monarchy that had occurred earlier in the Drama Conference, along with the attacks on 'patriotism, moral values, law and order, religion, Edinburgh, and "the bloody tattoo"'. He cited comments made by Lord Harewood that Scots were 'carping killjoys' and that his 'greatest enemy' was 'that old Presbyterian, John Knox', along with Harewood's observation that 'you Scots are still curiously reluctant to believe that the things you think are sinful really are not', while also drawing the reader's attention to the fact that Harewood was a first cousin of the Queen. These comments, and the perception that he had allowed seditious commentary against the monarchy to take place without comment, did not endear Harewood to moral reactionaries. Days after the happening, Morrison launched a campaign to have Harewood sacked as artistic director of the Festival.[146]

At the beginning of October an open letter, addressed to the Lord Provost, councillors, the EFS and 'the people of Scotland', was signed by 200 prominent individuals, including John Calder, Richard Demarco, Kenneth Tynan, Sir Laurence Olivier, Prof. G. M. Carstairs and Christopher Grieve (the real name of Hugh MacDiarmid). Noting dismay at the attacks on the Festival, the open letter stated:

> We believe that the Edinburgh Festival is a most important and vital cultural expression in Scotland today, and we believe that if it is in any way circumscribed or limited (whether for reasons of finance or prejudice) this would be an irreparable blow to the cultural life of the nation.[147]

The following day, an article in the *Express* by the Marquis of Graham responded to these 'artistic liberals'. Writing as a self-appointed spokesman for the Scottish people, Graham denied any attack on the Festival: 'What thousands of Scots have done is voice their disgust with the Drama Conference, which is but one tiny and sordid aspect of the Festival.' That same weekend in London, while addressing an MRA meeting at the Westminster Theatre (owned and run by MRA), Graham described the Drama Conference as having 'shaken and dismayed the people of Scotland', who he said were 'against the decadence, dirt and debt it has created'. Also that weekend, at an MRA meeting in Edinburgh, an open letter designed both to support the

Lord Provost and to counter the letter from the 'artistic liberals' was drawn up. Signed by 335 people from around Scotland, this letter included the statement: 'These gentlemen need to know that the people of Scotland do not want their godlessness and dirt imported across our border. They cannot use our Festival to foist this upon us in the name of culture.'[148]

This demonstrates the perceived power of the arts to corrupt morality. Jean-Jacques Lebel, a leading exponent of happenings, referred to 'the advent of sexuality' being the common factor in the spread of this new arts practice: 'Spontaneity is forbidden by the coercive morality which is at the very roots of our society.'[149] Happenings represented another challenge to prevailing sexual taboos in the 1960s. The Edinburgh happening focused the field of culture as a crucial location and the Edinburgh Festival as a stage for debate (and sometimes battle) between the self-appointed moral guardians of society and 'artistic liberals'. This clash was played out in the court case that resulted.

THE 'LADY MACCHATTERLEY' TRIAL

The trial of Anna Kesselaar, for 'acting in a shameless and indecent manner', took place on 9 December 1963 in the City of Edinburgh Corporation Burgh Court. Bailie Thomas McGregor, the only Edinburgh magistrate who was not a member of the EFS, presided. John Calder recalled that Finlay MacDonald, who then worked for the BBC in Scotland, told him: 'You must win this, John. Otherwise it will be a disaster for all the arts in Scotland.' Heeding his advice, Calder engaged Lawrence Dowdall, who he had been told was the best criminal lawyer in Scotland, and Nicholas Fairbairn, one of two successful and unconventional criminal barristers in Scotland at that time (Lionel Daiches was the other), as his legal team. Bernard Levin wrote about the trial for the *New Statesman*, calling it 'Lady MacChatterley' (Calder remarked of Levin's presence, 'It was a comic experience for an outsider'). As in the *Lady Chatterley* trial of Penguin Books, the defence produced a catalogue of witnesses that included the Scottish actor Duncan Macrae, a frequent Festival and Fringe performer; the historical playwright Robert McLellan, many of whose plays had been performed in the Gateway Theatre (and who later wrote a play inspired by the trial called *The Hypocrite*, premiered in 1967); Magnus Magnusson, a young journalist who had recently started writing for *The Scotsman*; David Jones, producer of the BBC television show that had filmed the conference (Jones was actually subpoenaed by the prosecution but his testimony had aided the defence); and, according to Calder, 'the most telling' witness, a housewife from Fife, who had found the last day of the Drama Conference 'entertaining, funny and very educational' and whose 'straight-forward honest evidence was a wonderful contrast to the put-up, obviously planted, prosecution witnesses'.[150]

There were five prosecution witnesses, led by the City Prosecutor, James Donaldson Heatly. According to Levin, Heatly 'made Mr Mervyn Griffith-Jones looked like a cultivated, well-read, polished and liberal-minded man of the world'.[151] Out of the five prosecution witnesses, four had been prominent in the anti-conference letters to the press in the months before the conference began and were, it seems, part of MRA. In fact, to Levin, the whole thing was an MRA campaign and it is difficult to refute his suspicion. As we have seen, the hallmarks of MRA pressure campaigns were clearly visible in the reaction to the happening, and the activities of the prosecution witnesses in the weeks leading up to the trial only serve to strengthen Levin's claim that the controversy and subsequent trial was conducted as part of an MRA campaign.

The key prosecution witnesses were Catherine Hotchkiss, a 76-year-old former church missionary in China, who said she was so shocked that she could not identify the girl, and 63-year-old Isabella McArthur, who was so 'shocked and angry' at the incident that she wrote to the *Express*. Hotchkiss declared at the trial: 'I was interested in the Drama Conference in the McEwan Hall because I knew the organisers believe in avant-garde theatre and no censorship. This idea is contrary to our heritage. I attended the conference each day [. . .] I disapproved of practically everything I heard.'[152] Remember, it was Hotchkiss who had written to the *British Weekly* asking for a 'clarion call', and she had also written to *The Scotsman* at the end of July 1963, criticising the forthcoming Drama Conference and asking that Calder invite authors and dramatists 'who will discuss how to bring a new renaissance to our stage so that people find faith, hope, and a vision of how to create a new kind of society'.[153] Levin noted that one of the witnesses had written from the same address as Revd John Morrison, who wrote many of the 'Godlessness and Dirt' articles that had appeared in the *Express* and was, like Hotchkiss, one of those who wrote to the *British Weekly* to defend MRA. In the first article to use the slogan, on 13 September, Morrison described some of the things that conference delegates had said, including Joan Littlewood's comment that 'the theatre is the soul and identity of the people. It is the opposite of religion and the cross.' He then told the story of one Edinburgh citizen who, when he rose from the audience to call for a theatre of 'greatness, faith and moral standards for which Edinburgh stands', was greeted with cries of 'Fascist!', 'Rubbish!' and 'Shame'. MRA's Michael Barrett had commented, 'We have reached a pretty pickle in Britain when anyone who calls for greatness and faith is greeted like that.'[154] That Edinburgh citizen was Henry MacNicol, another of those who wrote to the *British Weekly* to defend MRA, and another of the prosecution witnesses in the nudity trial (as was his wife).[155] His letter to *The Scotsman* complaining about Calder's statement that 'an absolute respect for conformism is one of the most dangerous tendencies of our time' had also appeared alongside the one from Hotchkiss in July 1963: 'Literature and the arts, as the founders of the Festival knew, can inspire and ennoble a nation's mind and purpose. The Writers' Conference last year did the opposite: it debased our city and the Festival.'[156] In some ways, then, this trial represented a clash between 'moral reactionaries' and 'artistic liberals', just as the Penguin trial had three years earlier.

In his final speech, Heatly tried to argue that according to the *Practical Treatise on the Criminal Law of Scotland*, 'all shamelessly indecent conduct was criminal'. An exhibition like that which had taken place might be alright in some places, like in a Paris nightclub, 'but in the McEwan Hall, at a Drama Conference, No!'[157] However, Fairbairn, for the defence, argued that Kesselaar had done nothing improper according to the ethics of modelling, and that there was no erotic motive in the happening.

In mid-October, when the date for the trial was fixed and initial pleas lodged, Dowdall put forward an objection on the grounds that there was insufficient evidence of a crime having taken place and quoted Lord Sands, who in 1931 had said that there was 'nothing indecent in the human frame: such a suggestion would be a libel on nature'. McGregor had repelled this.[158] During the trial, to help explain a point, Kenneth Dewey had produced 'a beautiful little terra-cotta statuette he had made, a female nude in the classical Greek style. The magistrate', Calder recalled, 'looked at it with interest, and I think with awe, and handed it back.'[159] During four hours of evidence, issues relating to nudity, art and the theatre were all raised; for readers of the *New Statesman*, Levin humorously recounted Heatly 'unwisely' straying into 'a discussion on the nature of the theatre' while he was cross-examining Dewey until Dewey began explaining Greek drama, at which point Heatly 'fled with a shriek of "Let it go, let it go!"'[160] In summing up, Fairbairn noted that there had never been a case in Scots law of an offence being constituted by a woman being seen naked, and claimed that any indecency attached to the happening was due to media involvement (with the *Scottish Daily Express* named as the main culprit): 'We are dealing in this case with witnesses who are very strait laced. We have no evidence at all of any erotic appeal.'[161]

After a full day's trial in the burgh court, judgement was reserved until 13 December, when Kesselaar was found not guilty. Consequently, the case against Calder, for being 'art and part' in Kesselaar's 'offence', was dropped.[162] McGregor read his 'most enlightened reserved judgement', the main part of which is worth repeating here:

> [Kesselaar] was not acting in a shameless and indecent manner. I am not concerned with whether the 'happening' is good theatre or an art form. I am content to leave the argument on this subject to those better equipped. What does concern me is the publicity given to the 'nude' incident by certain sections of the press which, to say the least, was not only sensational but in certain aspects bordering on the hypocritical. [. . .] It is my sincere hope that nothing detrimental to Edinburgh or the Festival will emerge from what has been stated or written on this matter. I find the accused 'Not Guilty'.[163]

In its editorial, the *Glasgow Herald* noted that it was 'difficult to decide which was sillier, the nude in the gallery or the prude in the press'.[164] The day after the trial, the *Express* reported the final verdict in a 1-inch-square box at the side of the front page, but inside ran an exclusive interview with Kesselaar and a large 'opinion' article titled 'Now that the nude case is over THE FESTIVAL IS ON TRIAL . . .'. The interview with Kesselaar stressed her modest life and need to make ends meet to support herself and her young son, whereas the opinion section asserted that, while the 'case of the Festival nude is closed', 'it is the Festival itself which must be put on trial'. It continued: 'For Edinburgh and for Scotland now is the time for new beginnings. To get back to the original aims of high entertainment and artistic endeavour. And on with the Festival – of art and music.'[165]

In 1963, the Festival found itself a stage for the most significant challenge to its definition of culture yet, one that undermined pronouncements about art being spiritual, a reaffirmation of order and a reflection of what was best in the world. The post-war alliance between the Church and the arts was strained due to an event that had occurred on the official Festival stage, although the Kirk itself did not set its face against the either the Festival or the arts more generally. In many ways, the happening and the reaction to it became one of the controversies that in the early 1960s 'forced taboo topics into the public sphere'. Hugh McLeod argues that 'the power and prestige' enjoyed by many churches in the post-war years and the 'associated atmosphere of moral conservatism' were increasingly challenged in the early 1960s, while from the mid-1960s, 'members of the counter-culture were flouting conventions of decency in a way that shocked many respectable citizens, but also accustomed them to new ways of thinking'.[166] In Scotland, this episode deserves a place in the narrative of liberalisation in the arts and society. As Dewey later wrote:

> To the member of the Edinburgh public making a plea for 'noble drama', there was a real opportunity for nobility by encouraging the personal examination of dark and fearful taboos to see if, in fact, they really are so dark and fearful.[167]

The happening of 1963 represents an important turning point in the history of the Festivals, and in the relationship between the Kirk and the arts. The day afterwards, Lord Provost Weatherstone tried to reaffirm the original aims of the Festival: 'a great experiment in the mystic influence of the Arts and letters and [. . .] an endeavour to maintain and, if possible, to raise the way of life which, because of the war, had gravely degenerated'. One letter to *The Scotsman* responded to this pronouncement: 'Without experimentation there can be no real progress, and with all experiments there is an element of danger.'[168] 'Culture' was an important space for challenging convention as well as a focus for those reacting against such challenges

(Magnus Magnusson had summarised the debate over the happening as 'ancients battl[ing] with moderns').[169] As one writer for the *British Weekly* asserted in August 1963:

> The artistic field is the most civilised one in which to express our differences and also to understand them. Fighting through art is the exact opposite of fighting on the battlefield, for the exchange of feeling and opinions, philosophy and way of life, through art, or simply the expression of what is important or alive to the artist, is constructive and helps understanding.[170]

The events at Edinburgh during 1963, especially the opening of the Traverse and the happening at the Conference, helped to set the stage for the experimental theatre that came to the fore in the mid-1960s, as well as to raise awareness of the challenge to traditional definitions of art being presented by a vanguard of young, radical artists. Barry Curtis has argued:

> The generation of the sixties had new ways of using culture. Deploying everyday ideas, objects and experiences as creative sources and materials indicates a rejection of Matthew Arnold's formulation of culture as an uplifting model of the best. The popular culture of the sixties saw a re-evaluation of transformative notions that drew on [. . .] an engagement with art as a model for everyday life.[171]

Through the happening, Dewey had challenged the traditional structure of theatre: 'My feeling about the pyramidical structure of the theatre – management, director, author, cast – is that it is not adequate to cope with what I want to deal with.' Magnusson noted that this prompted 'a reassessment of the fundamental definitions of words like "art" and "theatre", and forced on the audience an involvement that no other session had done'.[172] The happening fused ideas about poetry, jazz, assemblages and theatre, and in June 1964, Jean-Jacques Lebel organised a festival of happenings in London, at which he announced that 'the barrier between "artist" and "audience" is destroyed by forced involvement'.[173] It was clear that to remain relevant and attract new audiences the Edinburgh International Festival had to respond to these changes. Lord Harewood did respond, commenting during the 1963 event that the Festival 'cannot be static, repeating indefinitely the well known and well loved, but must be adventurous enough to explore new forms, new methods, new works.' Edinburgh had become an important space for cultural conflict. As Magnusson wrote, commenting on the post-happening debate, 'old friendships strained and snapped as people heatedly defended cherished concepts of art or defended the propriety of having them challenged. And isn't this one essential function of a conference like this, of a Festival like this?'[174]

NOTES

1. ECA, EIFMD Programme 1963.
2. *Housing the Arts in Britain* highlighted the concentration of resources in London and the need for investment in cultural buildings in the rest of the country. In Scotland, the main recommendation was for the 'speedy provision' of a National Gallery of Modern Art. *Housing the Arts in Britain*, 5, 65.
3. ECA, EIFMD Programme, 1963.
4. Brown, *Religion and Society in Scotland since 1707*, 224–43. See also McLeod, *The Religious Crisis of the 1960s*.
5. See e.g. Black, *Redefining British Politics*.
6. Donnelly, *Sixties Britain*, 69.
7. Seed, 'Hegemony Postponed', 15.
8. Levin, *The Pendulum Years*, 86.
9. Wheen, *The Sixties*, 94.
10. Carstairs, *This Island Now*, 55.
11. Rhymes, *No New Morality*, 7.
12. As outlined by McLeod, *The Religious Crisis of the 1960s*, 84.
13. Brown, *Religion and Society in Scotland since 1707*, 232.
14. *Reports to the GA 1963*, 401.
15. British theatre 'underwent a revolution of attitudes and practices' during this period. Shellard et al., *The Lord Chamberlain Regrets . . .* , 145.
16. The technical term should have been 'transverse'. McMillan, *The Traverse Theatre Story*, 15.
17. *Express*, 4 January 1963; McMillan, *The Traverse Theatre Story*, 9.
18. Sheila Colvin, 3 May 2005.
19. 'Richard Demarco: Beyond the Fringe'.
20. 'Richard Demarco: Beyond the Fringe'; Cordelia Oliver, 13 April 2005; Jim Haynes, 17 August 2003.
21. McMillan, *The Traverse Theatre Story*, 14.
22. Ibid., 11–16.
23. See Lane, *Side by Side*.
24. See e.g. McMillan, *The Traverse Theatre Story*; Haynes, *Thanks for Coming!* The minutes for the first meeting show that Mitchell, Malcolm, Lane, Haynes and Andrew Muir (representative for Calder in Scotland) formed the committee, joined at the second meeting by Demarco, Sheila Colvin and John Martin (graphic design artist and founder of Forth Studios, Scotland's first commercial art studio).
25. Haynes also states that he found the space and made arrangements with Tom Mitchell to turn it into a theatre space. See e.g. Haynes, 'A Love Story'. Tom Mitchell, on the other hand, credited Edinburgh College of Art teacher, Peter McGinn, with introducing him to the space. See Rudman, 'Edinburgh's Traverse', 125–7. Malcolm was asked to leave in December 1962, before the Traverse even opened. See McMillan, *Traverse*; Lane, *Side by Side*.

26. For Lane's perspective on the creation of the Traverse, see Lane, *Side by Side*, 89–117.
27. A Traverse press release stated that Lane's contract had been terminated as the Committee of Management did not feel that all of Lane's 'actions and policies are in accordance with the purposes with which the Traverse was founded', NLS, Traverse Theatre Club Archives (hereafter TTA), Acc. 4850, Box 1, press release, 20 January 1964.
28. Jim Haynes, 12 December 2003.
29. Green, *All Dressed Up*, 132.
30. In fact, Oliver said that it was because of the Traverse that she was offered a job reviewing theatre for the *Manchester Guardian* (which became *The Guardian* in 1959). Cordelia Oliver, 13 April 2005.
31. Hewison, *Too Much*, 105.
32. *The Herald*, 4 October 2004.
33. Hewison, *Too Much*, 105.
34. Richard Demarco, 2 March and 6 October 2004.
35. Haynes, 'C'est Ma Vie Folks!', 173.
36. Tom McGrath, 13 June 2005.
37. Nelson, *The British Counter-Culture*, 84.
38. McMillan, *The Traverse Theatre Story*, 32.
39. Jim Haynes, 12 December 2003; Sheila Colvin, 3 May 2005.
40. McMillan, *The Traverse Theatre Story*, 23.
41. NLS, TTA, Acc. 4850, Box 1 (1), Draft Constitution.
42. Sheila Colvin, 3 May 2005.
43. NLS, TTA, Acc. 4850, Box 1 (3), speech by Haynes for first AGM. For a full list of Traverse productions, see McMillan, *The Traverse Theatre Story*.
44. NLS, TTA, Acc. 4850, Box 1 (3), Speech by Haynes – AGM.
45. Findlater, *Banned!*, 201.
46. NLS, TTA, Acc. 4850, Box 1 (3), Speech by Haynes – AGM.
47. Elsom, *Theatre outside London*, 109.
48. *The Times*, 29 August 1963.
49. Ponsonby was no longer artistic director at this point; *Times*, 2 September 1963.
50. *Express*, 29 August 1963.
51. Kenneth Tynan, Foreword in Bruce, *How to Talk Dirty and Influence People*, vii.
52. Marowitz, 'The Confessions of Lenny Bruce', 252–6.
53. Kenneth Tynan, Foreword in Bruce, *How to Talk Dirty and Influence People*, x–xi.
54. Calder, *Pursuit*, 247.
55. ECA, EFP 1963, letters, 29 July 1963, 26 July 1963.
56. *The Times*, 6 September 1963.
57. *Express*, 6 September 1963.
58. Dewey, 'Act of San Francisco in Edinburgh'.
59. *Express*, 29 August 1963.

60. Green, *All Dressed Up*, 132.
61. Calder, 'Happenings in the Theatre', 7. See also Lebel, 'Theory and Practice'.
62. There is some contention over whether it was 'Big Ed' or 'Big Head'; it is plausible that over the years, 'Head' has been shortened to 'Ed' in some accounts.
63. Marowitz, 'Happenings at Edinburgh', 59–60. A full outline of the happening can be found in Dewey, 'Act of San Francisco at Edinburgh', 70–1.
64. Assemblages were constructions, usually made of rubbish, which 'acted as a potent anti-art, anti-establishment metaphor'. Elliott, 'Presenting Reality', 10.
65. Elliott, 'Presenting Reality', 11.
66. See Dewey, 'Act of San Francisco at Edinburgh', 70.
67. *The Scotsman*, 8 September 1963. Almost exactly fifteen years earlier, a *Times* writer had commented: 'Art is to-day one of the few affirmations of order and harmony in a distraught and angry world' (*The Times*, 3 September 1948).
68. Marowitz et al., *New Theatre Voices of the Fifties and Sixties*, 211.
69. Ibid.
70. Johnston, '"Happenings" on the New York Scene'. See also Calder, 'Happenings in the Theatre'.
71. Marwick, *The Sixties*, 185.
72. Wilson, 'Towards an Index for Everything', 45n117.
73. Haynes, 'C'est Ma Vie Folks!', 150.
74. See, for example, Laing, 'The Politics of Culture', 90; Hewison, *Too Much*, 105.
75. Quoted in Hewison, *Too Much*, 105.
76. Marowitz, 'Happenings at Edinburgh', 61.
77. Calder, *Pursuit*, 254.
78. Cordelia Oliver, 13 April 2005.
79. Aldgate, *Censorship and the Permissive Society*, 69.
80. *The Scotsman*, 8 September 1963.
81. Levin, *The Pendulum Years*, 308.
82. *The Scotsman*, 8 September 1963.
83. To Williams, art was intimately connected with the entire spectrum of human and social experience. Williams, *The Long Revolution*, 37–9.
84. *The Scotsman*, 8 September 1963.
85. Calder, *Pursuit*, 255.
86. Wilson, 'A Poetics of Dissent', 96.
87. Elliott, 'Presenting Reality', 11.
88. Wilson, 'A Poetics of Dissent', 97.
89. For more on the poetry scene in 1960s Scotland, see e.g. Bell, 'The Ugly Burds without Wings'.
90. *The Herald*, 4 October 2004.
91. Green, *Days in the Life*, 43, 70.

92. Hewison, *Too Much*, xv. See also Chapter 4 of the present volume.
93. Green, *Days in the Life*, 43.
94. Laing, 'The Politics of Culture', 90; Wilson, 'A Poetics of Dissent', 96; Henri, *Environments and Happenings*, 86, 116.
95. Hewison, *Too Much*, 115.
96. Dunn & Stout, 'Selected Chronology'.
97. Green, *Days in the Life*, 43.
98. Run by Peter Asher, Barry Miles and John Dunbar, the Indica became 'one of the hubs of London's emerging counter-culture'. See Wilson, 'Towards an Index for Everything', 49; Hewison, *Too Much*, 79.
99. *The Herald*, 10 June 2002.
100. Calder, *Pursuit*, 258; *GH*, 17 October 1963; *Express*, 9 September 1963.
101. Marowitz, 'Happenings at Edinburgh', 61.
102. Calder, *Pursuit*, 255; *Express*, 8 September 1963.
103. *Express*, 9 September 1963.
104. *Express*, 8 September 1963; 13 September 1963; 12 October 1963.
105. For more on MRA, see Brown, *Religion and Society in Scotland since 1707*, 198–201; Driberg, *The Mystery of Moral Re-Armament*.
106. *GH*, 14 September 1963; 17 October 1963.
107. *Express*, 13 October 1963; 14 October 1963. Like many other newspapers, the *Express* printed a picture of the naked model.
108. *BW*, 12 September 1963.
109. *Express*, 9 September 1963.
110. *BW*, 26 September 1963.
111. Duncan was managing editor of the *British Weekly* from 1957 until 1970 and an enthusiastic supporter of the arts.
112. *BW*, 12 September 1963.
113. *Life and Work*, October 1963.
114. *BW*, 29 August 1963. There was much discussion over what the term 'secular' actually meant in 1963 – see Brown, *Religion and Society in Scotland since 1707*, 232–6.
115. NRS, CH2/121/68, Church of Scotland Presbytery of Edinburgh Minute Book, 10 September 1963.
116. Ibid., 14 January 1964; 12 January 1965.
117. See e.g. Brown, *Religion and Society in Scotland since 1707*, chapter 6.
118. *BW*, 19 September 1963.
119. Ibid., 26 September 1963.
120. Driberg, *The Mystery of Moral Re-Armament*, 12.
121. *BW*, 26 September 1963.
122. Ibid.
123. *Express*, 15 October 1963.
124. Calder, *Pursuit*, 263; Driberg, *The Mystery of Moral Re-Armament*, 247.
125. Levin, 'Lady MacChatterley'.
126. ECA, EFP 1963, Letters concerning Drama Conference.
127. John Calder, 7 May 2005.
128. Levin, 'Lady MacChatterley'.

129. Inglis, *Private Conscience*, 44.
130. Driberg, *The Mystery of Moral Re-Armament*, 249, 296.
131. ECA, EFP 1963, letter, 17 September 1963.
132. Ibid., letter, 10 September 1963.
133. Brown, *Religion and Society in Scotland since 1707*, 201.
134. *Life and Work*, November 1963.
135. *The Scotsman*, 15 May 1956.
136. The editor referred to 'Our Moral Muddle' in *Life and Work*, September 1963.
137. ECA, EFP 1963, letters 10 September 1963; 30 September 1963; 9 September 1963; 10 September 1963; 17 September 1963.
138. Davidson & Davis, *The Sexual State*, 147.
139. *Reports to the GA 1963*, 383.
140. Brown, *The Death of Christian Britain*, 1; Brown, *Religion and Society in Scotland since 1707*, 159.
141. NRS, CH2/121/67, 4 October 1960, 282.
142. *Express*, 17 October 1963.
143. *Minutes of the Town Council of Edinburgh: Session 1963–1964*, 31 October 1963.
144. Davidson & Davis, *The Sexual State*, 216.
145. ECA, Edinburgh Festival Papers 1963, letters, 12 September 1963; 30 September 1963; 11 September 1963.
146. *Express*, 13 September 1963.
147. *Express*, 11 October 1963.
148. Ibid., 12 October 1963; 15 October 1963; *GH*, 16 October 1963.
149. Lebel, 'Theory and Practice', 29.
150. Calder, *Pursuit*, 264–6.
151. Griffith-Jones was the prosecutor in the *Lady Chatterley* trial of 1960. Levin, 'Lady MacChatterley'.
152. Levin, 'Lady MacChatterley'.
153. *The Scotsman*, 31 July 1963.
154. *The Scotsman*, 8 September 1963.
155. *GH*, 10 December 1963.
156. *The Scotsman*, 31 July 1963.
157. As cited in *GH*, 10 December 1963; Calder, *Pursuit*, 266.
158. *GH*, 17 October 1963.
159. Calder, *Pursuit*, 266.
160. Levin, 'Lady MacChatterley'.
161. *Express*, 10 December 1963.
162. ECA, Burgh Court Volumes, 13 December 1963.
163. Levin, 'Lady MacChatterley', 907; *GH*, 14 December 1963.
164. *GH*, 14 December 1963.
165. *Express*, 14 December 1963.
166. McLeod, *The Religious Crisis of the 1960s*, 67.
167. Dewey, 'Act of San Francisco at Edinburgh', 73.
168. *The Scotsman*, 11 September 1963.

169. Ibid, 8 September 1963.
170. *BW*, 29 August 1963.
171. Curtis, 'A Highly Mobile and Plastic Environ', 52.
172. *The Scotsman*, 8 September 1963.
173. Wilson, 'Towards an Index for Everything', 48.
174. *The Scotsman*, 2 September 1963, cited in letter to *The Scotsman*, 11 September 1963; 8 September 1963.

6

Cultural Explosion: The Arts and Moral Conflict in Edinburgh in the High Sixties, 1964–1967

In April 1966, London was dubbed capital of the world by America's *Time* magazine. In the front page feature, 'London: The Swinging City', *Time* spoke of 'how the capital had reinvented itself from being the centre of a once-mighty empire into a city that now set the social and cultural markers for the rest of the world'.[1] To a certain extent, Scotland's capital had also reinvented itself. Since the inaugural event of August 1947, the Festival had transformed Edinburgh, a city not previously renowned for its encouragement of the arts, into a world stage for culture, one of the 'greatest of the world's gatherings devoted to the Arts'. By May 1966, the Scottish actor and director Tom Fleming felt justified in commenting that 'something approaching a miracle has happened in Edinburgh'.[2] In June 1966, Irving Wardle described an 'altered Edinburgh' in *New Society*:

> In the past five years the place has undergone startling changes. At the end of the fifties there was only one commercial art gallery open all through the year; now there are several dozen. Boutiques have been burgeoning along Rose Street, discotheques springing up, and folk singers pouring in. The result to date may not be enough to excite another rave from *Time* magazine, but the change is unmistakeable – however firmly the city elders preserve the granite façade, and however the official Festival may have ignored it.[3]

The wider movement of experimental theatre from the fringes to the mainstream is evident in 'High Sixties' Edinburgh, from quite literally the fringe (and that 'fringe theatre', the Traverse, itself a product of the Festival Fringe) to Scotland's first civic theatre, the Lyceum Theatre, and the Edinburgh International Festival. Yet, as one *Times* journalist asked in March 1966, 'what, nowadays, is meant by experimental theatre?' His observation that 'with the arrival of the subsidized companies [. . .] it is no longer possible to draw a firm line between majority and minority drama' helps to demonstrate the complexities and contradictions in culture in High Sixties Britain.[4] Andrew Sinclair has written that by 1967 'an unspoken problem' for the Arts Council was the shifting meaning of 'the arts'. James McRobert, deputy secretary general from 1950 to 1971, observed that 'the boundaries shift and the markers get up and walk away like Alice's croquet hoops'.[5] This was a period of reflection and readjustment in British society, in light of the rapidly shifting attitudes to the arts, culture and morality which gained wider acceptance during this period. These can be explored by examining debates related to the funding of the arts, the growing prevalence of experimental theatre, and the increasingly fractured relationship between the Church of Scotland and the arts during the period 1964 to 1967.

CULTURE, THEATRE AND MORALITY IN THE HIGH SIXTIES

In 1965 the Labour government issued a White Paper, *A Policy for the Arts: the First Steps*. This was mainly the work of Jennie Lee, Britain's first Minister for the Arts, appointed in 1964. In the run-up to its publication there had been a noticeable shift in thinking about funding of the arts and to reflect that, between 1960 and 1964, the Arts Council's funding more than doubled.[6] Responsibility for arts expenditure was transferred from the Treasury to the Department of Education and Science, and a 'Housing the Arts' fund set up to allow the Arts Council to subsidise the buildings the arts were housed in. Given that education was a devolved area in Scotland, this transfer provoked opposition since it 'challenged Scotland's autonomy over the arts'. The Secretary of State for Scotland, Willie Ross, sought devolved responsibility for the Arts Council's Scottish Committee but was resisted by Lee and Prime Minister Harold Wilson: 'The Scottish and Welsh Secretaries would be consulted about appointments, but decisions would be made by the Secretary of State for Education.'[7]

The White Paper was the first major reappraisal of the role of culture in society since the Arts Council had been set up in 1946 and demonstrated Labour's attempts to develop a clear policy for the arts. It symbolised the renewed commitment of the state to patronage of the arts, but tried to diversify and widen the scope of its early commitments. One crucial difference was that funding was to be more widely disseminated:

> Most of Jennie's new money went not into London's national companies, but into Scotland, Wales and the regions (no one talked about 'provinces' in Jennie's presence). She encouraged local authorities to support not only libraries and museums but art, music, and drama in their schools; to aid amateur groups; to run local arts centres even in the smallest towns.[8]

Between 1964 and 1970, the proportion of total arts investment that went to Scotland 'almost doubled'. However, while the Goschen formula was reinstated in 1965 (after considerable pressure on the Arts Council chairman, Lord Goodman), in 1968/9 it was still a little short at 10.4 per cent (and did not reach 12 per cent until 1977/8). A new charter was drawn up too, which formally extended the remit of the Scottish and Welsh Arts Councils 'to exercise, or advise [. . .] on the exercise of [the Council's] functions in Scotland and Wales'.[9]

In the White Paper, artists were also offered support 'in the years before they have become established'.[10] This demonstrated a shift from the Arts Council's earlier policy of funding a narrow range of more established artists and companies, often summarised as the 'few, but roses' approach.[11] Furthermore, while the Arts Council had previously been guilty of support-ing what was traditionally termed 'high' culture, the White Paper aimed to widen its scope:

> It is partly a question of bridging the gap between what have come to be called the 'higher' forms of entertainment and the traditional sources – the brass band, the amateur concert party, the entertainer, the music hall and the pop group – and to challenge the fact that a gap exists. In the world of jazz the process has already happened; highbrow and lowbrow have met.[12]

A Policy for the Arts also showed that it was alert to youth culture. The introduction asserted: 'A younger generation [. . .] more self confident than their elders, and beginning to be given some feeling for drama, music and visual arts in their school years, are more hopeful material. They will want gaiety and colour, informality and experimentation.'[13] But despite what the White Paper said, and evidence that the 'Keynesian consensus' was breaking down after 1964, it has been argued that Labour still supported 'elite culture' and ultimately sought to improve access to the high arts to 'civilise' as well as to counter commercial, mass (and often American) culture.[14]

Experimental theatre grew in significance in the 1960s, yet remained a minority pursuit. Nonetheless, in May 1966 the theatre periodical *Plays and Players* emphasised that the 'tiny minority' that remained involved in the theatre 'almost certainly exercises an influence on the thoughts and feelings of the community out of all proportion to its numbers'.[15] Ideas that had been tried out and connections that had been made earlier in the decade began to come together, with the first 'outing' of the counter-culture often identified as the Albert Hall poetry reading of 1965 – although, as Chapters 4 and 5 show, the 1962 International Writers' Conference and 1963 International Drama Conference deserve due attention. Then came the launch of *International Times* in October 1966, which is often viewed as marking the true arrival of the counter-culture. In January 1967 another 'underground' newspaper, *Oz*, was launched, achieving success with its colourful psychedelic design, created by artist Martin Sharp, and its message that life was fun.[16] The influence of the West Coast of America also began to filter through to British youth culture. The 'Summer of Love' had kicked off in July 1967 and the Beatles' No. 1 single 'All You Need is Love' was its anthem. Drugs such as cannabis and LSD became openly linked with youth culture, with Paul McCartney publicly admitting to taking LSD (in June 1967), 5,000 people attending a

'Legalise Pot' rally at Hyde Park in London, and well-known names from a variety of backgrounds signing a full-page advert in *The Times* calling for the legalisation of cannabis (both July 1967). This was a real shift from 1962, when the very mention of drug taking at the International Writers' Conference had shocked the media and public alike. The Summer of Love was optimistic and colourful (the first BBC TV transmission in colour was made in July 1967), and symbolised a 'cultural explosion' of youth.

The counter-culture, and with it alternative notions of society, morality and culture, became increasingly visible and pervasive in the media. The moral campaigner Mary Whitehouse commented that in the 1960s 'we faced as grave a danger in the field of morals and faith as we faced on the battlefields of twenty years ago'.[17] Her campaign to 'clean up TV' was launched in 1964 (and reconvened as the National Viewers' and Listeners' Association in 1966), and was underpinned by the belief that television was bringing 'a tidal wave of filth' into the nation's homes and undermining Christian morality.[18] Indeed, it was widely acknowledged at the time that there was a link between the spread of communications and increasingly liberal attitudes towards morality in Britain. Hugh Carleton Greene, director general of the BBC between 1960 and 1969, supported the 'new ethos of questioning, taboo-breaking, and lack of respect for established institutions' and in his autobiography stated his wish to bring the BBC 'kicking and screaming into the Sixties'.[19] In 1965, the Kirk's Church and Nation Committee had published a report on the influence of television, titled *The New Impuritanism*.[20] Backed by the General Assembly, it called for the chairman and governors of the BBC 'to reverse the policy of Carleton Greene in order that its "high moral standards might be restored"'.[21] Historians of secularisation have often cited the spread of television and the shift in broadcasting from the Reithian position of moral guardianship as crucial factors in the rapid de-Christianisation of British society in the 1960s.[22] Whitehouse, who was open about her affiliation with and support for MRA, managed to gain fairly wide backing for her campaign and in doing so raised the issue of who actually represented the 'Christian position' with regard to morals.[23] This led churches, via the British Council of Churches (an ecumenical body founded in 1942), to combine efforts to respond to the 'heavy fire' that Christian teaching regarding chastity was coming under and to find a way of effectively communicating the 'Christian position'.

The 'explosive' report of the churches' working party, with its short and snappy title *Sex and Morality*, was published in October 1966. It divided opinion across the British churches, provoked debate on permissiveness, exposed conflicts within the Church of Scotland (particularly during the General Assembly of 1967) and sharply revealed the changing status of the Kirk in relation to wider Scottish society. Controversially, *Sex and Morality* asserted that it could not be assumed that 'even quite radical departures from traditional moral standards are proof of moral degeneracy'. It argued against fixed moral rules, called for churches to contribute to the development of moral values suitable for contemporary society, and requested the government to 'find more parliamentary time for bringing the law which affects sexual conduct into line with informed contemporary opinion'. A major shift did come in 1967, when the Abortion Act legalised medical terminations, the National Health Service (Family Planning) Act allowed local authorities to provide both contraception and contraceptive advice, and the Sexual Offences Act decriminalised homosexual acts between two consenting adults over the age of twenty-one in private in England and Wales (but not in Scotland). *Sex and Morality* had questioned whether there was still such a thing as a 'Christian position' in British society.[24] When the report was presented at the biannual meeting of the BCC in October 1966, two Church of Scotland representatives led a call to have it rejected in its entirety, stressing that no representative of the Church had been a member of the working party or had had a chance to see the report before details of its contents were released to the press.[25]

However, in its report to the 1967 General Assembly, the Committee on Moral Welfare described *Sex and Morality* as 'a carefully balanced and academically objective assessment of the forces at work in the field of sex and morality'.[26] Although the report was controversial in many ways, its essential message was that Church leaders should work on the principle that

> no rule can cover all the varied and complex situations in which men and women find themselves [. . .] an action which is in outward conformity with a rule may none-the-less be immoral because the motive and spirit behind it are wrong.[27]

The committee also considered the effects of the 'over-turning of long-held and cherished beliefs, the promulgation of "new moralities", [and] the readiness to experiment'. It also 'cautiously' gave its support to the Medical Termination of Pregnancy Bill, while a working party set up to consider the question of legalising homosexuality reported its feeling that the law should become in fact what it was then in practice (the Lord Advocate's Department had effectively stopped prosecuting consenting adults who committed homosexual acts in private).[28] This reflected the movement from public to private moral decision-making, and the sense that there was no longer a strict 'correct' moral code to be adhered to.[29] One contemporary journalist felt that the terms 'moral' and 'immoral' had 'become all but meaningless' in the confusion surrounding the debates on the 'new morality'.[30]

Nevertheless, despite the 'permissive' tone of the Committee on Moral Welfare report, the Church of Scotland, as represented by the General Assembly, remained a conservative body of opinion. Presented with the committee's proposal to support the decriminalisation of homosexual practices, the General Assembly instead rejected it and adopted a counter-motion that deplored the 'grave and growing evil' of homosexuality 'as a source of uncleanliness and deterioration in human Character, and of weakness and decadence in the Nation's life'. Indeed, unlike in England and Wales, in Scotland homosexual acts remained a criminal offence.[31] In response to the Committee on Moral Welfare's positive reaction to *Sex and Morality*, the General Assembly took the 'easy way out' after a heated debate by deleting the section of the committee's report which had asked it to note the committee's view 'and also to welcome this contribution towards the presentation to all sections of the community of a reasoned and positive statement of Christian insights into personal relationships'.[32] *The Scotsman* summed up the proceedings of the 1967 General Assembly: the Church of Scotland, it reported, had demonstrated that it would 'not encourage a permissive attitude to things which the Church has regarded as sins throughout its history'.[33]

It was clear by 1967 that the sea change in public opinion had been considerable, and that it was increasingly difficult for the Kirk to speak for or on behalf of the wider Scottish population. Although there remained a 'Presbyterian Establishment' in Scotland and the continuation of what publisher John Calder termed 'the old Scottish curse' of respectability, by 1967 there were quite open, and often quite radical, differences of opinion on contemporary issues (especially questions of morality) within the Kirk.[34] In 1966, in response to the General Assembly's reaction to the 'crippling lack of funds', a fall in membership and 'what looks like the beginning of a landslide among the young', one individual wrote to the *British Weekly*:

> Surely this was no time for the usual complacent dreary-go-round of sermonising, but rather one for new thinking and a readiness for radical changes [. . .] Do we make the best use of our ministers by requiring them to spend half their time preparing two sermons a week to preach to a handful of the elderly converted?[35]

There was recognition that the church had to make more effort to connect with youth and, indeed, many within the Kirk did try to engage with these issues. *Sex and Morality* triggered debate and exposed divides within the Church of Scotland over changing patterns of morality and raised questions about the place of the Kirk in Scottish society.

THE CHANGING NATURE OF THE FESTIVAL AND THE FRINGE

By the beginning of 1964 the Edinburgh International Festival was internationally acclaimed and, as a Scottish Tourist Board report on Festival publicity stated, there was a growing knowledge of Edinburgh throughout the world. This had to be expected since each year the EFS distributed brochures (over 900,000 in 1963), posters, and press statements to news-papers all over the world, and an estimated 450 journalists came to Edinburgh to cover the Festival.[36] However, Edinburgh was no longer the only regular festival centre in Britain (although it was still the biggest) and in 1966 *The Guardian* observed:

> The festival industry is grinding away more frantically than ever this summer. The committed festival follower could have spent the last few months at, variously, Buxton, Blackburn, Barnsgrove, Beverley, Dunferm-line, Keele, King's Lynn, Liverpool, Ludlow, Macclesfield, Malvern, Mat-lock, Morecambe, Plymouth, Port Sunlight, St Anne's, Windsor – and emerged, sated, dizzy and yet unaware that there were others he had missed.[37]

In 1964, another festival had even been established in Edinburgh, the Craigmillar Festival of Drama, Music and the Arts. This was chiefly con-cerned with people living in Craigmillar, one of Edinburgh's outlying housing estates that, like many dormitory schemes of the 1960s, lacked amenities. The festival was founded by a local resident, Helen Crummy, angry that her son was unable to get violin lessons at his school (the headmaster responded that it took all their time to teach the children 'the three Rs, far less music'!).[38] It aimed to 'knit together' different groups and associations in the area and 'encourage people to take a more active part in drama in its broadest sense, and music'. In this sense, the Craigmillar Festival symbolised the White Paper's concern for inclusive and participatory culture (we will return to this in Chapter 7).[39]

When Peter Diamand became artistic director of the International Festival in 1966, he inherited a more complicated and difficult situation than that faced by any of his predecessors. For one, there were many more arts festivals around in Britain as well as abroad, and therefore more competition for the best artists alongside a greater reluctance by other countries to subsidise visits to Britain by their artists and companies. *The Observer* had suggested in August 1965 that the official Festival was 'losing prestige', becoming more a Scottish national than an international event and no longer 'a great occasion for Europe's artistic *elite*'. The 'brilliant audiences', it reported, were now to be found at Salzburg or Glyndebourne, while in Edinburgh the audience was mainly Scottish bourgeois or students, a consequence, according to the writer, of the growth and prosperity of the Fringe.[40]

In 1964 the EFS and Edinburgh Corporation had shown that they were keen to distance themselves from the Fringe, by again refusing to recognise it on any official level or to allow it advertise any shows in the official Festival programme. The Festival publicity officer even encouraged the Lord Provost, Duncan Weatherstone, to 'take up the matter of the advertising of the Fringe in the *Scotsman*'s Festival Fanfare'.[41] Some of the reasons for maintaining this distance are revealed in the reaction to two petitions and a covering letter sent to the Lord Provost and Corporation of Edinburgh in September 1964. These followed an earlier meeting between Weatherstone and representatives of the Fringe, at which the former 'said it was manifestly impossible for the Festival Society to integrate the fringe in the festival or to become either directly or indirectly responsible for any of their productions'.[42] A group of Fringe artists sent petitions in response, although the FFS opposed the move. In fact, the treasurer of the FFS, Dr Patrick Brooks, wrote to Weatherstone in January 1965 to officially dissociate the society from the meeting and the 'unofficial attacks' by the poet Jon Silkin, who had led the delegation and the subsequent petitions. 'Mr Silkin', wrote Brooks, 'is not, and never had been, a member of F.F.S. and has absolutely no right to represent the Fringe'.[43]

These petitions raised issues relating to funding, publicity, support and accommodation and reveal the relationship between the Festival and the Fringe in 1964. Both asked that the Corporation and the EFS recognise the Fringe, mention it in the official programme, co-operate with it in ticket sales and publicity figures, and give more assistance with the provision of accommodation for Fringe performers. The second petition began:

> The Fringe is an integral part of the Edinburgh Festival; it provides more variety than the official Festival, and its presence is more vital. It would appear to be responsible for bringing many visitors to the Edinburgh Festival, tourists who come here for the Festival as a whole.[44]

Yet there was no funding for the Fringe, and no recognition of its role in attracting visitors to Edinburgh. Those who wrote the petitions complained that the value of the Festival as a 'tourist industry', a Festival which in 1964 received a total of £75,000 from Edinburgh Corporation and £20,000 from the Scottish Arts Council, was never weighed against the value of the Fringe as a tourist industry, a festival that received nothing except the rate of subscription for members of the FFS and registration fees from new members. The response of the EFS cemented the self-help element of the Fringe, by asking the Corporation to remind Fringe performers that the onus was on them to examine potential halls and consider financial implications, and also by refusing to accept any financial responsibility for the Fringe.[45]

During this period the Fringe was growing in both physical size and visibility. In August 1966, the number of groups appearing under the aegis of the FFS was the largest on record, with seventy productions across over thirty venues.[46] In response, the *Glasgow Herald* observed, 'If the official Festival were to come to an end – which God forbid – the Fringe was reaching the stage where it could carry on with its own Festival.' In 1966, the first American group (the University of Southern California School of Performing Arts) made the trip.[47] That a group from as far away as the USA should come to perform on the Fringe must have come as a shock to the city authorities. In response to the petitions from the Fringe in 1964, the publicity officer of the EFS had remarked:

> The image of Edinburgh, the gay, Festival city, has been built up by the Festival Society and the Corporation. It could never attract people from other countries on the basis of the Fringe – i.e. amateur or quasi-professional shows alone. People can see student drama etc. in their own country. There could be no 'Fringe' without the Festival itself. It is an adjunct to the Festival – not an integral part.[48]

But the 'transfer of ideas and talent' between the Festival and the Fringe, which had begun with *Beyond the Fringe* in 1960, continued.[49] In 1965, the first show to be dropped from the Festival programme, *Have Bird, Will Travel* (as its standards were not high enough), was adopted by the Fringe, while Larry Adler, who had appeared on the Fringe the week before, was drafted in to replace it in the official Festival line-up.[50] The Traverse was also invited to contribute to the official programme in 1965 (as we shall see). By 1966, that Fringe staple, the satirical revue, was also revitalised. One *Scotsman* critic had noted that 'Festival late-night revues have tended to become fossilised in format and scope' apart, he wrote, from the fresh, highly original and novel approach of the Scaffold, who 'have succeeded in breaking the mould which "Beyond the Fringe" imposed on its successors'.[51] Consisting of Liverpool poets Roger McGough, John Gorman and Michael McCartney (later changed to McGear to give some distance from his famous brother, Paul), the Scaffold brought together poetry, drama, songs and 'a unique brand of zany comedy' in an irreverent revue format that became a regular feature on the Fringe.[52]

Another reason the Fringe attracted so much attention in 1966 was due to 'the fringe fairytale', the premiere of Tom Stoppard's *Rosencrantz and Guildenstern Are Dead* by the Oxford Theatre Group. A professional version was performed by the National Theatre in London within a year, and from there the play went to Broadway, gathering rave reviews as it went and catapulting Stoppard to stardom. A *Guardian* critic recently wrote that 'Tom Stoppard's experience is the fantasy scenario that keeps the Edinburgh fringe alive. In 1966, so the story goes, a script by an unknown writer, performed by a ragged student company, transferred to the National Theatre.'[53] Although the reality was somewhat different, the romantic rags-to-riches myth persevered and the potential of the Fringe for 'making or breaking' those wishing to establish a career in the arts was cemented.[54]

There developed a more open and co-operative relationship between the Festival and the Fringe. After the Fringe petitions, there had been a tightening of hall regulations.[55] By 1966 stricter licensing regulations had resulted in a serious shortage of suitable venues for Fringe performances.[56] In April of that year, the FFS highlighted an 'acute' shortage of halls, attributing the problem to new, more stringent, fire regulations and difficulties with rating assessments, which had made many halls used in previous years unavailable for 1966.[57] In June 1966, the FFS noted that the Edinburgh Corporation Fire Department was to become even stricter in the application of fire regulations, but two weeks later noted that the Corporation was being co-operative over licences for Fringe shows. Peter Diamand appears to have been a crucial influence. He had written to the FFS in June 1966 informing them that he was considering the 'question of more official recognition of the Fringe'. He had even attended the annual opening of the Fringe Club in August 1966, the first Festival director to show such open support and encouragement towards the Fringe. This gave the FFS increased confidence and, after a meeting with Edinburgh Corporation in February 1967, its representatives reported that they had been 'favourably received and there would seem to be no friction between the official festival and the fringe'.[58] Patrick Brooks had helped to pave the way towards more cordial relations, pointing out in his letter to Weatherstone (in response to Silkin's petitions) that

> the Fringe Society is becoming increasingly alarmed at the unfortunate state of the relations between the Festival and the Fringe. We feel that it is childish, unnecessary and harmful to both parties for there to exist the state of 'cold war' [. . .] We believe that it should be possible for both parties to achieve a state of peaceful co-existence.[59]

Diamand deliberately set out to interest young people and saw that if the Festival were to maintain its position as an important international celebration of the arts, new ideas had to be tested and the contemporary landscape reflected. As George Bruce put it:

> The Fringe, by its nature, is presumed to be full of the joy of life, spontaneous, refreshing and daring, whereas the official Festival, by its nature, is presumed to be the choice of the Establishment, all dressed up and going nowhere.

Although Bruce declared the latter observation untrue, feeling that in many cases the Festival had provided for new or rare drama that the Fringe would have been unable to, he did note that the question was one of vitality, something that the Fringe had in abundance.[60]

However, in 1967 it appeared that sparks of vitality, although present in the official Festival programme, were missing from the atmosphere. The *Scottish Daily Express* reported on 'The Funeral Festival':

> Twenty-one years of Festivals! What an excuse for flamboyance in Edinburgh . . . Flags. Bunting. Fanfares. Massed bands down Princes Street. The old capital proving that it knows a thing or two about the carnival spirit.

Well, such were the hopes of Mr Peter Diamand, the Dutchman who is directing the 21st Edinburgh International Festival of Music and Drama which opens on Sunday. Today Mr Diamand is a disappointed man.

Diamand was reported as wondering if there was a 'streak of Puritanism which is prone to consider festivals wasteful'.[61] This was exactly the kind of atmosphere and artistic environment warned against in *A Policy for the Arts*:

> No greater disservice can be done to the serious artist than to present his work in an atmosphere of old-fashioned gloom and undue solemnity [. . .] If we are concerned to win a wider and more appreciative public for the arts, all this must be changed. A new social as well as artistic climate is essential.[62]

FUNDING CULTURE IN THE HIGH SIXTIES

During the 1960s, the question of funding for the Festival was repeatedly raised as sections of the press, members of the public and local government officials charged that municipal money was needed for civic repairs and amenities. In 1961 Edinburgh Corporation made a special contribution of £20,000 to the EFS in order to cover mounting deficits, then demanded more control over the administration of the Festival. One councillor asked for an investigation into the EFS before any more money was given, and stated: 'We are wholeheartedly in favour of the Festival, but we want to know what is happening to our investment. The public are very uneasy about money being poured into the Society.' A special sub-committee, appointed by the corporation in the run-up to the 1963 Festival in order to examine the Festival's finances, found that year's Festival had resulted in a 'record loss' and arranged for a review of the administrative arrangements by an international firm of management consultants. Although they found little to criticise in the way the Festival was managed, it was recommended that executive power be transferred from the EFC to the artistic director, in effect creating an 'overlord' with the title 'Festival Director'.[63]

This crucial issue of revenue underpinned the Festival's refusal to recognise the Fringe.[64] The EFS felt that 'to assist the Fringe by free advertising "boosts" as they suggest would [. . .] be unfair to the International Festival', while including listings in the programme and offering facilities in the Festival box office for Fringe ticket sales 'would be detrimental to the International Festival. If the Festival Society were to sell Fringe tickets some of the ticket revenue generally would be lost to the Festival "proper".'[65] In his memoirs, Lord Harewood recalled that, when he arrived as director, the Fringe 'was officially very much frowned on, as taking away money that could be spent on Festival tickets'.[66]

However, the Festival was not the only artistic venture that sought financial support from Edinburgh Corporation in 1964. Having applied for and been refused corporation funding in February that year, the chairman and artistic director of the Traverse Theatre, Jim Haynes, was informed in August that the Lord Provost's Committee had agreed to a grant of £200. Haynes also personally met with Lord Provost Weatherstone to discuss the problems of the club. After the meeting, Weatherstone had written to Haynes to indicate that the Lord Provost's Committee was both 'sympathetic and interested' and that he wished to be helpful.[67] Although a grant of £200 seemed rather paltry, that the Lord Provost was willing to support a theatre club, that in the pages of the *Express* had quickly assumed a reputation for 'Godlessness and Dirt', was in itself significant. Sheila Colvin, who collected the cheque for that first grant, recalled the City Treasurer saying 'This is quite an important moment' as he handed it over.[68] The city's financial contribution can partly be explained by increased emphasis on government funding for the arts.[69] Indeed, when the honorary treasurer of the Traverse, Andrew Elliott, wrote to the Lord Provost in March 1965 seeking corporation funding he referred to the White Paper's 'need for supporting cultural activities outside London'. His application was successful, and for 1965/6 the grant was increased to £350.[70]

The Traverse also received funding from the Scottish Committee of the Arts Council, which included a guarantee against loss (not exceeding £100) for the first professional stage production of new plays under the committee's Scheme for the Promotion of New Drama. However, only those plays deemed 'of a standard acceptable to the Scottish Committee's Play Panel' would be eligible for funding. The Traverse, as a theatre club, was effectively exempt from theatrical censorship, yet whether for reasons of censorship or personal dislike, representatives of the Play Panel turned down a number of plays submitted by the Traverse in 1965. This had prompted Haynes to write to Donald Mather, then chairman of the Scottish Committee of the Arts Council, that 'something was wrong':

> The growing international (and local) reputation of the Traverse over the past two and a half years should be an indication of our desires and future policies. One wonders if it is even necessary any more for our plays to be read by a play 'panel'. You know we are aiming for the highest qualities in production and content, and at the same time seeking new ways and new writers.

Haynes's letter was successful, perhaps because the White Paper had laid emphasis on exactly what the Traverse was providing: artistic experimentation (not only in theatre) and the support of new artists. On this basis, the Scottish Committee agreed that the Traverse no longer had to submit plays to the Play Panel.[71]

At the beginning of 1964, Edinburgh Corporation took on another significant responsibility when it purchased the Royal Lyceum Theatre for

£100,000 with the intention of running it as a civic theatre 'owned by and administered on behalf of the citizens of Edinburgh'.[72] On 29 May 1965, Edinburgh Civic Theatre Trust Ltd assumed responsibility for the administration of the theatre from the corporation. The opening of the Lyceum sealed the fate of the Gateway Theatre Company. Gateway member Moultrie Kelsall told the Civic Theatre Trust: 'The Gateway Company had held the torch of theatre alive in Edinburgh and it had always been their ultimate wish to pass it on to the stronger hands of the Town Council and the Civic Theatre'.[73] The trust consisted of eight town councillors, including Lord Provost Weatherstone, and four lay members: playwrights and former Gateway committee members Robert Kemp and Alexander Reid, John B. Rankin, former chairman of the Gateway and Bank of Scotland secretary, and Duncan Curr, who took on the role of secretary. The artistic director was named as Tom Fleming, a founder member of the Gateway Theatre Company.

On the official opening of the Lyceum in October 1965, *The Sunday Times* reported:

> Step by faltering step civilisation creeps over the face of Britain. Edinburgh, which likes to think of itself as a capital city, has some way to go before it can justify the claim; but change is in the air. Usually in the news when some fresh upsurge of philistinism seems about to imperil the Festival, it nevertheless buys more seats for that cultural jamboree than do visitors.

The writer of the article noted his suspicion that 'Official Edinburgh' had a 'slightly furtive and apprehensive pride in Mr Jim Haynes' bohemian Traverse Theatre Club; enough, along with a wish not to be left behind, to tempt them into the field – to the very gate of the fold'.[74] This helps to explain why Weatherstone showed some sympathy towards the Traverse and offered a token grant, but did not offer serious support or funding – large funds were already earmarked for the Lyceum, and in its first year, the corporation committed a staggering £42,000 to its new venture into the arts.[75]

The role of Edinburgh Corporation in forming this bold new venture has often been overlooked, or perceived as grudging. By 1963 it was seriously beginning to look as if the Lyceum might close for good in the face of the growing competition from television, meaning Edinburgh would have to endure the loss of another of its theatres.[76] Edinburgh businessman Meyer Oppenheim, who bought the theatre in 1960, planned to bulldoze it and build a new civic theatre alongside the Festival offices. This, according to theatre historian Donald Campbell, 'caused great alarm in the City Chambers'. This is because two of the Festival's key venues, the Lyceum and Usher Hall, would now be within a site that had become privately owned and their loss, even on a temporary basis while better facilities were created, could seriously affect the stability and future of the Edinburgh Festival.[77] In September 1961, the then Lord Provost, J. Greig Dunbar, announced that Edinburgh Corporation would buy the planned civic theatre but, after those plans were abandoned, the corporation purchased the existing Lyceum Theatre in January 1964.[78]

Since 1960, the corporation had been under pressure from the amateur dramatics field to provide a civic theatre after the main venue for amateur drama in Edinburgh, the Little Theatre, was threatened with closure. Its imminent demise attracted letters from the local wing of the SCDA. Furthermore, a 'Committee of Users' of the theatre pleaded with Edinburgh Town Council to step in and purchase the theatre as an 'ideal opportunity to meet the oft-expressed desire for a Civic Theatre in this our Festival City'. They went on:

> We feel that the time has now come for the Corporation to take the lead in the growing recognition of the fact that public leisure must receive public subsidy. This is already true of Golf, Bowls, Tennis, Swimming, Soccer, and is particularly true of the public libraries and Adult Education Scheme. As far as we know Amateur Theatre, Amateur Ballet and Amateur Dancing receives no support from the rates, and there is ample evidence that as a form of Further Education, it is of immense value to the Community.[79]

As Callum Brown argues, sport had been seen as an acceptable social policy objective since the 1930s, 'viewed as something in which the state would participate to further democratic access'.[80] However, in 1960 amateur artists had not received the same kind of support; one correspondent for *The Times* complained that the public hostility towards theatres of the eighteenth century had become public indifference, and that public funding tended to ignore the needs of amateur artists.[81] However, attitudes were beginning to change, and it is interesting that the government appointed Denis Howell its first Minister of Sport at the same time that Jennie Lee was made first Minister for the Arts.

Edinburgh Corporation responded to these changes and arranged for a five-man subcommittee to run the Lyceum for a period of twelve months while its future was decided.[82] But Weatherstone had already begun preparing the ground for a civic theatre. He had sent E. F. Catford, depute town clerk, to a one-day conference on civic theatres organised by Sunderland Borough Council in October 1963. In his report of the conference, Catford summarised those points made during the conference 'which seemed either to be of general interest, or to bear some relevance to Edinburgh's proposals for the Lyceum Theatre Development or the Morningside theatre project'.[83] This clearly demonstrates the corporation's serious attitude towards opening a civic theatre, and also shows that plans were being made fairly early to open what became the Churchill Theatre in Morningside. This theatre was originally Morningside High Church, but was bought, converted and reopened by the corporation in September 1965 as a venue for amateur drama, in order to fill the gap left by the demolition of the Little Theatre.[84] The conversion of this Edinburgh church into a theatre also symbolises the shifting status of organised religion in the 1960s.

What was different about the Lyceum is that it was not just going to be owned by the corporation and leased to theatre groups (like the Churchill Theatre was), but that the corporation itself was actually going to be involved in running it. When the news was first announced Duncan Macrae, then Scottish chairman of the British Actors' Equity Association, opposed anyone except a professional running the theatre, commenting: 'I have never believed public money requires public representation.'[85] But a shift in the balance of control in theatre in the mid-1960s is evident. In encouraging national and local government to take more responsibility for culture, one unintended effect of the White Paper was to shift control from those primarily interested in the arts themselves to administrators more concerned with finance and accountability. Andrew Sinclair has noted that, at the beginning of the 1960s, a 'slow and significant change was beginning in the membership of the Panels of the Arts Council from the doers to the administrators', while in Edinburgh, between 1961 and 1962, demands for 'a bigger control of Festival affairs by the business people of Edinburgh and the Corporation' grew from within the EFS. This led to the EFC's decision that, with the help of a programme advisory panel, it would in future 'control both the artistic and financial aspects of the Festival' and its composition was consequently reduced to decrease the number of art 'experts' and produce a majority of town councillors.[86]

The Edinburgh Civic Theatre Trust was also weighted towards town councillors, with arts practitioners in the minority. However, when Tom Fleming resigned from his post at the beginning of August 1966, it was in response to pressure to present better-known works that would attract Edinburgh ratepayers from the 'cultural' trust members. Fleming had been asked to submit plays to a Programme Advisory Panel, which would discuss the selection of plays and try to find ways of improving the theatre's financial performance, after 'too many Edinburgh ratepayers had demonstrated their lack of interest in the city's bold cultural experiment'. *The Scotsman* noted that there was a 'certain irony' in the stands taken by the two groups of trustees: the 'cultural' lay members reportedly felt that since the whole community supported the theatre, then it was in much the same category as a public library and as such 'had to cater for all its "proprietors"', while the councillors had given Fleming and the concept of artistic freedom for the artistic director 'whole-hearted support'.[87]

The Traverse was also experiencing pressures related to finance and a shifting balance of control. Tensions arose over Haynes's appointment of Jack Henry Moore as associate director, his increasing involvement in a London Traverse (which meant long absences from Edinburgh), and his alleged 'financial irresponsibility' at a time when the club was struggling for funds.[88] At the 1966 AGM, Andrew Elliott, now chairman, stated that Haynes's methods of running the Traverse 'had made it very difficult to control expenditure on theatre productions and to plan advance publicity'.[89] The crucial issue of trying to strike a balance between creativity on the one hand and financial responsibility on the other concerned the Committee of Management at a time when finances were critical, membership was declining, and there was increased competition for public subsidy (partly due to more experimental theatres opening in the aftermath of the White Paper).[90] Before the AGM, Haynes had distributed a circular to committee members that criticised the committee: 'The balance of control within the Traverse has moved from the artistic to the financial sector and creeping professionalism has set in.'[91]

Haynes had, as Joyce McMillan put it, 'effectively won a vote of confidence by appealing over the Committee's heads to his electorate, and by making a strong pitch on the issue of artistic freedom as opposed to nit-picking financial restraint'.[92] But he had inadvertently weakened his position on the committee by seeking a new and more supportive chairman.[93] This had led to the appointment of Nicholas Fairbairn (defence lawyer in the nudity trial), whose initial view was that 'there should be control without castration'.[94] However, the conflict over creative versus financial needs in the Traverse, and the feeling of the committee that Haynes was financially irresponsible, remained in the weeks following the AGM. At the first meeting of the new committee, on which only two original Traverse founder members were left (Richard Demarco, who continued as vice-chairman, and John Martin) the idea of an advisory Artistic Sub-committee was put forward. This sounded ominously like the Programme Advisory Panel suggested only weeks later by the Edinburgh Civic Theatre Trust. A week later, Martin, one of three guarantors of the club's bank accounts, resigned while the two others – Elliott, who had just been replaced as chairman, and James Walker – noted their lack of confidence in Haynes and asked to reduce their guarantees. The pressure was rising and the breaking point came when Haynes insisted on giving Moore an artistic position within the club. The committee disagreed, Haynes resigned, and the committee accepted his resignation, an action Demarco described as 'devastating'.[95] With Haynes's departure, and with Demarco the only original member of the Committee of Management left, the Traverse was 'run without exception by proper, professional theatre directors, in the manner of every other subsidised theatre of the day'.[96]

'THE JOY OF EXPERIMENT': THE RISING PROFILE OF EXPERIMENTAL ART

Within the 1965 White Paper, the British government emphasised a commitment to experimental and participatory culture: 'New ideas, new values, the involvement of large sections of the community hitherto given little or no opportunity to appreciate the best in the arts, all have their place.'[97] It also encouraged regional and local authorities to form new arts centres.[98]

Not long after, Edinburgh Corporation announced its plans for 'a complete cultural and conference centre unique in Scotland and probably Britain', while a Scottish Education Department circular sent out to local authorities in June 1965 asked for their support (financial and otherwise) in the creation and provision of arts centres in local communities.[99] Plans were also made to build a theatre specifically for experimental productions as experimental theatre established itself on the British arts scene, no doubt influenced by the Traverse. One journalist wrote: 'The light of the tiny Traverse Theatre has grown to be a bright beacon on Britain's theatrical scene.'[100]

During its first year, the repertoire at the Lyceum reflected Tom Fleming's recent work in theatres around Europe while a member of the Royal Shakespeare Company: exciting, varied and, above all, experimental. The programme was described as 'distinctly, almost defiantly international', his policy being to present the Lyceum 'as the logical outcome of the Edinburgh Festival' with its plays all new to Scotland and taken from as wide an international field as possible.[101] To Fleming, the theatre existed 'to break through the closed minds of people, to explore contemporary thought, and to pose moral questions'. He had put a ban on any plays about Scottish history during the first season, as he felt that Scottish theatre had 'failed in the past because of this image – namely, that the only interesting things that ever happened in Scotland happened years ago and [. . .] life has been very dull since'.[102] Even during the year that the theatre was operated by the corporation, before Edinburgh Civic Theatre Trust gained control, such 'controversial' writers as Bertolt Brecht and Jean Genet had been staged. Although Lord Provost Weatherstone was unfamiliar with them, he had reportedly commented that 'a little adventure can be a glorious thing'. It is hard to believe that this was the same Lord Provost who had so forcibly condemned the avant-garde happening less than two years before.[103]

In 1964 Jim Haynes, along with Michael Geliot, John Martin and Robin Richardson ('the best-known theatrical agent in Scotland'), had created Traverse Festival Productions Ltd in order to present the English-language premiere of Bertolt Brecht and Kurt Weill's *Happy End* outside the confines of the theatre club.[104] Since a large hall was required, *Happy End* was performed in Edinburgh's Pollock Hall as part of the Fringe.[105] Although Brecht had a 'pervasive, all-infecting influence' in the early 1960s, his work was still only gradually becoming known to the British theatre-going public by 1964, and one academic has argued that 'Brechtianism was more talked about than witnessed in British theatre until 1968, when it became crucial to the political end of the fringe'.[106] In putting on this significant, experimental piece by an influential figure in 1960s theatre, the Traverse was assured attention from the critics. Furthermore, that same year, the Traverse had also held an international poetry conference (which was to have been part of the official Festival programme until the reaction to the happening at the 1963 Drama Conference) and put on an exhibition of international contemporary art, both of which gained media interest and attention. The Traverse Art Gallery, run by Richard Demarco, was by then establishing a growing reputation for exhibitions of contemporary art and photography.

Indeed, it was almost as if the Traverse was putting on its own festival of the arts. A critic for the *Sunday Times* wrote:

> Edinburgh may count itself lucky in possessing its own extremely lively arts organisation in the shape of the Traverse Theatre Club. It is currently mounting an exhibition of international contemporary art. In its own theatre poetry reading, and folk-song in the small hours, supplement no fewer than four British premieres [. . .] Meanwhile, also in Edinburgh, the annual international festival is going on.[107]

Lord Harewood was also impressed with the production, telling *The Sun* 'I thought it was a very splendid production', although he refused to reveal whether Haynes would 'break through the official "culture barrier" of the 1965 Edinburgh Festival' and achieve official recognition.[108] But in October 1964, Haynes reported to the Traverse Committee of Management that Harewood had suggested the Traverse submit two plays for production in the Lyceum, and that the Traverse premises be used for the 'experimental side of the festival'.[109] The previous month, a Fringe Club meeting had described the Festival's drama offering as 'duller than ever' and called for Haynes to be appointed drama adviser to the official Festival, in order to redress the balance between music and drama. Harewood was mindful that drama 'was considered the poor relation in Edinburgh programming'.[110]

The Traverse was important to the growing network of experimental theatres throughout Britain and by December 1965, Haynes had made reciprocal arrangements with many of them.[111] In autumn 1965, he and Alexander Racolin, who ran a little theatre off Broadway, presented a number of shows in London's New Arts Theatre, which Haynes recalls were 'a big success – not financially, we broke even or lost a little money – but critically it was a major, major success'.[112] The venture's lack of financial success, attributed to the failure of New Arts Theatre members to attend, made some contemporaries conclude that Edinburgh was an important location for experimental theatre. *The Scotsman* commented of the New Arts Theatre season: 'But it has, at least, proved one thing – that Edinburgh, despised, provincial Edinburgh, is much more capable of supporting a dynamic, adventurous theatre than much-vaunted London is.'[113] This was partly a riposte to an American theatre director, Charles Marowitz, who in June 1965 had asked: 'Is Scotland ready for Theatre of Cruelty? One would sooner ask, is Scotland ready for serious theatre of any sort? [. . .]

Figure 6.1 Richard Demarco pictured during the Traverse Exhibition of International Contemporary Art in the Traverse Art Gallery, 1964.
(© Richard Demarco, the Demarco Archives)

Culturally speaking, is Scotland worth salvaging?' One individual wrote in response:

> In Scotland, the area Mr Marowitz would have us believe worries him, there is the only avant-garde theatre in Britain with a consistent policy – the Traverse Theatre Club. In its short life it has established a record in the production of new plays by modern European, American and British writers which cannot be reached at the stretch by its nearest rival, the Hampstead Theatre Club.[114]

In August 1965, Haynes was also negotiating to take over a London theatre on a long-term basis to allow transfers from Edinburgh to London, and later from London to Paris. One reporter for *The Observer* commented: 'This sudden expansion mirrors the growth of the Traverse in Edinburgh itself – a success story without equal in the arts in post-war Britain outside London.'[115] In 1966, Haynes raised the profile of the Traverse in London by establishing a London Traverse, based at the Jeanetta Cochrane Theatre, and intended as a 'sister theatre' to the original Traverse.

The Richard Demarco Gallery, which sprang out of the Traverse Art Gallery, opened its doors in August 1966 and quickly established a reputation as a cutting-edge venue for contemporary art. It was originally intended that the gallery be called The Traverse Art Gallery, in essence a bigger and more flexible space than the critically acclaimed, but extremely cramped and in many ways unsuitable, existing gallery located above the theatre in James Court. However, the Traverse Committee of Management soon made it clear that Demarco would not be allowed to use the name 'Traverse' in connection with this new gallery. After much deliberation, the gallery was named after its director, and developed into something more than a contemporary art gallery in the usual sense of the word by engaging with other art forms, particularly theatre.[116] The new venture quickly became a success and its opening exhibition, 'which expressed its commitment to bringing the world of Bond Street and Cork Street galleries to Scotland', attracted excited reviews:

> The London critics are apparently falling over themselves in excitement; the Spanish cities are for the first time taking an interest in the Edinburgh Festival; and the genuine amazement of Sr. de Marcis, co-curator of the Italian Gallery of Modern Art in Rome, on his visit yesterday, that the 150 works by international artists (valued at more than £40,000) had been assembled in Edinburgh explains why Mr Demarco felt able to claim that his three-storey gallery in Melville Street ranks with the best of London, Paris and New York.[117]

At the beginning of November 1966, Demarco contacted the EFS to inform it of a competition that his gallery was holding, and to invite it to donate a prize. This was the Open 100, in which all UK-resident visual artists (professional or otherwise) were invited to enter their paintings, with the best hundred to be chosen by judges and exhibited during the Festival at Edinburgh University, which had agreed to offer financial support and a monetary prize, and to sponsor public lectures. The EFC was initially uninterested but after one judge, David Baxandall, pointed out that the Festival had been 'criticised in the past for failing to encourage contemporary art', the matter was remitted to the Programme Advisory Panel. With the backing of Peter Diamand, who was 'of the opinion that the Society should give its moral and financial support' to the exhibition, the EFS agreed to include Open 100 in its programme. The competition attracted 1,500 entries and led to Demarco being invited to direct the Festival's exhibitions of contemporary art (which he did from 1967 to 1994) on the proviso that he bore the burden of the costs involved.[118]

With the shift to experimental theatre across Britain, and the emphasis on new ideas in cultural production, the Festival simply had to adapt in order to stay relevant in a world so vastly different from the immediate post-war era in which it had been born. In his first press conference as Festival director, Diamand noted his awareness that the drama side of the Festival was subject to 'quite a bit of criticism'.[119] However, in 1967 he responded to the rising profile of 'little theatres' by compiling a drama programme predominantly made up of productions by theatre clubs from around the world, prompting Allen Wright, *The Scotsman*'s drama critic, to proclaim, 'Edinburgh Plans Real Drama Festival at Last.' Miller argued that it was 'one of the strongest drama programmes of any Festival so far' with seventeen plays scheduled, including experimental productions by groups such as La Mama Theatre Group of New York, the Marionetteatern puppet theatre of Stockholm, Hampstead Theatre Club of London, Glasgow's Close Theatre Club and Edinburgh's own Traverse Theatre Club.[120] In preparation, the assistant director of the Festival, Alexander Schouvaloff, had explored places including off-Broadway, Montparnasse in Paris, Poland, Sweden and a number of theatre clubs in Britain to find new plays, commenting: 'It's in these places that the discoveries are being made [. . .] They are not standing still, and they can do things which the commercial theatres cannot afford to do.' *The Scotsman* announced: 'It would seem that, at long last, the official programme is absorbing some of the radical qualities of the Fringe.'[121]

Diamand had asserted that his intention was to attract and engage with young people, but there were also more practical reasons for compiling a programme of experimental theatre companies in 1967. For one, Edinburgh Corporation was reluctant to increase its grant to the Festival.[122] However, more pressing was the growing crisis over the dwindling number of theatres available for official Festival productions. Indeed between July and December 1966 (when organisation for the 1967 Festival programme was taking place) Festival Society records show an increasingly difficult situation in Edinburgh with regard to theatre accommodation. By December 1966, the management of the King's Theatre had yet to confirm whether it would be available for the 1967 Festival, there was no certainty that the Empire Theatre would be available, and the amount available from the budget was not going to be enough to cover the cost of the programme.[123] The management of the King's were seeking financial support from the corporation as they felt that the Lyceum would, before long, put the King's out of business.[124] The Empire had become a bingo hall in 1963, and negotiations for ballet to be performed there for the duration of the Festival had centred on making sure that the bingo and its accompanying paraphernalia were cleared up in time for the performances.[125] Diamand did not want a repeat of what had befallen the Hungarian State Opera and Ballet in 1963, the last time the Festival had used the Empire for ballet, when the Saturday night bingo session had continued until after 11 p.m. (amid 'much crude humour directed against the Festival') and the performers had had to wait while the stage was cleared of bingo apparatus before going on.[126] The size of some of the theatres available to the Festival was also a cause for concern while another, noted at a Programme Advisory Panel meeting in January 1967, concerned funding: 'Bearing in mind the financial position of the Society [. . .] an appropriate amount of new and experimental drama should be presented at the Gateway and Church Hill Theatres.'[127] Inviting a number of smaller theatre companies that did not have high production costs, and were generally used to producing on a tight budget and to performing in small spaces, was a means of easing both the financial and accommodation pressures on the Festival while staying true to the aim of making the twenty-first Festival attractive to younger audiences.

'IF ART IS OFFENSIVE, IS IT NOT STILL ART?'

In the immediate aftermath of the Second World War, churches had seized on the arts as an evangelistic and teaching tool. Then, in the late 1950s and on into the 1960s, the arts offered a point of contact with young people and the intelligentsia. In the midst of a growing 'cultural revolution', the relationship between religion and the arts became strained, and to some observers it seemed as if the arts were beginning to take the place of religion – some churches were even converted to theatres. Throughout the 1960s attempts were made to find a 'new morality' to replace the loss of the Christian moral code. The Kirk's Committee on Moral Welfare had attributed the 'violent' reaction that *Sex and Morality* provoked among many Christians to its unexpected content: 'Some were looking for a clarion cry to rally round the old standards and to preserve the bastions of morality against the sometimes insidious and often brash assaults of a soul-destroying array of novelists, broadcasters, publicists and irreligious egg-heads'.[128] This is a telling statement, since it sums up the widespread feeling among religious groups that the blame for the move from Christian to secular morals and ethics lay with the intelligentsia, specifically those involved in media and the arts.[129] It also shows the crucial role that the arts were seen to be playing in the social, cultural and moral changes of the 1960s.

The reverberations of the 1963 Drama Conference and the ensuing controversy over the nude girl on the balcony were still being felt in 1964. In November that year, the head of MRA, Peter Howard, criticised, among other things, the Edinburgh Festival, the Traverse Theatre Club and the Lord Provost of Edinburgh during a speech given in Newcastle. In reference to an occasion days before, in which he had suggested that it was still possible to present a great festival of the arts 'without resort to filth and godlessness', Howard remarked:

> I was rebuked by the Lord Provost of Edinburgh. He says it is impertinence to give these views. I am in the dilemma of giving offence either to the Lord Provost of Edinburgh or to the Lord God Almighty. So reluctantly I must risk the displeasure of the elected ruler of Edinburgh rather than incur the wrath of the eternal ruler of the earth.

Howard also told his audience that plays by Joan Littlewood, who had said in a press conference during the 1963 International Drama Conference that the 'theatre can be a marvellous world since God is dead and religion is dead', had been presented by the Festival in 'the home of the General Assembly of the Church of Scotland'. Moreover, he exclaimed, the Traverse had been awarded 'a substantial financial grant' by Edinburgh Corporation and 'nakedness seems to have an appeal to those who handle art in Edinburgh'. Howard was not just referring to the nude model on the balcony. In 1964, the hugely successful African ballet company Les Ballets Africains appeared as part of the Festival. Howard described their performance as 'naked African ladies dancing publicly in ways which no white women would be allowed to do up there' and repeated the 'godlessness and dirt' accusations of the previous year.[130, 131] However, this time there was no outburst from the Lord Provost, no press (or even *Express*) campaign, and no sign of protest from Church of Scotland representatives.

Those who had written in to support Weatherstone in his comments against the happening in 1963 were dismayed to see him clash with Howard, with one who wrote to complain suggesting that Howard 'would be a most natural ally in restoring the high reputation of the Edinburgh Festival'. But Weatherstone was not to be persuaded. When the *Scottish Daily Express* asked Weatherstone to comment on accusations made by Hugh MacDiarmid that he represented 'the voice of Scottish Philistinism and the voice of the conspiracy of the Moral Rearmament people which has been designed to oust Lord Harewood', Weatherstone had refused, remarking: 'I don't want to listen to any second-hand statements.'[132] Furthermore, the *Express*, which had led the 'Godlessness and Dirt' campaign after the happening, had reported favourably on Les Ballets Africains, and had printed two large full-frontal photographs of the topless dancers. Under the headline, 'Africa Girls! – As Edinburgh Sees Them', the paper reported:

> Topless skirts came to Edinburgh in 'Les Ballets Africains'. These, with deafening drums, terrifying witch-doctors and mad, mad dancing, caused astonishment at the Lyceum. The topless display need not dismay, for the girls are so like bronze sculptures animated. They leapt about the stage in frenzied ecstacies [*sic*] [. . .] What an amusing break from the decorum of all the rest of the Festival!

No moral controversy occurred around these sell-out performances. This raises interesting questions about the persistence of colonial views in the mid-1960s, but more obviously shows how out of touch MRA were with public opinion. Revd Donald Davidson, of the Kirk's Social and Moral Welfare Board, commented under the headline 'Kirk Leader Backs the Topless Show': 'If we are to get a natural presentation of folk dancing, what right have we to cover the dancers' bodies? If we went to see them in Africa they would not cover their chests for us.' Prior to the performance, the sociologist John Highet had asked Harewood whether he intended to 'tone down' the show for Edinburgh audiences, writing:

> I would like the show to be presented as it was in London so that we can see how the Edinburgh City fathers, the Church and the public will react in view of the protests at the Festival nude incident last year.[133]

A year was a long time in sixties Britain. Attitudes to morality, 'controversial' theatre and the arts more broadly had become more complex and fractured, and there was evidence of some liberalisation.

In April 1966, Denis Duncan, editor of the *British Weekly*, wrote an open letter to Jim Haynes asking for his stance on a number of issues. Duncan began his front-page letter by noting that it would be a 'contemporary tragedy' if a 'further rift' developed between the church and the arts, boldly stating:

> The contemporary prophets may more be found in you, the writers and artists, than from people like me in the pulpits. We need new ideas, new ideas [*sic*], radical ideas, bold and courageous thinking and expression [. . .] and this may well come from the stage in our time.[134]

That year, *Sex and Morality* had identified the arts as having an important role in the field of morality and for sex education. Painting and sculpture, it commented, showed the human body as something other than the 'exaggerated symbol of the "girlie" magazine' (the defence had used sculpture to make a similar point at the 1963 nudity trial), while drama and poetry offered 'a language for inarticulate feeling which actually extends and deepens the range of feeling itself'.[135] Duncan sought Haynes's stance on points that he said 'genuinely puzzle people who want to be sympathetic to the theatre as an art form':

> Why do you seem to need to have the 'vulgarity', 'crudity' (or do you call it 'reality') which so persistently and deliberately turn up in your productions? It is a valid complaint that you and your colleagues often make that the churches too often equate immorality and sex. Is it not possible for your critics to feel that the theatre is not equally obsessed with sex?[136]

In February 1966, the House of Lords had set up a joint select committee to look into the question of stage censorship. Lord Annan, who brought the motion, emphasised the arbitrary nature of theatrical censorship.[137] In Edinburgh in 1966, for example, the Lord Chamberlain had banned a drama group from performing parts of Geoffrey Chaucer's *The Miller's Tale* at that year's Fringe festival, even advising them to drop the piece altogether:

> The Lord Chamberlain regrets he cannot allow the piece to be played on the stage as it contains certain words and phrases which he cannot allow on stage. Because of the nature of the piece, the Lord Chamberlain would be reluctant to cut any of the words and phrases.

As the *Glasgow Herald* reported, the group went ahead with their modern production 'without certain four-letter words and phrases used by Chaucer (1340–1400) that might cause objection in 1966'.[138]

In March that year, Duncan wrote to Peter Diamand inviting him to meet with a group of 'churchmen' in order to discuss the Church and the arts, with particular reference to the Edinburgh Festival:

> As you know in Scotland there appears to be a judgemental kind of approach to drama and entertainment, yet at the same time within the Church there are many who feel Church and Arts must talk with each other about basic issues, believing that they are, in fact, concerned with the same kind of problems.

Duncan referred obliquely to a 'situation' concerning the Church and the arts as the reason for suggesting this meeting (and noted he had already contacted Haynes, John Calder, Tom Fleming, and the playwright John Arden).[139]

On 9 February 1966, a Revd J. B. Longmuir contacted William Grahame, secretary and administration manager of the EFS, to say that he and a Dr Sanderson, as representatives of the General Administration Committee of the Church of Scotland's Assembly Hall, had read the plays that the EFS had proposed be performed there in the forthcoming Festival. Longmuir noted that, while they did not approve of the choices 'whole-heartedly', they were 'not disposed to turn them down' and asked that in one of them the 'more bawdy scenes [. . .] be treated with restraint'. These plays were due to be performed by Pop Theatre, a new project founded by Frank Dunlop and due to be launched at the 1966 Edinburgh Festival. Pop Theatre brought comedians, jazz musicians and pop singers together with classical actors and aimed to bring accessible classical work to wide – especially young – audiences.[140] Enclosed with Longmuir's letter was *The Scotsman*'s review of the adaptation of Alan Sillitoe's *Saturday Night and Sunday Morning*, presented in London in February 1966 to raise money; an excerpt read: 'Every sexual nuance is played up, the language is foul, the atmosphere unreal.' In response, Longmuir warned: 'One does not need to be a prophet to foresee the loss of the Assembly Hall altogether to the Festival if these plays are produced in a similar style.' A week later, Longmuir wrote another letter to Grahame in response to a further two plays, noting objection to one of them:

> Dr Sanderson and I were given authority to grant or refuse the use of the hall if, in our opinion, the plays proposed were either suitable or unsuitable. The view was expressed that the Assembly Hall was not the place for experimental plays or those which might be considered 'strong meat' or, indeed, for companies or producers whose ideas are too advanced for the Church to approve.[141]

When the Festival had begun in the immediate post-war period, it had been easy to see the cultural values shared by the Kirk and the EFS. But, during the upheaval of rapid change, these were diverging.

Diamand was prompted by these objections to write a strongly worded letter to Herbert Brechin, newly elected as Lord Provost following the end of Weatherstone's tenure, in which he outlined the three options he considered open to the EFS: think of a number of plays that might be considered suitable for the Assembly Hall and 'hope' one might be approved; ask Longmuir to explain why he objected to the last play, or give up using the Assembly Hall altogether. Diamand's tone was one of incredulity, and he made it clear that his preferred course of action was not to use the Assembly Hall, at least for the 1966 Festival, and to let the press know exactly why. In all, Diamand summarised his reaction to the events with the comment 'To qualify it as "surprise" and "disappointment" would be a euphemism'.[142]

But this was not the first time that the Kirk had disapproved of plays that the EFS wanted to present in the Assembly Hall. The Traverse had been invited to present a play as part of the official 1965 Festival programme. Every one of the plays proposed by the Traverse were rejected by the Edinburgh Festival Society, a decision that Haynes later attributed to the plays being 'too scary for them'.[143] But what was not revealed at the time was that it was the General Administration Committee of the Assembly Hall that objected, not the EFS. This actually influenced the decision of one EFS member, Colin Chandler, to resign – mainly on account of his heavy workload, but also because of 'certain recent decisions made by the Council with which I am quite out of sympathy, notably the manner in which "The Assembly" was withdrawn from this year's programme'. This play, he went on, had been recommended by the Drama Panel, approved by the Programme Panel and accepted by the EFC, before the General Administration Committee of the Assembly Hall asked that it be withdrawn 'as they objected to a certain bawdiness in its content'. Although Chandler agreed with the right of any body to make an objection, he noted: 'I have the strongest possible feeling against censorship of any kind by any body other than the Lord Chamberlain's Office, and cannot continue conscientiously to serve on any committee where this is condoned.'[144]

The General Administration Committee might have thought that the danger of bawdiness within property belonging to the Church of Scotland had been averted when the EFS asked the Traverse to put on the 'safe' option of *Macbeth*. But this was the Traverse, which in Edinburgh had quickly become 'a powerful focus for respectable Edinburgh's fantasies and fears about the new "permissive" age'.[145] In May 1965 a writer for the *Glasgow Herald* began his review of three Traverse plays with his observation that the 'now socially accepted sexual revolution' was evident in this triple bill.[146] Arthur Marwick, in his study of the 1960s, wrote that 'the Traverse was a place where one could practically observe the sexual revolution taking place. The whole building, bar, dining room, tiny theatre, art gallery, seemed suffused by sex'.[147] Sheila Colvin laughed when recalling that she was sure that the press 'thought we had nightly orgies'.[148] In keeping with its reputation, the Traverse production of *Macbeth* grabbed headlines with a new take on the three witches – 'Bikini-clad Witches in Unethical "Macbeth",' read *The Scotsman*. What had been originally 'seized on as an innocuous last minute choice for the Assembly Hall' had become, in the words of actor Duncan Macrae, a performance that was 'very black, bloody, pagano [*sic*], libidinous and completely unethical'.[149] The EFS acknowledged the attention it had received, noting in a draft report for the 1966 AGM that some of the press and public 'were even able to keep their eye on an imaginatively produced "Macbeth" without being distracted by the novel and un-hag-like sinuosity of the Witches'.[150] The witches were played by 'beautiful, athletic young women' wearing bikinis (the tops of which were flesh coloured to give the impression of nudity) and during the play they squirmed 'obscenely through the smoke that drifts over the stage'. The director, Michael Geliot, commented: 'I've tried to make them evil and blasphemous . . . Creatures that are half moral as they were regarded at the time.'[151]

Concerns grew about the suitability of using public money to support plays or ventures that could be seen as immoral or controversial in any way. The Traverse had even been mentioned in the House of Commons in 1965, when the MP for Edinburgh West had expressed his

> grave misgivings about the way in which public money was being spent at Edinburgh's Traverse Theatre Club [. . .] and in staging plays in theatre clubs which are barred from performance in the ordinary theatres of the country on the grounds of obscenity or for any other reasons.[152]

In February 1967, Diamand was forwarded a copy of a letter from Revd John Morrison, initially addressed to the Lord Provost, complaining about experimental theatre clubs being part of the official Festival. Diamand replied:

> When you refer to the Close Theatre Club, the Hampstead Theatre Club and the Traverse Theatre Club as 'organisations' operating as 'clubs in order to circumvent the Lord Chamberlain's ban on the type of production they seem to favour' I think you misunderstand the purpose of these theatres.

The purpose of the theatres, and of the Festival in inviting them, wrote Diamand, was 'to discover interesting plays by new, promising or even by well-known authors' and not to 'do harm to the Edinburgh Festival's international reputation by inviting companies to perform sordid offerings'. Morrison was particularly concerned about the Traverse appearing as part of the official programme: 'Valuable as the Traverse Club's experimental work may be on a Fringe level, it is clearly not of Edinburgh Festival level.' However, despite Morrison's best efforts – he wrote back to both the Lord Provost and Diamand asking for changes to the drama programme – no change was forthcoming. In fact, the Lord Provost's response to Morrison's first letter had been simply: 'There have always been controversial features associated with the Festival.'[153]

THE 'FUTZ FURORE'

During the 1967 Festival, the main elements of Revd Morrison's concerns were brought together in a controversy referred to variously as the 'lust and bestiality play', the 'lust play', and the 'Futz furore'. This involved a play described as 'shocking', the Traverse Theatre and the experimental theatre troupe La MaMa Company, from New York's Café La MaMa. This was an

Off-Off-Broadway theatre club, founded in 1961 and run by the 'dynamic' Ellen Stewart (as contemporary journalists described her). 'Off-Off-Broadway' refers to a type of theatre that 'challenged social, literary and theatrical convention' and offered directors, playwrights and actors 'freedom of expression in a non-commercial environment'.[154] By June 1967, just before their appearance at the Edinburgh Festival, the café had developed its reputation as *the* place for new American plays to originate and had, to date, discovered 130 new playwrights and given 175 premieres.[155] In short, Café La MaMa had become a leading light in contemporary and experimental theatre on the international stage. The Traverse Theatre Club presented and La MaMa performed Rochelle Owens's play *Futz* as part of the Fringe. On the surface, this was a play about a farmer (the Futz of the title) who had a love affair with a pig before his bestiality disgusted the local community so much that they lynched him, giving it all the ingredients for a moral controversy.

It is not surprising that the *Scottish Daily Express*, which had launched the 'Godlessness and Dirt' campaign of 1963, brought the matter to the attention of the public under the banner 'Filth on the Fringe'. Journalist Brian Meek described the performance in a way designed to evoke public outcry:

IN ONE SCENE the leading character appears to be suggesting sexual intercourse with a sow.
IN ANOTHER a girl is handled intimately by two men at once.
IN YET ANOTHER an actress bares her bosom before her mentally defective son who has just murdered a girl.

Warning of the danger that the Fringe would turn into a 'vehicle for plays which disgust and offend a large majority of the theatre-goers', Meek directed his anger in a long tirade against the Traverse (which endured regular criticism from the *Express* throughout the 1960s) for inviting La MaMa to take part in the Fringe. Meek pointed out that the Traverse was heavily supported by public money and claimed that it shocked 'even the most liberal minded'. His article prompted one of Edinburgh's bailies, Mary Robertson-Murray, to obtain special permission to appear before the Lord Provost's Committee. Neither Meek nor Robertson-Murray had seen the play: Meek based his outrage on what a colleague had told him was 'the most shocking play I have ever seen' while Robertson-Murray remarked: 'If it portrays bestiality then I wouldn't waste my time.' Both pointed out that the play was not part of the official Festival, and Meek called for it to be looked at by the city magistrates since 'such scenes as I have described would not be allowed in even the most sleazy London strip clubs'. 'Why then', he asked, 'should they be allowed in Scotland's capital city?'[156]

It looked like another moral storm was brewing in Edinburgh. Meek's article, in conjunction with Roberson-Murray's efforts, succeeded in the

Traverse being reported to the police, who visited the club – but only to ensure membership regulations were not being circumvented. Rather than gathering support for his stance against 'Filth on the Fringe', Meek instead gave extra publicity to *Futz*, La MaMa and the Traverse, and there was a long queue of members of the public outside the performance on the day the first 'Filth on the Fringe' article was published. Less than a week after the 'Futz furore' began, the *Express* reported 'Famous Watch Lust Play "Futz"' after David Frost, the then well-known film actor Anton Diffring and the Scottish Office minister Norman Buchan and his wife Janey (among others) joined hundreds packing the theatre to watch *Futz*.[157]

There are a number of reasons for the lack of real scandal. For one, by 1967 experimental theatre had attained new levels of support from the 'Establishment' and the importance of theatre clubs in encouraging new plays and new methods of performance had become widely recognised. La MaMa was at the same time performing the world premiere of *Tom Paine* on the official Festival programme, at the corporation-owned Church Hill Theatre (organised by the Traverse). La MaMa had established an international reputation for cutting-edge theatre, presenting plays that 'yield meanings that take us far beyond their rather ordinary surfaces', and by 1967 this was recognised by the 'Establishment' as a significant function of the arts.[158] In the first 'Filth on the Fringe' article, La MaMa's American director, Tom O'Horgan, explained: 'We intend to produce a very physical theatre by pushing the limits of physicality to the ultimate,' stating that an audience could no longer be preached to and that instead, an indirect method should be used to produce 'subliminal rumblings' on the part of the audience, in order to engender a personal involvement in the performance.[159] The director of the Traverse, Gordon McDougall, invited Meek to take part in a discussion about censorship and to talk about the 'moral implications' of his article, which Meek duly accepted. During the discussion, O'Horgan accused Meek of failing to understand that the play was about a 'man's struggle for personal freedom'. Meek retorted that surely this point could be made without obscenity, and asked that if he was going to push 'physicality to the limit' like he claimed, then why didn't he use a real pig? 'Oh we have,' answered O'Horgan, to 'wild laughter'.[160]

Secondly, the whole nature of morality, on which the objections had been focused, had changed in the public discourse. Meek and Robertson-Murray objected to *Futz* because of its immoral content, but the play attracted attention from theatre critics for its moral message. One writer for *The Scotsman* wrote: 'We knew that *Futz* must be a very moral play because all plays that are dismissed as pornographic in intent turn out to have a high moral content. That is axiomatic.'[161] Reviewing the play for *The Times* during its subsequent run in London, Irving Wardle described it as 'a highly moral piece', commenting that it is the rest of the community, not Farmer Futz, 'who emerge as the bestial ones', an observation shared in the *Scotsman* review:

A farmer with a reprehensible but at least exclusive aberration is pilloried by an indignant society – the same society responsible, of course, for the much less exclusive bestialities of Belsen, Viet-Nam, any civil war, or the fighting 'pub' on Saturday night.[162]

Questions of morality had gone beyond simple shocks with regards to sex and nudity on stage. Hugh McLeod highlights how *New Christian*, a journal founded in October 1965 and run by liberal representatives of the Christian denomination, went beyond 'traditional "moral issues"' and 'showed a complete lack of panic' with regard to sex. In response to the controversy over Kenneth Tynan becoming the first person to say 'fuck' on television in November 1965, *New Christian* denounced censorship and pointed out that 'the real obscenities are being enacted in Vietnam and Rhodesia.'[163] The Vietnam War was attracting more coverage and condemnation in Britain from the mid-1960s. In general, the role of the arts as a forum for exploring contemporary ethical and moral opinions had become recognised. This was acknowledged by the *British Weekly* in 1966 and connected to the growing gap between religion and the arts and the drop in the number of young people attending church.

Churches were also divided and lacking a central sense of what morality actually meant in late 1960s Britain. In a letter to the *British Weekly* on the subject of the arts, religion and morals, John Calder suggested that morality was the issue that offered the greatest chance of co-operation between religion and the arts, since churches were torn on moral issues in the much same way that artists were.[164] In April 1966, Jim Haynes responded to Denis Duncan's open letter:

Every theatre gets scripts from playwrights and a lot of them are in their original form unproduceable for either commercial or censorship reasons. The difference is that other theatres' artistic policies are geared to keeping 500 seats full, and no one must be offended. If art is offensive, is it not still art?

For Duncan, Haynes's letter was evidence that the gap between the church and the arts 'is at present enormous':

We do not really speak the same language. This is surely true in our relationship to younger people. The gap between ourselves and our sons has widened until we are not sure if we understand in any way their likes, their interests, their fashions or their ways. We literally do not speak the same language.

Duncan was particularly concerned about the General Assembly recommendation that the Americans be 'moderate in their conduct of war in Vietnam', a stance that he felt would not satisfy 'our modern young people or pull them to the churches!' The moral implications of the Vietnam War provoked much debate in the pages of *The British Weekly* during 1966 and 1967.

Michael Geliot wrote a lengthy letter to the *British Weekly* titled 'What are the Moral Issues?' in which he attacked the position of the Church:

> I write now with some of the bitterness of one who sought in the Church, as a young adult, some explanation of, and some reconciliation to the world's manifest evils. I found, find, only cowardly evasion and obsession with relatively petty sexual morality.

Concern about what Geliot termed 'relatively petty sexual morality' was still evident, and letters written to the *British Weekly* continued to highlight the 'degrading' nature of Traverse productions. Yet it is clear that there had been a fundamental shift in attitudes to morality and the arts from within the churches by 1967. Duncan was keen to address concerns raised by artists and 'modern youth', and he particularly respected Calder, whose 'shrewd comments [. . .] sometimes go much more to the heart of current ethical questions than many sermons and TV epilogues'.[165] During the 1960s, Duncan used the *British Weekly* to encourage its Christian readers to consider the challenges made by artists and the counter-culture, noting that it was imperative that churches did not 'simply line up to defend the "status quo" society' but gave space to discussion of culture and the arts in modern society, and their relationship with established religion.[166]

The lack of any real furore over *Futz* highlights the step change in public attitudes to the arts, culture and morality that had occurred in the years 1963 to 1967. That an important function of the arts was to challenge ideas, attitudes and values had become widely acknowledged and this was reflected in the willingness of the state, local authorities, churches and organisations like the EFS to support and encourage experimental theatre. Just as a wider context of fears over sexual immorality and the assaults on 'cherished concepts of art' had made the 'Festival nude' controversy, so the more 'permissive' climate and state sanction of challenging art (particularly drama) diminished the '*Futz* furore'. To Stuart Laing, the enactment of permissive legislation between 1967 and 1969 'both created and reflected the acceptance of an increasing breadth of social behaviours and moral stances in the areas of sexuality and artistic expression'.[167]

In July 1967, Allen Wright, drama critic for *The Scotsman*, explored the parallels between the Edinburgh of 1967 and the Edinburgh of 200 years before in an article titled 'In Pursuit of Sin'. He was motivated to explore the ways in which opposition to the arts in the two centuries compared by the performances of Robert McLellan's *The Hypocrite* at the Lyceum, a play set in eighteenth-century Scotland but inspired by the nudity trial of 1963. Wright argued that 'the artists of today encounter a more sophisticated opposition than the physical violence of the Reformers' and noted McLellan's concern that the prudishness of eighteenth-century magistrates and ministers had persisted: 'He feels strongly about the Scottish weakness for seeking out sin and deploring it in other people. The eagerness to purge and condemn has been much in evidence in recent years, so far as the arts are concerned.'[168]

The *British Weekly* review of *The Hypocrite* showed dismay at the way generalisations were made about the Church: 'It is true that there are, as there were, hypocrites in the churches. But this does not mean all churchmen are hypocrites.'[169] This applied outside the Church of Scotland too. In 1967, the minister of St Mark's Unitarian Church in Edinburgh held a special service on 'Arts and Morality' in which he referred to the 'mild furore' over *Futz*. Revd Bruce Findlay told the congregation:

Any living art must be allowed to reach beyond the mores of any particular society. I am against any form of censorship of the arts and prepared to accept that a few hundred or a few thousand people will be shocked or offended, and am prepared to be shocked or offended myself.[170]

Findlay's views reflected the changing contemporary opinion on censorship with regards to the theatre. In February 1968, the Bill to abolish theatre censorship was widely welcomed in the House of Commons (see Chapter 7). The criticisms that were expressed were few and were concerned more with safeguarding the Royal Family 'against offensive stage representation' than with protecting audiences from sexual content or nudity.[171]

Central to the social and cultural changes of the High Sixties was the increasing visibility and influence of experimental theatre. McLeod outlines how theatre, in conjunction with various *causes célèbres*, the media, and other art forms, broke taboos and exposed people to new ways of thinking and living.[172] In Edinburgh, experimental theatre began to move from the Fringe and the Traverse to the Festival, and the corporation-run Lyceum Theatre became involved through its civic theatre. Central to this broad shift was the increasing visibility and attraction of the Fringe to performers, critics and audiences alongside the growing international recognition of the Traverse, all of which were underpinned by the sanctioning of the experimental arts encouraged by the 1965 White Paper.

The idea that so-called 'Establishment' individuals and institutions adapted and adopted new ideas from the fringes reflects and supports Raymond Williams's theory of the transmission of culture, in terms of the creative act of artists. To Williams, the key activity of the artist was the actual work of transmission: 'Communication is the crux of art, for any adequate description of experience must be more than simple transmission, it must also include reception and response.' Despite identifying a tension between the artist and audience (for example, that between Haynes at the Traverse and the readers of the *British Weekly*), the 'lag' between the artists' expressions and their adoption or understanding by an audience were, to Williams, what makes us 'conscious of the fact of change'.[173] We can see this unfold in Edinburgh, the 'Festival City'.

NOTES

1. Donnelly, *Sixties Britain*, 92.
2. NLS, TTA, Acc. 4850, Box 21 (3) Newspaper Cuttings January–August 1966, *Morning Advertiser*, 23 August 1966; ECL, Royal Lyceum Theatre Press Cuttings Vol.1: 1963–5; *The Scotsman*, 21 May 1966.
3. *New Society*, 30 June 1966.
4. *The Times*, 22 March 1966.
5. Sinclair, *Arts and Cultures*, 151.
6. Donnelly, *Sixties Britain*, 99.
7. Galloway and Jones, 'The Scottish Dimension of British Arts Government', 31. See also McArthur, *Scotland, CEMA and the Arts Council*.
8. Hollis, *Jennie Lee*, 258.
9. This was 'close enough to count as a hit' (the Goschen level was 12.08 per cent). McArthur, *Scotland, CEMA and the Arts Council*, 210, 220. McArthur provides a rich and detailed analysis of the Scottish dimension of arts governance until 1967.
10. Hewison, *Too Much*, 57–8.
11. Sinclair, *Arts and Cultures*, 77.
12. *A Policy for the Arts*, para. 71, reproduced in Jenkins, *The Culture Gap*, Appendix 1.
13. Hollis, *Jennie Lee*, 258; *A Policy for the Arts*, para. 7.
14. Black, 'Making Britain a Gayer and More Cultivated Country?', 330–1.
15. *Plays and Players*, May 1966.
16. Nelson, *The British Counter-culture*, 45, 53.
17. Whitehouse, *Cleaning-up TV*, 50. For more on Whitehouse and the NVLA, see Black, *Redefining British Politics*, chapter 5.
18. The phrase is Malcolm Muggeridge's, another outspoken defender of traditional morality (who had started the decade in the liberal camp and, indeed, had chaired one of the 1962 Writers' Conference sessions). See his foreword in Whitehouse, *Who Does She Think She Is?*, 8.
19. Cited in McLeod, *The Religious Crisis of the 1960s*, 71.
20. *The Times*, 20 April 1965.
21. See Davidson and Davies, *The Sexual State*, 246–52.
22. Brown, *The Death of Christian Britain*, 175–80. See also McLeod, *The Religious Crisis of the 1960s*.
23. See Whitehouse, *Cleaning-up TV*.
24. Machin, 'British Churches and Moral Change in the 1960s', 225; British Council of Churches (hereafter BCC), *Sex and Morality*.
25. *The Times*, 18 October 1966.

26. *Reports to GA 1967*, 508.
27. BCC, *Sex and Morality*, 62.
28. *Reports to GA 1967*, 501–14; Davidson & Davis, *The Sexual State*, Parts I & II.
29. See McLeod, *The Religious Crisis of the 1960s*.
30. Inglis, *Private Conscience*, 45.
31. Homosexual acts also remained a criminal offence until 1982 in Northern Ireland, and 2000 in the armed forces. See Davidson & Davis, *The Sexual State*, for a full examination of sexuality and Scottish governance between 1950 and 1980.
32. *The Scotsman*, 25 May 1967.
33. See *Reports to GA 1967*, 525; *The Scotsman*, 25 May 1967.
34. Kellas, *Modern Scotland*, 74; John Calder, 7 May 2005. See Davidson & Davis, *The Sexual State* for analysis of the Church of Scotland's continuing influence on Scottish governance.
35. *BW*, 9 June 1966.
36. ECA, Lord Provost's Committee (hereafter LPC), Note on Publicity from Edinburgh Festival Society Ltd to City Chamberlain, 20 February 1964.
37. NLS, TTA, Acc. 4850, *The Guardian*, 6 August 1966.
38. Crummy, *Let the People Sing!*, 39.
39. ECL, Craigmillar Press Cuttings, *Edinburgh News & Dispatch*, 7 October 1964, *EEN*, 15 March 1966. See also ECL, Crummy, *People in Partnership*.
40. *The Observer*, 28 August 1965.
41. ECA, EFP 1964, letter from EFS Publicity Officer to Lord Provost's Secretary.
42. *The Times*, 3 September 1964.
43. *Express*, 3 September 1964; ECA, EFP 1965, letter from Brooks to Weatherstone, 15 January 1965.
44. ECA, LPC, Petition to Lord Provost of Edinburgh and Corporation of the City of Edinburgh, 4 September 1964. There was a separate petition from those in the Oxford Theatre Group because they did not agree with asking for subsidy (the second petition asked for one).
45. Ibid., EFS Ltd re Petitions from Festival Fringe Society, 13 November 1964.
46. Compare this to the 2012 Fringe Festival, which boasted a record-breaking 2,695 shows across 279 venues. See www.edfringe.com (last accessed 30 November 2012).
47. *GH*, 22 August 1966; Moffat, *The Edinburgh Fringe*, 69.
48. ECA, LPC, 'Petitions from Fringe' from Publicity Officer of EFC to Depute Town Clerk, 28 October 1964.
49. Moffat, *The Edinburgh Fringe*, 51.
50. *The Times*, 2 September 1965.
51. NLS, TTA, Acc. 4850 Box 21, *The Scotsman*, 8 September 1966.
52. McGough, *Said and Done*, 155.
53. *The Guardian*, 6 August 2003.
54. See Moffat, *The Edinburgh Fringe*.

55. This was reported to a meeting of the EFC in October 1964. ECA, LPC, EFS Ltd re Petitions.

56. Moffat, *The Edinburgh Fringe*, 52.

57. After the Valuation and Rating (Scotland) Act was passed in 1956 a number of church authorities had become fearful that they would become liable for rates if they allowed the use of church halls for concerts or other cultural purposes. This led to a gradual decrease in the number of church halls available for Fringe groups during the 1960s. See *Housing the Arts*, 83; STA, GB247, La1/24 (c) Edinburgh Festival Fringe, FFS Minutes of Meetings, 12 April 1966.

58. Ibid., 14 June 1966; 28 June 1966; 30 May 1966; 10 February 1967.

59. *Express*, 3 September 1964; ECA, EFP 1965, Letter from Brooks to Weatherstone, 15 January 1965.

60. Bruce, *Festival in the North*, 222–3.

61. *Express*, 18 August 1967.

62. *A Policy for the Arts*, paras 5–6.

63. *The Times*, 26 August 1964; Miller, *The Edinburgh International Festival*, 55–63.

64. See Miller, *The Edinburgh International Festival*, chapter 5 for more on Festival finances at this time.

65. ECA, LPC, Petition Note 'Petitions from Fringe'.

66. Harewood, *The Tongs and the Bones*, 187.

67. NLS, TTA, Dep. 206, Box 5 (d) Edinburgh Corporation (Grants etc.), letter from Depute Clerk to Haynes, 11 August 1964; letter from Traverse Theatre Club (hereafter TTC) to Edinburgh Corporation, 14 August 1964; letter from Weatherstone to Haynes, 26 August 1964.

68. Sheila Colvin, 3 May 2005.

69. NLS, TTA, Dep. 206, Box 5 (c) Arts Council (Grants) 1964–7, circular to TTC members, 24 September 1964.

70. Ibid., letter from Elliott to Weatherstone, 1 March 1965; letter from Depute City Chamberlain to Colvin (TTC secretary), 22 June 1965.

71. Ibid., letter from Arts Council to Haynes, 27 March 1964; letter from Arts Council to Colvin, 29 March 1965; Arts Council of Great Britain Scottish Committee, Scheme for the Promotion of New Drama: Guarantees against Loss 1963/4; letter from Haynes to Mather, 15 May 1965.

72. ECL, Lyceum, *Edinburgh Evening News and Dispatch*, 17 January 1964.

73. ECA, LPC, Edinburgh Civic Theatre Trust Ltd – Lyceum Theatre, Part 1, Minutes of Meeting, 2 March 1965.

74. ECL, Lyceum, *Sunday Times*, 10 October 1965.

75. *The Scotsman*, 15 January 1965. Using the Retail Price Index, the equivalent in 2010 would be £634,000. See Measuring Worth, www.measuringworth.com (last accessed 30 November 2012).

76. ECA, LPC, 4 March 1967.

77. Campbell, *A Brighter Sunshine*, 166–7.

78. ECL, Lyceum, *Evening News and Dispatch*, 17 January 1964.

79. ECL, copies of letters received by town council in connection with Little

Theatre 1960; letter from Edinburgh District of SCDA, 6 October 1960; letter from Committee of Users of Little Theatre, 30 September 1960.

80. See Brown, 'Sport and the Scottish Office'.
81. *The Times*, 5 May 1960; Jenkins, *The Culture Gap*, 53.
82. *The Scotsman*, 17 January 1964.
83. ECL, Civic Theatres: conference in Sunderland 31 October 1963, notes by depute town clerk.
84. Royle, *A Diary of Edinburgh*, 25 September 1965.
85. *The Scotsman*, 17 January 1964.
86. Sinclair, *Arts and Cultures*, 125; Miller, *The Edinburgh International Festival*, 55.
87. *The Scotsman*, 6 August 1966.
88. Moore was a young American Haynes met while in Dublin in 1964. NLS, TTA Acc. 4850, Box 2, copy of letter to Committee of Management signed by J. O. R. Martin, A. K. Elliott and on behalf of J. Walker.
89. Elliott, who had been part of the committee as well as honorary treasurer since the inception of the Traverse, had replaced Haynes as chairman in September 1965 to allow Haynes to separate his artistic and administrative duties. NLS, TTA, Acc. 4850 Box 2, Minutes, 10 September 1965; Minutes, AGM, 27 April 1966.
90. During the AGM it was revealed that 60 per cent of members had not renewed their subscriptions for 1966/7. See NLS, TTA, Minutes, AGM ,27 April 1966.
91. *Express*, undated (estimated April 1966) in Haynes, *Thanks for Coming!*
92. McMillan, *The Traverse Theatre Story*, 29.
93. Haynes, *Thanks for Coming!*, 65.
94. NLS, TTA, Acc. 4850, Minutes, 1 May 1966.
95. Ibid., Minutes, 6 June 1966; Richard Demarco, 2 March 2004.
96. McMillan, *The Traverse Theatre Story*, 31–2.
97. *A Policy for the Arts*, para. 92.
98. A number of arts centres had been funded by the Arts Council in the years following the Second World War, but funding was cut and association withdrawn in 1952. See e.g. Hutchison, *The Politics of the Arts Council*, 47–8.
99. See Chapter 7. NRS, CO1/5/883, Scottish Arts Council 1965–1973, Policy Files, Scottish Education Department (hereafter SED) Circular No. 589: *A Policy for the Arts*.
100. ECL, Lyceum, *EEN*, undated (September 1965).
101. *The Scotsman*, 29 July 1965.
102. *The Scotsman*, 2 August 1965.
103. *The Scotsman*, 22 February 1965; 2 August 1965; 2 March 1964.
104. Calder, *Pursuit*, 279.
105. Hewison, *Too Much*, 88.
106. Brecht's *The Caucasian Chalk Circle* was performed by the Royal Shakespeare Company in 1962. Marowitz et al, *New Theatre Voices*, 135; Priestman, 'A Critical Stage', 129.

107. Copy of TTC brochure in Haynes, *Thanks for Coming!*
108. *The Sun* (undated – estimated September 1964) in Haynes, *Thanks for Coming!*
109. NLS, TTA, Acc. 4850, Minutes, 12 October 1964.
110. *Express*, 5 September 1964; Harewood, *The Tongs and the Bones*, 187.
111. NLS, TTA, Acc. 4850, Minutes, 8 December 1965.
112. Jim Haynes, 17 August 2003.
113. Moffat, *The Edinburgh Fringe*, 59.
114. *The Scotsman*, 19 June 1965; *Wolverhampton Express & Star*, 30 June 1966.
115. *The Observer*, 29 August 1965.
116. Richard Demarco, 2 March 2004.
117. Demarco, ' "Too Rough to Go Slow" '; *The Scotsman*, 19 August 1966.
118. ECA, EFC, Meetings of Programme Advisory Panel, 2 November, 10 November, 15 November and 20 December 1966; Demarco, ' "Too Rough to Go Slow" '.
119. *The Times*, 11 May 1965.
120. Miller, *The Edinburgh International Festival*, 69.
121. *The Scotsman*, 18 February 1967.
122. After increasing its grant in 1964 to £75,000, Edinburgh Corporation 'dropped a bombshell' in July 1967 and cut it to £50,000. Miller, *The Edinburgh International Festival*, 70.
123. ECA, EFP 1965–6, letter from Diamand to Brechin, 2 December 1966.
124. ECA, EFP 1967, 'Future of the King's Theatre, Edinburgh', Notes of a Private Meeting between the Lord Provost, Councillors McLaughlin and Kane, and Mr Peter Donald, Chairman of Howard & Wyndham Limited, 6 October 1966.
125. Ibid., Correspondence re Empire Theatre, August–December 1966.
126. Miller, *The Edinburgh International Festival*, 59.
127. ECA, EFC Programme Advisory Panel, 20 January 1967.
128. *Reports to GA 1967*, 508.
129. See e.g. McLeod, *The Religious Crisis of the 1960s*.
130. ECA, EFP 1965–6, Copy of Address by Peter Howard, Newcastle upon Tyne, 9 November 1964.
131. Les Ballets Africains was created in 1952 in France by Guinean poet Keita Fodeba 'to showcase a vision of justice for Africa by giving witness to the humanity of the black man through its choreography'. When Guinea became independent from France in 1959, the company became the National Ensemble of the Republic of Guinea. Les Ballets Africains de Keita Fodeba, as it was originally known, had also appeared at the Empire Theatre during the 1957 Festival. See 'Les Ballets Africains'.
132. *Express*, 24 August 1964.
133. *Express*, 1 September 1964.
134. *BW*, 21 April 1966. Haynes's reply was published in the following week's issue. See p. 181.
135. BCC, *Sex and Morality*, 74.
136. *BW*, 21 April 1966.

137. Annan also outlined the damage it could do to the theatre, and 'pleaded for the freedom of artistic expression'. *Times*, 22 March 1966; 18 February 1966.
138. *GH*, 15 August 1966.
139. ECA, EFP 1965–6, letter from Duncan to Diamand, 24 March 1966. During the 1960s, Scottish Churches' House in Dunblane ran a series of meetings on cultural themes between representatives of the church and public life. See Fraser, *Ecumenical Adventure*, 25–68.
140. Chambers, *The Continuum Companion to Twentieth Century Theatre*, 231. Dunlop was subsequently director of the Edinburgh International Festival (1983–91).
141. ECA, EFP 1965–6, letter from Revd Longmuir to W. Grahame, 9 February 1966; letter, 16 February 1966.
142. Ibid., letter from Diamand to Lord Provost Brechin, 16 February 1966.
143. Jim Haynes, 12 December 2003.
144. ECA, EFP 1965–6, letter from Colin Chandler to EFS Ltd, 19 February 1965.
145. McMillan, *The Traverse Theatre Story*, 40.
146. *GH*, 6 May 1965.
147. Marwick, *The Sixties*, 352.
148. Sheila Colvin, 3 May 2005.
149. *The Scotsman*, 23 August 1965.
150. ECA, EFC Agendas and Minutes 1966, Draft Report for 1966 AGM.
151. *The Scotsman*, 23 August 1965.
152. NLS, TTA, Acc. 4850, Minutes of TTC, 20 July 1965.
153. ECA EFP 1967, letter from Diamand to Revd John Morrison, 1 March 1967; letter from Morrison to Diamand, 2 March 1967; letter from Lord Provost Brechin to Morrison, 17 February 1967.
154. Chambers, *The Continuum Companion to Twentieth Century Theatre*, 564.
155. *The Times*, 21 June 1967.
156. Meek later became a Conservative councillor for Colinton in Edinburgh. *Express*, 23 August 1967.
157. Buchan had been involved in the People's Festivals of the 1950s (see Chapter 3). *Express*, 30 August 1967.
158. *The Times*, 27 February 1967.
159. *Express*, 23 August 1967.
160. *Express*, 24 August 1967.
161. *Scotsman*, 25 August 1967.
162. *The Times*, 12 September 1967; *The Scotsman*, 23 August 1967.
163. McLeod, *The Religious Crisis of the 1960s*, 87–9.
164. *BW*, 28 April 1966; 12 May 1966.
165. *BW*, 29 June 1967.
166. See *BW* 1960–1970.
167. Laing, 'Economy, Society and Culture in 1960s Britain', 23.
168. *The Scotsman*, 22 July 1967.

169. *BW*, 10 August 1967.
170. *Express*, 4 September 1967.
171. *Times*, 23–24 February 1968.
172. McLeod, *The Religious Crisis of the 1960s*, 67.
173. Williams, *The Long Revolution*, 29–33.

7

Cultural Crisis? Protest and Reaction, 1968–1970

The world appeared to erupt in 1968. Major upheavals and a wave of rebellion unfolded across the globe: increasing levels of opposition to the Vietnam War (in the aftermath of the Tet Offensive, which had been launched in January), the Prague Spring (March), *les événements* in Paris (May), violent struggles during the Democratic Convention in Chicago (August), major student revolts (including in Belgrade, Tokyo and Mexico City), and student protests and sit-ins in a number of British universities (including Leeds, the LSE and Sussex). Also in 1968, Martin Luther King and Robert Kennedy were assassinated, and Enoch Powell made his famous 'Rivers of Blood' speech.[1] The year came to be seen as a 'watershed' for the peaceful 'love' revolution of 1967, as 'the contradictions between what the post-war generation had been educated to expect and the reality of the world around them' was revealed.[2] Growing economic difficulties in Britain contributed to a sense that the consensus and affluence of the post-war years were coming to an end.[3] Catherine Itzin remarked:

> Rarely can one year be singled out as an isolated turning point, but in the case of 1968 so many events coincided on a global scale that it clearly marked the end of an era in a historically unprecedented fashion, and the beginning of a period of equally unprecedented political consciousness and activism.[4]

The very nature of what was 'political' was being fundamentally redefined, captured in the expression 'the personal is the political'.[5] This, combined with the influence of the high-profile counter-culture, reintroduced a clear political agenda in the arts and helped to unleash a new generation of artists and theatre practitioners who sought to use new forms to express challenge and conflict. The ideas and forms experimented with in the late 1950s and early 1960s, and developed through the counter-culture of the High Sixties, were developing in new ways. The Situationist International, central to *les événements* in Paris, argued that society was but a spectacle, 'a false projection which masks our alienation from our true selves'.[6] But, as Michael Billington has asked, 'if society was becoming a theatrical spectacle, where did that leave the theatre? What was its role in the newly liberated High Sixties?'[7]

These questions were being asked in the Festival City. By the time the Festival had responded to the changes of the mid-1960s and included experimental theatre in its programme in 1967, another cultural shift was underway. There was a 'theatrical outburst' of street theatre, community and theatre-in-education movements, touring and communal troupes, and 'arts labs', influenced by American and European experimental theatre, the ethos of the 1960s counter-culture and earlier assaults on barriers between 'art' and 'life'.[8] These groups had less need for conventional theatre spaces, and put more emphasis on spontaneity and less on the text (and on directors and performers more than playwrights). The People Show (founded in 1966), for example, favoured starting with 'creative ideas' over a script.[9] The increasing emphasis on improvisation was aided by the passing of the Theatres Act in July 1968, which finally freed theatre from the control of the Lord Chamberlain's office and its requirement that scripts be approved in advance, putting it on the same footing as literature.[10] The musical *Hair*, directed by Tom O'Horgan, opened in London on 27 September 1968, the day after the Lord Chamberlain's jurisdiction ended. With its naked cast members, swearing and strong anti-Vietnam war message, *Hair* symbolised a sense of liberation. But these developments were not universally welcomed, and from 1967 there was a backlash against the liberalisation of arts and society. In Edinburgh, this came to be seen in regular scandals over drama on the Festival, Fringe and Traverse Theatre stages.

ARTS LABS AND FRINGE THEATRE

In July 1967, Jim Haynes created the Arts Lab in London. Based in a warehouse in Drury Lane, Covent Garden, the Arts Lab formed an experiment in 'art-and-life-style' that hosted multi-media events, films, drama and all manner of artistic experiments. Its aim was to provide 'a participatory creative and community environment within which there is enough latitude to include every type of spectacle and experience that a particular group can conceive of or organise'.[11] In *New Society*, James Allen reported that activities at the London Arts Lab included 'solitary guitar-playing in the first-floor café-gallery, Warhol-type films viewed lying on one's back in the basement, and the all-encompassing spectacle of the People Show (leaping lights, amplified music, projected film and bouncing, ubiquitous actors).'[12] The Arts Lab had 'an enormous impact', providing a base for the growing fringe theatre movement, and was either the impetus for or home of groups such as Portable Theatre, Freehold, Pip Simmons and the People Show.[13] After it closed in October 1969, groups like these helped to create 'a nationwide circuit of arts labs, campuses and youth clubs in which to display their highly individual wares to young and enthusiastic audiences'.[14]

This 'new' fringe theatre was particularly associated with the London counter-culture and inspired by its mediums (demonstrations, rock music, the underground press) and oppositional ethos.[15] During the late 1960s, the meaning of 'fringe' had widened. In arts terms, it was no longer simply a shorthand description for something that was not part of the official Edinburgh International Festival but also encompassed a type of theatre or performance, approach to the performing arts, emphasis on new writing or experimental work, or ethos.[16] It is difficult to pinpoint exactly when this shift occurred. The producer of the Oxford Theatre Group had reflected on their experiences in Edinburgh in 1955, and referred to a planned 'attempt, based on the lesson learned by amateurs at Riddles Court, to work out a new and distinctive style' as a result of the 'unified style which we have accidentally come across through living and working together at Riddles Court'.[17] This hothouse way of living and working together, necessary to avoid financial ruin while on the Edinburgh Fringe, became increasingly common from the mid-1960s. Groups like Living Theatre and The People Show began living and working together as a collective (often while travelling around), leading to new ways of creating theatre, and extending the act of breaking down the distinctions between 'art' and 'life' so associated with the cultural shifts of the 1960s.[18] The boundaries between art forms were increasingly fluid too. Links between the music scene and the new performing arts scene were especially pronounced at this time. These could be seen, for example, in the work of Mark Boyle and Joan Hills, whose performance-based light projections found a new audience in underground clubs such as UFO and Middle Earth, and with groups like Soft Machine and Pink Floyd. During the 1967 Fringe, Boyle and Soft Machine had performed at the Traverse Theatre Club in a show described as an 'all action, lights, music, noise, colour, freak-out'.[19] Theatre increasingly drew upon dance and other forms of physical performance, influenced in part by the American alternative theatres like Joseph Chaikin, Living Theatre and La MaMa.[20]

Despite this American input to fringe theatre, it is the Edinburgh connection that deserves most attention. John Ashford, theatre editor of *Time Out* between 1969 and 1973, said that when he introduced the new category of 'Fringe Theatre' to the magazine's theatre listings, he named it after the Edinburgh Festival Fringe:

> Edinburgh has 'invitees' at the main Festival and a Fringe of the uninvited who shack up in any old village hall. The latter was an appropriate model for what was happening in London, where people were taking over spaces not designed for theatre.[21]

The emphasis at the Festival Fringe on experimentation with new ideas in conjunction with 'the right to fail' made Edinburgh 'an important area of fertilisation for alternative theatre' and also contributed to the ethos of fringe theatre.[22] The importance of the Festival City as a 'laboratory' for new ideas and space that fostered directors, playwrights and performers cannot be emphasised enough.

Of course, Edinburgh was not the only place in Britain where artistic experiments were being conducted during the early 1960s. New writing and performance ideas were encouraged at a range of theatres, including Joan Littlewood's Theatre Workshop (established in 1945), Stephen Joseph's Theatre in the Round in Scarborough (1955), the Hampstead Theatre Club (1960), Arnold Wesker's Centre 42 (1960), the Royal Shakespeare Company (1961) and the Close Theatre Club in Glasgow (1965). Yet, over 1965–6 regular complaints were made about a lack of new voices and ideas. Charles Marowitz told *Plays and Players* that the theatre magazine *Encore*, which folded in November 1965, had done so due to a 'malaise in theatre':

> Up to the present, no new or distinctive voices have risen out of the smouldering sixties to challenge or disrupt proceedings, and the Alternative Theatre, those fervent groups of artistic discontents on which the health of any theatre relies, are – as yet – nowhere to be found.[23]

But many new ideas were at this time being tried out at the Edinburgh Festival Fringe and the Traverse Theatre.

In an interview with Haynes in May 1966, *Plays and Players* reported that the policy of presenting new plays at the Traverse drew national press attention, in turn attracting new scripts, directors and performers. This had also tempted commercial managements to Edinburgh and helped increase transfers to London (for example, *Happy End* transferred to the Royal Court in 1964). The Traverse had quickly become a 'beacon' in the theatre scene in 1960s Britain. Max Stafford-Clark, who started out as a stage manager at the Traverse in spring 1966, commented that the smaller size of the Traverse meant that you could 'take many more risks'. Furthermore, 'Edinburgh was a city which, because of its annual Festival, was accustomed to experiment and so it welcomed that'.[24] Although not a theatre director per se, Haynes had 'cut his teeth' in Edinburgh, and later became one of the central figures in the 'explosion' of arts labs and experimental theatre in the late 1960s.[25] The Arts Lab, too, was a model for many of the arts centres that sprang up around Britain from the late 1960s. Major directors such as Marowitz, Geoff Moore and Tom O'Horgan all stage-managed or directed work at the Traverse during its early years.[26] Marowitz regularly worked at the Traverse between 1964 and 1966, including the London Traverse season at the Jeanetta Cochrane Theatre in 1966, and had also been involved in creating the happening at the 1963 International Drama Conference. In 1964, he had worked with Peter Brook on the seminal Theatre of Cruelty season at LAMDA, and in 1968 founded the influential Open Space Theatre in London as a hub for international new writing and experiments in acting and design. Moore, who had a stint as a stage manager in the Traverse in

1965, was in 1969 the founder director of Moving Being, a mixed-media experimental theatre group. Dig a little deeper, and you find that many figures well known in the dramatic arts were influenced by attending the Festival, or even did a show on the Fringe in their youth. The first British appearance of La MaMa was in Edinburgh in 1967, at which a number of theatre practitioners experienced their first encounter with their influential style.[27] La MaMa's success in Edinburgh 'led directly' to a transfer to London's Mercury Theatre, and from there to the larger Vaudeville Theatre in the West End. Playwright John Arden wrote to *The Times*:

> What they have managed to do with both *Futz* and *Tom Paine* is to arouse a quite remarkable degree of excitement among informed and receptive theatre workers in this city [. . .] La MaMa Troupe's visit here is going to have a very great effect upon the work done in England over the next few years. I know my writing is already being influenced considerably.[28]

The critical acclaim received during their visits to Edinburgh and London in 1967 also opened doors for La MaMa in their native America, and led to transfers to Off-Broadway as well as a film version of *Futz* (released in 1969).[29]

O'Horgan and La MaMa also profoundly influenced Stafford-Clark during their time in Edinburgh in 1967, when Stafford-Clark was in the role of associate director of the Traverse (he became assistant director from spring 1968, when Gordon McDougall left). Both McDougall and Stafford-Clark had directed a series of pieces by Paul Foster, a regular writer for Café La MaMa, in spring 1967.[30] Stafford-Clark took leave at the beginning of 1968 to work with La MaMa in the USA, and on his return pitched the idea of engaging 'a permanent theatre workshop to experiment and improvise and, from time to time, present plays'.[31] In a memo for the Traverse Committee of Management, he pointed out that in addition to continuing to encourage and develop new playwrights,

> I feel it's time the Traverse experimented in another direction as well. For some time different groups in Europe and America have been trying to find a new theatre language and new ways of presenting plays. Simply, there's a growing dissatisfaction with actors standing on a stage making speeches and people sitting in an audience listening. This 'movement' is growing towards additional methods of expressing emotion and feeling, through voices, through dance movement, and through a much greater physical involvement.[32]

A permanent company of actors was formed to explore workshop-style productions in 1968, with its first production, *Dracula*, in February 1969. During Stafford-Clark's time as artistic director, the Traverse tried out more workshop-style techniques and improvisation in theatre production. Stafford-Clark told the 1968 AGM that he aimed 'to maintain an avant-garde theatre in Edinburgh, not just a small theatre with a new-play policy'.[33] It embarked upon tours outside Britain, including to Boston, Baalbek (Lebanon) and Amsterdam.[34] Links were also made with the new experimental theatre spaces in London, with transfers to the Open Space and the Arts Lab. Fringe theatre came north too, with groups such as the Pip Simmons Theatre Group, the Freehold, American Theatre Project and the People Show performing in Edinburgh – the latter appearing frequently at the Traverse throughout 1968. But, after initial successes, there was a 'slide' in both audiences and membership of the Traverse from spring 1969.[35] Furthermore, the club was forced to move from Kelly's Paradise after internal floors in the James Court building were declared 'unsafe' in early 1969. The Committee of Management had to move quickly to find and refit suitable premises in time for the 1969 Festival, with the Minister for the Arts, Jennie Lee, formally opening the new, larger Traverse Theatre at 112 West Bow in the Grassmarket area of the city on 24 August 1969. Stafford-Clark resigned in November 1969 to be director of the Traverse Workshop Company, which based itself in the 'old Traverse' and whose first productions opened on 30 July 1970, and Michael Rudman was appointed artistic director of the Traverse in February 1970.[36]

The elements that had made the Traverse so distinctive and exciting when it first opened were becoming more widespread and, to some extent, institutionalised, as theatre clubs and experimental drama became standard in the world of subsidised theatre. In 1969, for example, the Royal Court opened its Theatre Upstairs, one of the first 'black box' studios opened by a mainstream theatre, although the critic B. A. Young pointed out in 1971 that the Traverse was still 'arguably the most influential theatre in our island, from which so many of the Theatre Upstairs's successes emanate, and others too, like those at the Open Space'.[37] With the development of the Lyceum Theatre in Edinburgh, too, the Traverse 'no longer had the automatic kudos of being the only serious, internationally-aware theatre in the Festival City'.[38] Under first Tom Fleming and then, from 1966, Clive Perry, the Lyceum followed 'a brave and restless policy' as it presented a wide range of drama that included international contemporary writing. Richard Eyre, the Lyceum's associate director, also opened it up to a range of other activities, including poetry readings (many organised by Alan Bold) and folk concerts.[39] When he resigned as artistic director of the Traverse, Stafford-Clark commented that it 'now stands uneasily somewhere between an Arts Lab and a conventional repertory theatre'. It acted as a base for visiting theatre groups as well as producing its own plays, but there was some uncertainty about its future – perhaps, McMillan mused, reflecting 'a general unease among organisations that had grown up in the 60's as the decade drew to a close'.[40]

Being the site of a summer holiday arts festival sometimes worked against

Edinburgh. During August, it attracted critics, performers, journalists and audiences from all over the world for a three-week cultural feast. But for the rest of the year, critical attention remained largely focused upon the London metropolis rather than the Scottish capital (or, indeed, any other 'regional' city). In August 1968, *New Society* observed:

> Edinburgh comes to life for three brief weeks during the festival and spends the rest of the year in a sort of all-season hibernation: that's the conventional view of the place, and, in spite of isolated efforts like the Traverse Theatre, there's a great deal of justice in it.[41]

A number of plays first performed in the Festival City were described as premieres when performed later in London. McDougall complained about this to the editor of *Plays and Players* in April 1967. Citing the recent examples of Alfred Jarry's *Ubu Roi* and D. H. Lawrence's *The Daughter in Law*, both 'premiered' at the Royal Court in London after having already been performed at the Traverse in Edinburgh, he pointed out that the pretence continued that 'a play is not worth looking at until it has been given the seal of approval of a London theatre'. He continued:

> [The fact that] Britain has other cities – even capital cities – and that some theatres in these cities have for many years been doing more adventurous work than any London theatre, has so far not penetrated outside the cities themselves and certain parts of the theatre profession.[42]

McDougall also raised this with the Scottish Arts Council (SAC). The 1966 production of *Ubu Roi* at the Royal Court was announced as the British public premiere, despite the Traverse having produced the play in both April and August 1963. Furthermore, *The Daughter-in-Law* had been 'discovered' by McDougall in 1965, granted rights for its first performance at the Traverse in 1966, and first performed in January 1967. It got 'excellent notices', leading to invitations from both the International Theatre Club and a commercial management to present the play in London. However, while the play was still being performed at the Traverse in Edinburgh, the rights for London were offered to and accepted by the Royal Court and, like *Ubu Roi*, billed as the first 'public performance' with no acknowledgement of the Traverse production. Part of the problem stemmed from the Traverse being a club, therefore its premieres were not strictly 'public'. But, argued McDougall, there must be 'some protection and safeguard for the interests and reputation of a theatre which does not have the publicity pull of the Court, but is doing original work which is then usurped'. Such billings, he said, were 'deliberately misleading'.[43] Edinburgh, in some ways, was viewed as a dress rehearsal for the 'real' audiences of London. Certainly, McDougall had sought to continue (and extend) the pattern of transferring Traverse productions to London, which could bring in extra funds. The 'discovery myth' of the Fringe had been underlined with the so-called 'Fringe fairytale' of *Rosencrantz and Guildenstern are Dead* in 1966, which attracted those looking for their big break or to see the 'next big thing'.[44] In September 1968, a writer for *Tribune* magazine had pointed out being 'struck [. . .] on one of those interminable Scottish sabbaths, how much better equipped London has recently become to accommodate a "fringe" of its own'. In the summer, he noted, artists 'inexplicably decamp' to Edinburgh, despite there being better facilities than 'drill halls' in London: 'Personally I enjoy an annual busman's holiday across the border: but objectively, a south drift would make better economic artistic sense.'[45] But, clearly, the Festival City retained its pull, and despite the proliferation of fringe theatre in London, the Scottish capital still drew fringe groups throughout the year.

The winds of change affected the Church of Scotland, too. In summer 1967, the Home Board decided to close down the Gateway Theatre. In many ways, the Lyceum civic theatre was the 'lineal continuation' of the Gateway Theatre Company, which had been wound up when the Edinburgh Civic Theatre Trust was established.[46] Although the Gateway was still functioning as a theatre, the Kirk felt that it had become outdated. The situation in 1967, the Home Board noted, is 'radically different from that of 1945', when it was first donated the Elm Row property. 'This new situation demands a new kind of initiative.' Reporting to the General Assembly in 1968, the Home Board stated:

> The Kirk, through the Home Board, believes as strongly as ever that there is a continuing service which it can render to the Arts, and plans are being laid to initiate another enterprise which, it is hoped, will be a relevant expression of the Church's concern in this field during the 'seventies'.[47]

All public performances at the Gateway ceased in December 1967, and the main part of the building was sold to Scottish Television in autumn 1968 (and developed as the first colour television studio in Scotland). Later that year, the Home Board decided to use the proceeds of the sale to build an arts centre on the site of the recently demolished Moray-Knox Church in the High Street, situated on the Royal Mile next to John Knox House. The Board felt that it could provide a 'window on the Church' for the thousands of visitors who passed up and down the High Street of Edinburgh each year.[48] Suitable workrooms for the Home Board Audio Visual Production Unit were also required. The General Assembly of 1969 approved the decision of the Home Board to build in Edinburgh's Royal Mile, (almost exactly) at the old Netherbow.[49] 'A most imaginative concept' was submitted by Home Board architect Harry Taylor and unanimously approved. The building, which would have a 'recognisable relationship' with John Knox House, was to include an open court with a coffee room and exhibition space at street level,

'an intimate auditorium, with seventy permanent seats and an "end stage"'
below street level, and projection and lighting control rooms at the rear of the
auditorium. Upper floors were to include a medium-sized hall and several
rooms as well as premises for the AV Production Unit.[50] The Netherbow, as
it was named, was to form a space for those interested in the arts to meet and
share ideas, and was designed to be flexible to changing needs:

> Meetings, dialogues and talks will certainly be considered, as will film
> programmes and conferences. It is hoped that 'workshop' groups will be
> formed in drama and music or 'multi-media' (acting, mime, films, stills, etc.).
> These activities may not end in public presentation – or they may – but those
> taking part will have experienced and benefited.[51]

The proposed videotape recording and closed-circuit television could be used
for exhibitions and meetings, or a 'group might be formed to rehearse and
ultimately record on video tape a short play, programme or "happening"'.[52]
The Kirk had updated its engagement with the arts to reflect the new artistic
climate of the late 1960s and early 1970s.[53]

THE FESTIVAL CITY AND ARTS GOVERNANCE IN A NEW CLIMATE

Iain Crawford, first publicity director of the Festival from 1973, wrote that
the 'advent of the 1968 Festival was ponderous with ill omens'. These
included the loss of two British opera premieres due to the lack of a proper
opera house in the city, petty bickering with the corporation over EFS
building signs, and ongoing financial problems.[54] Peter Diamand also
experienced difficulties planning the 1969 Festival programme due to the
'uncertainty' of the corporation grant to the Festival, and throughout 1968
had his attention drawn to a 'growing resistance within Edinburgh Corporation to the Festival, and particularly to the allocation of funds'.[55] The Festival
had also lost out on Pop Theatre, which had been so successful in 1967, when
it opted to go elsewhere, but had engaged the revolutionary Polish director
Jerzy Grotowski and his Laboratory Theatre to present *Acropolis*. *The Times*
described it as 'by far the biggest theatrical catch' for the Festival, telling
readers that 'Grotowski enjoys a god-like status among the experimental
troupes of the west'.[56] This was the first appearance of Grotowski and
Laboratory Theatre in Britain, and was completely booked out. However, as
part of what Crawford called 'the jinx element' of the 1968 Festival, the
opening night had to be cancelled and the audience turned away when
specially balanced wheelbarrows required for the performance disappeared
en route to Edinburgh.[57]

That year, the Festival was also the scene of angry protest when the
invasion of Czechoslovakia by Soviet troops on 20 August called into
question the engagement of the USSR State Orchestra for two concerts,

due to take place days later. Although requests to cancel or boycott the concerts failed, demonstrators were able to make their feelings known with loud protests and pickets outside the performances.[58] The Citizens' Theatre Company production of Bertolt Brecht's *The Resistible Rise of Arturo Ui*, part of the official Festival drama programme, included in their last caption slide not Hitler (as expected), but the Russians entering Czechoslovakia.[59] *The Times* drama critic, Irving Wardle, praised the play, pointing out it 'has taken on a fresh and astounding timeliness in the light of the Czech invasion'.[60]

By the late 1960s, contemporary theatre had become more conspicuous on the official Festival stage. The Fringe also began to attract more professional groups, performers from further afield, and companies formed specifically for the Fringe Festival. It became trickier to easily distinguish between Festival and Fringe drama offerings, as the same groups often performed on the 'official' and 'unofficial' programmes (like La MaMa in 1967), transfers took place between the Festival and the Fringe, and the Festival included more contemporary experimental theatre. In 1970, Peter Diamand even put on the Festival's first rock musical, *Stomp*, in Haymarket Ice Rink. Performed by the Combine, a young American company, Michael Billington wrote for *The Times*: 'Even if the cast have been prevailed on not to strip during their Edinburgh run, it still counts as something of a break-through for this multi-media rock musical to be staged as part of the official festival.'[61] Teatro Libero's *Orlando Furioso*, which also took place in Haymarket Ice Rink in 1970, produced 'an entirely new experience in the theatre'.[62] One critic reported:

> There are no seats; we wander at will over the floor, running for our lives when one of the great trollies, bearing a Knight on horseback, or a sea monster, or a hollow mountain, comes swooping down on us, swift and silent under the control of the army of stage hands.[63]

Referring to these productions, B. A. Young wrote in the *Financial Times* that Edinburgh's official programme was 'notably more adventurous than usual' whereas the Fringe 'seems to be relaxing into conservatism'.[64]

The Fringe had by 1969 reached fifty-seven groups presenting more than 100 shows, and by 1971, there were seventy-eight companies. This was beginning to overwhelm the FFS, which was still staffed by volunteers. After seeking professional advice, the Edinburgh Fringe Society Ltd was created on 22 May 1969 and in December 1970, John Milligan was appointed as the first professional (part-time) Fringe administrator. This was to mark a major shift, as the Fringe became professionalised and, with increased administration and organisation, grew in size – in 1974, it outsold the official Festival for the first time, and has continued to do so almost every year since. After a long period of opposition and 'bureaucratic cold war' between Festival and

Fringe, the growing 'artistic co-operation' between the two developed into a recognition that each was part of the same whole, and in 1969 the Fringe was finally allowed a mention in the official Festival programme.[65] While the official Festival had tended to focus more on music, and the Fringe on the dramatic arts, by the late 1960s a wider range of art forms could be seen in both. Chamber music was part of the Fringe offerings in 1968, and it increasingly began to attract professional music groups acquiring 'a reputation for complementing the Festival's interest in large scale popular works with small scale, unusual pieces for those with an informed interest in music'. There was also an increase in mime, dance (including ballet), and contemporary visual arts on the Fringe.

The Festival, too, widened its parameters to include more contemporary visual art. After the success of the Open 100 exhibition in 1967, Richard Demarco was given responsibility for the Festival's contemporary art exhibitions. His seminal event came in 1970 with Strategy: Get Arts. André Thomkins created the palindrome, which Tom Normand writes 'caused nearly as much consternation as the array of artists included in the show'.[66] Organised by Demarco in conjunction with the Kunsthalle Düsseldorf, this ground-breaking exhibition brought a number of avant-garde artists from Düsseldorf to Edinburgh College of Art, including Bernd and Hilla Becher, Sigmar Polke, Gerhard Richter and Joseph Beuys.[67] Strategy: Get Arts was to be hugely influential in Scotland, Britain and further afield. It was the first exhibition of contemporary German art in Britain since 1938, and the first time that the work of Beuys, now a hugely influential and internationally admired contemporary artist, had been shown to the English-speaking world.[68] This major exhibition of new work offered a powerful example of how the visual arts and performance were being combined in new ways, and showcased the work of a number of artists associated with the international Fluxus movement. This originated in New York in the 1950s and brought together spontaneity, playfulness, protest, anti-art, happenings, 'unity of art and life' and other features. It is complex and difficult to define. Fluxus artist Dick Higgins wrote that 'Fluxus is not a moment in history, or an art movement. Fluxus is a way of doing things, a tradition, and a way of life and death.'[69]

Strategy: Get Arts attracted a great deal of media attention. *The Scotsman* described it as a 'massive happening'. John Martin, co-founder of the Demarco Gallery and designer of the exhibition programme, recalled:

Like many who saw it when it opened, I was amazed at the wonderland of the German avant-garde art scene which had transformed the staid art college building where I had previously studied [. . .] Lasting impressions included: Rinke's 'water-snake' which you had to dodge past at the entrance (firemen from the neighbouring fire station had a field-day helping to set it up!); Weseler's furry objects in a darkened studio which suddenly (and alarmingly!) twitched as you looked at them; Daniel Spoerri's 'Banana Trap' Dinner where mashed potato was made up to look like ice cream – the caterer, Ann Smith, had to deal with a revolt by her staff over the use of chicken embryos in one of the dishes; one was vaguely aware of the intermittently slamming door engineered by Günther Uecker, and his 'wall of knives (blunted by police)' made a threatening passage to negotiate [. . .] Beuys and Henning Christiansen did their mesmerising performances of 'Celtic (Kinloch Rannoch) Scottish Symphony' in one of the ground floor studios watched intently by, among others, Robin Philipson; the entrance stairway was littered with Wewerka's broken chairs, with Palermo's primary-coloured stripes around the frieze high above; and Beuys' 'The Pack' of course was unforgettable.[70]

Cordelia Oliver wrote that Strategy: Get Arts 'marked a significant, immensely influential milestone in the arts in Scotland. Yet, at the time, the art establishment of Edinburgh for the most part found itself in a state of shock.'[71] Demarco called it 'explosive', a 'turning point in the development of twentieth century art'.[72] Beuys was inspired by the landscape of Scotland, having been taken on a tour around the Highlands by Demarco, and this was to inform his work both during Strategy: Get Arts and in the following years. Responding to shifts like that highlighted by Strategy: Get Arts, the SAC announced plans in 1972 to create an arts workshop centre for Scotland, as exhibitions in formal galleries were no longer

> the type most favoured by younger people or by some others involved with the arts who prefer a less formal atmosphere and the possibility of combining visual arts with other media and with social contacts. We know that the now prevalent idea that the value of art is in the doing and not the production of objects [. . .] blurs the distinction between the studio/workshop and the exhibition space, and has created a demand for the arts workshop or arts laboratory.[73]

In 1968, in the introduction to that year's annual report of the Arts Council, the chairman, Lord Goodman, wrote:

> I believe that the last thirty years in this country has demonstrated a profound social change. Within our society there is now a widespread feeling that the provision of drama and music and painting and culture in all its broadest aspects is no longer to be regarded as a privilege for a few but is the democratic right of the entire community.[74]

The recommendations of A Policy for the Arts were being implemented. Between 1965/6 and 1968/9, the funds available to the Arts Council doubled, new arts buildings were springing up across the country, and a wider range of arts and artists were being funded.[75] In Scotland, the creation of the SAC in

1967 in conjunction with the reintroduction of the Goschen formula in 1965 had increased the funding available to support the arts, while the extension of the Royal Charter in 1967 allowed the SAC to more effectively encourage and support activity in Scotland.[76]

Figure 7.1 Richard Demarco and Joseph Beuys, pictured in Inveraray, 1970. (© Richard Demarco, the Demarco Archives)

From its first festival in 1964, the Craigmillar Festival of Drama, Music and the Arts had developed to combine the arts and sport with social action. One of its objectives was 'to make the residents of Craigmillar more aware of the talent which exists in the district, and to encourage people to take a more active part in drama in its broadest sense, and music'.[77] It also focused political and social issues and politicised many locals. Its slogan was 'Community concern, care and action for social change through culture'.[78] In 1968, with rising unemployment and poverty badly affecting the scheme, the Festival Society offered support not just through the opportunity to become involved in the Festival, but also by organising playgroups and playschemes for children. That year, the Craigmillar Labour Party (in which the festival's founder, Helen Crummy, was also active) produced a play called *The Emancipation of Women* to celebrate fifty years of the vote as well as to 'rally women and show just how great had been the female contribution to the life of our country'. In 1969, Craigmillar had even had street theatre when Edinburgh Theatre Workshop worked with 'Mr Magic', the circus performer Reg Bolton.[79] The Craigmillar Festival was to develop in the

1970s into an influential and widely cited example of how culture and community action could work in practice.

The shift from private patronage to public subsidy in the arts resulted in more attention being given to the importance of community engagement. In March 1969, the Saltire Society held a weekend conference on the community and the arts in Scotland, inviting representatives of local and planning authorities, development corporations and interested societies.[80] The flowering of community arts in the 1970s was partly a reaction against the social and professional exclusivity that characterised much of the activity supported by the Arts Council. The work of community artists cut across the distinctions between professional and amateur, and sought to stimulate wider participation in the arts.[81] This was to become a more central aim of the Arts Council as the shifts that began in the 1960s took hold (although spending on these was curbed as economic difficulties gripped in the mid-1970s).

The Arts Council also experienced difficulties in trying to keep up with the shift from the kind of experimental theatre that had developed in the High Sixties to the more politicised and spontaneous forms that spread in the aftermath of the watershed events of 1968. The social and cultural upheavals that had taken place in the post-war period also called for different responses. The Education Act (1944) had come to fruition, with an expansion in higher education. Twenty-two new universities were founded in Britain between 1961 and 1969, which Robert Hutchison points out is equal to the number founded in the 700 years between 1249 and 1954.[82] More emphasis was also being put on children's theatre and coverage of the arts in the school curriculum. In 1968, James Kellas wrote that 'the notion of a liberal education has never in modern times included cultivation of the Arts such as painting and sculpture, music, drama and modern literature', leading directly to a shortage of creative artists in Scotland. Time on these subjects was largely 'grudged' and seen as 'non profitable in academic terms'. 'The attitudes of teachers to the arts', continued Kellas, 'is transmitted to Scottish life as a whole, and materialism and puritanism combine to strangle many cultural pursuits. Such ventures as the Edinburgh Festival and the repertory theatres, for example, are frequently attacked and are directed mainly by non-Scots.'[83] But, as Euan McArthur highlights, these problems were beginning to be addressed by the Scottish Committee of the Arts Council (SAC from 1967), who, brought closer to the Scottish Education Department after the 1965 White Paper, were exploring ways of stimulating interest in the arts in Scotland by engaging with schoolchildren and looking into the formation of regional arts associations.[84]

The spread of television also played a part. Tom Fleming referred in November 1967 to audiences becoming much more 'critically minded in recent years', attributed in part to television, which had helped to develop 'the sincerity of acting. The theatre's function', he went on, 'had suddenly been sharpened and made more exciting.'[85] The Arts Council had to respond, and make sure that young people and more experimental work were catered for (as Jennie Lee had argued in her White Paper). At the end of 1968, it set up its first subcommittee to investigate new activities. This produced an interim report in May 1969, after which a full New Activities Committee, which required half of its members to be young people, was created. In 1970, it reported: 'New Activities, in almost all their manifestations, can be seen as a concerted response and reaction by a section of the present younger generation – together with certain intellectuals and artists of an older generation – to the prevailing established culture.'[86] But despite the interest and activity stimulated by the New Activities Committee between 1968 and 1970, the Arts Council ultimately made no separate allocation for new activities or experimental projects in 1970/1 and the panel was wound up.[87]

THE BACKLASH AGAINST PERMISSIVENESS

An increasingly concerted reaction against many of the social and cultural shifts of the 1960s was becoming apparent. In 1968, John Calder had created the Society for the Defence of Literature and the Arts in response to a growing reaction against permissiveness.[88] In London, the Metropolitan Police even had a vigorous Obscene Publications Squad and regular raids took place on the underground press, high-profile musicians and counter-cultural venues (including the Arts Lab).[89] Robert Hewison has argued that as 'the guardians of traditional culture became more and more alarmed, drugs were increasingly the issue over which the authorities and the avant-garde came into critical conflict'.[90] After an Appeal Court ruling that allowed Calder to publish *Last Exit to Brooklyn* in June 1968, the Arts Council responded to increasing anxieties about obscenity by convening a conference and setting up a working party to explore existing obscenity laws in Britain. Reporting in July 1969, it argued that the obscenity laws should either be repealed or withdrawn for a period of five years, but when its report was offered to the Labour government, its recommendations were ignored.[91] This helped to set the scene for the major obscenity trials of the early 1970s. The new Minister for the Arts, David Eccles, who replaced Jennie Lee when the Conservatives took power in 1970, spoke out in Parliament against the Arts Council's use of public money to support 'works which affront the religious beliefs or outrage the sense of decency of a large body of tax-payers' and frequently clashed with Lord Goodman over the issue.[92] In November 1970, three of *IT*'s editors were taken to court on a charge of 'conspiring to corrupt morals and public decency' by printing personal ads placed by homosexuals. The following year, the 'longest obscenity trial in history' took place when three editors of *Oz* were charged after the 'School Kids Issue', put together in conjunction with schoolchildren, resulted in a number of charges, including conspiracy to corrupt young children.[93] High profile groups like the National Viewers' and Listeners' Association and the Festival of Light attempted to return to a morality founded upon traditional Christian values. 'This backlash', argue Roger Davidson and Gayle Davies, 'was also experienced in Scotland where the puritan lobby south of the Border attracted significant support from both church and civic leaders'.[94]

The arrival of the 'permissive society' was both recognised and resisted in Scotland. In 1970, the introduction to the Church of Scotland's Moral Welfare Committee report noted that the content of the report 'afford[s] ample evidence of the existence of what is most often referred to as our "permissive society"'. It continued:

> For better or worse, we have entered upon an era when men and women will claim the right to decide, free from all dictation and direction by any authority, how they will conduct themselves and live their lives. Need the Church always deplore this new 'permissiveness' as an unalloyed disaster? If the sanctions of commandment and convention are gone, people are set free to respond to goodness for its own sake, under no compulsion, constrained and sustained by the love of Christ and not by the fear of a lost respectability.[95]

But to what extent had permissiveness made a mark on Scottish society? In 1969, the Report of the Social and Moral Welfare Board stated that 'one of the big battles for the soul of modern man is being fought on the field of personal morality, and not least where drink, drugs, money and sex are concerned', with the purveying of these on the 'vast scale of today' causing concern.[96] Between 1968 and 1970, the Kirk's Moral Welfare Committee laid bare evidence of the permissive society in Scotland. The reports referred to growing problems with alcoholism, family breakdown and gambling, and even the appearance of a 'drug scene' in Scotland. In 1968, the Moral Welfare Committee had not been too concerned about drug addiction in Scotland, and although it highlighted a problem 'of some magnitude' among married women taking amphetamines, it noted that it was difficult to gauge levels of drug use.[97] By 1970, three types of LSD had been found in Glasgow (Strawberry Fields, Purple Haze and Osley's), cannabis addiction was on the rise, and there was also a 'critical rise in [alcohol] addiction among young people'.[98] In 1971, under the heading 'Drug Scene', references to the counter-culture pervaded the Report of the Committee on Moral Welfare.[99] Referring to the challenges being faced by the Kirk, it stated: 'Timothy Leary asks of us: "If your adviser is against LSD, what is he for? If he forbids you the psychedelic key to revelation, what does he offer you instead?" It is a fair question.' There was 'no ultimate answer' to the protests of the young 'against the dull respectability of traditional values' but for the Church to show the importance of Christ: 'It is not without relevance to note that it was within a rejected sub-culture that the message and the ministry of Jesus came with telling force.'[100]

Representatives of local government increasingly took it upon themselves to try to police obscenity. Throughout the 1960s, the Edinburgh City Prosecutor had actively enforced the obscene publications clauses of local Corporation Acts. Some local powers were extended and 'more vigorously exercised'. In 1973, Edinburgh even experienced its own 'obscenity trial' when the publishers of the underground magazine *Cracker* 'were successfully prosecuted under the Edinburgh Corporation Act for publishing an indecent cartoon'.[101] Less formal policing took place too. At the opening of the Canada 101 exhibition, one of the official 1968 Festival art exhibitions (organised by Richard Demarco), Bailie George Theurer spotted a couple of four-letter words in an exhibit by Greg Curnoe and immediately complained to Lord Provost Brechin, resulting in the 'offending parts' of the exhibit being removed. Despite letters of protest, these were not replaced.[102]

There were similar conflicts over theatre. The controversies over the 1963 happening and the resulting nudity trial, the sexualised witches in *Macbeth* in 1965, and the furore over *Futz* in 1967 were joined annually by scandals revolving around the Fringe and the Traverse Theatre, often encapsulated in the expression 'Filth on the Fringe'. We have seen instances of local officials, bodies hiring halls out to Fringe groups, and even police in the city vetting the scripts of plays, alongside a move in the mid-1960s towards committees made up of both theatre professionals and lay members in both the Traverse and Lyceum Theatres. Asked his views on censorship late in 1967, Tom Fleming responded that while he did not believe in it, he was not sure what might take its place: 'I would rather have this anachronistic office in London deciding what I was going to see than a sub-committee of the Town Council.'[103] Earlier in 1967, Clive Perry had agreed to a request from an Edinburgh Corporation councillor to make copies of play scripts available to any member of the Edinburgh Civic Theatre Trust Board who 'wished to read the play where it was a controversial one', as long as it did not affect the selection of the Programme Committee. During the same board meeting, ex-Lord Provost Weatherstone expressed disquiet about the choice for the next production – the John McGrath play *Events While Guarding the Bofors Gun* – mainly because he felt it was libellous against the British army.[104] In response, an Arts Council assessor, A. C. Mather, warned that, while he understood Weatherstone's concerns, 'establishment art is a very dangerous thing'.[105]

The Lord Chamberlain's office had even begun requesting that private theatre clubs submit scripts for approval prior to performance.[106] In February 1968, Gordon McDougall pointed out to the director of the SAC, Ronald Mavor, that this would have a 'completely stultifying effect' on the evolution of new drama in theatres like the Traverse – 'not, I stress, because the plays we do are obscene, or we want to present experiments in nudity etc., but purely and simply because of the script problem'.[107] Days before, the Traverse had been the focus of a major scandal concerning 'filth' on its stage.

In February 1968, a play by Edinburgh Experimental Group, *Mass in F*, caused a widely publicised controversy that almost resulted in the withdrawal of funding from the theatre and threats from the university of disciplinary action against the students involved. For the *Scottish Daily Express*, Brian Meek reported:

> A young girl, naked from the waist up, sits muttering sexual obscenities . . . another near-naked girl crawls towards a man with a whip . . . a man and a woman exchange clothes . . . two women portray acts of lesbianism. It could only happen at Edinburgh's Traverse Theatre . . . AND IT DID.[108]

The play attracted the attentions of local government officials such as Councillor John Kidd ('then Edinburgh's leading scourge of permissiveness') and Bailie Robert Knox, with the former calling upon the Church of Scotland to 'take action' over the production and the latter asking the Lord Provost's Committee not to renew the corporation's grant to the Traverse. Meek appealed to his readers, pointing out that it was they who contributed 'towards this juvenile club', through the Arts Council and, for those living in Edinburgh, the corporation grant. These should be re-examined, argued Meek:

> And this can be achieved by local folk putting pressure on their Councillors and MPs [. . .] The town council can certainly find something better to do with the money. And there are plenty of decent theatres in need of Arts Council support. If we must have this gutter theatre then let the organisers provide the cash for it.[109]

The *Daily Record* reported that four days later, the sixty-seat Traverse was 'packed' with over 120 people there to see *Mass in F*, including a representative sent by the Kirk's Social and Moral Welfare Board and an Edinburgh bailie. Instead, they saw the chairman of the Traverse, Nicholas Fairbairn, and McDougall, who presented a 'talk-in' titled *F in Mass*, which the *Express* described as 'a skit on the production and the public's violent reaction to it'.[110] McDougall told the *Daily Record*: 'I think the obscenity has been greatly overplayed.'[111] The SAC made it clear to the Traverse that it would not support plays that did not have a licence from the Lord Chamberlain, although Mavor was keen to emphasise that the future of the Traverse was 'not threatened in any way by productions of this kind for any other reasons'.[112] Dependent upon subsidy and experiencing financial difficulties, the Traverse was forced to withdraw the production (and also banned the group from ever performing there again).[113] Calling upon those who had become temporary members of the Traverse for the 1968 Festival period for donations towards the cost of the new Traverse Theatre in the Grassmarket in 1969, Andrew Leigh, the theatre's administrator, wrote that 'it would be a triumph for the forces of philistinism if we cannot succeed through failing to show that people all over the country want us to continue'.[114]

The latest scandal at the Traverse followed hot on the heels of Malcolm Muggeridge's high profile resignation as rector of the University of Edinburgh in mid-January. The Student Representative Council had called for the contraceptive pill to be made available to students at their health centre. The university newspaper, *The Student*, had asked Muggeridge to agree with the demand or resign. The following week, Muggeridge quit as rector in a move 'believed to be unprecedented in modern times.'[115] He gave a 'sensational address' in St Giles' Cathedral in which 'he lashed out at the "slobbering debauchery of dope and bed"'.[116] Muggeridge, who became a Christian sometime between 1966 and 1969, was 'macabrely sad' that the students should demand 'pot and pills for the most tenth-rate sort of escapism and indulgence'.[117]

In the foreword to the 1968 Edinburgh International Festival Programme, Lord Provost Brechin welcomed visitors to a 'City which seeks to establish a way of life and a style of living more in accordance with the virtues, rather than the vices of humanity'.[118] Brechin was perhaps mindful of the scandals over Muggeridge's resignation and *Mass in F*. The 1968 Theatres Bill 'had met with a cautious, if not hostile, response from Scottish policy makers, attuned to the somewhat heightened moral sensitivities of Scottish public opinion'.[119] Scotland was still seen as distinctive from the rest of Britain in terms of morality and social conservatism. In 1968, backtracking on his optimistic assessment of Edinburgh in 1966, Irving Wardle wrote in *The Times*: 'Edinburgh, for all the spread of commercial galleries, the folk singing, and the little theatre movement, is not going to change. For everything except the most orthodox culture, the atmosphere of moral suspicion will persist.'[120]

The reputation that the Edinburgh Festivals still have as a site of scandal was consolidated during the late 1960s. The idea of dour, humourless city officials and Presbyterian church representatives decrying the scandal of this-or-that Fringe production has become part of the cultural narrative of the Fringe, and is anticipated each year. In 1969, Councillor John D. Kidd wrote to the chief constable of Edinburgh, asking that the Festival production of Shakespeare's *Edward II* (in which Ian McKellen played the title role) be prosecuted for obscenity: 'A disgrace to the city with male members of the cast kissing on stage. Shocking and degrading with the scene where the king is killed with a red-hot poker, just brutality.'[121] Peter Diamand had also 'felt it necessary' to draw attention to a scene in the final act of *The Fiery Angel* by Frankfurt Opera where 'there was a scene of holy hysteria in which three nuns stripped to the waist'. In early 1970, a delegation from the Festival Council – made up of Lord Provost McKay, Bailie Theurer and James Dunbar-Nasmith, an architect – went to Frankfurt to view the production for themselves ('A censorious posse [. . .] sent themselves on a moral inspection tour,' wrote Iain Crawford). Nonetheless, they reported favourably and the production went ahead without the need to partially dress the characters.[122] In September 1970, representations made to the Scottish Education Department alleged that avant-garde plays at the Edinburgh Festival were imitating more sexually explicit London productions like *Hair* and *Oh! Calcutta.*[123]

In a letter to *The Scotsman* Mavor wrote: 'Can we not agree that adult human beings should be allowed to do what they like within the law and without that moral censoriousness for which the marvellous city of Edinburgh is in danger of becoming a byword?'[124] The 'permissive society', with its more open discussion about what were previously taboo subjects, social trends that pointed to liberalisation in various aspects of people's personal lives, and the enactment in law of 'permissive legislation' formed the backdrop to increased concern about obscenity and sexual explicit content in drama, in Edinburgh as elsewhere.

THE FESTIVAL OF THE DEAD?

In 1967, Tom Nairn penned the blistering piece 'The Festival of the Dead', published in the *New Statesman*, in which he condemned the 'tartanry' and 'kailyard' myths that characterised Scotland and, above all, the stultifying weight of Presbyterianism:

> By and large, it was the odious hell-religion of Scottish Calvinism which endured, and still endures, as the cultural substratum of the country. The three-week Festival is exactly like an interminable church fete in atmosphere. People comment ceaselessly on how little effect it has had upon the real, continuing life of the city, but what do they expect? The soil Scotland offers to this fragile festival culture is mildewed religiosity a mile deep, and what could thrive in this? Edinburgh's soul is Bible-black, pickled in boredom by centuries of sermons, swaddled in the shabby gentility of the Kirk – what difference could 21 years of Festival make to this?[125]

Slowly but surely, however, the Festival was beginning to make a difference, even if that was not immediately evident in 1967. Its influence on the Scottish arts scene could be seen more clearly as Scottish nationalism swelled from the late 1960s. The Union relationship was put under pressure by economic crises, the shortcomings of regional planning, major cuts in public investment and the first signs of deindustrialisation as Scotland's heavy industries (coal mining, shipbuilding and steel) all experienced difficulties.[126] The once 'impregnable' relationship faltered, the Unionist Party experienced decline (becoming the Conservative and Unionist Party in 1965), and the victory of Winnie Ewing in the Hamilton by-election in 1967 gave the Scottish National

Party its first seat in Westminster.[127] This sense of growing nationalism was initially seen as largely political. In 1969, in an interview with the new periodical *Scottish Theatre*, Sir Tyrone Guthrie felt that talk of Scottish nationalism was taking place in an almost entirely political context with theatre seemingly having 'no place in the expression of political ferment'. This, Guthrie said, was partly because of a narrow sense of nationalism but also a feeling in Scotland 'that the theatre is frivolous at best, licentious at worst'.[128]

But there was a growing recognition of the need for Scotland to have its own national companies in cultural terms too. Aided by public funding for the arts, national professional arts companies and institutions were created and developed during the post-war years. The Scottish National Orchestra was formed in 1950, the Scottish National Gallery of Modern Art in 1960, Scottish Opera in 1962 (in a country 'with no indigenous operatic tradition to boast of'), and Scottish Theatre Ballet in 1969.[129] The Glasgow College of Dramatic Art's change of name to the Royal Scottish Academy of Music and Drama was approved in 1968.[130] The Scottish Committee of the Arts Council was 'reinvigorated' by the arrival of Ronald Mavor as director in 1965.[131] Euan McArthur reveals how the decision to rename the Scottish Committee in 1967 actually emanated from growing Welsh nationalism, particularly Labour's by-election loss of Carmarthen to Plaid Cymru in July 1966, Welsh local government reform, and the *Report on the Arts in Wales*. Published in May 1966, one of its recommendations was that the public perception of the Welsh Committee 'might be improved' by changing its title to 'The Arts Council for Wales'. In response, the Scottish and Welsh Committees were renamed the Scottish Arts Council and the Welsh Arts Council at 'the eleventh hour'. The Scottish Office was amenable to the change 'because it too was looking over its shoulder at a nationalist advance'.[132]

There was a growing recognition of Scottish theatre too. In 1966, the Department of Theatre Studies was founded at the University of Glasgow. In 1969, it presented an interdisciplinary revival of *The Thrie Estaitis* (first revived by the Edinburgh International Festival in 1948). Adrienne Scullion has noted that 'the challenge of the production was to declare theatre and drama – and, indeed, Scottish theatre and Scottish drama – as a legitimate locus for the academic exploration of place, image, representation and identity'.[133] The Gateway had acted as a nursery for Scottish theatrical talent in Edinburgh, particularly in the form of the Gateway Theatre Company active between 1953 and 1965. The latter had made a 'serendipitous transition' into the Royal Lyceum Theatre Company, whose first director, Tom Fleming, planned a theatre 'which, while rooted firmly in Scotland, would never fail to exhibit an international awareness'.[134] The Traverse, too, sought to provide a space for new writers, and to engage with Scottish themes and playwrights. Cecil P. Taylor and Stanley Eveling, two 'resident' playwrights at the Traverse, 'brought new political, social and philosophical perspectives to Scottish theatre'.[135] Some argue that the Traverse, however, has had only a 'slight' impact on the Scottish national repertoire (partly due to 'the structural inability of mainstream Scottish theatres to capitalise on the gains' made by the Traverse and other small studio theatres), although Randall Stevenson points out that its 'long-sustained policy of encouraging new writing has been highly effective locally'.[136] In its 1970 report *Theatre in Scotland*, the SAC defended the use of public funds to support club theatres. In reference to the Traverse, it stated that 'in presenting essentially programmes of new plays it serves an absolutely vital function of the theatre'.[137]

Whether the 1950s and 1960s were a period of growth or stagnation for Scottish theatre remains contested. There is general agreement, however, that it was during the 1970s that there was a dramatic renaissance in Scotland. This, Donald Smith has argued, was in part a reaction against the 'often vapid' internationalism of the 1960s and a 'new emphasis on the importance of cultural difference and identity [. . .] Whatever political disappointments lay ahead, the 1970s began a cultural shift in which Scottishness reshaped and reasserted itself against both external forces and its own stereotypes.'[138]

The Edinburgh Festivals were significant to this resurgence, right from the very first event in 1947 when Glasgow Unity made a high-profile stand for Scottish drama:

> It was the first Scottish theatre movement to demonstrate a strong interest in international plays and theatrical forms and the first to insist that Scottish theatre expose itself to international criticism and influence by taking part in the First Edinburgh Festival [. . .] it set an important ball rolling, because without permitting the international theatre to have a stronger influence on its plays and their chosen theatrical form, Scottish theatre would otherwise have remained tied to its English neighbour's apron strings and condemned to a provincial half-life.[139]

The presentations of *Ane Satyre of the Thrie Estaitis* on the official Festival stage in 1948 and 1949 were important, too, in successfully presenting native Scottish drama on an international platform.[140] Over the ensuing years, the Festival and Fringe became increasingly important platforms for the arts in Scotland. In 1971, Peter Diamand wrote that after twenty-five years, 'I believe that the Festival, while having sustained and perhaps enhanced its international reputation, is now even more deeply rooted in Edinburgh and Scotland than it was – also perhaps because more Scottish artists than ever are involved in it'.[141]

The importance of the Edinburgh Festivals was to grow in conjunction with the mood of Scottish nationalism in the 1970s. A 'living guide' to Edinburgh, published in 1976, observed:

A Scotland growing closer to independence has to be a Scotland proving herself more international than London, not less. Hence the Edinburgh Festival, which used to be comfortably dismissable as an alien incursion, is now becoming a large claim on Scottish identity.[142]

A pivotal influence was John McGrath's 7:84 group, formed to bring theatre to working-class people and to 'relate political theatre to political realities' (its name came from the statistic that 7 per cent of the population owned 84 per cent of the wealth). Inspired by the events in Paris in May 1968, McGrath wanted to 'oppose bourgeois theatre by creating a truly revolutionary theatre, in order to help bring about a change in society and in our own art'.[143] Its first productions were of McGrath's *Trees in the Wind* and Trevor Griffiths's *Apricots* at the Festival Fringe in 1971. In 1973, it split into two companies covering England and Scotland separately. 7:84 Scotland soon became a major force, and modern Scottish theatre is sometimes dated as beginning with its production of McGrath's *The Cheviot, the Stag and the Black, Black Oil* in 1973. A major aim was to 'present the realities of working class life and history directly to working class audiences'.[144]

Parallels could be seen between the work of 7:84 Scotland and that of Glasgow Unity more than twenty years earlier. Linda Mackenney has argued that Unity's post-war Scottish working-class plays

> reject specific categories of Scottish drama which project specific images of Scotland. Unity rejects tartanry and, with it, the kind of Scottish historical dramas that mythologise the past, but it also rejects the kinds of plays that over-idealise rural and, in particular, Highland life, which are likewise divorced from contemporary reality.[145]

To Michael Coveney, 'the avowedly left wing of Scottish theatre was facing the future by confronting the past'.[146] Existing experimental theatre spaces such as the Traverse Theatre Club were joined by new initiatives in Edinburgh like the Young Lyceum Company (formed in 1972) and the Pool Lunch Hour Theatre Club (begun in 1971). The Royal Lyceum Theatre Company, with Clive Perry directing, and Richard Eyre and then Bill Bryden as associate directors, was 'at the time something of a powerhouse of Scottish theatre making and writing'.[147] Donald Campbell sees Bryden as partly responsible for 'the greatest upsurge of native dramatic writing that Scotland has ever known'.[148] The Glasgow Citizens, too, was making a mark here. The appointment in 1970 of Giles Havergal, with co-directors Philip Prowse and Robert David Macdonald, 'initiated a radical policy' at the Citizens Theatre.[149] Its controversial production of *Hamlet* in 1970 'represented a calculated assault on Scottish Calvinism and the spirit of John Knox [and] also declared war on the narrow nationalist aspirations of Scottish theatre'.[150] To Donald Smith, the short-lived Scottish Actors Company (1970–3) was also influential, through 'its sense of the Scottish identity as a challenging and, to a large extent, unexpressed vehicle for theatre'.[151]

It is no surprise that the idea of a Scottish National Theatre was once again in the air. In 1964, the then Lord Provost, Duncan Weatherstone, had announced his intention to develop an all-round Festival centre on the Castle Terrace site, where the Lyceum was situated, in time for the 1971 Festival. In 1970, the SAC had begun exploring the idea of creating a major drama company ('tentatively' called the Scottish Theatre Company) that would use this multi-purpose arts centre as a base (as, it was anticipated, would Scottish Opera and Scottish Ballet).[152] Its report, *Theatre in Scotland*, remarked that the Edinburgh Opera House would 'open a new era for the arts in Scotland [. . .] In all of this may be the seeds of a theatre company which might approximate to what for years enthusiasts have described as a National Theatre for Scotland.'[153] Despite plans being in place, and support for the project coming from both the Minister for the Arts, Jennie Lee, and the chairman of the Arts Council, Lord Goodman, Lord Provost Brechin, Weatherstone's successor, showed more interest in developing infrastructure for the 1970 Commonwealth Games, which took place in Edinburgh. Even with new Prime Minister Edward Heath's promise of £2.5 million from the government towards the cost of building an opera house for Edinburgh, the plans did not go ahead due to misgivings over the design, inflation, local government reorganisation and ever-changing plans for the site.[154] The 'entire strategy' planned by the SAC (in conjunction with the Lyceum) was 'linked directly' to the completion of this building, which floundered as a result of the ongoing problems.[155]

Wider changes also suggest a shift from one era to another. Labour were in power from October 1964 until, to their shock and surprise, they lost the election to the Conservatives in June 1970. A growing distrust of Labour, after economic difficulties like the devaluation of the pound in 1967 and a major economic crisis in 1968, and a sense of frustration with Britain's declining status (and embarrassment at Charles de Gaulle again vetoing Britain's application to join the European Economic Community) combined with growing concerns about the loss of morality and standards in British society. The overriding reason for the Conservative's surprise victory related to the worsening economic crisis, but fears linked to the social upheavals of the 1960s, for example, about family breakdown, permissiveness, drug-taking, alcoholism, pornography and obscenity, also contributed to their electoral success. To Michael Billington, the election of Heath as Prime Minister and the Conservatives into a clear majority government (with 330 seats against 300 for all the other parties combined) 'marked the end of the liberalising Sixties reform and signalled that the party was officially over'.[156] Unemployment increased, inflation rose, and in 1970 and 1971 there were major strikes across British industry (the worst since 1926).

Furthermore, many of the promises of the 1960s counter-culture were also turning to dust. A letter to *IT* commented that the underground had 'split up into factions [and] failed to make any worthwhile progress as a generation, to consolidate gains, and to force out more'.[157] John Seed argued that the counter-culture 'disintegrated rapidly after 1970'.[158] The achievements of the counter-culture remain contested, and some of its inherent contradictions have been widely criticised. But it helped give birth to new movements that were to influence social attitudes in Scotland, as further afield. Frustrations with the continuation of chauvinistic attitudes and the double standards of the counter-culture and political movements of the 1960s underpinned the development of the new Women's Liberation movement, for example.[159] The Gay Liberation movement, too, grew out of the late 1960s counter-culture, the limitations of existing political activity and debates surrounding the permissive society.[160] In Scotland, the Scottish Minorities Group was founded in January 1969 to work towards the decriminalisation of homo-sexual activities in Scotland, in line with the Sexual Offences Act (1967) enacted in England and Wales – the word 'minorities' was initially used to avoid explicit reference to homosexuality – and decriminalisation was finally achieved in 1980.[161] To Robert Hewison, 'political failure thrust the issue of "culture and society" back into the cultural arena, thus making it even more of a political battleground'.[162]

It is clear that the major shifts that occurred from 1968, and the changing political, social and artistic context of the 1970s, demand dedicated exam-ination. They mark a step change in the history of the Edinburgh Festivals, and they show the development of a new artistic climate that was to underpin the flourishing of community arts movements in the late 1970s, grassroots social action through culture, and a growing professional Fringe that was to pose new questions about the arts and culture in the 1970s. The SAC also, in 1971, responded to growing interference in the Festival by members of Edinburgh Corporation. In the EFS, out of a composition of twenty-one members, twelve were representatives of Edinburgh Corporation, who, the SAC noted, confused the function of supporting an artistic enterprise with that of organising and running it. It was suggested that their role be reduced and a higher proportion be made up of 'individuals interested in the arts'.[163] In terms of Scotland, the role of the Festival and Fringe as a space for questioning Scottishness and Scottish national identity grew apace during the 1970s. The Traverse and Lyceum, too, became important spaces for ques-tioning Scots, Scotland and the relationship to the wider world. The impact of social movements 'unleashed' during the 1960s was to have consequences for expressions of Scottish identity, as were the painful shift from Scotland as an industrial nation to a service-based economy and the impact of Con-servative rule under Prime Minister Margaret Thatcher from 1979. There were also changes in arts governance as, by the mid-1970s, 'the brief period of expansion in national arts funding was over, replaced by harsh cuts in local government spending which hit arts and leisure badly'.[164]

When reflecting on 'an altered Edinburgh' in 1966, Irving Wardle had mused:

> The reason for the awakening, I suppose, is that Edinburgh is one of the last remaining European cities that possesses all the amenities of a capital without reducing its inhabitants to insect life – and thus exerts a similar appeal to that of Paris in the [1890s] and Dublin after the last war.[165]

Until the mid-1960s, the sheer size of London had meant that its literary and artistic network was more dispersed than in a small, compact city like Edinburgh. Tom McGrath has recalled:

> London was different because it was so much bigger. London is so many little villages, you know. You could be in one part and wouldn't be influenced at all with what was happening somewhere else. When we did *IT*, the newspaper, we brought a lot of different far-flung things in England together.[166]

In the High Sixties, London became seen as the creative capital of Britain and was the site of the high-profile counter-culture with its ideas about alternative arts and ways of living, multi-purpose arts spaces, and new forms of social protest.[167]

But, if London was host to a 'cultural explosion', Edinburgh was the 'bubbling volcano'. To Jim Haynes,

> Edinburgh was just like a small little bubbling-away volcano but it exploded in London with the Beatles and the Rolling Stones and '68, certain art colleges were taken over by the students and, you know, it exploded in London whereas it hadn't exploded in Edinburgh when I was there. It was bubbling away but it hadn't exploded.[168]

The Festivals clearly had an important role to play in lighting sparks in the 1960s 'cultural explosion' and in providing a space conducive to experimentation, and one that attracted some of the most influential figures in the arts scene to its environs. Even the very landscape of the city was important. The need for groups to improvise with different types of performance spaces due to the lack of theatres in Edinburgh helped to give the Fringe Festival its distinctive identity, influenced other theatre companies and Fringe theatre groups, and played a part in the broader shift away from traditional proscenium arch theatre spaces in Britain.

Nonetheless, despite culture becoming more widely based and a more diverse range of arts and artists given state subsidy (and approval), its definition was still problematic. As Lawrence Black points out, however, 'an elitist vision of what arts were worthy of funding prevailed' and, despite wishes to extend access to and enjoyment of the arts in society, this was not to be at the expense of standards. Jennie Lee stated in the Commons in 1970 that 'there should be no cutting back on metropolitan standards in order to spread the available money more evenly throughout the country'. 'The equation of culture, civilization and "high" Western art held good,' observed Black, 'just as for Keynes in the 1940s.'[169]

NOTES

1. On 1968 see e.g. Fink et al., *1968*; Kurlansky, *1968*; Marwick, *The Sixties*. On responses to the Vietnam War in Britain, see Thomas, 'Protests against the Vietnam War in 1960s Britain'. On student protests, see Thomas, 'Challenging the Myths'. In 2008, the fortieth anniversary of '68 provoked a wide range of exhibitions, publications and media coverage reflecting on its significance.
2. Nelson, *The British Counter-culture*, 116.
3. The 'rediscovery' of poverty in the mid-1960s also contributed to this. See e.g. Abel-Smith & Townsend, *The Poor and the Poorest*. A number of sociological studies of youth also began to show how, despite the widespread belief in a new generation of classless, affluent youth, class continued to have a significant role in young people's lives – see e.g. Willmott, *Adolescent Boys of East London*.
4. Itzin, *Stages in the Revolution*, 1.
5. Moore-Gilbert & Seed, *Cultural Revolution?*, 9.
6. Hewison, *Too Much*, 190, 150.
7. Billington, *State of the Nation*, 165.
8. Rees, *Fringe First*, 9.
9. The People Show had started out with scripts and some improvisation, but gradually abandoned scripts in favour of improvisation after its first year or so. See interview with Mark Long, co-founder (with John Darling, Laura Gilbert, Jeff Nuttall and Sid Palmer) in Rees, *Fringe First*, 30.
10. Performances could still be proceeded against if deemed obscene and able to be shown to 'deprave or corrupt'.
11. Nelson, *The British Counter-culture*, 130.
12. *New Society*, 21 November 1968.
13. Itzin, *Stages in the Revolution*, 9.
14. Ansorge, *Disrupting the Spectacle*, 1, 47.
15. Ronald Rees prefers the term 'new theatre' to 'fringe' for theatre whose origins lie in the 1960s, arguing that fringe theatre does not have 'a historical role to play' until the late 1970s. Rees, *Fringe First*, 10.
16. Shrum, *Fringe and Fortune*, 67.
17. Moffat, *The Edinburgh Fringe*, 28.
18. Of course, travelling performing groups were not a new phenomenon – they had existed for hundreds of years – but in the context of the late 1960s they developed a new identity and ethos.
19. TTA, Dep 206, 21st EIF Traverse Theatre Club Brochure.

20. See e.g. Rees, *Fringe First*; Priestman, 'A Critical Stage'; Ansorge, *Disrupting the Spectacle*; Hewison, *Too Much*.
21. Ashford reflecting on 1969, cited in Rees, *Fringe First*, 9.
22. Moffat, *The Edinburgh Fringe*, 39; Itzin, *Stages in the Revolution*, 9.
23. *Plays and Players*, December 1965. The periodical became *Plays and Players and Theatre World* from January 1966, and *Plays and Players, Theatre World and Encore* from March 1966. However, in this work it will be referred to as *Plays and Players* throughout.
24. Roberts & Stafford-Clark, *Taking Stock*, 4.
25. Itzin, *Stages in the Revolution*, 9.
26. *Plays and Players*, May 1966; McMillan, *The Traverse Theatre Story*; Itzin, *Stages in the Revolution*.
27. For personal perspectives on this, see Unfinished Histories.
28. Arden, cited in Bottoms, *Playing Underground*, 202.
29. Bottoms, *Playing Underground*, 201–2.
30. Joyce McMillan notes that Stafford-Clark's interest in Paul Foster and La MaMa was prompted by John Calder. See McMillan, *The Traverse Theatre Story*, 39.
31. NLS, TTA, Minutes, 25 March 1968, cited in Roberts & Stafford-Clark, *Taking Stock*, 7.
32. Memo from Max Stafford-Clark, 25 March 1968, cited in Roberts & Stafford-Clark, *Taking Stock*, 7.
33. Stafford-Clark, cited in McMillan, *The Traverse Theatre Story*, 47.
34. Moffat, *The Edinburgh Fringe*, 63.
35. On membership, see McMillan, *The Traverse Theatre Story*, 47–54.
36. Stafford-Clark left the Traverse in 1972, becoming resident director of the Royal Court in 1973 and founding the Joint Stock Theatre Group in 1974. See Roberts & Stafford-Clark, *Taking Stock*.
37. See website of the Royal Court Theatre, www.royalcourttheatre.com (last accessed 3 December 2012); Young, writing in 1971, cited in Moffat, *The Edinburgh Fringe*, 65.
38. McMillan, *The Traverse Theatre Story*, 38.
39. Campbell, *A Brighter Sunshine*, 194–8.
40. McMillan, *The Traverse Theatre Story*, 55.
41. It was reported that plans were being made for a year-round theatre focusing on revue. *New Society*, 29 August 1968.
42. *Plays and Players*, 26 April 1967.
43. NLS, TTC, Dep 206 letter from McDougall to SAC, 20 May 1967.
44. See e.g. Shrum, *Fringe and Fortune*, chapter 5.
45. *Tribune*, 13 September 1968.
46. Brown, 'The New Writing Policies of Clive Perry and Stephen MacDonald at the Royal Lyceum Theatre', 2.
47. *Reports to GA 1968*, 389.
48. *Reports to GA 1969*, 402–14.
49. The Netherbow Port was a large gatehouse between High Street and Canongate, demolished in 1764.

50. *Reports to GA 1970*, 320–1.
51. *Reports to GA 1971*, 309.
52. Ibid.
53. The Netherbow was officially opened on 19 September 1972, but was not fully operational until the following year. Its director was named as Revd George Candlish, who had been director of the Gateway Theatre.
54. Crawford, *Banquo on Thursdays*, 92.
55. Miller, *The Edinburgh International Festival*, 70; Crawford, *Banquo on Thursdays*, 95.
56. *The Times*, 24 August 1968.
57. Crawford, *Banquo on Thursdays*, 93.
58. Miller, *The Edinburgh International Festival*, 72.
59. See Crawford, *Banquo on Thursdays*, 95.
60. *The Times*, 7 September 1968.
61. *The Times*, 31 August 1970.
62. Miller, *The Edinburgh International Festival*, 76.
63. *Financial Times*, 2 September 1970.
64. Ibid., 1 September 1970.
65. See Moffat, *The Edinburgh Fringe*.
66. Normand, '55° North 3° West'.
67. For a complete list of the artists who participated, see 'Some Memories of the 1970 Edinburgh Festival Exhibition'.
68. For more on Beuys, see e.g. Ray, *Joseph Beuys*.
69. Friedman, *Fluxus Reader*, viii–ix.
70. John Martin cited on 'Some Memories of the 1970 Edinburgh Festival Exhibition'.
71. Oliver, 'Strategy: Get Arts'.
72. Demarco, *The Artist as Explorer*, 16.
73. NRS, ED61/75, SAC press release, 'The SAC and the Visual Arts in Scotland', 24 March 1972.
74. Introduction to *Twenty-Fourth Annual Report of the Arts Council, 1968–9*, cited in Morgan, *People's Peace*. 31.
75. Hutchison, *The Politics of the Arts Council*, 107.
76. See McArthur, *Scotland, CEMA and the Arts Council*.
77. *Evening News and Dispatch*, 3 June 1967.
78. ECL, Crummy, *People in Partnership*, 36.
79. Crummy, *Let the People Sing!*, 63.
80. NRS, CO1/5/883, 'The Community and the Arts in Scotland'.
81. The Arts Council produced reports on community arts in 1974 and 1977. Hutchison, *Politics of the Arts Council*, 52. For more on community arts, see Hewison & Holden, *Experience and Experiment*.
82. Hutchison, *The Politics of the Arts Council*, 106.
83. Kellas, *Modern Scotland*, 97.
84. McArthur, *Scotland, CEMA and the Arts Council*, 277–8. See also NRS, CO1/5/883, SED Circular, 24 June 1965.
85. *The Scotsman*, 28 November 1967.

86. Hutchison, *The Politics of the Arts Council*, 107.
87. A Fringe and Experimental Drama Committee was created in 1971. Hutchison, *The Politics of the Arts Council*, 109.
88. See Calder, *Pursuit*.
89. See e.g. Travis, *Bound and Gagged*.
90. Hewison, *Too Much*, 131.
91. Ibid., 171. See also Arts Council, *The Obscenity Laws*.
92. Moore-Gilbert & Seed, *Cultural Revolution?*, 8.
93. Hewison, *Too Much*, 171–5.
94. Davidson & Davies, *The Sexual State*, 262, 276–7. This continued throughout the 1970s (see chapter 11). Other underground magazines in Edinburgh included *Four the Wardrobe* (1970–1), *Press-Ups* (1970–1) and *Roots* (1971–4). See Noyce, *The Directory of British Alternative Periodicals*.
95. *Reports to GA 1970*, 398–9.
96. *Reports to GA 1969*, 493.
97. *Reports to GA 1968*, 497.
98. *Reports to GA 1970*, 415, 423–4.
99. The Committee on Moral Welfare and the Committee on Social Service originally came under the umbrella of the Social and Moral Welfare Board. They were reconstituted as separate entities at the 1970 General Assembly.
100. *Reports to GA 1971*, 410.
101. Davidson & Davies, *The Sexual State*, 262, 276–7.
102. Miller, *The Edinburgh International Festival*, 71.
103. *Scotsman*, 28 November 1967.
104. The play was premiered by the Hampstead Theatre Club in 1966, and made into a film in 1968.
105. ECA, LPC, Lyceum Theatre, Board Meeting 3 February 1967.
106. Until the mid-1960s, the Lord Chamberlain's office had generally avoided getting involved with private members' clubs, but the growing practice of turning theatres into private clubs for performances of plays unable to secure a licence saw it extending its remit. See e.g. Shellard, *British Theatre since the War*, 136–46.
107. NLS, TTC, Dep 206, letter from McDougall to SAC, 15 February 1968.
108. *Express*, 6 February 1968.
109. Ibid.
110. NLS, TTC, Acc. 4850, *Daily Record*, 7 February 1968; *Express* (n.d.).
111. *Daily Record*, 7 February 1968.
112. *Express*, 9 February 1968.
113. Moffat, *The Edinburgh Fringe*, 61; NLS, TTA, Acc. 4850, newspaper cuttings for February 1968. See also McMillan, *The Traverse Theatre Story*.
114. NLS, TTC, Dep 206, circular, 15 August 1969.
115. *The Times*, 15 January 1968.
116. Muggeridge had taken the role of rector in 1966. *Express*, 15 January 1968.

117. *Express*, 15 January 1968. For more on debates over birth control in Scotland, see Davidson & Davis, *The Sexual State*.
118. EIFMD Programme, 1968.
119. Davidson & Davies, *The Sexual State*, 278. See pp. 240–6 for a detailed examination of the Scottish response to the Theatres Bill.
120. *The Times*, 7 September 1968.
121. Crawford, *Banquo on Thursdays*, 101.
122. See Crawford, *Banquo on Thursdays*, 103–4; Miller, *The Edinburgh International Festival*, 75.
123. Cited in Davidson & Davies, *The Sexual State*, 278.
124. NLS, TTA, Acc. 4850, Demarco Gallery, letter from Ronald Mavor to *The Scotsman*, 29 July 1970.
125. Nairn, 'The Festival of the Dead', 276–7.
126. For more on the Scottish economy, see Saville, *The Economic Development of Modern Scotland*.
127. Devine, *Scotland and the Union*, 14.
128. *Scottish Theatre*, March 1969.
129. Scottish Opera was led by the Scottish-born composer Sir Alexander Gibson, and based in Glasgow. It first performed at the Edinburgh International Festival in 1967, and thereafter appeared regularly. See Oliver, *It Is a Curious Story*.
130. In 2011, its name was changed again to the Royal Conservatoire of Scotland.
131. Jones & Galloway, 'Arts Governance in Scotland'.
132. McArthur, *The Arts Council in Scotland*, 212, 218; chapter 7 outlines the reason for these changes and provides detailed analysis of the Scottish Committee of the Arts Council between 1961 and 1967.
133. Scullion, 'Political Theatre or Heritage Culture?', 222–4.
134. Campbell, *A Brighter Sunshine*, 171.
135. Smith, '1950–95', 269–70.
136. Fisher, 'From Traverse to Tramway', 53; Stevenson, 'Snakes and Ladders, Snakes and Owls', 13.
137. SAC, *Theatre in Scotland*, 17.
138. Stevenson, 'Snakes and Ladders, Snakes and Owls', 8; Smith, '1950–95', 269–70.
139. Mackenney, *The Activities of Popular Dramatists and Drama Groups in Scotland*, 245.
140. See e.g. Scullion, 'Political Theatre or Heritage Culture?'
141. NLS, EFS, Dep 378, EIFMD Programme, 1971.
142. Campbell, *Another Edinburgh*, 50.
143. Itzin, *Stages in the Revolution*, 119. See also McGrath, *The Bone Won't Break*.
144. McGrath, cited in Moffat, *The Edinburgh Fringe*, 89.
145. Mackenney, *The Activities of Popular Dramatists and Drama Groups in Scotland*, 198.
146. Coveney, *The Citz*, 85.

147. Scullion, 'Political Theatre or Heritage Culture?', 224.
148. Campbell, *A Brighter Sunshine*, 207.
149. Shellard, *British Theatre since the War*, 174.
150. Coveney, *The Citz*, 45–6.
151. Smith, '1950–95', 285.
152. Ibid., 210.
153. SAC, *Theatre in Scotland*, 11.
154. Ultimately, it took until 1994 for the initial idea of a new purpose-built theatre for Edinburgh to come to fruition, when the Festival Theatre was created out of what had been the Empire Theatre. Eileen Miller refers to this as the 'hole in the ground'. See Miller, *The Edinburgh International Festival*, 151–5. For more on the SAC, see McArthur, *Scotland, CEMA and the Arts Council*.
155. Campbell, *A Brighter Sunshine*, 211.
156. Billington, *State of the Nation*, 205.
157. Cited in Nelson, *The British Counter-culture*, 136.
158. Seed, 'Hegemony Postponed', 38.
159. For Scotland, see Browne, ' "A Veritable Hotbed of Feminism" '.
160. See e.g. Robinson, *Gay Men and the Left*; Weeks, *Sex, Politics and Society*.
161. The group was renamed the Scottish Homosexual Rights Group in 1978. See Cant, *Footsteps and Witnesses*; Davidson & Davies, *The Sexual State*.
162. Hewison, *Culture and Consensus*, 158.
163. NRS, ED61/75, 'Composition of the SAC', SED, January 1971.
164. Jones & Galloway, 'Arts Governance in Scotland', 229.
165. 'Arts in Society', *New Society*, 30 June 1966.
166. Tom McGrath, 13 June 2005.
167. See e.g. Green, *Days in the Life*; Hewison, *Too Much*; Miles, *London Calling*.
168. Jim Haynes, 17 June 2005
169. Black, 'Making Britain a Gayer and More Cultivated Country', 326–32.

8

Conclusion

In 1971, the Edinburgh International Festival and Edinburgh Festival Fringe celebrated their twenty-fifth seasons. In his foreword to the International Festival Programme the Lord Provost, Sir James W. McKay, quoted a statement made by his predecessor Sir John Falconer in 1947: 'The human mind needs an occasional stretch into an overflowing fountain of grace and beneficence to confirm its weak faith and to anchor it to something higher than itself.' McKay continued:

> It was on this charter of idealism that the Festival was launched. Over a period of twenty-five years detail changes have been inevitable. Successive Lord Provosts, as Chairman of the Festival Society, have been inspired by Sir John Falconer's concept of the grand design and have striven to maintain the standards that have been the touchstone of success. And now looking forward twenty-five years – we shall have new members of the Festival Society, new audiences and new directors. In the midst of such a natural course of events the Festival must remain true to the idealism of its founders. It must not be the instrument of ribald or derisive jests nor the vehicle of extreme experimental phenomena. Rather it should be permitted to acquire the patina of tradition and reflect some of Edinburgh's golden age of Arts and Letters.[1]

To thank the people of Edinburgh for their support to the Festival, the EFS put on a free concert that was 'almost a replica' of the opening concert, with tickets given out by ballot to Edinburgh citizens.[2] Drama at the Festival was relatively 'clean', and included a staging of James Hogg's *The Private Memoirs and Confessions of a Justified Sinner*, directed by Richard Eyre at the Lyceum Theatre, and a hugely popular production of Shakespeare's *The Comedy of Errors* by Frank Dunlop and the Young Vic at Haymarket Ice Rink. But the Fringe made up for this with plenty that was 'ribald' and experimental. 'Sex is alive and in decent health this year on the Edinburgh Festival Fringe,' reported *The Guardian*, while Alistair Moffat observed that 'nudity, buggery, fetishism, voyeurism and even heterosexuality seem to have been very much in evidence'.[3] Despite McKay's plea to 'remain true to the idealism of its founders' and to 'acquire the patina of tradition', there was no denying that major changes had occurred in the intervening years, changes that altered the shape of the Festival, the landscape of the arts and arts policy across the western world, and the very fabric of modern Scotland.

During the first twenty-five years of the Edinburgh Festivals, ideas about culture in society underwent startling changes. In the optimistic flush of the immediate post-war world, the state took significant financial responsibility for the arts for the first time. Widening access to the arts had been conceived of as a means of 'improving' individuals, a 'civilising process' that had its roots in nineteenth-century attitudes to arts and society. It was also seen as part of the wider welfare state and underpinned by social-democratic ideals during post-war reconstruction. But in practice, the Arts Council of Great Britain had continued to direct most funding to the most expensive and elite arts (namely opera and ballet) and to focus most attention and financial support on the metropolis. Broader support was given in Scotland, where 'the double arm's length' position of the Scottish Committee of the Arts Council (and from 1967, the Scottish Arts Council) had given the organisation considerable autonomy. The growing challenge to existing classifications and barriers in the arts introduced by artists from the mid-1950s brought about a shift in opinion and led to a more diverse, inclusive and flexible conception of culture. This was particularly true after the publication in 1965 of the government White Paper *A Policy for the Arts*, which emphasised the need to provide wider access to culture, and to encourage innovation and creation among younger generations. 'Culchah' was no longer only the preserve of the 'grand masters', although high culture did (and still does) retain its association with class.[4]

The Festivals played a part in democratising culture. The unintentional creation of the Fringe in 1947 created a significant 'laboratory' for experimenting in the arts and influenced and inspired many theatre practitioners and other artists. It also helped to develop the form, content and ethos of fringe theatre, which, once pollinated by the 1960s counter-culture, became a force all of its own. This created the conditions for the community arts and fringe theatre movements that flourished in the 1970s, and made wider access to and participation in the arts an important policy goal at local, regional and national levels. As the 1960s became the 1970s, local authorities were encouraged to recognise the value of the arts and culture to their populations and invest accordingly.[5] Fringe theatre was born and raised in Edinburgh, a city that has provided a model for the arts festivals that are now ubiquitous in the modern world. The Fringe has played a crucial role in the democratisation of arts festivals, and modern festivals now have a 'fringe' element, including many 'high-brow' festivals. There are even standalone fringe festivals that are not part of any 'official' festival all over the world.

In 1947, one *Times* critic ventured: 'Upon Scottish music and drama the festival may [. . .] have a stimulating effect.'[6] In fact, between 1947 and 1970, the Festival was the catalyst for a number of significant developments in Scottish culture. For one, the Edinburgh Festival Fringe became a vital space for Scottish drama and for the expression of Scottish identities in theatre and other art forms. This grew more important as a sense of national identity increased from the late 1960s, with a 'rising tide of cultural nationalism' evident in the 1970s.[7] The programme of the official Festival was repeatedly criticised for not presenting enough Scottish drama, and the exclusion of Scottish theatrical representation in the inaugural event had, of course, sparked the creation of the Fringe in the first place. The Festivals instigated cultural contest and inspired cultural production. Many early Fringe groups were keen to show that there existed a living Scottish theatre, and to show that the host nation could contribute its own (worthwhile) art. Even when the Festival programme did include Scottish drama, it was often criticised as being dated and looking backwards instead of engaging with contemporary Scotland. But here, too, the Festival provided stimulation. The opportunities presented by the annual Festivals – whether as a stage to present upon or as something to rail against – and the 'annual pollination' they brought with them 'bore rich fruit'.[8]

The roots of the Scottish folk song revival could also be found in the Edinburgh Festivals, specifically the Edinburgh People's Festivals of the early 1950s. The revival was to make a rich contribution in Scotland, as well as being intimately connected to the wider folk song revival of the 1960s. As Hamish Henderson recalled:

What made this inaugural People's Festival ceilidh so important was the fact that this was the first time such a masterly group of authentic traditional musicians and ballad-singers from rural Scotland had sung together to a city audience; the result was a veritable cultural explosion, for a number of the 'folk' virtuosi of the future were present in the audience.[9]

Theatres in Edinburgh played a part too. The Traverse Theatre Club had, like the Fringe, encouraged and inspired cultural production. It gave new and untested writers the opportunity to have their work staged, brought international and avant-garde theatre, performance and visual arts, and provided a space for debate and discussion – as well as somewhere to go on the Scottish Sabbath. The Gateway and Lyceum theatres also provided training grounds for theatrical talent, staged many works that brought new influences to Scottish soil, and provided spaces for the presentation of Scottish themes and content.

When the Festival began in 1947, there were few playwrights, actors, directors and artists who could stay and work in Scotland, rather than having to move to London or further afield to work. It would, of course, be grossly inaccurate to argue that the Festival single-handedly changed this state of affairs. The Arts Council played a crucial role in developing infrastructure in Scotland and in encouraging the arts, as did some local authorities (although often much less than they could have done). Nevertheless, where it did occur, the development of local authority-funded ventures like civic theatres and arts centres also contributed to cultural infrastructure and talent in Scotland, as did the development of regional broadcasting, and the formation of the College of Dramatic Art (1950) and the Drama Department of the University of Glasgow (1966).[10]

It is difficult to fully capture the influence that the Edinburgh Festivals have had on the arts, in Scotland as well as further afield. George Bruce put it eloquently when he wrote: 'It is true the Festival begins as "pleasure for a minority", but its impact is like the widening circles of the stone dropped from a height into water.'[11] Richard Demarco was in the audience of *L'École des femmes* in 1947 as young schoolboy, which he credits with his decision to live his life in the arts:

> I was absolutely amazed that I was being told that I had to go to a play performed in French . . . because I failed my French [. . .] I was lucky as a seventeen-year-old boy to be sitting listening to the world's greatest French-speaking theatre company, Comédie-Française, and it was *L'École des femmes*. And the greatest actor in the history of French theatre of modern times was performing, Louis Jouvet [. . .] a great theatre in Paris and here it was landed like a spaceship, this entire company, in Edinburgh of all places [. . .] *It changed my life* and I wanted more.[12]

Playwright Robert Kemp was also in the audience of *L'École des femmes* in 1947 'ripe for reception of the seed of an idea which came to fruition in a pawky Scots adaptation of Molière's play, which we have come to know as *Let Wives Tak' Tent*'.[13] The young Brian McMaster, who became director of the Edinburgh International Festival in 1991, visited the Festival when a young law student in 1962, referring to it as a 'life-changing experience' that influenced his decision to go into arts administration.[14] Frank Dunlop, already an experienced director when he founded Pop Theatre for the Festival in 1966, was able to try out new approaches to theatre direction and production, becoming a regular contributor to the Festival programme thereafter and becoming director of the International Festival between 1984 and 1991. Pondering its impact, the artist Alexander Moffat has said:

> I suppose the whole way that Scotland has developed, both culturally and politically, I think owes a great deal to the Edinburgh Festival because it put us in touch with the world in a very important moment, yes, in the aftermath of World War Two. And the idea, if I remember, it first struck me when I started to specialise in art at school, after seeing that Moltzau Collection [in 1958] and realising that the Festival was this huge thing, massive thing in our cultural, artistic life, the very fact that all these people came to Edinburgh. Okay . . . there was tremendous resistance by a lot of silly people in Edinburgh, tremendous resistance to all this. It's just culture, it's just new

arts, but understanding that it played this huge role and without doubt [it was] moving our thinking forward, and over a period of time it would completely re-educate the way that we ourselves as artists looked at ourselves. And that in itself would change everything, yes. So the role of the Festival is inestimable, isn't it, in this kind of Scotland and the world . . . We should stress the importance of the Edinburgh Festival; it's almost impossible to measure it, aye.[15]

The relationship between the visual arts and the Festival City demands more attention.

The impact on the city of Edinburgh, too, has been important. Assessing the inaugural Festival, the Scottish Tourist Board magazine *Take Note!* reported that over 120,000 visitors had come to Edinburgh in 1947, making the Festival a 'cultural triumph' and putting Edinburgh and Scotland on the world's map 'as never before'.[16] By the 1960s, the Festival City was firmly on the map as host of a major international festival of the arts. Some observers were proclaiming an 'altered Edinburgh' and lauding the 'miracle' that was changing the face of the city. In June 1965, Jim Haynes even referred to Edinburgh as 'the San Francisco of Britain, the second cultural capital.'[17] But these assessments were a little premature, and it took some time for a truly Festival City to emerge (some would argue it never has). In October 1955, L. J. Bell had despaired in the *Scots Magazine* about the failure of the Festival as a 'spontaneous *fiesta*', despite being an 'artistic triumph': 'Where, oh where', she asked, 'is the spirit of Paris, or Brussels, or Barcelona [where] cafes open til after midnight [. . .] Is it too much to ask that Edinburgh should go continental for all time?'[18] The Festival and Fringe Clubs, as well as ventures like the Paperback Bookshop and the Traverse Theatre Club, had sought to create festival atmospheres and offer somewhere to go when local bars and cafés closed (especially later at night and on Sundays).[19] Licensing regulations were not relaxed in Scotland until the Licensing Act of 1975, although some venues had been able to obtain extended licensing hours for the duration of the Festival. Although the 'interminable Scottish Sabbath' was to last well into the 1970s (and far beyond in some parts of the country), the Festivals and associated ventures played a part in opening up Sundays to a wider range of activities.[20]

The whole post-war period was one of awakening in Scotland, in which the long shadow of John Knox began to be shaken off. Edinburgh's reputation as puritan, stifled by its Presbyterianism, persisted among many journalists, critics, visitors and residents throughout the 1960s and into the 1970s (and hangs around still). But it was undoubtedly undermined, sometimes by events at the Festivals and other cultural ventures in Edinburgh, and sometimes by broader social shifts. Alexander Moffat, recalling the scandal over the 1963 happening, has mused:

I suppose that was the last stand in a way of what we used to call the Church of Scotland, that kind of moral straitjacket that was clamped down upon us, or seemed to be. I remember we talked about that a lot when we were students.[21]

In 1973, Hamish Henderson said in an interview with the musical weekly *Melody Maker*:

The folk revival has been a tremendous catalyst [. . .] releasing new energies, giving place for new feelings and creative imagination and everything. In breaking this terrible, hard, coarse mould of the old Kirk thing which lays so heavily on Scotland you can't believe it.[22]

Every year, this major arts jamboree brought with it challenges to philistinism and moral conservatism in Scotland, helping to undermine what in 1966 Revd Denis Duncan had termed the 'judgemental' approach to drama in Scotland.[23] The Festival began at a time when spiritual renewal was foremost, conservative values were strong, traditional morals based on Victorian mores were still persuasive, and the Church of Scotland held a strong position in Scottish society. By 1970, as a consequence of a significant shift in public attitudes, morality was becoming liberalised from Victorian mores as responsibility for decision-making began to move from public to private spheres, conservative values were under assault (and often undermined), and the Church of Scotland was experiencing declining authority and a crisis in its membership. But church representatives consistently sought to engage with youth through the arts, as well as with the artists themselves, in order to defend organised religion and to maintain some sort of connection with a section of the population being lured away by the excitement of new cultural forms and activities. In part due to its experiment with the Gateway Theatre and to the challenges mounted by a young artistic vanguard to its teaching and values, the Kirk accepted the arts as a space for asking questions and debating ideas. In 1971, the Kirk's Committee on Moral Welfare remarked: 'Sometimes these issues for which guidance is sought arise from the so-called "underground" who question the established order. The Church cannot be unsympathetic since it is part of her perennial role to do the same.'[24] In this way, the Festivals give us an unusual insight into the forces of secularisation in Scottish society, the responses of Scotland's national church to these, and what Hugh McLeod refers to as 'the gradual loosening of the ties between church and society'.[25]

The Edinburgh Festivals provided a 'prism' through which important social and cultural shifts, like changing attitudes to morality, challenges to censorship, and the breaking down of barriers in the arts, could be engaged with and explored. The attentions of local government, the national church, the press, moral reactionaries and artists were focused on Edinburgh for a three-week period each year. These made the Festival City the site of numerous 'culture wars' and a high-profile arena in which social and cultural tensions in British society were given space for confrontation. It should be clear, by now, that Scotland was neither peripheral to nor unaffected by the cultural upheavals of 'the sixties'. Richard Finlay's casual comments about the 'Swinging Sixties' passing Scotland by ignore the very real battles that were taking place in the field of culture, and his suggestion that the excitement of the 1960s took place elsewhere overlooks the creative force of ventures like the Fringe and the Traverse Theatre Club, and the significant challenges to traditional ideas and values in culture and morality that were expressed during the Festivals. We have seen that even the Kirk was not immune to these challenges and upheavals.

As Raymond Williams argued back in 1961, culture is a process and not a conclusion.[26] The debate over the roles, definitions and challenges of culture are still being played out in Edinburgh, in Scotland and, indeed, across the world. The Festivals remained contested, too. In Edinburgh, the People's Festival was resurrected in 2002, initially as a one-off celebration of Hamish Henderson but, from 2003, also to challenge the perceived elitism and expense of the Fringe. After devolution in 1999, and in the midst of current debates about Scottish national independence, culture has become even more important and the site of continuing, vigorous debate.[27]

The Edinburgh Festivals came to represent the very hub of new 'liberal' culture in Scotland. They played a valuable role in fracturing the atmosphere of moral austerity that Presbyterianism had imposed on Scottish culture, provided an exciting space for taking risks and experimenting in the arts, gave birth to a new brand of theatre in the form of fringe theatre (and the Fringe Festivals), and provided a focal point and arena for 'culture wars' in Britain during the middle decades of the twentieth century. I sometimes wonder how different things might have been had Sir Rudolf Bing's original proposal for an international arts festival been welcomed in Oxford, or any of the other towns and cities he considered before he stumbled upon Edinburgh . . .

NOTES

1. NLS, EFS, Dep 378, EIFMD Programme, 1971.
2. Miller, *The Edinburgh International Festival*, 77.
3. Moffat, *The Edinburgh Fringe*, 86.
4. Williams, *Keywords*, 92; Sinfield, *Literature, Politics and Culture in Postwar Britain*, 55.
5. In 1970, the Arts Council and SAC reports on theatre both showed an increase in local authority subsidy of the theatre during the 1960s, but highlighted that more could be done. See ACGB, *The Theatre Today*; SAC, *Theatre in Scotland*.

6. *The Times*, 23 August 1947.
7. Maley, 'Representing Scotland in the 1970s', 85.
8. Harvie, *No Gods and Precious Few Heroes*, 156.
9. Henderson, cited in Bort, *'Tis Sixty Years Since*, 189.
10. Playwright Stanley Eveling complained in November 1971 that Scottish television did not actively encourage Scottish work. Eveling, *The Total Theatre*, 13.
11. Bruce, *Festival in the North*, 214.
12. Richard Demarco, 6 October 2004.
13. Oliver, *Magic in the Gorbals*, 10.
14. *Guardian*, 5 August 2006.
15. Alexander Moffat, 15 March 2012.
16. *Take Note!*, October 1947.
17. *Scotland*, June 1965.
18. *Scots Magazine*, October 1955.
19. The Traverse had also pioneered Sunday closing and Monday opening in theatres, something that did not become mainstream until Jennie Lee and Hugh Jenkins were able to get it on the statute books in 1972 (after a private member's bill to legalise Sunday opening was defeated in 1968), Black, 'Making Britain a Gayer and More Cultivated Country', 331.
20. See also Brown, 'Spectacle, Restraint and the Twentieth-century Sabbath Wars'.
21. Alexander Moffat, 15 March 2012.
22. Hamish Henderson cited in Bort, *'Tis Sixty Years Since*, 189.
23. ECA, EFP 1965–6, letter from Duncan to Peter Diamand, 24 March 1966 (see Chapter 6).
24. *Reports to GA 1971*, 392.
25. Rather than a process of secularisation, McLeod argues for a 'decline of Christendom' in order to take account of the emergence of new forms of religion and spirituality. Locating this in a longer-term process, he argues that this loosening was the final and most complex stage. McLeod, *The Religious Crisis of the 1960s*, 18–19.
26. Williams, *Culture and Society*, 295.
27. See e.g. Bartie, 'Culture in the Everyday', and the ongoing, lively debates about Creative Scotland, the body created in 2010 to replace the Scottish Arts Council (which had achieved independence from the Arts Council in 1994).

Appendix 1

List of Lord Provosts/Chairs of the Edinburgh Festival Society and Artistic Directors of the Edinburgh International Festival, 1947–1970

For the duration of their three-year posts, Edinburgh's Lord Provosts also chaired the Edinburgh Festival Society. Artistic directors (the title was changed to 'festival director' in 1962) were appointed by the EFS and stayed in their posts until they either resigned or were dismissed.

Lord Provosts/Chairs

1944–7: Sir John Falconer
1948–50: Sir Andrew Murray
1951–3: Sir James Miller
1954–6: Sir John Banks
1957–59: Sir Ian Johnson-Gilbert
1960–2: Sir J. Greig Dunbar
1963–5: Sir Duncan Weatherstone
1966–9: Sir Herbert Brechin
1970–2: Sir James McKay

Artistic/Festival director

1947–9: Rudolf Bing
1950–5: Ian Hunter
1956–60: Robert Ponsonby
1961–5: George Lasselles,
   Earl of Harewood
1966–78: Peter Diamand

Appendix 2

Short Biographies of Oral History Interviewees

CALDER, JOHN (b. 1927)

Born into a conservative Scottish landed family (his mother's side were wealthy Canadian industrialists), John Calder grew up in Britain and Canada. He attended university in Canada and Switzerland and was destined to join the family business, a timber company. However, Calder had other ideas. In 1949, he set up his first publishing company and by the late 1950s was making a name for publishing avant-garde European and American writers, including Beckett, Ionesco, Burroughs and Miller. During the 1960s, he continued to publish, led organisation of the International Writers' and Drama Conferences of 1962 and 1963 respectively, became involved in the Traverse Theatre Club and also ran his own arts festival, Ledlanet Nights, in Kinross-shire from 1963 to 1974. Calder still writes and in 2002 co-founded the Godot Company. He lives in Edinburgh and Paris.

COLVIN, SHEILA (b. 1935)

Born in Lancashire, Sheila Colvin moved to Edinburgh when she was ten years old. After leaving school, Colvin worked in the arts, beginning at the BBC then moving to New York to work both in theatre and for a television channel. She returned to Edinburgh for the summer of 1962 for a short holiday. Here she met Richard Demarco (q.v.), who introduced her to his friends, and 'just got caught up in Edinburgh'. Colvin became involved in the Traverse Theatre Club, becoming its first secretary and then general manager (from 1964), before moving to London in 1966 to work for a theatrical agency as well as London Weekend Television. In 1979, Colvin joined the EIFMD, becoming associate director in 1985, the first woman to do so, where she stayed until 1989. Her next post was as general director of the Aldeburgh Foundation (1990–9). Colvin remains actively involved in the arts in Scotland and lives in Edinburgh and Paris.

DEMARCO, RICHARD (b. 1930)

Edinburgh born and raised, and a graduate of Edinburgh College of Art, Richard Demarco became an art teacher at Duns Scotus Academy in

Edinburgh. He got involved in the Paperback Bookshop and the Traverse Theatre, founding the Traverse Art Gallery in 1963. The Demarco Gallery was established in 1966, and Demarco became increasingly involved with directing official Festival exhibitions of contemporary art. In 1970 the famous Strategy: Get Arts exhibition introduced the avant-garde German artist Joseph Beuys to Britain, and later exhibitions brought many artists from 'behind the Iron Curtain'. Demarco continues to live and breathe the arts, organising exhibitions and theatrical events, collaborating with international artists, and working to ensure the long-term survival of the Demarco Archive.

HAYNES, JIM (b. 1933)

Born and brought up in Louisiana, with his teenage years spent in Venezuela (where his father worked in the oil fields), Haynes attended Louisiana State University. He arrived in Edinburgh as part of his US military service in 1956, opened the Paperback Bookshop in 1959, and co-founded the Traverse Theatre in 1962. Haynes then moved to London, where he helped set up and run the underground newspaper *International Times* (*IT*) in 1966, followed by the alternative arts space the Arts Lab in 1967. In 1969, Haynes co-founded *Suck*, Europe's first 'sexpaper', and then the Wet Dream Film Festivals of 1970–1 (all based in Amsterdam). Also in 1969, he moved to Paris (where he still lives) to teach media and sexual politics at the University of Paris. Since 1978, Haynes has been hosting Sunday Salons at his atelier, to which all are welcome – for full details, see www.jim-haynes.com.

MCGRATH, TOM (1940–2009)

Brought up in Rutherglen and Glasgow, on leaving school McGrath immersed himself in the jazz and poetry scene, becoming both a jazz pianist and a poet. He left for London in 1962 and worked for *Peace News*, performed at the seminal Albert Hall poetry reading of 1965 and was the first editor of *International Times* from 1966. Having become a heroin addict, McGrath returned to Glasgow in 1969, overcame his addiction, and went to Glasgow University to study English and drama. In 1972 he was musical director of *The Great Northern Welly Boot Show* (by Billy Connolly and John Byrne), Two years later he co-founded the Third Eye Centre (now the Centre for Contemporary Arts) and was its first director, until 1977. In 1976 he achieved success as a playwright with *Laurel and Hardy*, his first play. A major playwright in Scotland, McGrath's other plays include *The Hard Man*, *Animal* and *Dream Train*.

MOFFAT, ALEXANDER (b. 1943)

Alexander Moffat grew up in the Kingdom of Fife and went to Edinburgh College of Art in 1960. There, he met John Bellany and, together with his friend, the poet Alan Bold, they mounted a challenge to what they saw as the bourgeois and conservative nature of Scottish art. Their famous exhibitions on Castle Terrace took place during the Festival period in 1963, 1964 and 1965. After being inspired by his attendance at the 1962 International Writers' Conference, Moffat became interested in Hugh MacDiarmid and the Scottish renaissance, becoming known as a Scottish realist painter. He has painted many famous Scottish writers and artists, including Bold, MacDiarmid and Muriel Spark. His most famous work remains *Poet's Pub* (1980). Moffat became chair of the New 57 Gallery (1975–8) and began teaching at Glasgow College of Art in 1979, where he was made head of painting in the 1980s. In 1985, he curated the exhibition New Image: Glasgow, which featured paintings by six young artists (most of whom had been his students): Stephen Barclay, Steven Campbell, Ken Currie, Peter Howson, Mario Rossi and Adrian Wiszniewski. Moffat retired from the School of Art in 2005, but continues to paint and speak publicly on the arts, and has recently co-authored *Arts of Resistance: Poets, Portraits and Landscapes of Modern Scotland* (with Alan Riach and Linda MacDonald-Lewis).

OLIVER, CORDELIA (1923–2010)

Born and brought up in Glasgow, Cordelia Patrick attended Glasgow School of Art. Marrying photographer and writer George Oliver in 1948, she lived in London for a year before moving to Edinburgh, and then finally back to Glasgow in 1959. During the 1950s, Oliver drew artistic performers for the *Glasgow Herald* before becoming 'our art critic' (in the days before it was seen as acceptable for women to be newspaper critics). In 1961 she was appointed Scottish art and theatre critic for the *Manchester Guardian*, a position which she held for twenty-five years. Oliver also helped to found the Third Eye Centre in Glasgow (now the Centre for Contemporary Arts) and wrote books on the artist Joan Eardley, Scottish Opera and the Citizens Theatre.

Sources and Select Bibliography

ORAL HISTORY INTERVIEWS

All interviews are archived at the Scottish Oral History Centre, University of Strathclyde, Glasgow, and were conducted by the author.

John Calder, 7 May 2005 (Edinburgh)
Sheila Colvin, 3 May 2005 (Glasgow)
Richard Demarco, 2 March 2004 (Edinburgh)
Richard Demarco, 6 October 2004 (Edinburgh)
John Flattau (and Jim Haynes), 17 August 2003 (Edinburgh)
Jim Haynes, 17 August 2003 (Edinburgh)
Jim Haynes, 12 December 2003 (Paris)
Jim Haynes, 17 June 2005 (Paris)
Tom McGrath, 13 June 2005 (Kingskettle, Fife)
Alexander Moffat, 15 March 2012 (Glasgow – additional interviewer, Eleanor Bell)
Cordelia Oliver, 13 April 2005 (Glasgow)

ARCHIVE SOURCES

Edinburgh Central Library
Booksellers and Publishers: Press Cuttings, Vol. 1, 1932–64
Civic Theatres: Conference in Sunderland 31 October 1963, Notes by E. F. Catford, Depute Town Clerk.
Copies of letters received by Town Council in connection with Little Theatre, 1960.
Edinburgh International Festival of Music and Drama, Press Cuttings
'Edinburgh Notes', collection of press cuttings made by Elizabeth Mein, 1944–64
Moral Re-Armament Mission, Press Cuttings
Royal Lyceum Theatre: Press Cuttings, Vol. 1 (1963–5), Vol. 2 (1966), Vol. 3 (1967)
Scottish Association of the Lord's Day Observance Society, Press Cuttings

Edinburgh City Archives
Burgh Court Volumes
Early Festival Papers, 1944–7
Edinburgh Festival Council Agendas and Minutes, 1947–70
Edinburgh Festival Papers, 1946–68
Edinburgh International Festival of Music and Drama Programmes 1947–71
General Purposes Committee Files
Lord Provost's Committee Files
Minutes of the Town Council of Edinburgh, 1945–6

Gallacher Memorial Library
Communist Party Culture Reports
Edinburgh Labour Festival Committee Papers
Plan of Work of National Cultural Committee up to Summer of 1953

National Library of Scotland: Manuscripts
Traverse Theatre Club Archives
James Bridie Papers
Edinburgh Festival Society Papers

National Records of Scotland
CH2/121/62–69: Church of Scotland Presbytery of Edinburgh Minute Book, Vols. V (1943–7), X (1959–61), XI (1962–4), XII (1965–7).
CH2/136/82: Minute Book, St Giles Kirk Sessions, 1945–52.
CO1/5/883: Scottish Arts Council 1965–73, Policy Files.
ED61/45: Scottish Education Department, Art Files, Bodies Concerned with the Arts, Edinburgh Festival Society: General 1946–72.
ED61/75–76: Scottish Arts Council 1965–73: Minutes of Meetings and Papers.

Scottish Theatre Archives
Edinburgh Festival Fringe Archives
Edinburgh Gateway Theatre Company Limited Council Minutes
Glasgow Unity Theatre Papers

Victoria and Albert Museum
Arts Council of Great Britain Archives

NEWSPAPERS, JOURNALS AND MAGAZINES

Akros: Special Hugh MacDiarmid Issue
British Weekly: A Journal of Social and Christian Progress
British Weekly and Christian World
Daily Worker

Edinburgh Evening News
Evening Dispatch
Evening News and Dispatch
Financial Times
Glasgow Herald
The Guardian
The Herald
Life and Work: The Record of the Church of Scotland
New Statesman
New Society
Our Heritage
Plays and Players
Scotland
Scots Magazine
The Scotsman
Scottish Daily Express
Scottish International
Scottish Theatre
Take Note!
The Times

BOOK CHAPTERS AND JOURNAL AND MAGAZINE ARTICLES

Bartie, A., 'Culture in the Everyday', in L. Abrams & C. G. Brown (eds), *A History of Everyday Life in Twentieth-century Scotland* (Edinburgh: Edinburgh University Press, 2010), 206–28.

Bartie, A., 'EXPLORER: Into the Sixties with Tom McGrath', in E. Bell & L. Gunn (eds), *The Scottish Sixties: Reading, Rebellion, Revolution?* (Amsterdam: Rodopi, 2013).

Beecham, T., 'The Edinburgh Festival 1949', in O. Dudley Edwards & G. Richardson (eds), *Edinburgh* (Edinburgh: Canongate, 1983), 270–3.

Bell, E., 'Experimenting with the Verbivocovisual: Edwin Morgan's Early Concrete Poetry', *Scottish Literary Review*, forthcoming.

Bell, E., 'The Ugly Burds without Wings: Reactions to Tradition since the 1960s', in P. Mackay et al. (eds), *Modern Irish and Scottish Poetry* (Cambridge: Cambridge University Press, Cambridge, 2011), 238–50.

Bennett, O., 'Cultural Policy in the United Kingdom: Collapsing Rationales and the End of a Tradition', *European Journal of Cultural Policy*, 1:2 (1995), 199–216.

Birch, L., 'Edinburgh's Festival', *Picture Post*, 20 September 1947.

Black, L., 'Arts and Crafts: Social Democracy's Cultural Resources and Repertoire in 1960s Britain', in J. Callaghan & I. Favretto (eds), *Transitions in Social Democracy: Cultural and Ideological Problems of the Golden Age* (Manchester: Manchester University Press, 2007), 149–62.

Black, L., 'Making Britain a Gayer and More Cultivated Country: Wilson, Lee and the Creative Industries in the 1960s', *Contemporary British History*, 20:3 (2006), 323–42.

Bradby, D. & M. Delgado, 'Editorial', *Contemporary Theatre Review*, 13:4 (2003), 1–4.

Brown, C. G., ' "Each Take Off Their Several Way"? The Protestant Churches and the Working Classes in Scotland', in G. Walker & T. Gallagher (eds), *Sermons and Battle Hymns: Protestant Popular Culture in Modern Scotland* (Edinburgh: Edinburgh University Press, 1990), 69–85.

Brown, C. G., 'Religion and Secularisation', in A. Dickson & J. H. Treble (eds), *People and Society in Scotland Volume III, 1914–1990* (Edinburgh: John Donald, 1992), 48–79.

Brown, C. G., 'Spectacle, Restraint and the Twentieth-century Sabbath Wars: The "Everyday" Scottish Sunday', in L. Abrams & C. G. Brown (eds), *A History of Everyday Life in Twentieth-century Scotland* (Edinburgh: Edinburgh University Press, 2010), 153–80.

Brown, C. G., 'Sport and the Scottish Office in the Twentieth Century: The Control of a Social Problem', *European Sports History Review*, 1 (1999), 164–82.

Brown, I., 'The New Writing Policies of Clive Perry and Stephen MacDonald at the Royal Lyceum Theatre, 1966–79', *International Journal of Scottish Theatre*, 2:2 (2001).

Brown, P., 'The Gateway, Edinburgh' (1961).

Browne, S., ' "A Veritable Hotbed of Feminism": Women's Liberation in St Andrews, Scotland, c. 1968–c. 1979', *Twentieth Century British History*, 23:1 (2012), 100–23.

Bruce-Watt, J., 'Edinburgh's Cultural Catalyst', *Scotland*, June 1965.

Buchan, N., 'Folk and Protest', in E. J. Cowan (ed.), *The People's Past: Scottish Folk, Scottish History* (Edinburgh: Edinburgh University Student Publications Board, 1980), 165–90.

Burns, M., 'The Presbytery and the Play', *Saltire Review*, 3:7 (1956).

Calder, J., 'Alexander Trocchi', *Edinburgh Review*, 70 (1985), 32–5.

Calder, J., 'Happenings in the Theatre', in J.-J. Lebel et al., *Plays and Happenings* (London: Calder & Boyars, 1967), 7–10.

Campbell, I., 'Music against the Bomb', in J. Minnion & P. Bolsover (eds), *The CND Story: The First 25 Years of CND in the Words of the People Involved* (London: Allison & Busby, 1983), 115–17.

Crossland, J. B., 'Festival City', *Edinburgh Tatler*, 1962.

Davie, G., 'Religion in Post-War Britain: A Sociological View', in J. Obelkevich & P. Catterall (eds), *Understanding Post-war British Society* (London: Routledge, 1994), 165–78.

Curtis, B., 'A Highly Mobile and Plastic Environ', in C. Stephens & K. Stout (eds), *Art & the 60s: This Was Tomorrow* (London: Tate, 2004), 47–63.

Davie, G., 'Religion in Post-war Britain: A Sociological View', in J. Obelkevich &

P. Catterall (eds), *Understanding Post-war British Society* (London: Routledge, 1994), 165–78.

Dawson, S. T., 'Selling the Circus: Englishness, Circus Fans and Democracy in Mid-twentieth-century Britain', in B. Bebber (ed.), *Leisure and Cultural Conflict in Twentieth-century Britain* (Manchester: Manchester University Press, 2012), 84–108.

Dewey, K., 'Act of San Francisco at Edinburgh', in J.-J. Lebel et al., *Plays and Happenings* (London: Calder & Boyars, 1967), 67–76.

Dunn, H. & K. Stout, 'Selected Chronology: 1956–69', in C. Stephens & K. Stout (eds), *Art and the 60s: This Was Tomorrow* (London: Tate, 2004), 138–44.

Edwards, O., 'Cradle on the Tree-top: The Edinburgh Festival and Scottish Theatre', in R. Stevenson & G. Wallace (eds), *Scottish Theatre since the Seventies* (Edinburgh: Edinburgh University Press, 1996), 34–48.

Elliott, P., 'Presenting Reality: An Introduction to the Boyle Family', in P. Elliott et al., *Boyle Family* (Edinburgh: National Galleries of Scotland, 2003), 9–19.

Fisher, M., 'From Traverse to Tramway: Scottish Theatres Old and New', in R. Stevenson & G. Wallace (eds), *Scottish Theatre since the Seventies* (Edinburgh: Edinburgh University Press, 1996), pp. 49–56.

Gallagher, T., 'The Press and Protestant Popular Culture: A Case Study of the *Scottish Daily Express*', in G. Walker & T. Gallagher (eds), *Sermons and Battle Hymns: Protestant Popular Culture in Modern Scotland* (Edinburgh: Edinburgh University Press, 1990), 193–212.

Galloway, S. & H. D. Jones, 'The Scottish Dimension of British Arts Government: A Historical Perspective', *Cultural Trends*, 19:1 (2010), 27–40.

Garattoni, M., 'Scottish Drama at the Edinburgh Fringe until the Seventies', in V. Poggi & M. Rose (eds), *A Theatre that Matters: Twentieth-century Scottish Drama and Theatre – A Selection of Critical Essays and Interviews* (Milan: Unicopli, 2000), 171–87.

Gibson, C., ' "Tomorrow, Songs / Will Flow Free Again, and New Voices / Be Born on the Carrying Stream": Hamish Henderson's Conception of the Scottish Folk-song Revival and Its Place in Literary Scotland', *The Drouth*, 32 (2009), 48–59.

Glasgow, M., 'The Concept of the Arts Council', in M. Keynes (ed.), *Essays on John Maynard Keynes* (London: Cambridge University Press, 1975), 260–72.

Harvie, J., 'Cultural Effects of the Edinburgh International Festival: Elitism, Identities, Industries', *Contemporary Theatre Review*, 13:4 (2003), 12–26.

Hayes, N., 'More than "Music-While-You-Eat"? Factory and Hostel Concerts, "Good Culture" and the Workers', in N. Hayes & J. Hill (eds), *'Millions Like Us'? British Culture in the Second World War* (Liverpool: Liverpool University Press, 1999), 209–35.

Henderson, H., 'The Edinburgh People's Festival, 1951–1954', in E. Bort (ed.), *'Tis Sixty Years Since: The 1951 Edinburgh People's Festival Ceilidh and the Scottish Folk Revival* (Ochtertyre: Grace Note, 2011), 35–44.

Henderson, H., ' "It Was in You that It A' Began": Some Thoughts on the Folk

Conference', in E. J. Cowan (ed.), *The People's Past: Scottish Folk, Scottish History* (Edinburgh: Edinburgh University Student Publications Board, 1980), 4–15.

Hill, J., 'Glasgow Unity Theatre: The Search for a "Scottish People's Theatre"', *New Edinburgh Review*, 40 (1978), 27–31.

Hill, J., '"When Work Is Over": Labour, Leisure and Culture in Wartime Britain', in N. Hayes & J. Hill (eds), *Millions Like Us? British Culture in the Second World War* (Liverpool: Liverpool University Press, 1999), 236–60.

Hutchinson, D., 'Scottish Drama 1900–1950', in C. Craig (ed.), *The History of Scottish Literature, Volume 4: Twentieth Century* (Aberdeen: Aberdeen University Press, 1987), 163–77.

Jamieson, K., 'Edinburgh: The Festival Gaze and Its Boundaries', *Space and Culture*, 7:1 (2004), 64–75.

Johnson, K., 'Apart from *Look Back in Anger*, What *Else* Was Worrying the Lord Chamberlain's Office in 1956?', in D. Shellard (ed.), *British Theatre in the 1950s* (London: Sheffield Academic Press, 2000), 116–35.

Johnston, G., 'Revisiting the Cultural Cold War', *Social History*, 35: 3 (2010), 290–307.

Johnston, J., '"Happenings" on the New York Scene', in C. Marowitz et al. (eds), *New Theatre Voices of the Fifties and Sixties: Selections from Encore Magazine, 1956–1963* (London: Eyre Methuen, 1981), 260–5.

Jones, H. D., '"An Art of Our Own": State Patronage of the Visual Arts in Wales, 1945–1967', *Contemporary British History*, published online May 2012.

Jones, H. D. & S. Galloway, 'Arts Governance in Scotland: the Saga of Scottish Opera, 1962–2007', *Journal of Scottish Historical Studies*, 31:2 (2011), 220–41.

Laing, S., 'Economy, Society and Culture in 1960s Britain: Contexts and Conditions for Psychedelic Art', in C. Grunenberg & J. Harris (eds), *Summer of Love: Psychedelic Art, Social Crisis and Counterculture in the 1960s* (Liverpool: Liverpool University Press, 2006), 19–34.

Laing, S., 'The Politics of Culture: Institutional Change', in B. Moore-Gilbert & J. Seed (eds), *Cultural Revolution? The Challenge of the Arts in the 1960s* (London: Routledge, 1992), 72–95.

Lebel, J.-J., 'Theory and Practice', in J.-J. Lebel et al., *Plays and Happenings* (London: Calder & Boyars, 1967), 13–48.

Leventhal, F. M., '"The Best for the Most": CEMA and State Sponsorship of the Arts in Wartime, 1939–1945', *Twentieth Century British History*, 1:3 (1990), 289–317.

Levin, B., 'Lady MacChatterley', *New Statesman: The Weekend Review*, 20 December 1963.

Logue, C., 'Alexander Trocchi and the Beginning of Merlin', *Edinburgh Review*, 70 (1985), 59–65.

Louvre, A., 'The New Radicalism: The Politics of Culture in Britain, America and France, 1956–73', in B. Moore-Gilbert & J. Seed (eds), *Cultural Revolution? The Challenge of the Arts in the 1960s* (London: Routledge, 1992), 45–71.

McArthur, E., 'The Cultural Front: Scotland and Northern Ireland, 1940–42', in F. Cullen & J. Morrison (eds), *A Shared Legacy: Essays on Irish and Scottish Art and Visual Culture* (Aldershot: Ashgate, 2005), 191–206.

McGrath, T., 'Remembering Alex Trocchi', *Edinburgh Review*, 70 (1985), 36–47.

McGuigan, J., '"A Slow Reach Again for Control": Raymond Williams and the Vicissitudes of Cultural Policy', *European Journal of Cultural Policy*, 2:1 (1995), 105–15.

Machin, G. I. T., 'British Churches and Social Issues, 1945–60', *Twentieth Century British History*, 7:3 (1996), 345–70.

Machin, I., 'British Churches and Moral Change in the 1960s', in W. Jacob & N. Yates (eds), *Crown and Mitre: Religion and Society in Northern Europe since the Reformation* (Woodbridge: Brydell Press, 1993), 223–41.

MacNaughton, A., 'The Folksong Revival in Scotland', in E. J. Cowan (ed.), *The People's Past: Scottish Folk, Scottish History* (Edinburgh: Edinburgh University Student Publications Board, 1980), 180–93.

Maley, W., 'Representing Scotland in the 1970s', in B. Moore-Gilbert (ed.), *The Arts in the 1970s: Cultural Closure?* (London: Routledge, 1994), 78–98.

Marowitz, C., 'The Confessions of Lenny Bruce', in C. Marowitz et al. (eds), *New Theatre Voices of the Fifties and Sixties: Selections from Encore Magazine, 1956–1963* (London: Eyre Methuen, 1981), 251–9.

Marowitz, C., 'Happenings at Edinburgh', in J.-J. Lebel et al., *Plays and Happenings* (London: Calder & Boyars, 1967), 57–66.

Marshall, J., 'Festival Cities: A Comparison', *Scots Magazine*, 1957.

Marwick, A., 'The Arts, Books, Media and Entertainments in Britain since 1945', in J. Obelkevich & P. Catterall (eds), *Understanding Post-war British Society* (London: Routledge, 1994), 179–91.

Mitchell, G., 'A Very "British" Introduction to Rock 'n' Roll: Tommy Steele and the Advent of Rock 'n' Roll Music in Britain, 1956–1960', *Contemporary British History*, 25:2 (2011), 205–25.

Morgan, E., 'Alexander Trocchi: A Survey', *Edinburgh Review*, 70 (1985), 48–58.

Morris, J., 'The Strange Death of Christian Britain: Another Look at the Secularization Debate', *Historical Journal*, 46:4 (2003), 963–76.

Nairn, T., 'Festival of the Dead', in O. Dudley Edwards & G. Richardson (eds), *Edinburgh* (Edinburgh: Canongate, 1983), 275–9.

Newton, C. C. S., 'The Sterling Crisis of 1947 and the British Response to the Marshall Plan', *Economic History Review*, 37:3 (1984), 391–408.

Nicholson, 'Foreign Drama and the Lord Chamberlain in the 1950s', in D. Shellard (ed.), *British Theatre in the 1950s* (London: Sheffield Academic Press, 2000), 41–52.

Normand, T., '55° North 3° West: A Panorama from Scotland', in D. Arnold & D. P. Corbett (eds), *A Companion to British Art: 1600 to the Present* (Chichester: Wiley-Blackwell, forthcoming. Copy sent by Tom Normand, with grateful thanks).

Prentice, R. & V. Andersen, 'Festival as Creative Destination', *Annals of Tourism Research*, 30:1 (2003), 7–30.

Priestman, M., 'A Critical Stage: Drama in the 1960s,' in B. Moore-Gilbert & J. Seed (eds), *Cultural Revolution? The Challenge of the Arts in the 1960s* (London: Routledge, 1992), 118–38.

Quinn, B., 'Art Festivals and the City', *Urban Studies*, 42:5–6 (2005), 927–43.

Quinn, B., 'Changing Festival Places: Insights from Galway', *Social & Cultural Geography*, 6:2 (2005), 237–52.

Quinn, B., 'Symbols, Practices and Myth-making: Cultural Perspectives on the Wexford Festival Opera', *Tourism Geographies*, 5:3 (2003), 329–49.

Reid, A., 'Has the Festival "Stuck"?', *Scotland*, August 1957.

Reid, A., 'The Three Estates', *Scotland's Magazine*, 1959.

'Reports on the International Writers' Conference', *The Bookseller*, 1 September 1962.

Rosie, G., 'Religion', in M. Linklater & R. Denniston (eds), *Anatomy of Scotland: How Scotland Works* (Edinburgh: Chambers, 1992), 78–96.

Rudman, M., 'Edinburgh's Traverse, Now and Then', in S. Morley (ed.), *Theatre '72: Plays, Players, Playwrights, Theatres, Opera, Ballet* (London: Hutchinson, 1973), 123–31.

Scullion, A., 'Glasgow Unity Theatre: The Necessary Contradictions of Scottish Political Theatre', *Twentieth Century British History*, 13:3 (2002), 215–52.

Scullion, A., 'Political Theatre or Heritage Culture? *Ane Satyre of the Thrie Estaitis* in Production', in C. Gribben & D. G. Mullan (eds), *Literature and the Scottish Reformation* (Aldershot: Ashgate, 2009), 213–32.

Seed, J., 'Hegemony Postponed: The Unravelling of the Culture of Consensus in Britain in the 1960s', in B. Moore-Gilbert & J. Seed (eds), *Cultural Revolution? The Challenge of the Arts in the 1960s* (London: Routledge, 1992), 15–39.

Shellard, D., '1950–54', in D. Shellard (ed.), *British Theatre in the 1950s* (London: Sheffield Academic Press, 2000), 28–40.

Smith, D., '1950–1995', in B. Findlay (ed.), *A History of Scottish Theatre* (Edinburgh: Polygon, 1998), 253–308.

Smith, D., 'Kirk and Theatre', in I. Brown (ed.), *Journey's Beginning: The Gateway Theatre Building and Company, 1884–1965* (Bristol: Intellect, 2004), 29–36.

Steele, T., 'Hey Jimmy! The Legacy of Gramsci in British Cultural Politics', in G. Andrews et al. (eds), *New Left, New Right and Beyond: Taking the Sixties Seriously* (Basingstoke: Palgrave, 1999), 26–41.

Stevenson, R., 'Scottish Theatre, 1950–1980', in C. Craig (ed.), *The History of Scottish Literature, Volume 4: Twentieth Century* (Aberdeen: Aberdeen University Press, 1987), 349–67.

Stevenson, R., 'Snakes and Ladders, Snakes and Owls: Charting Scottish Theatre', in R. Stevenson & G. Wallace (eds), *Scottish Theatre since the Seventies* (Edinburgh: Edinburgh University Press, 1996), 1–20.

Stiles, K., 'The Story of the Destruction in Art Symposium and the "DIAS affect"', in S. Breitwieser (ed.), *Gustav Metzger: Geschichte Geschichte* (Ostfildern: Hatje Cantz, 2005), 41–65.

Thomas, N. 'Challenging the Myths of the 1960s: The Case of Student Protest in Britain', *Twentieth Century British History*, 13:3 (2002), 277–97.

Thomas, N., 'Protests against the Vietnam War in 1960s Britain: The Relationship between Protesters and the Press', *Contemporary British History* 22:3 (2008), 335–54.

Upchurch, A. R., 'Keynes's Legacy: An Intellectual's Influence Reflected in Arts Policy', *International Journal of Cultural Policy*, 17:1 (2011), 69–80.

Varon, J. et al., 'Time Is an Ocean: The Past and Future of the Sixties', *The Sixties*, 1:1 (2008), 1–7.

Waterman, S., 'Carnivals for Elites? The Cultural Politics of Arts Festivals', *Progress in Human Geography*, 22:1 (1998), 54–74.

Wehle, P., '"Avignon, Everybody's Dream"', *Contemporary Theatre Review*, 13:4 (2003), 27–41.

Whipple, A., 'Speaking for Whom? The 1971 Festival of Light and the Search for the "Silent Majority"', *Contemporary British History*, 24:3 (2010), 319–39.

Wilson, A., 'A Poetics of Dissent: Notes on a Developing Counterculture in London in the Early Sixties', in C. Stephens & K. Stout (eds), *Art & the 60s: This Was Tomorrow* (London: Tate, 2004), 92–111.

Wilson, A., 'Towards an Index for Everything: The Events of Mark Boyle and Joan Hills, 1963–71', in P. Elliott et al, *Boyle Family* (Edinburgh: National Galleries of Scotland, 2003), 45–80.

Wilson, M., 'Your Reputation Precedes You: A Reception Study of *Naked Lunch*', *Journal of Modern Literature*, 35:2 (2012), 98–125.

BOOKS

Abel-Smith, B. and P. Townsend, *The Poor and the Poorest: A New Analysis of the Ministry of Labour's Family Expenditure Surveys of 1953–54 and 1960* (London: G. Bell, 1965)

Aldgate, A., *Censorship and the Permissive Society: British Cinema and Theatre, 1955–1965* (Oxford: Clarendon Press, 1995).

Allen, T. (ed.), *Crusade in Scotland: Billy Graham* (London: Pickering & Inglis, 1955).

Allsop, K., *The Angry Decade: A Survey of the Cultural Revolt of the Nineteen-fifties* (London: Peter Owen, 1958).

Ansorge, P., *Disrupting the Spectacle: Five Years of Experimental and Fringe Theatre in Britain* (London: Pitman, 1975).

Arnold, M., *Culture and Anarchy*, ed. J. D. Wilson (Cambridge: Cambridge University Press, 1932).

Arts Council of Great Britain, *The Obscenity Laws: A Report by the Working Party Set Up by a Conference Convened by the Chairman of the Arts Council of Great Britain* (London: André Deutsch, 1969).

Atkinson, H., *The Festival of Britain: A Land and Its People* (London: I. B. Tauris, 2012).

Bain, A. (ed.), *The Fringe: 50 Years of the Greatest Show on Earth* (Edinburgh: Scotsman, 1996).

Bannister, W., *James Bridie and His Theatre: A Study of James Bridie's Personality, His Stage Plays and His Work for the Foundation of a Scottish National Theatre* (London: Rockliff, 1955).

Bartie, A. & E. Bell (eds), *The International Writers' Conference Revisited: Edinburgh, 1962* (Glasgow: Cargo, 2012).

Bell, E. & L. Gunn (eds), *The Scottish Sixties: Reading, Rebellion, Revolution?* (Amsterdam: Rodopi, 2013).

Bennett, A. et al., *Beyond the Fringe* (London: Souvenir Press, 1963).

Billington, M., *State of the Nation: British Theatre since 1945* (London: Faber & Faber, 2007).

Bing, Sir R., *5,000 Nights at the Opera* (London: Hamish Hamilton, 1972).

Birrell, R. & A. Finlay (eds), *Justified Sinners: An Archaeology of Scottish Counter-culture (1960–2000)* (Edinburgh: Pocketbooks, 2001).

Black, L., *Old Labour, New Britain? The Political Culture of the Left in 'Affluent' Britain, 1951–64* (Basingstoke: Palgrave Macmillan, 2002).

Black, L., *Redefining British Politics: Culture, Consumerism and Participation, 1954–70* (Basingstoke: Palgrave Macmillan, 2010).

Bold, A., *MacDiarmid: Christopher Murray Grieve – A Critical Biography* (London: John Murray, 1988).

Booker, C., *The Neophiliacs: A Study of the Revolution in English Life in the Fifties and Sixties* (London: Collins, 1969).

Bort, E. (ed.), *'Tis Sixty Years Since: The 1951 Edinburgh People's Festival Ceilidh and the Scottish Folk Revival* (Ochtertyre: Grace Note, 2011).

Bottoms, S. J., *Playing Underground: A Critical History of the 1960s Off-Off-Broadway Movement* (Ann Arbor: University of Michigan Press, 2004).

British Council of Churches, *Sex and Morality: A Report to the British Council of Churches, October 1966* (London: SCM Press, 1966).

Brown, C. G., *The Death of Christian Britain: Understanding Secularisation, 1800–2000* (London: Routledge, 2000).

Brown, C. G., *Religion and Society in Scotland since 1707* (Edinburgh: Edinburgh University Press, 1997).

Brown, C. G., *Religion and Society in Twentieth-century Britain* (Harlow: Pearson Longman, 2006).

Brown, G. et al. (eds), *Alternative Edinburgh: A City Guide with a Difference* (Edinburgh: Edinburgh University Student Publications Board, 1972).

Bruce, G., *Festival in the North: The Story of the Edinburgh Festival* (London: Robert Hale, 1975).

Bruce, L., *How to Talk Dirty and Influence People: An Autobiography* (London: Peter Owen, 1966).

Calder, A., *The People's War: Britain, 1939–1945* (London: Pimlico, 1992).

Calder, J., *Pursuit: The Uncensored Memoirs of John Calder* (London: Calder, 2001).

Callaghan, J., *Cold War, Crisis and Conflict: The History of the Communist Party of Great Britain, 1951–68* (London: Lawrence & Wishart, 2003).

Cameron, E., *Impaled upon a Thistle: Scotland since 1880* (Edinburgh: Edinburgh University Press, 2010).

Campbell, B. (ed.), *Another Edinburgh: A Living Guide* (Edinburgh: Edinburgh University Student Publications Board, 1976).

Campbell, D., *A Brighter Sunshine: A Hundred Years of the Edinburgh Royal Lyceum Theatre* (Edinburgh: Polygon, 1983).

Campbell, D., *Playing for Scotland: A History of the Scottish Stage, 1715–1965* (Edinburgh: Mercat Press, 1996).

Cant, B. (ed.), *Footsteps and Witnesses: Lesbian and Gay Lifestories from Scotland* (Edinburgh: Polygon, 1993).

Carpenter, H., *That Was Satire That Was: The Satire Boom of the 1960s* (London: Victor Gollancz, 2000).

Carstairs, G. M., *This Island Now: The BBC Reith Lectures 1962* (London: Hogarth Press, 1963).

Chambers, C. (ed.), *The Continuum Companion to Twentieth Century Theatre* (London: Continuum, 2002).

Chambers, C., *The Story of Unity Theatre* (London: Lawrence & Wishart, 1989).

Collins, M. (ed.), *The Permissive Society and its Enemies: Sixties British Culture* (London: Rivers Oram, 2007).

Conekin, B. E., *'The Autobiography of a Nation': The 1951 Festival of Britain* (Manchester: Manchester University Press, 2003).

Coveney, M., *The Citz: 21 Years of the Glasgow Citizens Theatre* (London: Nick Hern, 1990).

Cowan, E. J. (ed.), *The People's Past: Scottish Folk, Scottish History* (Edinburgh: Edinburgh University Student Publications Board, 1980)

Crawford, I., *Banquo on Thursdays: the Inside Story of Fifty Edinburgh Festivals* (Edinburgh: Goblinshead, 1997).

Crummy, H., *Let the People Sing! A Story of Craigmillar* (Edinburgh: Helen Crummy, 1992).

Daiches, D., *Edinburgh* (London: Hamish Hamilton, 1978).

Dale, M., *Sore Throats and Overdrafts: An Illustrated Story of the Edinburgh Festival Fringe* (Edinburgh: Precedent, 1988).

Davidson, R. & G. Davis, *The Sexual State: Sexuality and Scottish Governance, 1950–80* (Edinburgh: Edinburgh University Press, 2012).

Davies, C., *Permissive Britain: Social Change in the Sixties and Seventies* (London: Pitman, 1975).

Demarco, R., *The Artist as Explorer* (Edinburgh: Richard Demarco Gallery, 1978).

Devine, T. M. (ed.), *Scotland and the Union, 1707–2007* (Edinburgh: Edinburgh University Press, 2008).

Donaldson, F., *The British Council: The First Fifty Years* (London: Jonathan Cape, 1984).

Donnelly, M., *Sixties Britain: Culture, Society and Politics* (Harlow: Pearson Education, 2005).

Driberg, T., *The Mystery of Moral Re-Armament: A Study of Frank Buchman and His Movement* (London: Secker & Warburg, 1964).

Drummond, P., *The Provincial Music Festival in England, 1784–1914* (Farnham: Ashgate, 2011).

Dudley Edwards, O., *City of a Thousand Worlds: Edinburgh in Festival* (Edinburgh: Mainstream, 1991).

Dudley Edwards, O. & G. Richardson (eds), *Edinburgh* (Edinburgh: Canongate, 1983).

Dworkin, D., *Cultural Marxism in Postwar Britain: History, the New Left, and the Origins of Cultural Studies* (Durham, NC: Duke University Press, 1997).

Edinburgh Corporation, *Edinburgh Official Guide* (1960–2).

Eliot, T. S., *Notes towards the Definition of Culture* (London: Faber & Faber, 1948).

Elliott, P. et al., *Boyle Family* (Edinburgh: National Galleries of Scotland, 2003).

Elsom, J., *Theatre outside London* (London: Macmillan, 1971).

Eveling, S., *The Total Theatre* (Edinburgh: Heriot-Watt University, 1971).

Fielding, S., *The Labour Governments 1964–70, Volume I: Labour and Cultural Change* (Manchester: Manchester University Press, 2003).

Findlater, R., *BANNED! A Review of Theatrical Censorship in Britain* (London: MacGibbon & Kee, 1967).

Findlay, B. (ed.), *Scottish People's Theatre: Plays by Glasgow Unity Writers* (Glasgow: Association for Scottish Literary Studies, 2008).

Fink, C. et al. (eds), *1968: The World Transformed* (Cambridge: Cambridge University Press, 1998).

Finlay, A. (ed.), *The Armstrong Nose: Selected Letters of Hamish Henderson* (Edinburgh: Polygon, 1996).

Finlay, R., *Modern Scotland, 1914–2000* (London: Profile, 2004).

Fountain, N., *Underground: the London Alternative Press, 1966–74* (London: Routledge, 1988).

Fraser, I. M., *Ecumenical Adventure: a Dunblane Initiative* (Glasgow: ACTS, 2003).

Friedman, K. (ed.), *The Fluxus Reader* (Chichester: Academy Editions, 1998).

George-Warren, H. (ed.), *The Rolling Stone Book of the Beats: The Beat Generation and American Culture* (New York: Hyperion, 1999).

Gray, C., *The Politics of the Arts in Britain* (Basingstoke: Macmillan Press, 2000).

Green, J., *All Dressed Up: The Sixties and the Counterculture* (London: Pimlico, 1999).

Green, J., *Days in the Life: Voices from the English Underground, 1961–1971* (London: Pimlico, 1998).

Grunenberg, C. (ed.), *Summer of Love: Art of the Psychedelic Era* (London: Tate, 2005).

Hall, S. & Whannel, P., *The Popular Arts* (London: Hutchinson Educational, 1964).

Hardy, F., *Slightly Mad and Full of Dangers. The Story of the Edinburgh Film Festival* (Edinburgh: Ramsay Head Press, 1992).

Harewood, Earl of, *The Tongs and the Bones: The Memoirs of Lord Harewood* (London: Weidenfeld & Nicolson, 1981).

Harker, B., *Class Act: The Cultural and Political Life of Ewan MacColl* (London: Pluto Press, 2007).

Harvie, C., *No Gods and Precious Few Heroes: Twentieth Century Scotland* (Edinburgh: Edinburgh University Press, 1998).

Harvie, J., *Staging the UK* (Manchester: Manchester University Press, 2005).

Hayes, N. & J. Hill (eds), *'Millions Like Us'? British Culture in the Second World War* (Liverpool: Liverpool University Press, 1999).

Haynes, J., *Thanks for Coming! An Autobiography* (London: Faber & Faber, 1984).

Henri, A., *Environments and Happenings* (London: Thames & Hudson, 1974).

Hewison, R., *Culture and Consensus: England, Art and Politics since 1940* (London: Methuen, 1995).

Hewison, R., *Footlights! A Hundred Years of Cambridge Comedy* (London: Methuen, 1983).

Hewison, R., *In Anger: Culture in the Cold War, 1945–60* (London: Weidenfeld & Nicolson, 1981).

Hewison, R., *Too Much: Art and Society in the Sixties, 1960–1975* (London: Methuen, 1986).

Hewison, R., *Under Siege: Literary Life in London, 1939–1945* (London: Weidenfeld & Nicolson, 1977).

Hewison, R. & J. Holden, *Experience and Experiment: The UK Branch of the Calouste Gulbenkian Foundation, 1956–2006* (London: Calouste Gulbenkian Foundation, 2006).

Highet, J., *The Scottish Churches: A Review of Their State 400 Years after the Reformation* (London: Skeffington, 1960).

Hinchliffe, A. P., *British Theatre, 1950–70* (Oxford: Basil Blackwell, 1974).

Hoggart, R., *The Uses of Literacy: Aspects of Working-class Life, with Special Reference to Publications and Entertainments* (London: Chatto & Windus, 1957).

Hollis, P., *Jennie Lee: A Life* (Oxford: Oxford University Press, 1997).

Howard, P., *Britain and the Beast* (London: Heinemann, 1963).

Hutchison, D., *The Modern Scottish Theatre* (Glasgow: Molendinar Press, 1977).

Hutchison, R., *The Politics of the Arts Council* (London: Sinclair Browne, 1982).

Inglis, B., *Private Conscience: Public Morality* (London: Four Square, 1964).

Itzin, C., *Stages in the Revolution: Political Theatre in Britain since 1968* (London: Eyre Methuen, 1980).

Jarvis, M., *Conservative Governments, Morality and Social Change in Affluent Britain, 1957–64* (Manchester: Manchester University Press, 2005).

Jenkins, H., *The Culture Gap: An Experience of Government and the Arts* (London: Marion Boyars, 1978).

Kellas, J. G., *Modern Scotland: The Nation since 1870* (London: Pall Mall Press, 1968).

Kurlansky, M., *1968: The Year that Rocked the World* (London: Jonathan Cape, 2004).

Lane, T., *Side by Side: The Traverse Theatre Before and After* (Roma: Duca della Corgna, 2007).

Levin, B., *The Pendulum Years: Britain and the Sixties* (London: Pan, 1972).

Lord's Day Observance Society, *Our Yearbook: Annual Report of the Lord's Day Observance Society* (1944–52).

McArthur, E., *Scotland, CEMA and the Arts Council, 1919–1967: Background, Politics and Visual Art Policy* (Aldershot: Ashgate, 2013).

MacColl, E., *Journeyman: An Autobiography* (London: Sidgwick & Jackson, 1990).

McCrone, D., *Understanding Scotland: The Sociology of a Nation* (London: Routledge, 2001).

MacDiarmid, H., *The Company I've Kept* (London: Hutchinson, 1966).

MacDonald, C. M. M., *Whaur Extremes Meet: Scotland's Twentieth Century* (Edinburgh: John Donald, 2009).

McGlone, J., *(Behind the) Fringe: Conversations with Leslie Bennie (Treasurer 1972–2002) and Andrew Kerr (Company Secretary 1969–2002)* (Edinburgh: Festival Fringe Society, 2003).

McGough, R., *Said and Done: The Autobiography* (London: Century, 2005).

McGrath, J., *The Bone Won't Break: On Theatre and Hope in Hard Times* (London: Methuen Drama, 1990).

McKay, G., *Circular Breathing: The Cultural Politics of Jazz in Britain* (Durham, NC: Duke University Press, 2006).

Mackenney, L., *The Activities of Popular Dramatists and Drama Groups in Scotland, 1900–1952* (Lewiston, NY: Edwin Mellen Press, 2000).

McLeod, H., *The Religious Crisis of the 1960s* (Oxford: Oxford University Press, 2007).

McMillan, J., *The Traverse Theatre Story, 1963–1988* (London: Methuen Drama, 1988).

MacMillan, P. R., *Censorship and Public Morality* (Aldershot: Gower, 1983).

Marowitz, C. et al. (eds), *New Theatre Voices of the Fifties and Sixties: Selections from Encore Magazine, 1956–1963* (London: Eyre Methuen, 1981).

Martin, B., *A Sociology of Contemporary Cultural Change* (Oxford: Basil Blackwell, 1981).

Marwick, A., *The Arts in the West since 1945* (Oxford: Oxford University Press, 2002).

Marwick, A., *British Society since 1945*, 3rd ed. (London: Penguin, 1996).

Marwick, A., *The Sixties: Cultural Revolution in Britain, France, Italy, and the United States, c.1958–c.1974* (Oxford: Oxford University Press, 1998).

Miles, B., *In the Sixties* (London: Jonathan Cape, 2002).

Miles, B., *London Calling: A Countercultural History of London since 1945* (London: Atlantic, 2010).

Miller, E., *The Edinburgh International Festival, 1947–1996* (Aldershot: Scolar Press, 1996).

Minihan, J., *The Nationalization of Culture: The Development of State Subsidies to the Arts in Great Britain* (London: Hamish Hamilton, 1977).

Minnion, J. & P. Bolsover (eds), *The CND Story: The First 25 Years of CND in the Words of the People Involved* (London: Allison & Busby, 1983).

Minutes of the Town Council of Edinburgh: Session 1963–1964 (Edinburgh: William Nimmo, 1965).

Moffat, A., *The Edinburgh Fringe* (London: Johnston & Bacon, 1978).

Moore-Gilbert, B. and J. Seed (eds), *Cultural Revolution? The Challenge of the Arts in the 1960s* (London: Routledge, 1992).

Morgan, K. O., *Britain since 1945: The People's Peace* (Oxford: Oxford University Press, 2001).

Morgan, K. O., *The People's Peace: British History, 1945–1989* (Oxford: Oxford University Press, 1990).

Morgan, T., *Literary Outlaw: The Life and Times of William S. Burroughs* (New York: Henry Holt, 1988).

Munro, A., *The Democratic Muse: Folk Music Revival in Scotland* (Aberdeen: Scottish Cultural Press, 1996).

Nelson, E., *The British Counter-culture, 1966–73: A Study of the Underground Press* (Basingstoke: Macmillan Press, 1989).

Noyce, J., *The Directory of British Alternative Periodicals* (Hassocks: Harvester Press, 1979).

Nuttall, J., *Bomb Culture* (London: MacGibbon & Kee Ltd, 1968).

Oliver, C., *It Is a Curious Story: The Tale of Scottish Opera, 1962–1987* (Edinburgh: Mainstream, 1987).

Oliver, C., *Magic in the Gorbals: A Personal Record of the Citizens Theatre* (Ellon: Famedram, 1999).

Osgerby, B., *Youth in Britain since 1945* (Oxford: Blackwell, 1998).

Pym, B., *Pressure Groups and the Permissive Society* (Newton Abbot: David & Charles, 1974).

Ray, G. (ed.), *Joseph Beuys: Mapping the Legacy* (New York: DAP, 2001).

Rees, R., *Fringe First: Pioneers of Fringe Theatre on Record* (London: Oberon, 1992).

Reid, A., *Kirk and Drama: An Artist's View of the Gateway* (Edinburgh: Gateway Theatre, 1958).

Reports to the General Assembly of the Church of Scotland with the Legislative Acts (Edinburgh: Wm Blackwood and T. & A. Constable, 1945–1967).

Rhymes, D., *No New Morality: Christian Personal Values and Sexual Morality* (London: Constable, 1964).

Roberts, P. & M. Stafford-Clark, *Taking Stock: The Theatre of Max Stafford-Clark* (London: Nick Hern, 2007).

Robinson, L., *Gay Men and the Left in Post-war Britain: How the Personal Got Political* (Manchester: Manchester University Press, 2007).

Rolfe, H., *Arts Festivals in the UK* (London: Policy Studies Institute, 1992).

Rolph, C. H. (ed.), *The Trial of Lady Chatterley: Regina v. Penguin Books Limited* (Harmondsworth: Penguin, 1961).

Royle, T., *A Diary of Edinburgh* (Edinburgh: Polygon, 1981).

Sandbrook, D., *Never Had It So Good: A History of Britain from Suez to the Beatles* (London: Little, Brown, 2005).

Sandbrook, D., *White Heat: A History of Britain in the Swinging Sixties* (London: Little, Brown, 2006).

Saville, R., (ed.), *The Economic Development of Modern Scotland, 1950–1980* (Edinburgh: John Donald, 1985).

Scott, A. M., *Alexander Trocchi: The Making of the Monster* (Edinburgh: Polygon, 1991).

The Scotsman, Festival City: A Pictorial History of the Edinburgh Festivals (Derby: Breedon, 2009).

The Scotsman Presents the Edinburgh Story: Seventy-eight Pages on Scotland's Capital (1960).

Shellard, D., *British Theatre since the War* (London: Yale University Press, 1999).

Shellard, D. (ed.), *The Golden Generation: New Light on Post-war British Theatre.* (London: British Library, 2008).

Shellard, D. et al., *The Lord Chamberlain Regrets . . . : A History of British Theatre Censorship* (London: British Library, 2004).

Shrum, W. M., *Fringe and Fortune: The Role of Critics in High and Popular Art* (Princeton: Princeton University Press, 1996).

Sinclair, A., *Arts and Cultures: The History of the 50 Years of the Arts Council of Great Britain* (London: Sinclair-Stevenson, 1995).

Sinfield, A., *Literature, Politics and Culture in Postwar Britain* (Oxford: Basil Blackwell, 1989).

Sissons, M. & P. French (eds), *Age of Austerity* (London: Hodder & Stoughton, 1963).

Spender, S., *Eliot* (Glasgow: Fontana, 1975).

Stephens, C. & K. Stout (eds), *Art & the 60s: This Was Tomorrow* (London: Tate, 2004).

Stevenson, R. & G. Wallace (eds), *Scottish Theatre since the Seventies* (Edinburgh: Edinburgh University Press, 1996).

Storey, J., *Cultural Studies and the Study of Popular Culture*, 3rd ed. (Edinburgh: Edinburgh University Press, 2010).

Storey, J., *Cultural Theory and Popular Culture: A Reader* (Hemel Hempstead: Harvester Wheatsheaf, 1994).

Sutherland, J., *Offensive Literature: Decensorship in Britain, 1960–1982* (London: Junction, 1982).

Thornton-Duesbery, J. P., *The Open Secret of MRA: An Examination of Mr Driberg's 'Critical Examination' of Moral Re-Armament* (London: Blandford Press, 1964).

Travis, A., *Bound and Gagged: A Secret History of Obscenity in Britain* (London: Profile, 2000).

Vall, N., *Cultural Region: North East England, 1945–2000* (Manchester: Manchester University Press, 2011).

Warr, C. L., *The Glimmering Landscape* (London: Hodder & Stoughton, 1960).

Weeks, J., *Sex, Politics and Society: The Regulation of Sexuality since 1800* (London: Longman, 1981).

Wheen, F., *The Sixties: A Fresh Look at the Decade of Change* (London: Century, 1982).

Whitehouse, M., *Cleaning-up TV: From Protest to Participation* (London: Blandford Press, 1967).

Whitehouse, M., *Who Does She Think She Is?* (London: New English Library, 1971).

Whitley, H., *Thorns and Thistles* (Edinburgh: Edina Press, 1976).

Williams, R., *Culture and Society, 1780–1950* (London: Penguin, 1961).

Williams, R., *Keywords: A Vocabulary of Culture and Society*, rev. ed. (London: Fontana, 1988).

Williams, R., *The Long Revolution* (London: Hogarth Press, 1992 [1961]).

Willmott, P., *Adolescent Boys of East London* (London: Routledge & Kegan Paul, 1966).

Wilmut, R., *From Fringe to Flying Circus: Celebrating a Unique Generation of Comedy, 1960–1980* (London: Eyre Methuen, 1980).

Wishart, R., *Celebration! Edinburgh International Festival – 50 Years in Photographs* (Edinburgh: Edinburgh Festival Society, 1996).

Wolrige Gordon, A., *Peter Howard: Life and Letters* (London: Hodder & Stoughton, 1969).

Wright, B. & C. Worsley (eds), *Alternative Scotland: A Passport to Scotland* (Edinburgh: East March Press/Bozo, 1975).

REPORTS AND OTHER PUBLICATIONS

Crummy, H., *People in Partnership: The Report of the Craigmillar Festival Society, 1973–4*.

Edinburgh Corporation Committee Minutes: Lord Provost's Committee Session 1963–64 (Edinburgh: William Nimmo, 1965).

Edinburgh Festival: A Review of the First Ten Years of the Edinburgh International Festival, Its Aims and Its Origins, Its Achievements and Its Hopes for the Future (Edinburgh: Edinburgh Festival Society, 1956).

Housing the Arts in Britain: Report by the Arts Council of Great Britain, Part 1: London, Scotland, Wales (London: Arts Council of Great Britain, 1959).

Ingham, Councillor A. G., *Our Beautiful City: The Story of How It Is Run* (5th ed.), 1963–4.

A Policy for the Arts: The First Steps (London: HMSO, 1965).

Report of the Committee on Broadcasting 1960 (London: HMSO, 1962).

Scotland in Festival Year 1951 (Festival of Britain Programmes and Catalogues).

Scottish Arts Council, *Theatre in Scotland* (1970).

Scottish Tourist Board, *A Report by the Manager and Secretary, The Scottish Tourist Board, on Some of the Advantages Accruing to Edinburgh, to Scotland and to Britain through the Promotion of the Edinburgh Festival* (1956).

Scottish Tourist Board, *Report on the Advantages of the Festival to Edinburgh* (1956).

Submission on Behalf of Edinburgh Festival Society for Nobel Peace Prize, January 1952.

UNPUBLISHED THESES, ARTICLES AND OTHER ACCOUNTS

Bell, E., 'Resisting "Prickly Isolation" in the Scottish 60s', paper given at 'Reading, Rebellion, Revolution' seminar, Edinburgh Napier University (October 2009).

Bold, A., 'Introduction to the Paintings of Alexander Moffat and John Bellany At Castle Terrace Railings' (1963).

Breitenbach, E, 'Empire and Civil Society in 20th Century Scotland: Imperial Decline and National Identity c. 1918–c. 1970', End of Award Report, RES-062-23-1790 (2012), Economic and Social Research Council.

Demarco, R., ' "Too Rough to Go Slow" (on the Road to Meikle Seggie): An Autobiographical Essay' (March 2005).

Hill, J., 'Glasgow Unity Theatre', MA dissertation, University of Glasgow (1975).

Jarman, D., 'Mirror of the Nation? The Edinburgh Festivals and Scottish National Identity', MA (Hons) undergraduate dissertation, University of Edinburgh, 2001.

Jarman, D., 'Nascent Fringe: The Edinburgh Festival Fringe 1956–1963 – Continuity, Evolution and Legacy', MSc dissertation, University of Edinburgh, 2005.

Haynes, J., 'A Love Story or How the Traverse Came to Be' (February 2001).

Haynes, J., 'C'est Ma Vie Folks! Bits from a Participatory Autobiography, Volume 1: 1933–1969', unpublished manuscript.

International Writers' Conference, original transcript, Edinburgh, August 1962.

McArthur, E., 'The Council for the Encouragement of Music and the Arts (CEMA) and the Development of the Arts Council in Scotland: Background,

Politics, Visual Art Policy, 1919–1947', PhD thesis, University of Dundee, 2005.

Oliver, C., 'Strategy: Get Arts', printed information sheet for Strategy: Get Arts Revisited exhibition, National Gallery of Modern Art, Edinburgh, 22 October 2005–8 January 2006.

'Richard Demarco: Beyond the Fringe', *Artworks Scotland*, BBC2, first transmitted 17 August 2003.

Vall, N., 'Northern Arts, 1961–1975: Regional Culture and the Politics of Improvement', paper given at Social History Society Conference, University of Reading (March 2006).

WEB-BASED SOURCES

Les Ballets Africains: Cultural Ambassadors, http://www.danceforpower.org/balletafricains.html (last accessed 6 December 2012).

Forbes, E., 'Bing, Sir Rudolf Franz Joseph (1902–1997)', *Oxford Dictionary of National Biography*, www.oxforddnb.com/view/article/68105 (last accessed 6 December 2012).

Linklater, E., 'Mavor, Osborne Henry [James Bridie] (1888–1951)', *Oxford Dictionary of National Biography*, www.oxforddnb.com/view/article/34950 (last accessed 6 December 2012).

Measuring Worth, http://www.measuringworth.com (last accessed 6 December 2012).

Royal Court Theatre, http://www.royalcourttheatre.com (last accessed 6 December 2012).

'Some Memories of the 1970 Edinburgh Festival Exhibition', Strategy: Get Arts, http://www.eca.ac.uk/palermo/history_strategy_get_arts.htm (last accessed 6 December 2012).

Unfinished Histories: Recording the History of Alternative Theatre, http://www.unfinishedhistories.com (last accessed 6 December 2012).

Index